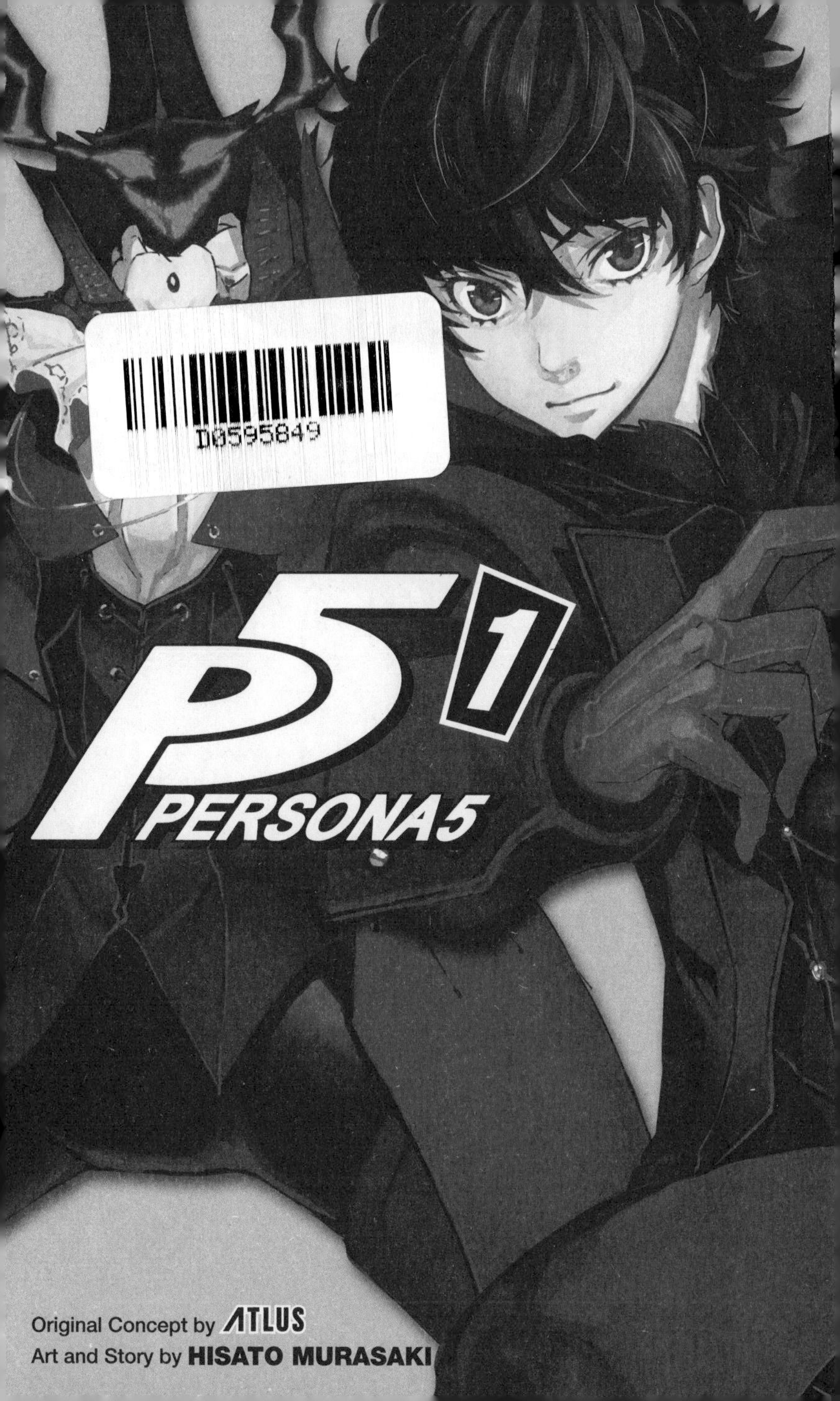
P5
1
PERSONA5
Original Concept by ATLUS
Art and Story by HISATO MURASAKI

PERSONA5

VOLUME 1

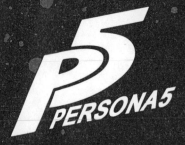

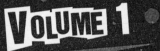

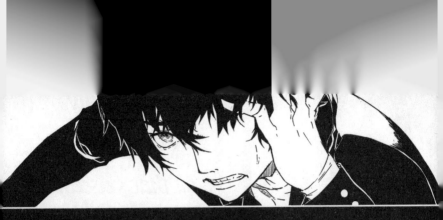

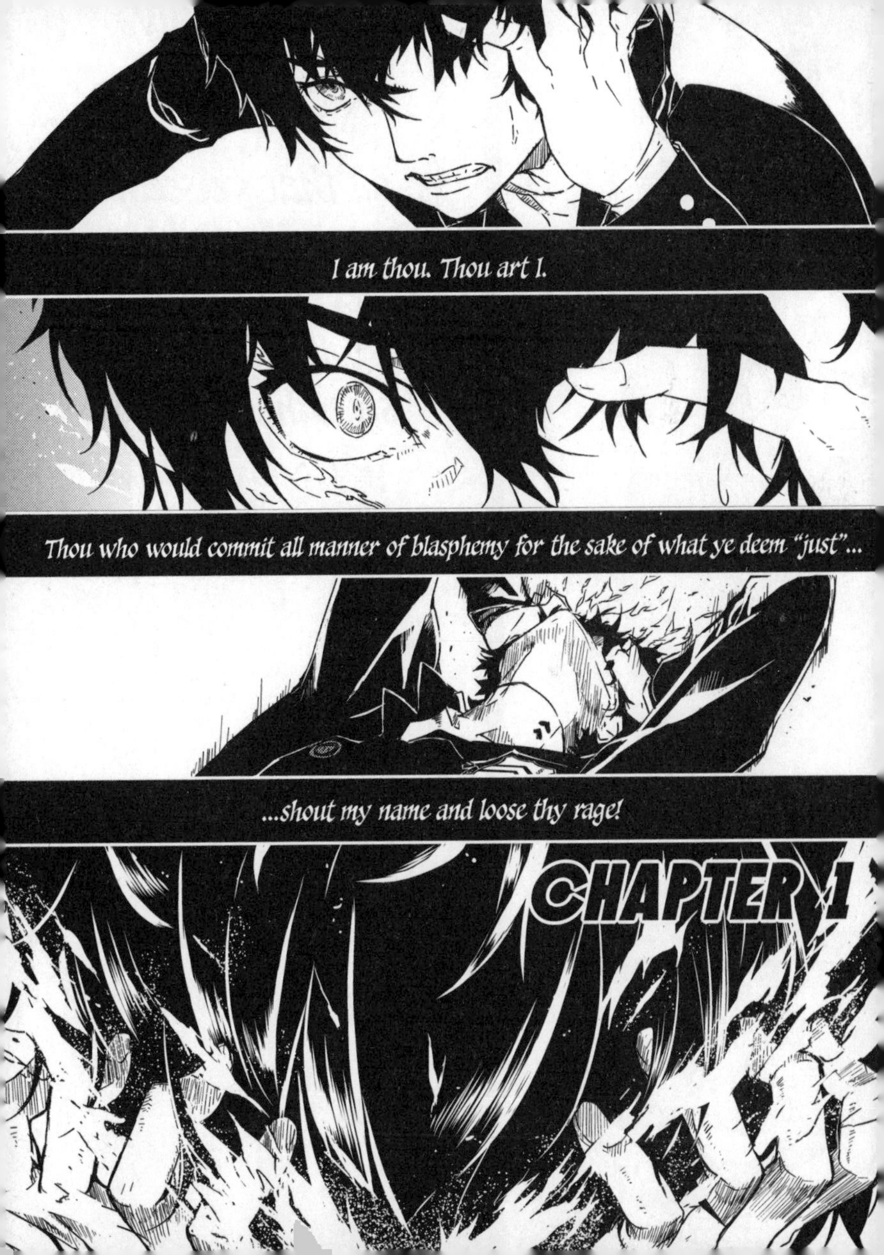
I am thou. Thou art I.
Thou who would commit all manner of blasphemy for the sake of what ye deem "just"...
...shout my name and loose thy rage!
CHAPTER 1

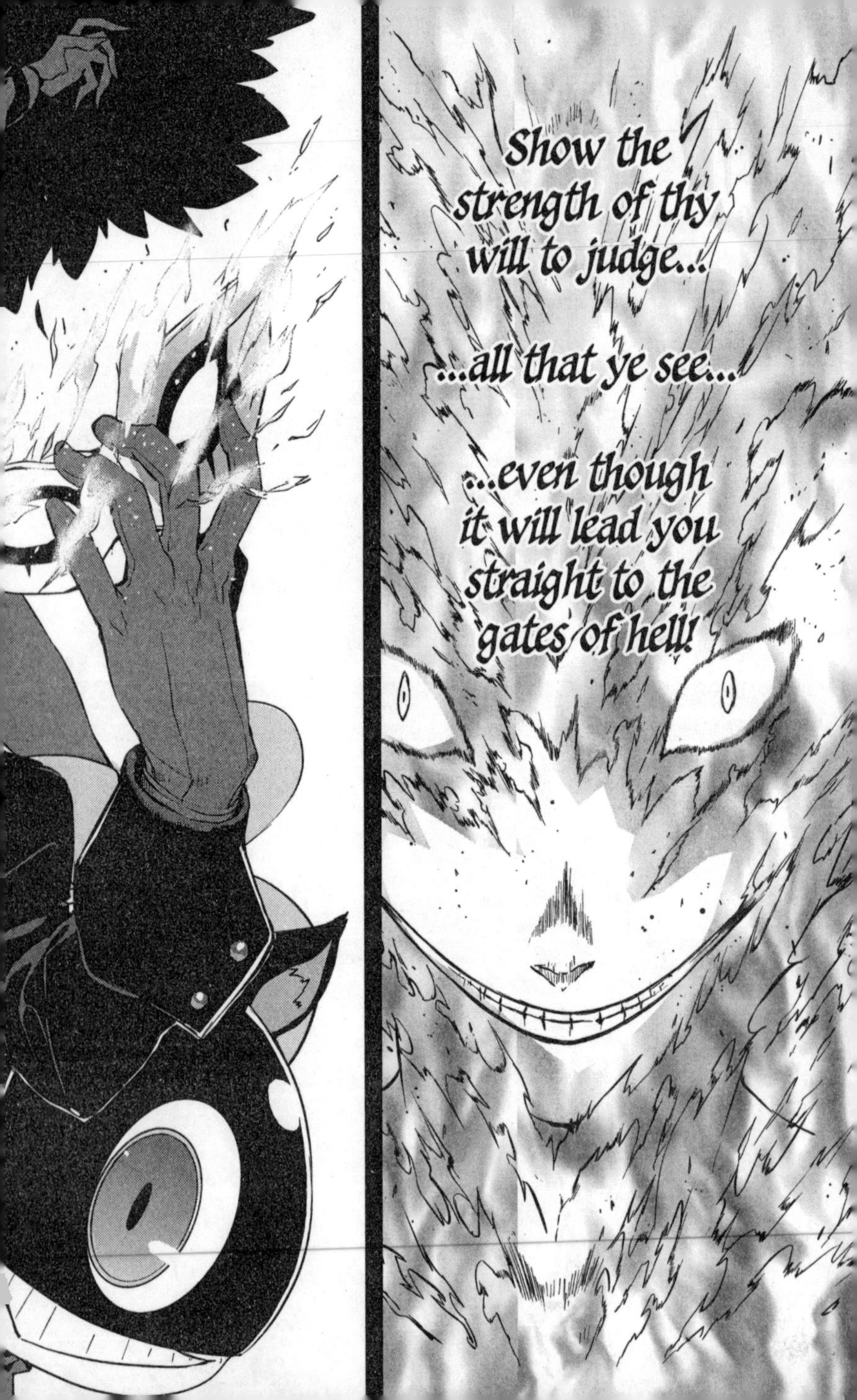
Show the strength of thy will to judge...
...all that ye see...
...even though it will lead you straight to the gates of hell!

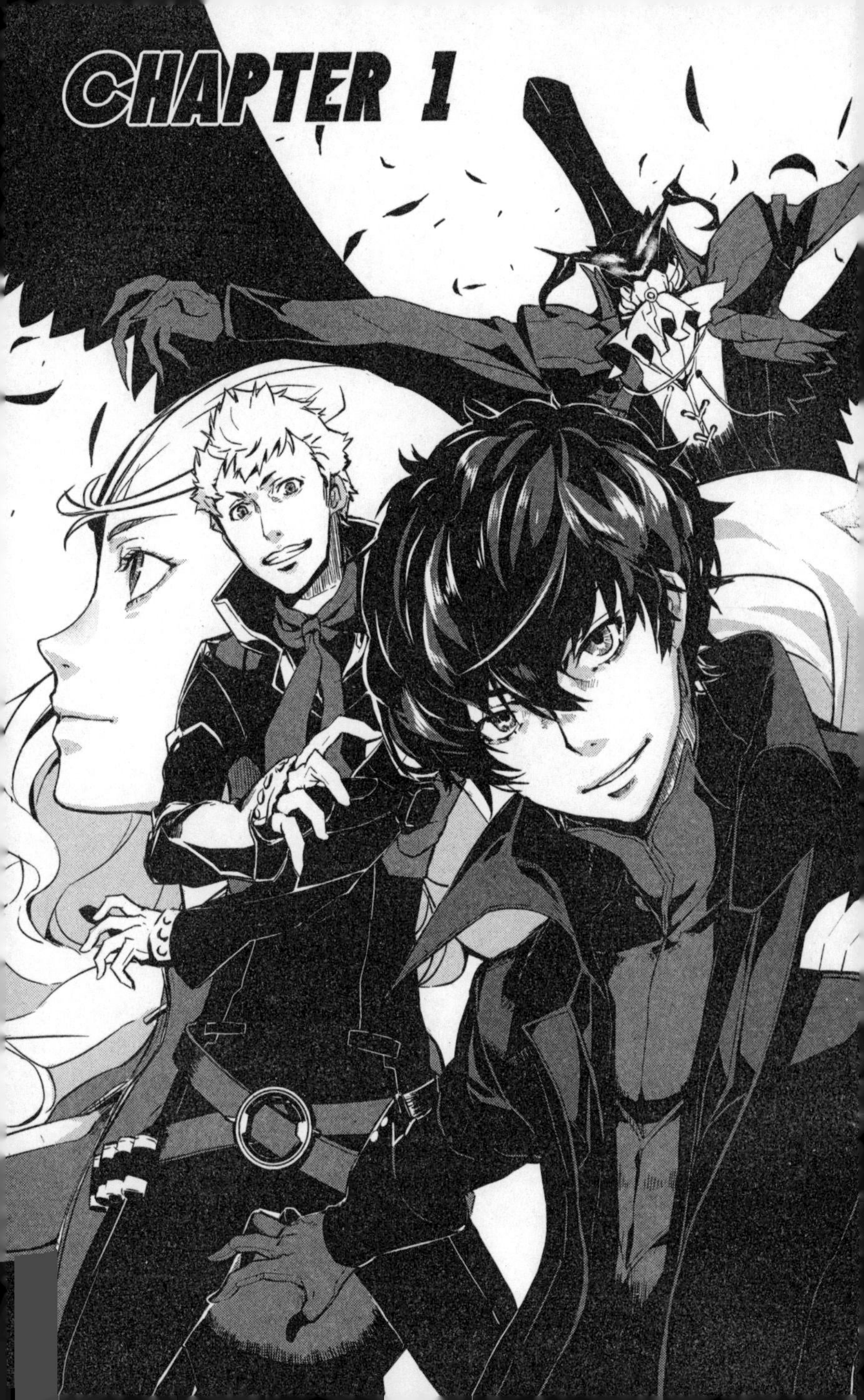
CHAPTER 1

PERSONA5

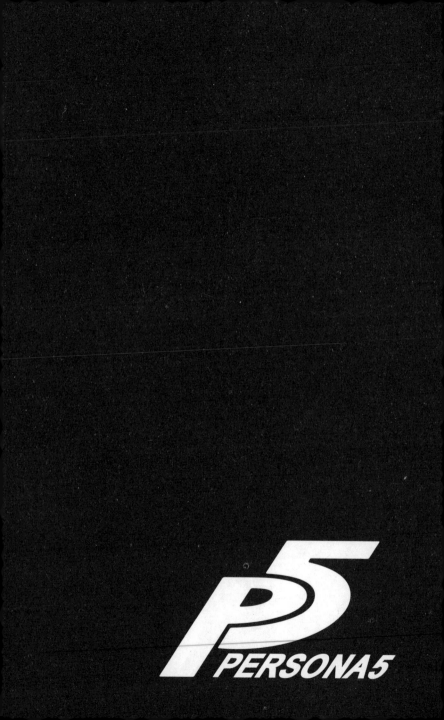

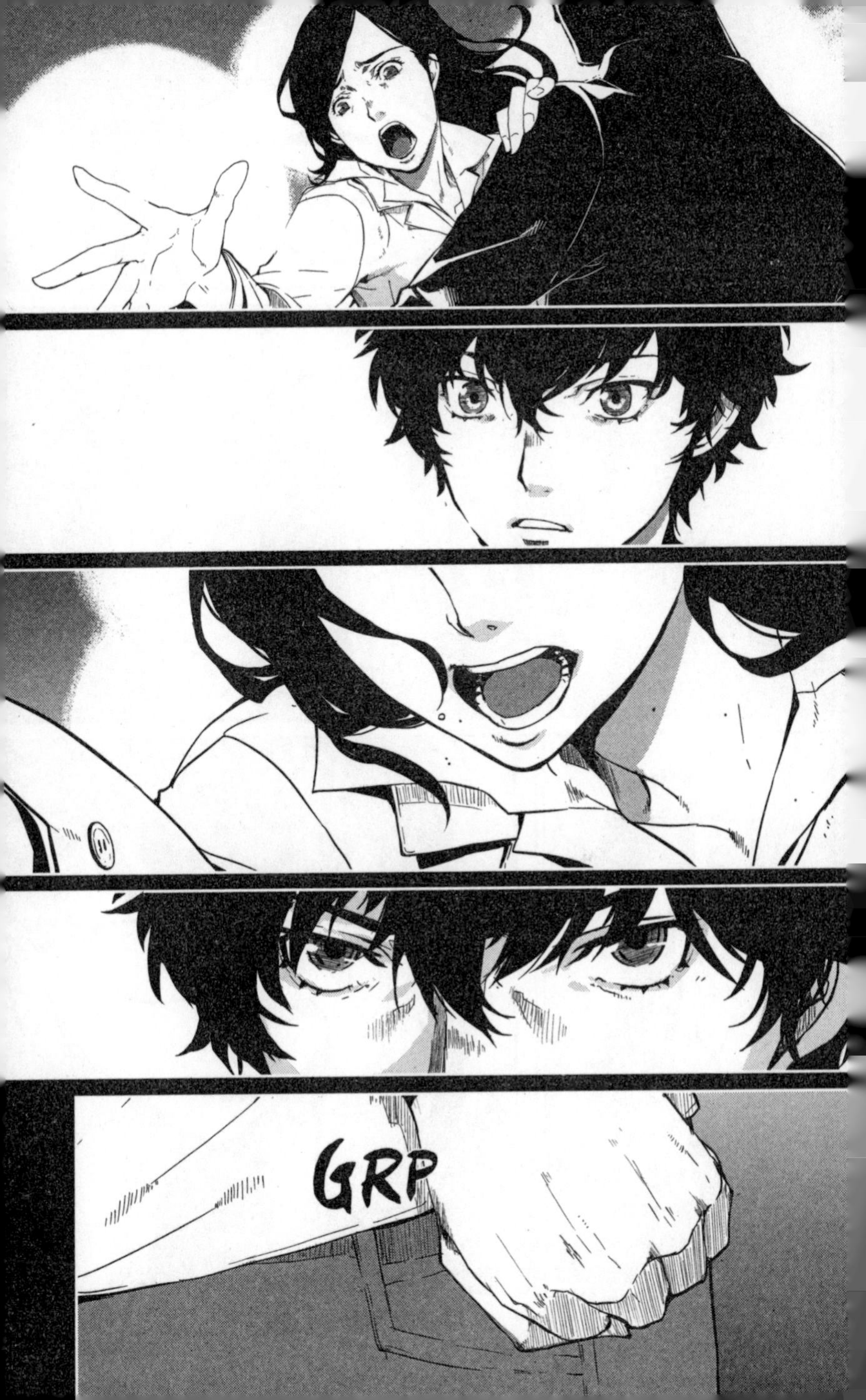
GRP

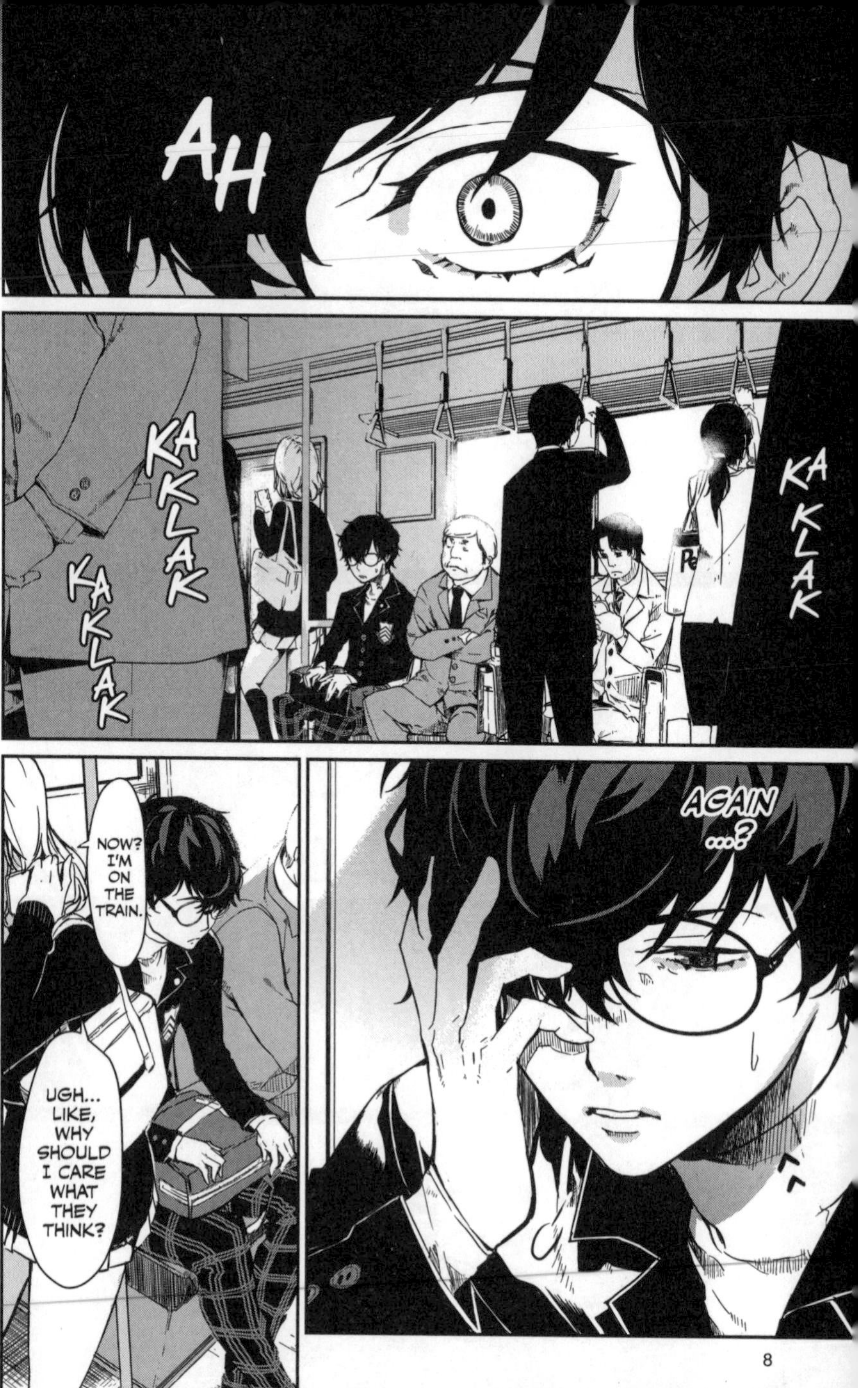
AH
KA KLAK
KA KLAK
KA KLAK
AGAIN ...?
NOW? I'M ON THE TRAIN.
UGH... LIKE, WHY SHOULD I CARE WHAT THEY THINK?

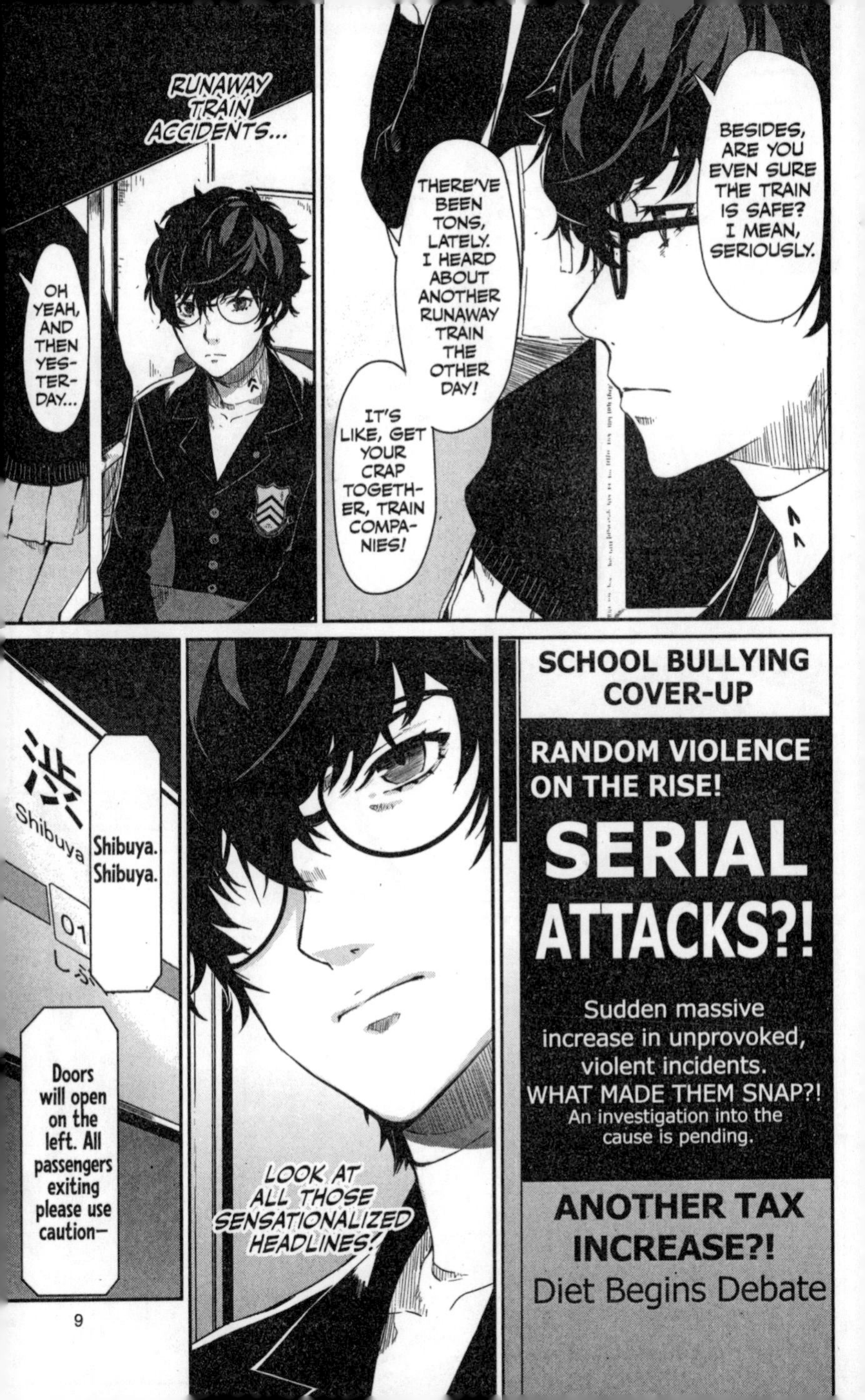
BESIDES, ARE YOU EVEN SURE THE TRAIN IS SAFE? I MEAN, SERIOUSLY.
THERE'VE BEEN TONS, LATELY. I HEARD ABOUT ANOTHER RUNAWAY TRAIN THE OTHER DAY!
IT'S LIKE, GET YOUR CRAP TOGETHER, TRAIN COMPANIES!
RUNAWAY TRAIN ACCIDENTS...
OH YEAH, AND THEN YESTERDAY...
SCHOOL BULLYING COVER-UP
RANDOM VIOLENCE ON THE RISE!
SERIAL ATTACKS?!
Sudden massive increase in unprovoked, violent incidents. WHAT MADE THEM SNAP?! An investigation into the cause is pending.
ANOTHER TAX INCREASE?! Diet Begins Debate
LOOK AT ALL THOSE SENSATIONALIZED HEADLINES!
渋
Shibuya
01
Shibuya. Shibuya.
Doors will open on the left. All passengers exiting please use caution—

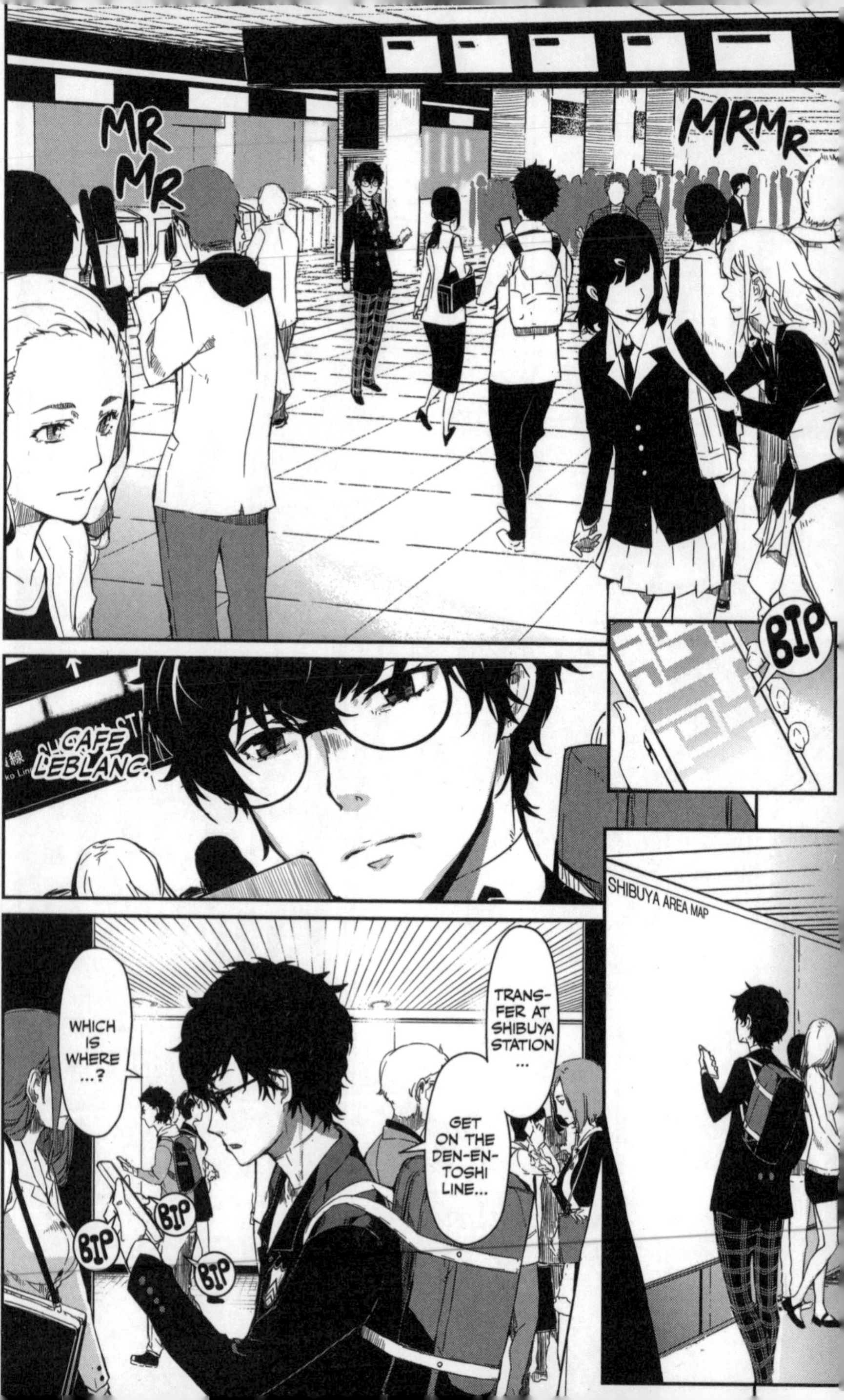
MRMR
MR MR
BIP
CAFE LEBLANC
SHIBUYA AREA MAP
TRANSFER AT SHIBUYA STATION...
GET ON THE DEN-EN-TOSHI LINE...
WHICH IS WHERE...?
BIP
BIP
BIP

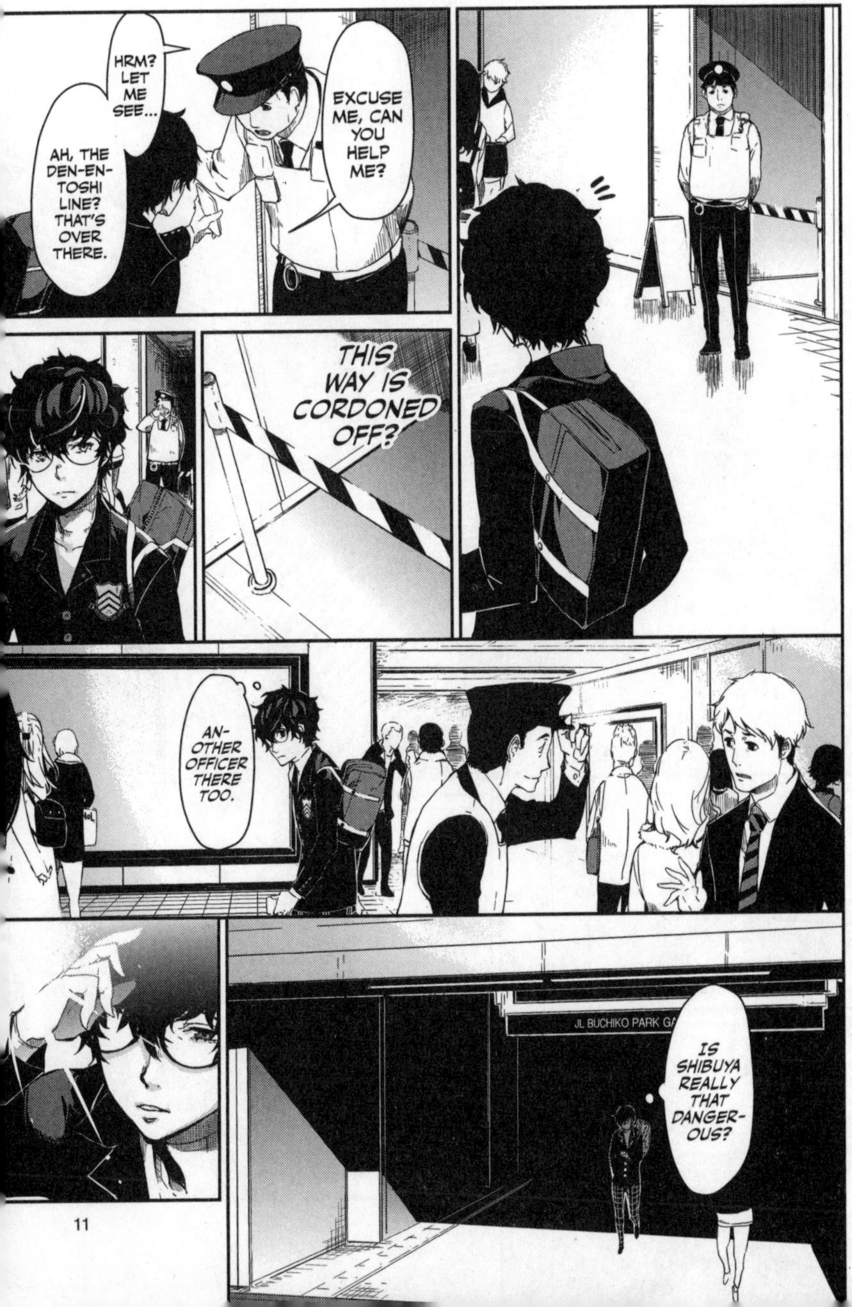
EXCUSE ME, CAN YOU HELP ME?
HRM? LET ME SEE...
AH, THE DEN-EN-TOSHI LINE? THAT'S OVER THERE.
THIS WAY IS CORDONED OFF?
AN-OTHER OFFICER THERE TOO.
JL BUCHIKO PARK GA
IS SHIBUYA REALLY THAT DANGER-OUS?

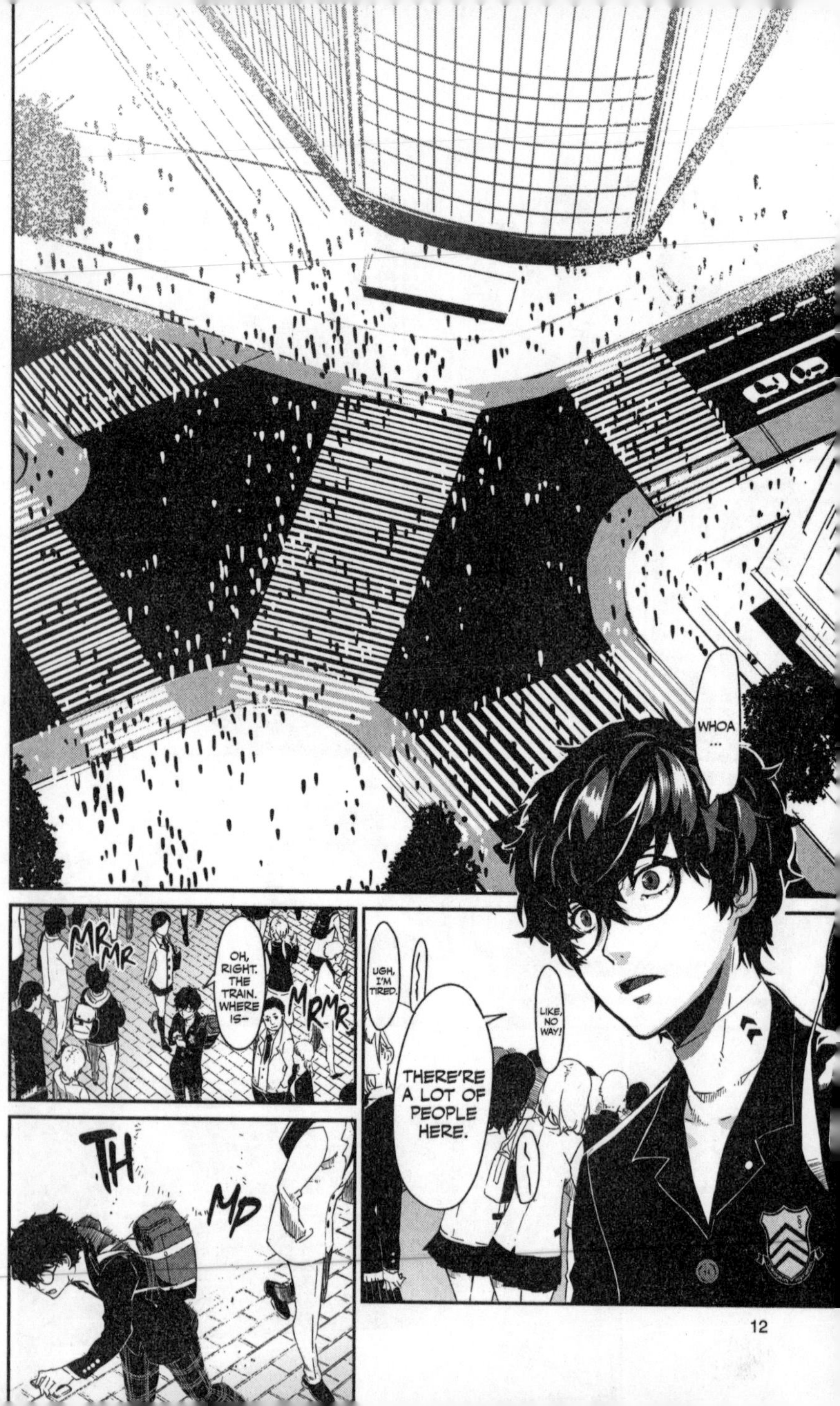
WHOA...
LIKE, NO WAY!
UGH, I'M TIRED.
THERE'RE A LOT OF PEOPLE HERE.
MRMR
OH, RIGHT. THE TRAIN. WHERE IS—
MRMR
THMP

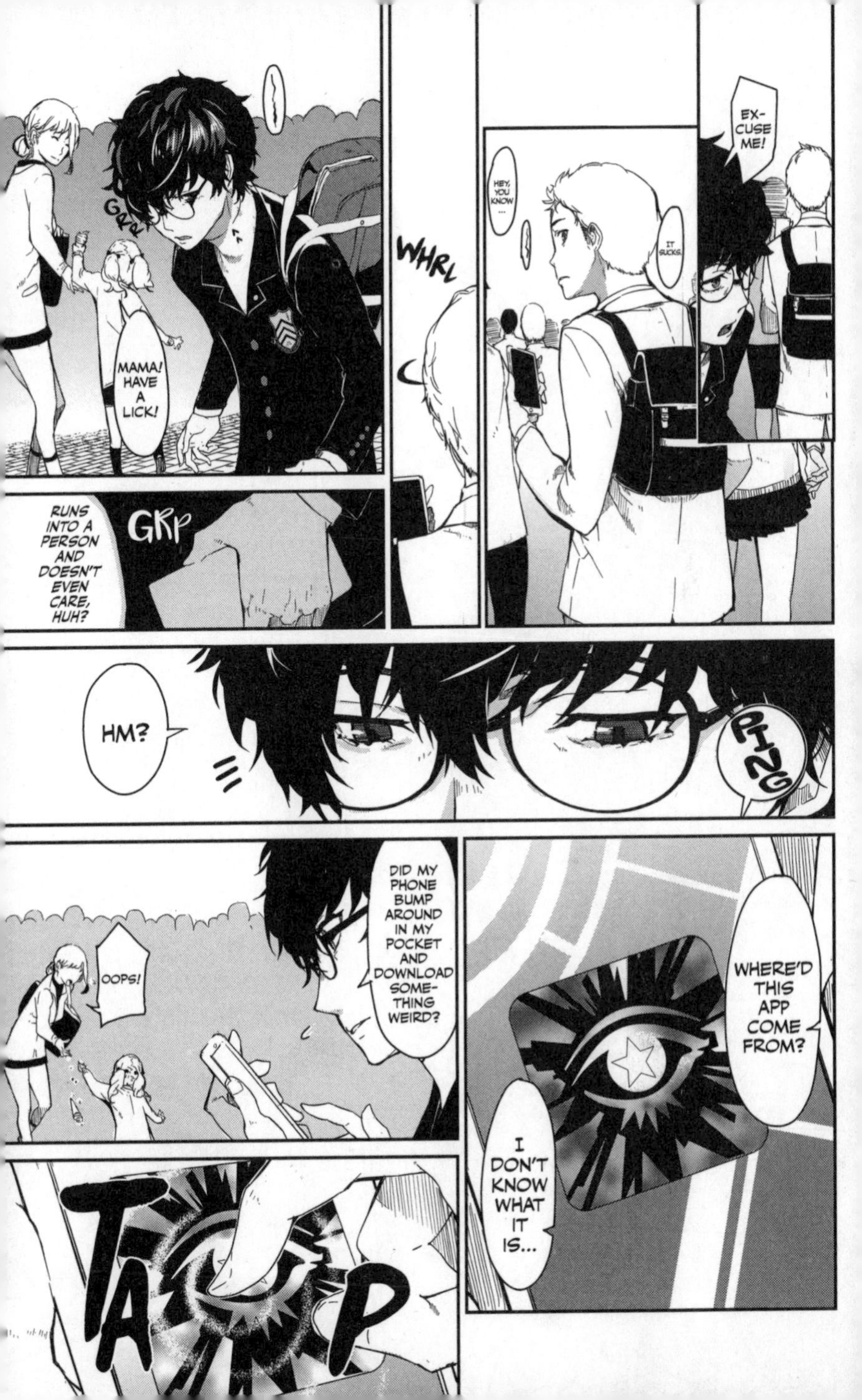
EX-CUSE ME!
HEY, YOU KNOW ...
IT SUCKS.
WHRL
GRR
MAMA! HAVE A LICK!
GRP
RUNS INTO A PERSON AND DOESN'T EVEN CARE, HUH?
PING
HM?
WHERE'D THIS APP COME FROM?
I DON'T KNOW WHAT IT IS...
DID MY PHONE BUMP AROUND IN MY POCKET AND DOWNLOAD SOME-THING WEIRD?
OOPS!
TAP

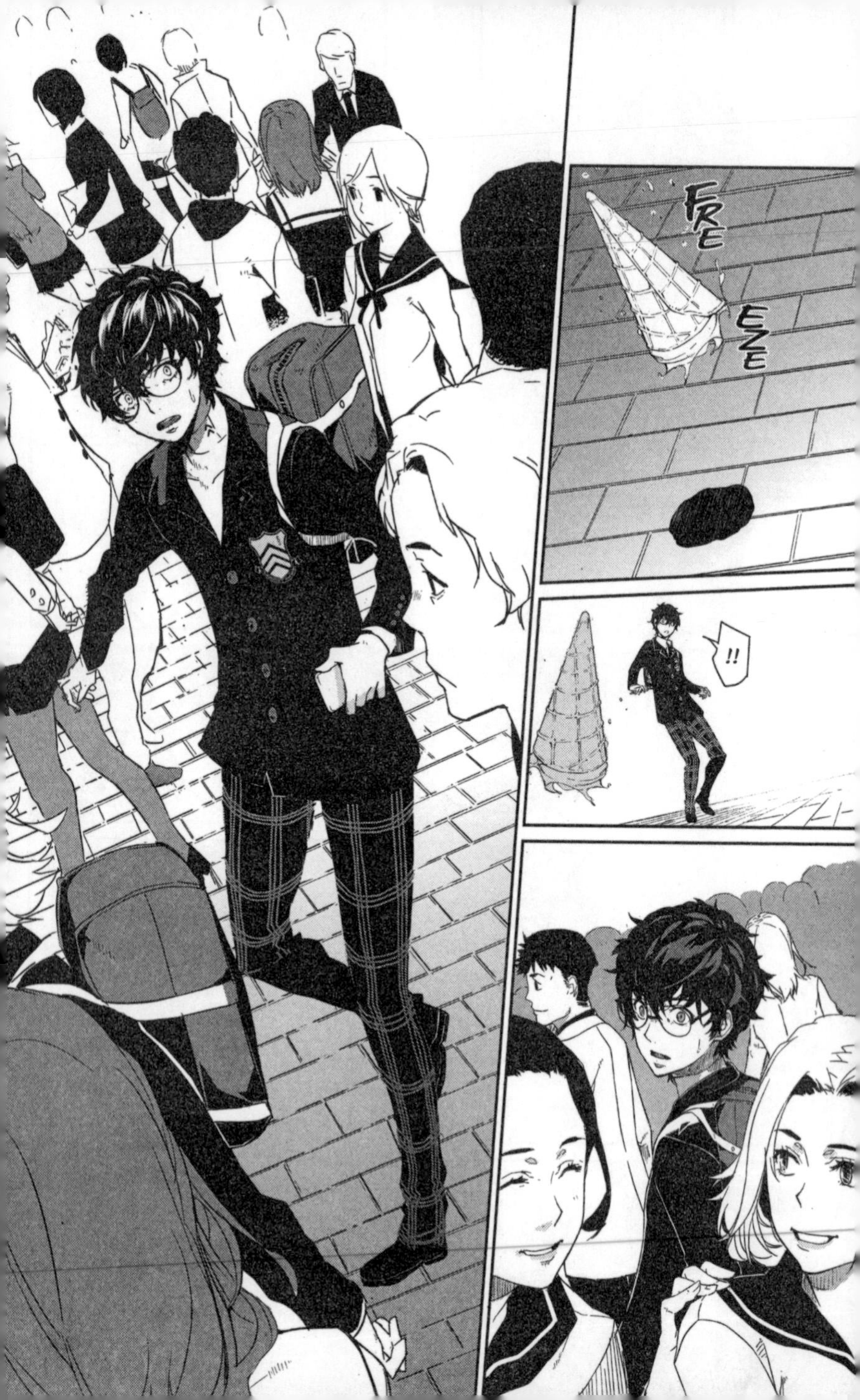
FREEZE
!!

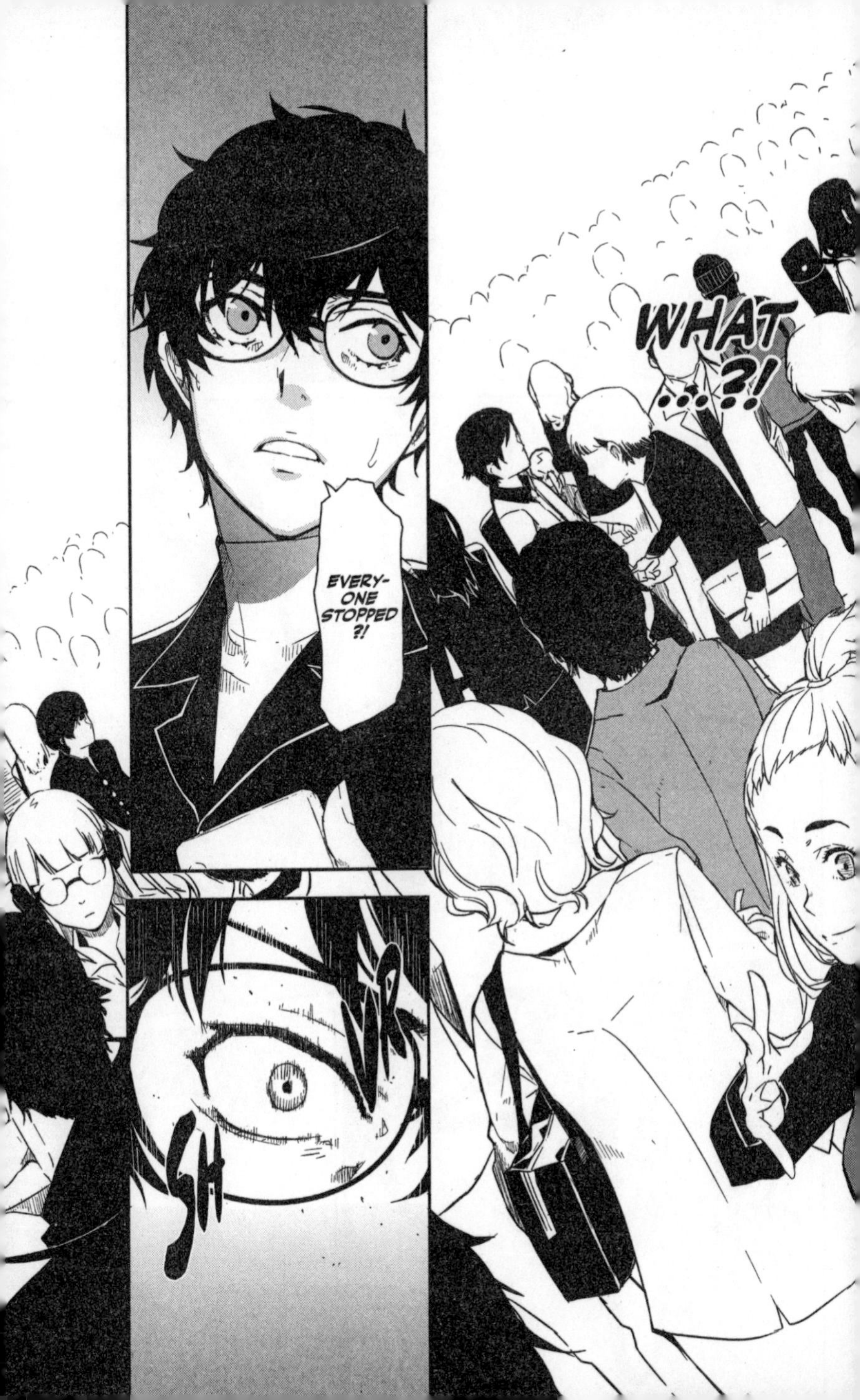
WHAT ...?!
EVERY-ONE STOPPED ?!
SH

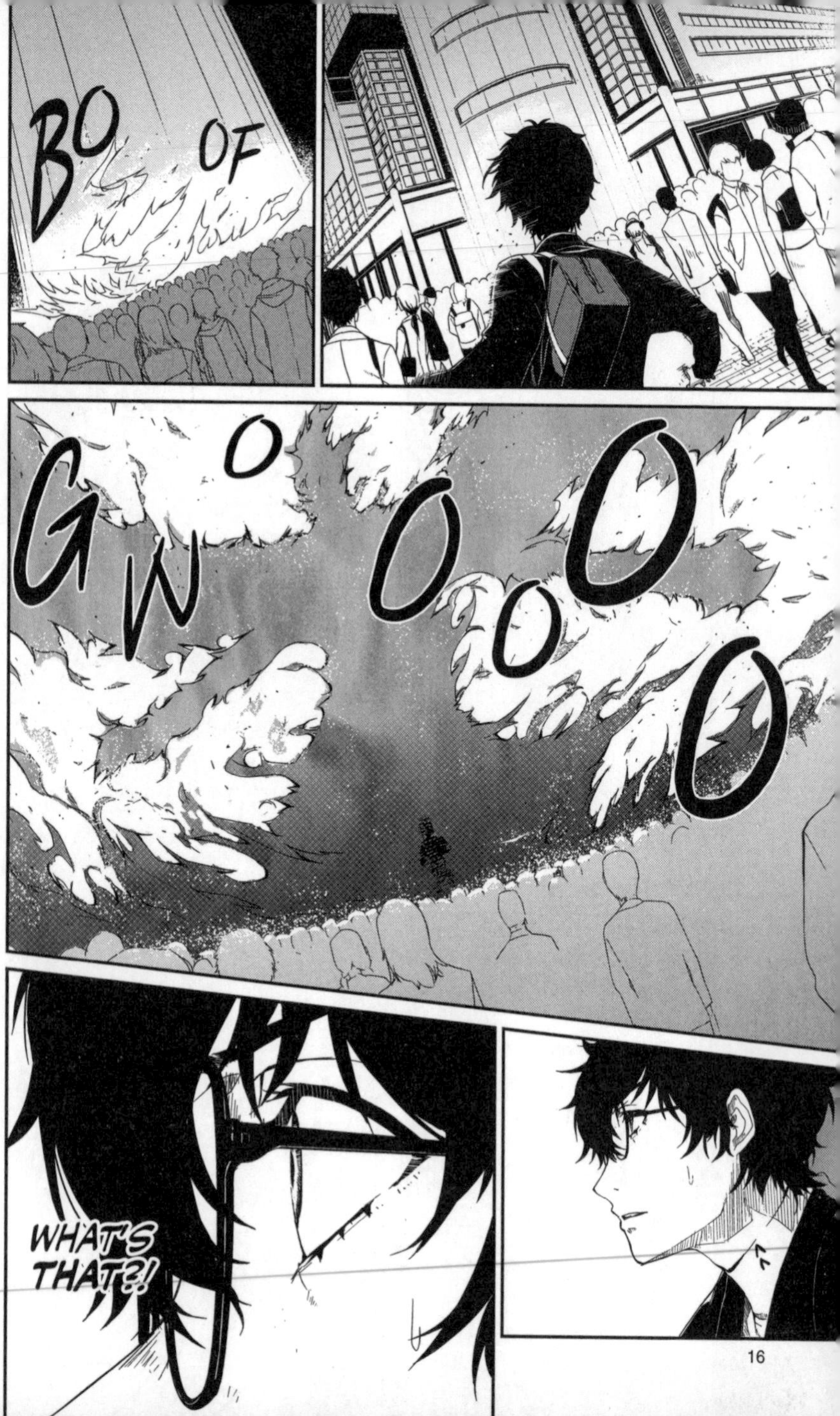
BO OF
GWOOOOOO
WHAT'S THAT?!

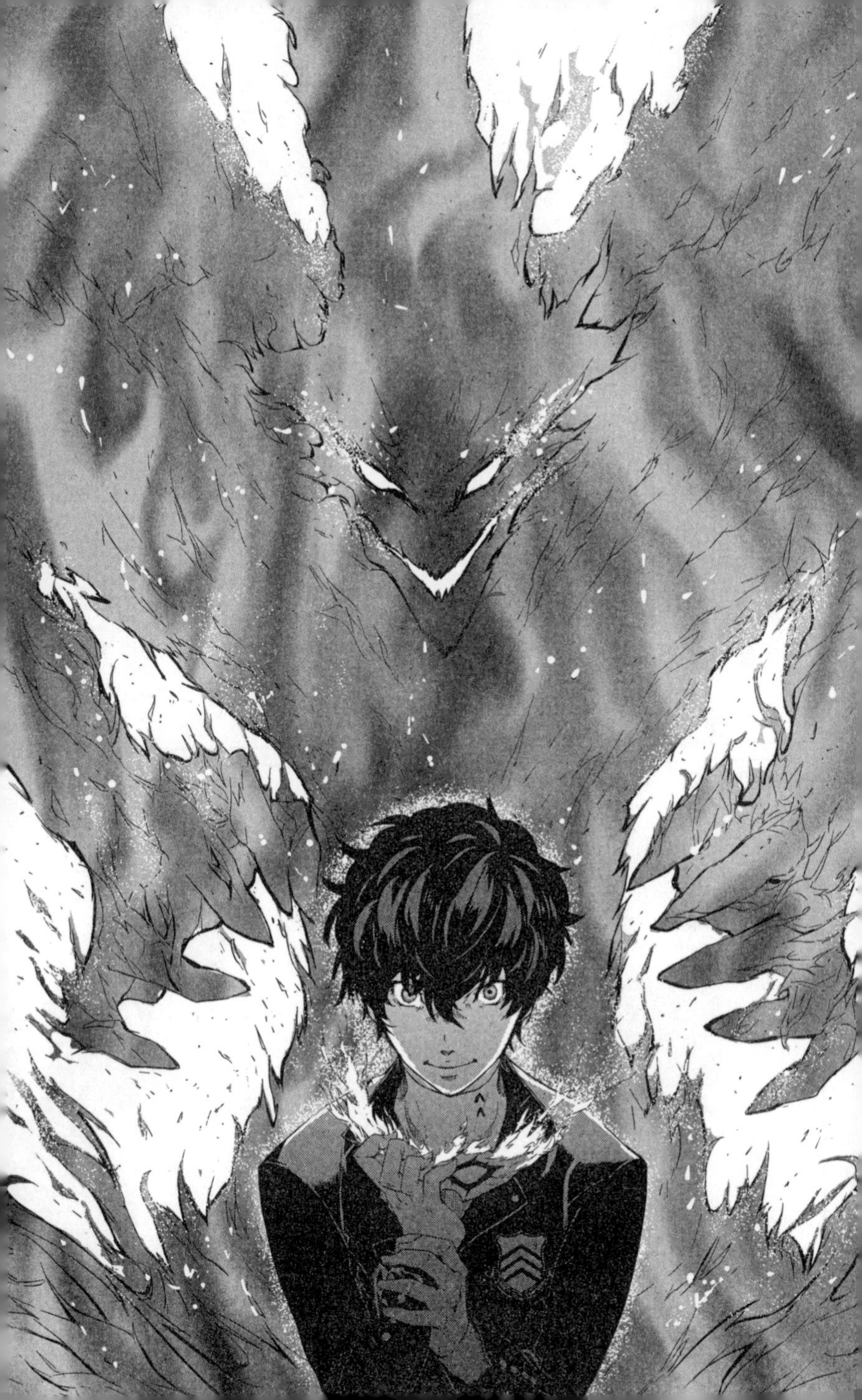

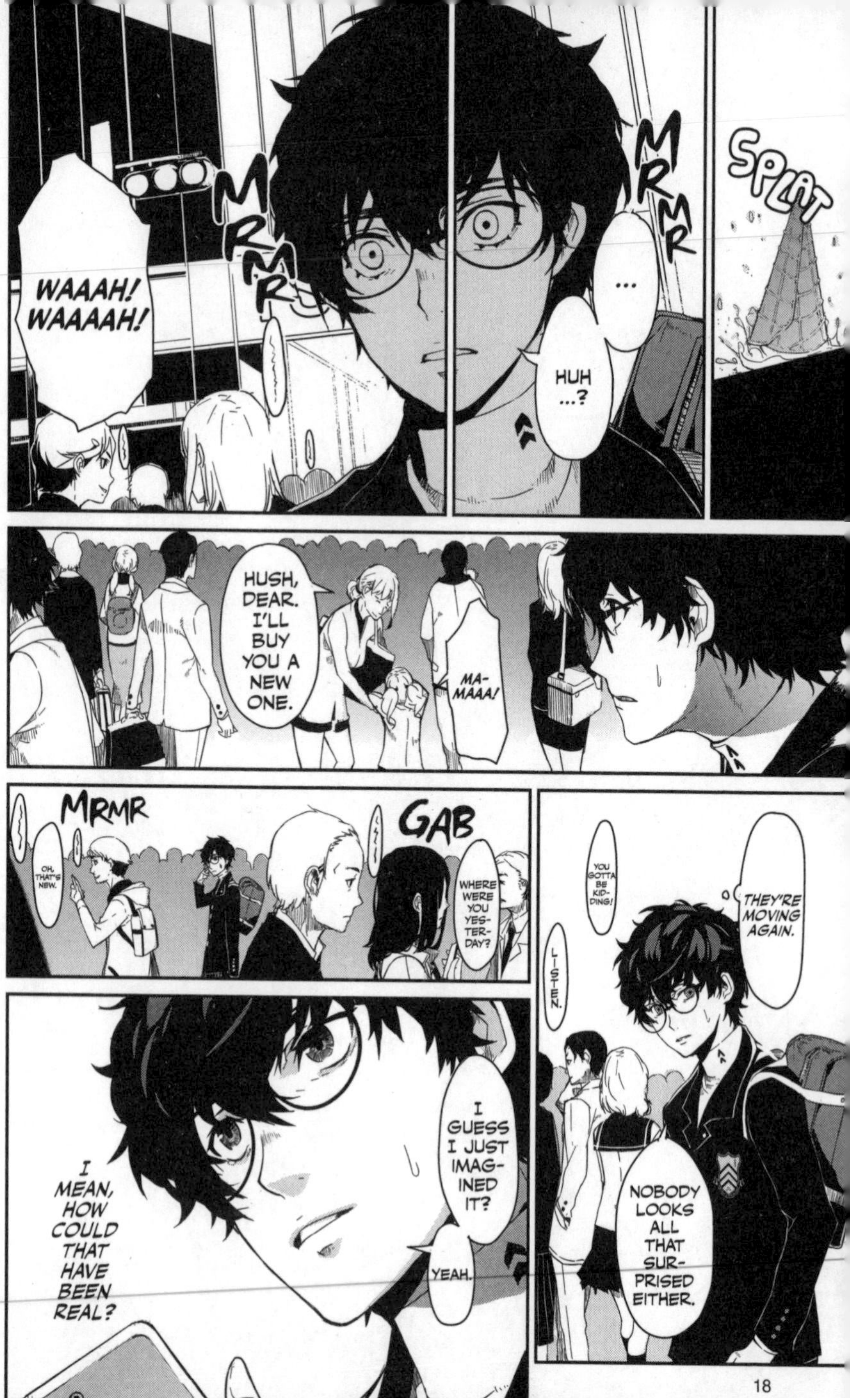
SPLAT
MRMR
...
HUH ...?
MRMR
WAAAH! WAAAH!
HUSH, DEAR. I'LL BUY YOU A NEW ONE.
MA-MAAA!
THEY'RE MOVING AGAIN.
YOU GOTTA BE KID-DING!
LISTEN.
NOBODY LOOKS ALL THAT SUR-PRISED EITHER.
GAB
WHERE WERE YOU YES-TER-DAY?
MRMR
OH, THAT'S NEW.
I GUESS I JUST IMAG-INED IT?
YEAH.
I MEAN, HOW COULD THAT HAVE BEEN REAL?

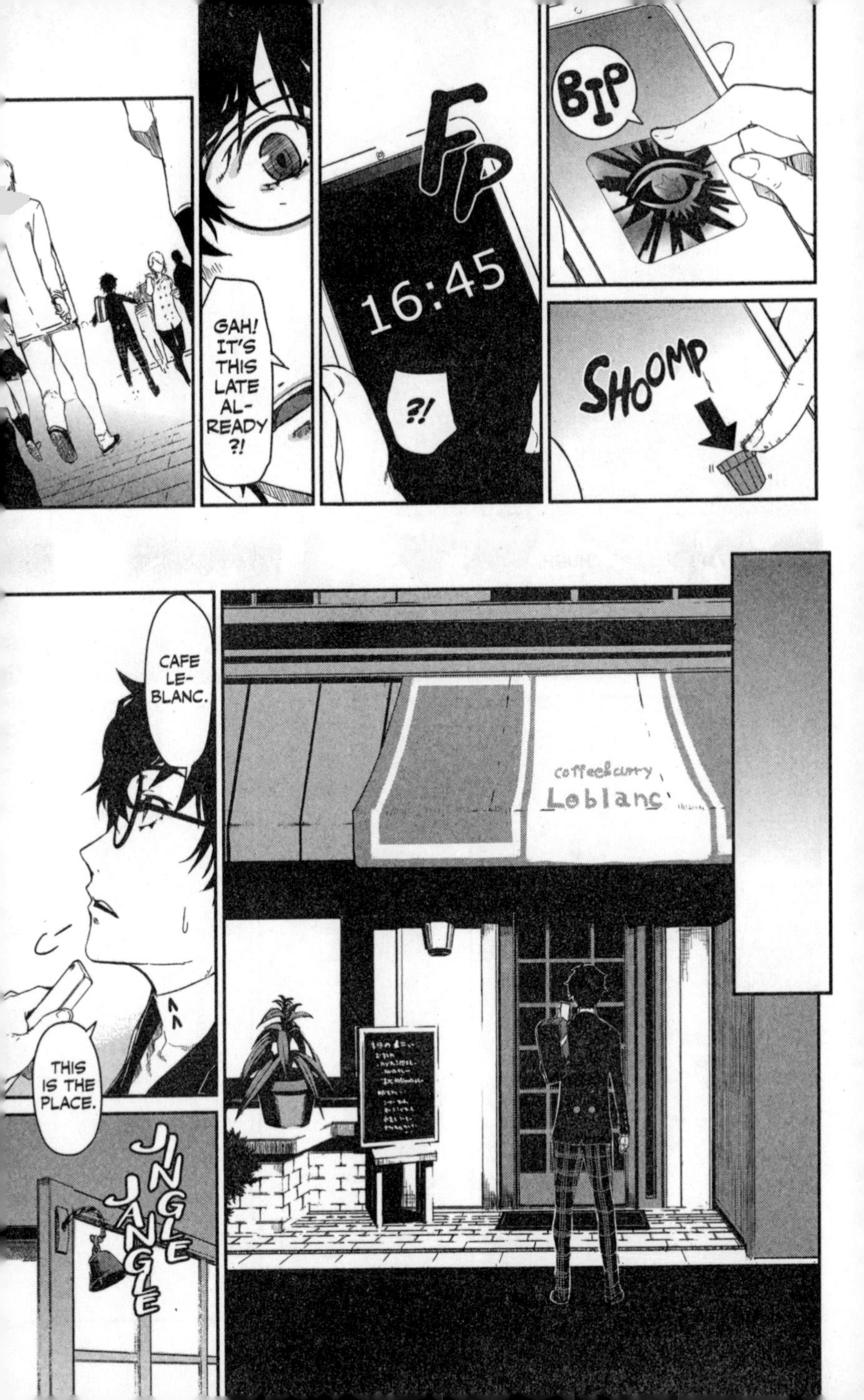
BIP
SHOOMP
FP
16:45
?!
GAH! IT'S THIS LATE AL-READY?!
coffee&curry
Leblanc
CAFE LE-BLANC.
THIS IS THE PLACE.
JINGLE JANGLE

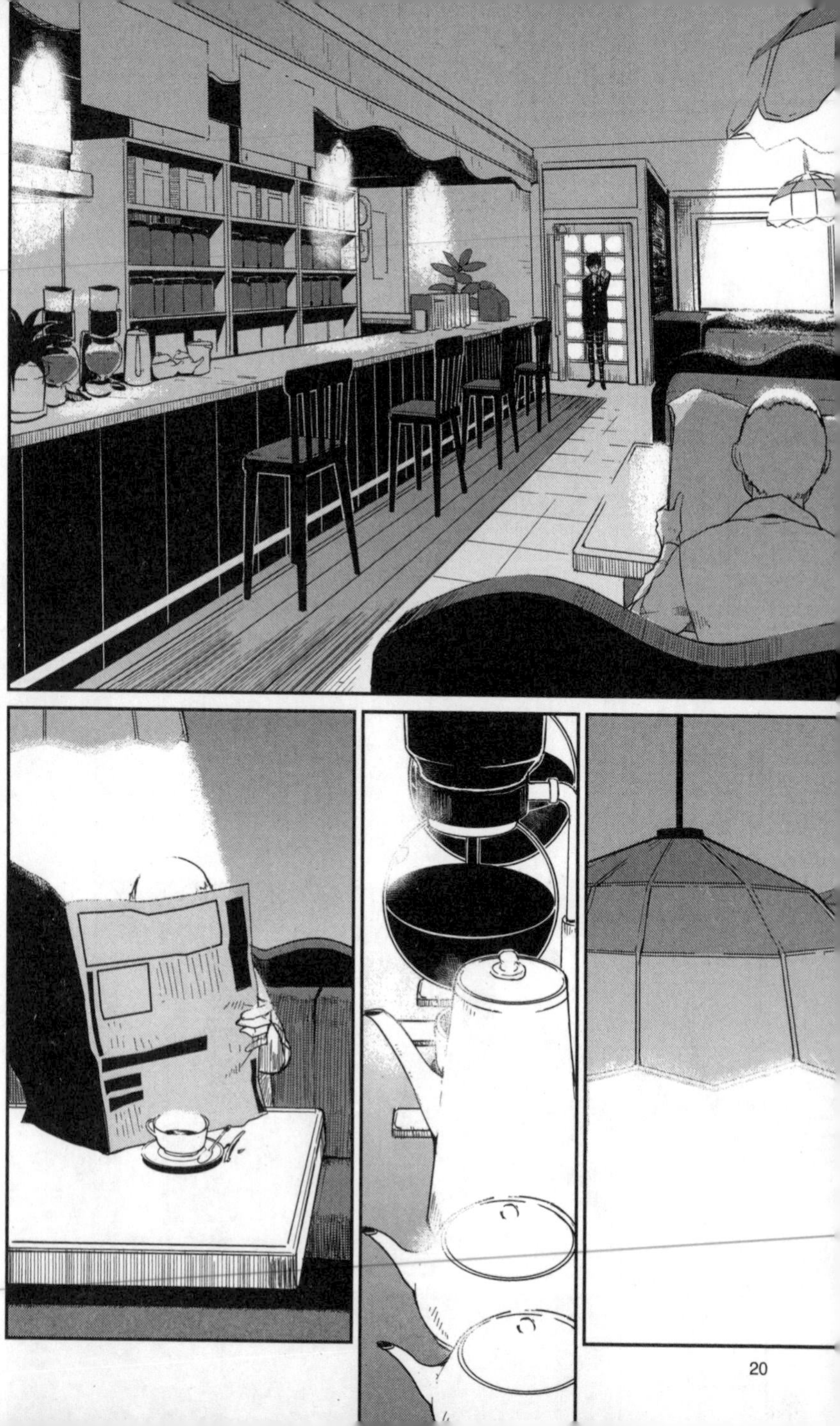

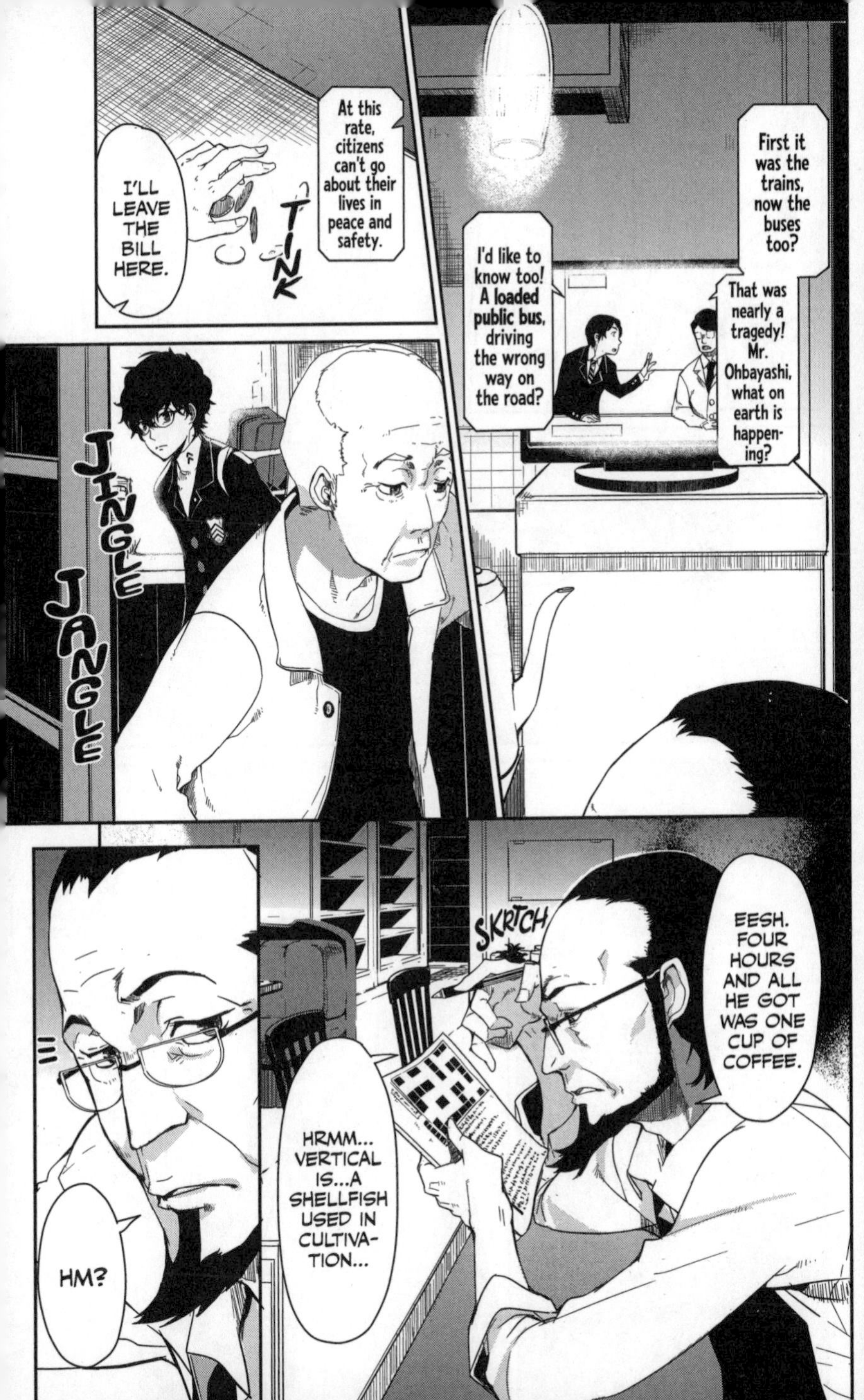
First it was the trains, now the buses too?
That was nearly a tragedy! Mr. Ohbayashi, what on earth is happening?
I'd like to know too! A loaded public bus, driving the wrong way on the road?
At this rate, citizens can't go about their lives in peace and safety.
TINK
I'LL LEAVE THE BILL HERE.
JINGLE JANGLE
EESH. FOUR HOURS AND ALL HE GOT WAS ONE CUP OF COFFEE.
SKRTCH
HRMM... VERTICAL IS...A SHELLFISH USED IN CULTIVATION...
HM?

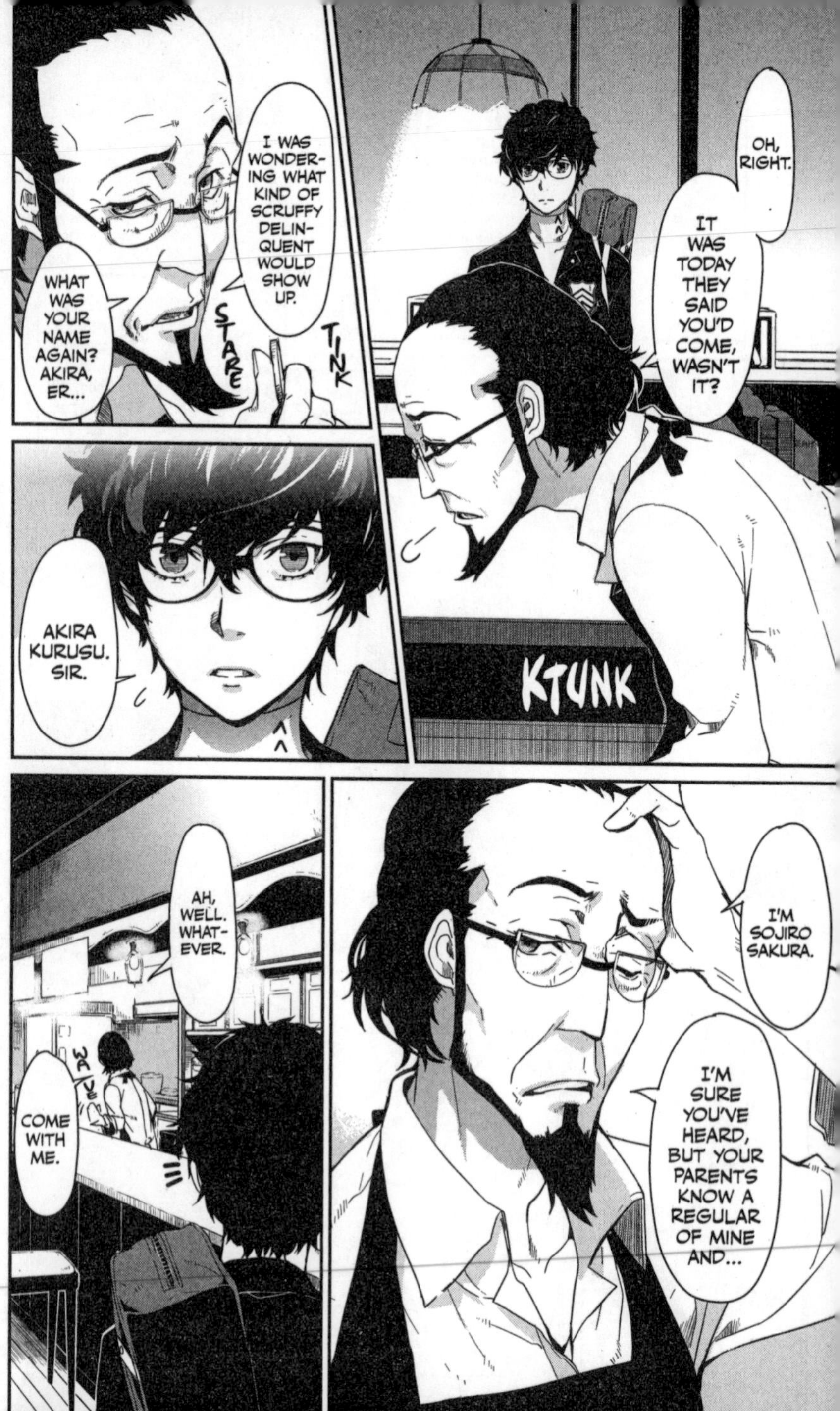
OH, RIGHT.
IT WAS TODAY THEY SAID YOU'D COME, WASN'T IT?
KTUNK
I WAS WONDERING WHAT KIND OF SCRUFFY DELINQUENT WOULD SHOW UP.
TINK
STARE
WHAT WAS YOUR NAME AGAIN? AKIRA, ER...
AKIRA KURUSU. SIR.
I'M SOJIRO SAKURA.
I'M SURE YOU'VE HEARD, BUT YOUR PARENTS KNOW A REGULAR OF MINE AND...
AH, WELL. WHATEVER.
WAVE
COME WITH ME.

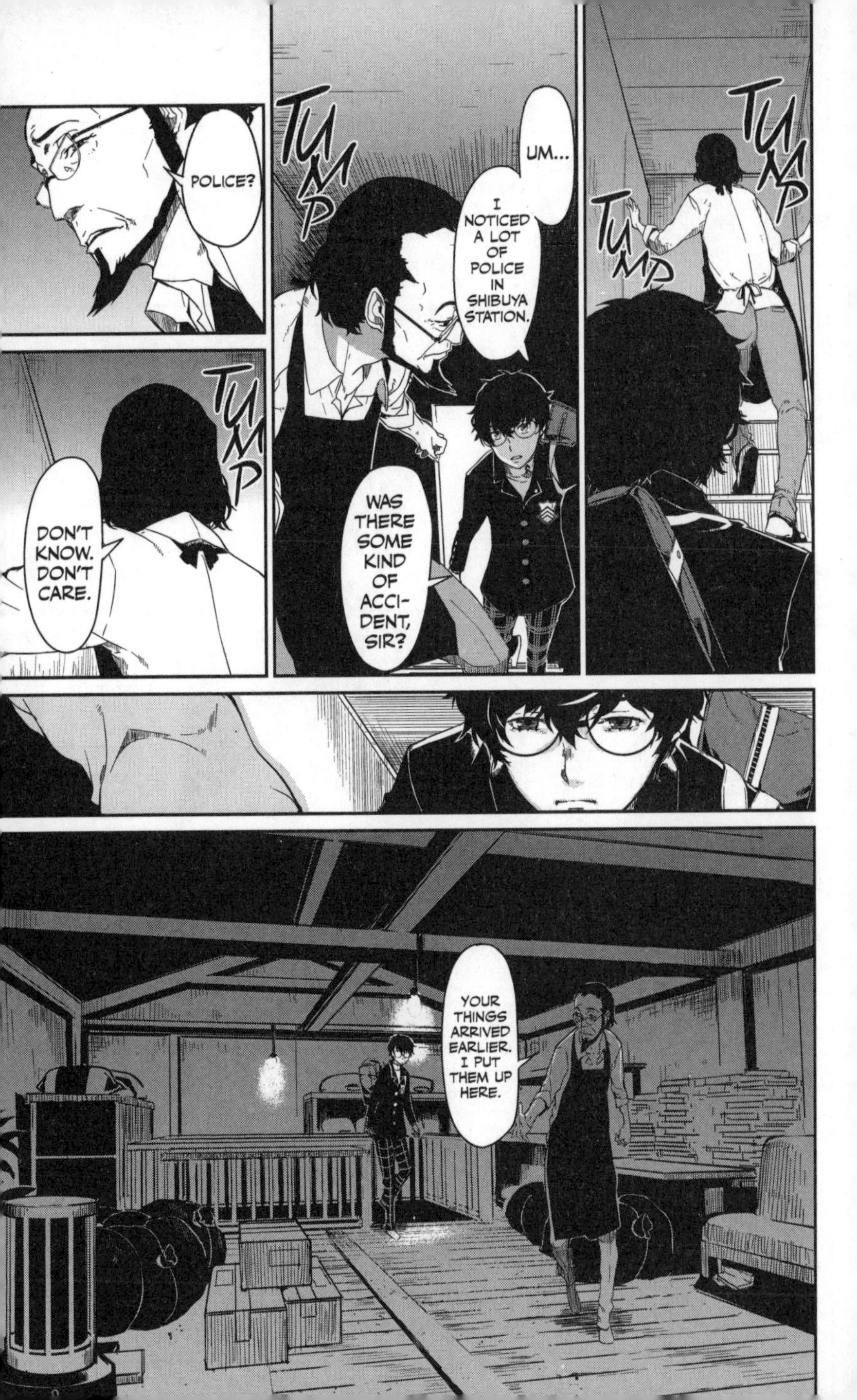
TUMP
TUMP
TUMP
UM...
I NOTICED A LOT OF POLICE IN SHIBUYA STATION.
WAS THERE SOME KIND OF ACCI- DENT, SIR?
POLICE?
TUMP
DON'T KNOW. DON'T CARE.
YOUR THINGS ARRIVED EARLIER. I PUT THEM UP HERE.

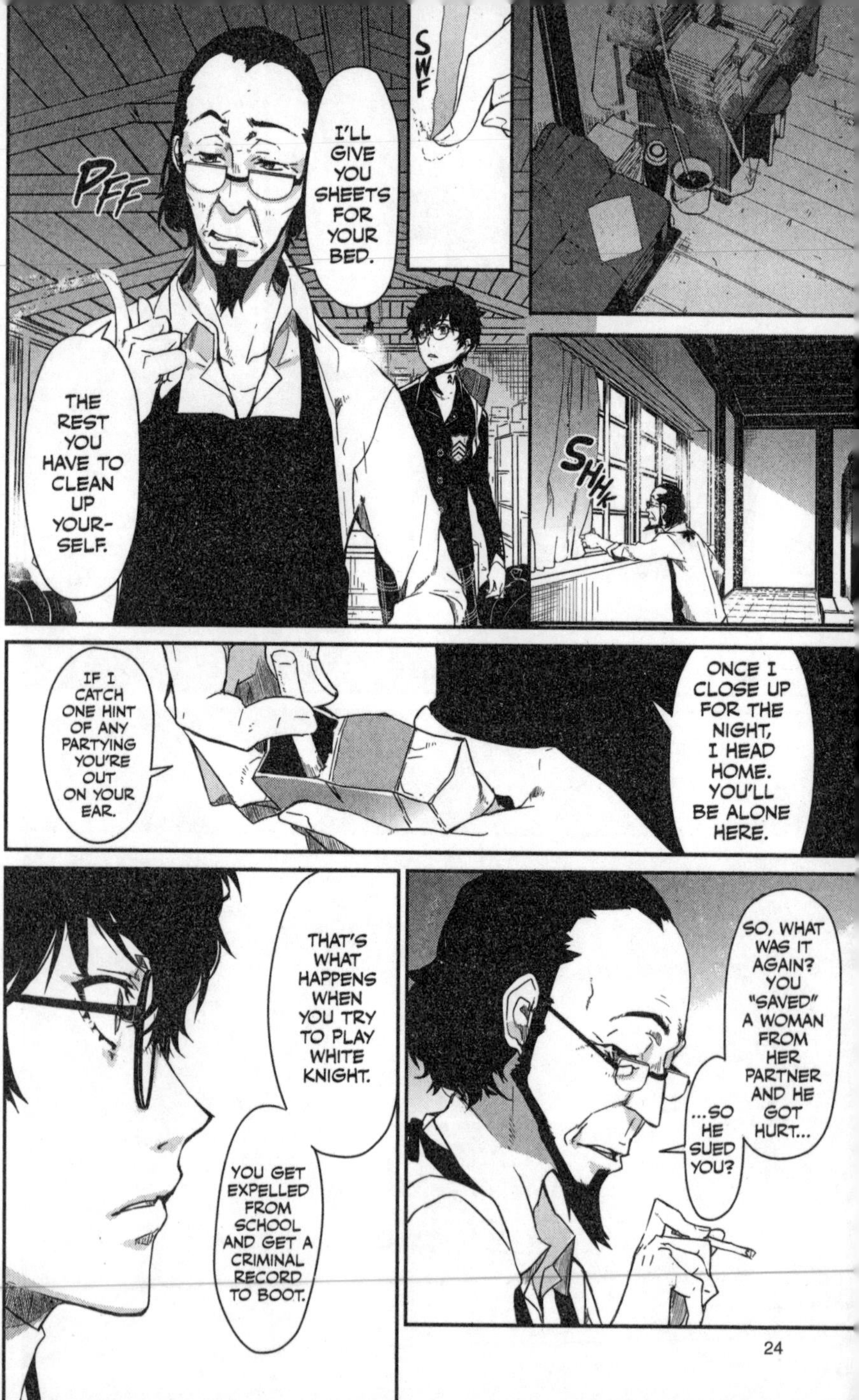
SWF
SHHK
I'LL GIVE YOU SHEETS FOR YOUR BED.
PFF
THE REST YOU HAVE TO CLEAN UP YOUR-SELF.
ONCE I CLOSE UP FOR THE NIGHT, I HEAD HOME. YOU'LL BE ALONE HERE.
IF I CATCH ONE HINT OF ANY PARTYING YOU'RE OUT ON YOUR EAR.
SO, WHAT WAS IT AGAIN? YOU "SAVED" A WOMAN FROM HER PARTNER AND HE GOT HURT...
...SO HE SUED YOU?
THAT'S WHAT HAPPENS WHEN YOU TRY TO PLAY WHITE KNIGHT.
YOU GET EXPELLED FROM SCHOOL AND GET A CRIMINAL RECORD TO BOOT.

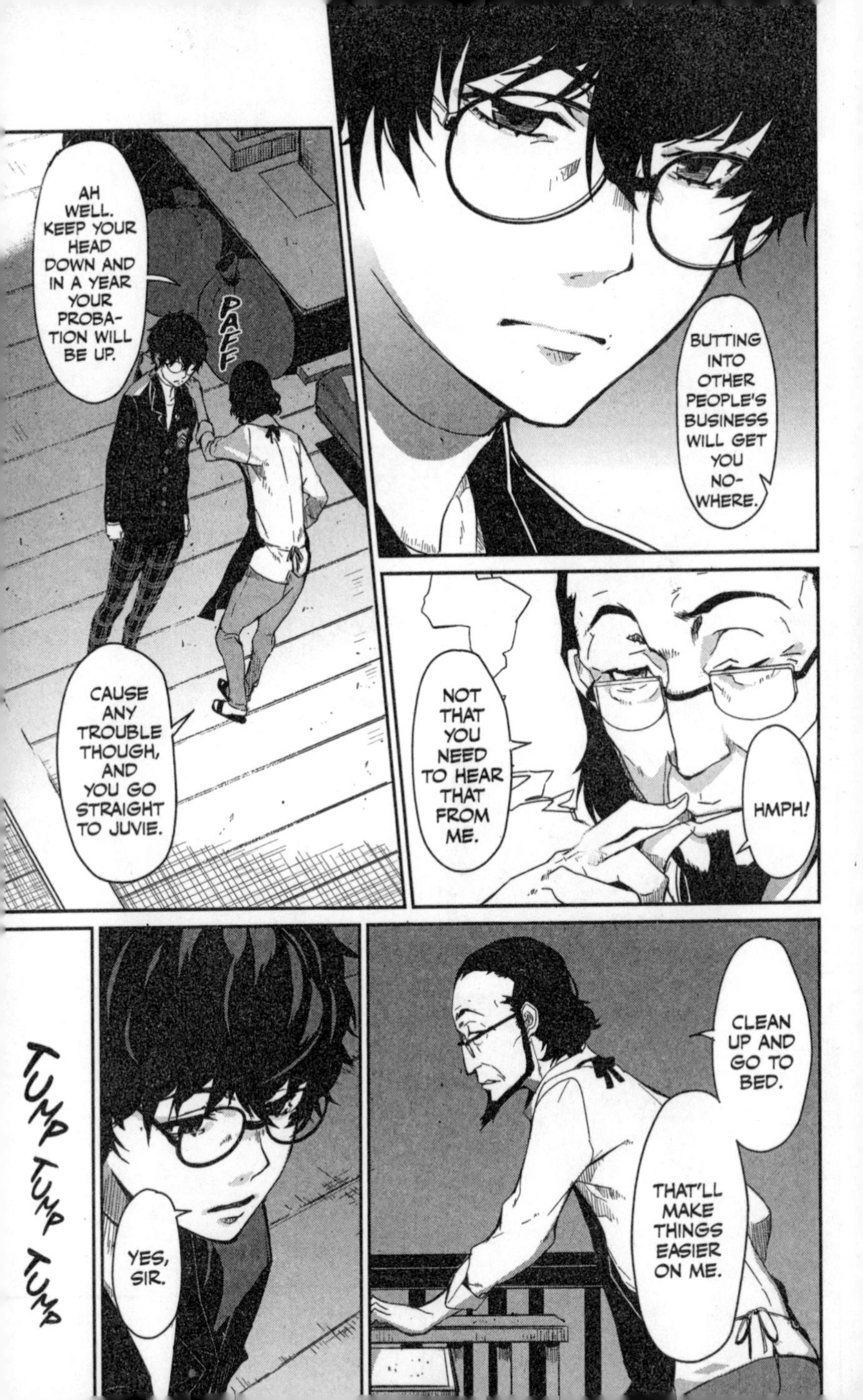
BUTTING INTO OTHER PEOPLE'S BUSINESS WILL GET YOU NO-WHERE.
NOT THAT YOU NEED TO HEAR THAT FROM ME.
HMPH!
AH WELL. KEEP YOUR HEAD DOWN AND IN A YEAR YOUR PROBA-TION WILL BE UP.
PAFF
CAUSE ANY TROUBLE THOUGH, AND YOU GO STRAIGHT TO JUVIE.
CLEAN UP AND GO TO BED.
THAT'LL MAKE THINGS EASIER ON ME.
YES, SIR.
TUMP TUMP TUMP

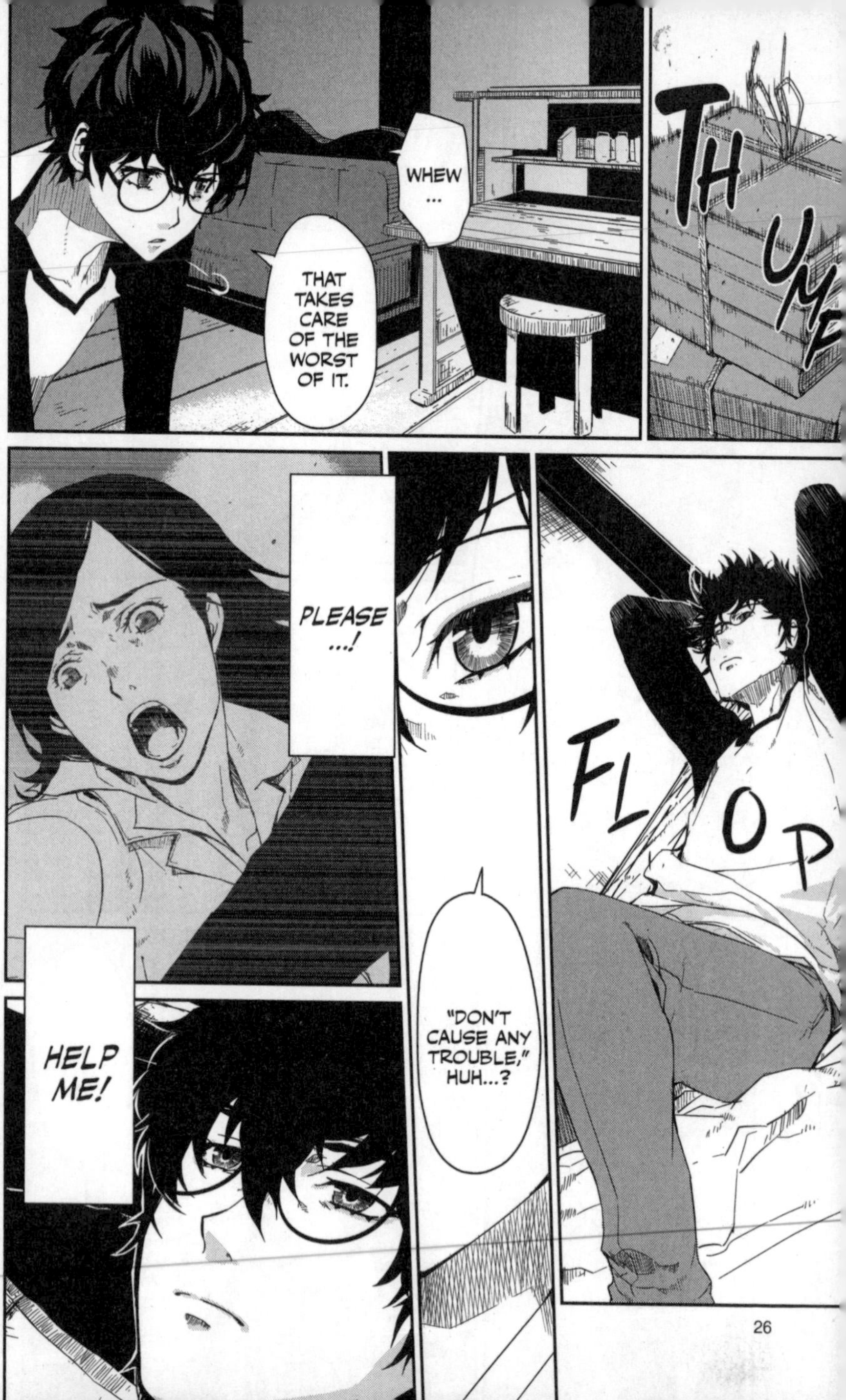
THUMP
WHEW...
THAT TAKES CARE OF THE WORST OF IT.
FLOP
"DON'T CAUSE ANY TROUBLE," HUH...?
PLEASE...!
HELP ME!

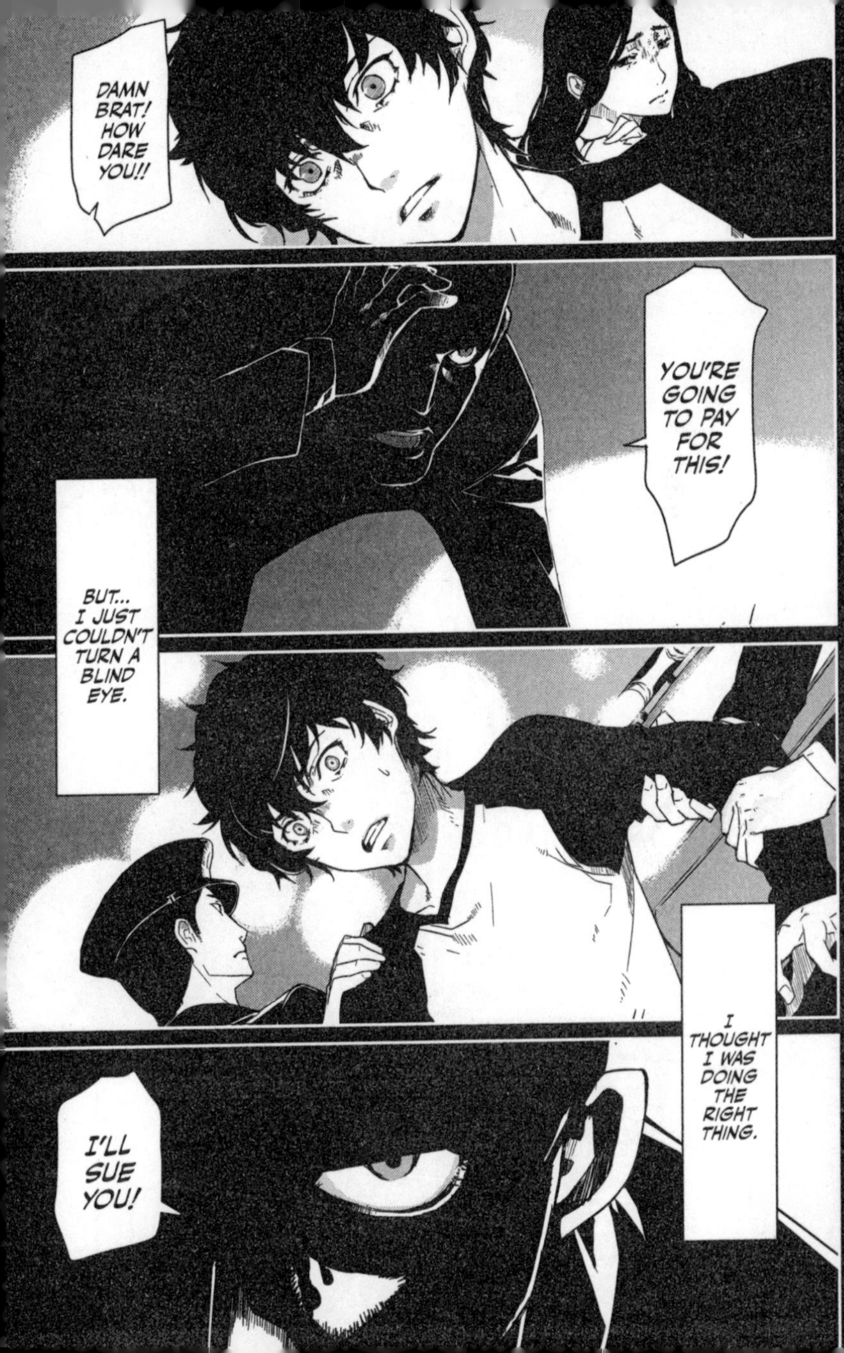
DAMN BRAT! HOW DARE YOU!!
YOU'RE GOING TO PAY FOR THIS!
BUT... I JUST COULDN'T TURN A BLIND EYE.
I THOUGHT I WAS DOING THE RIGHT THING.
I'LL SUE YOU!

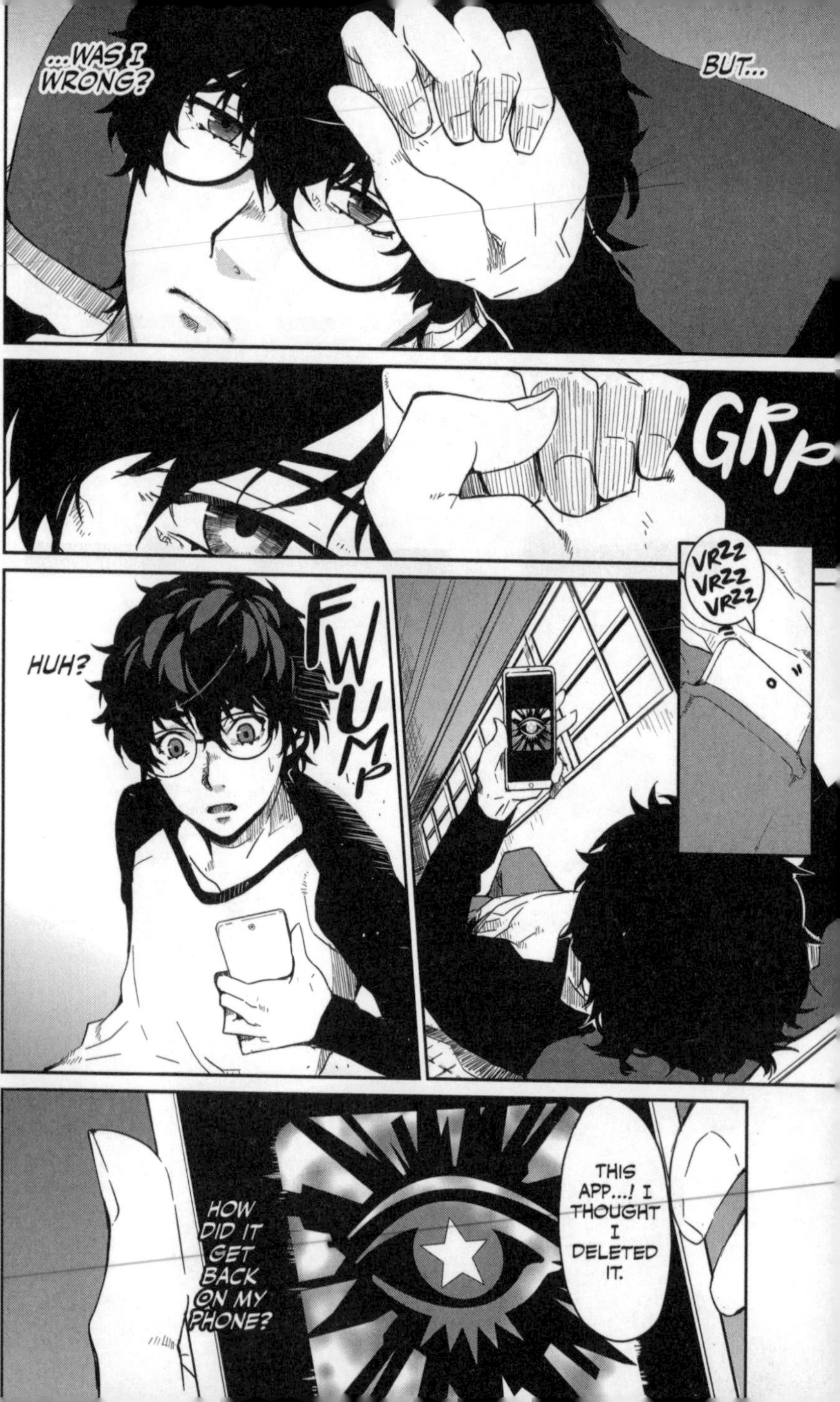
BUT...
...WAS I WRONG?
GRIP
VRZZ VRZZ VRZZ
FWUMP
HUH?
THIS APP...! I THOUGHT I DELETED IT.
HOW DID IT GET BACK ON MY PHONE?

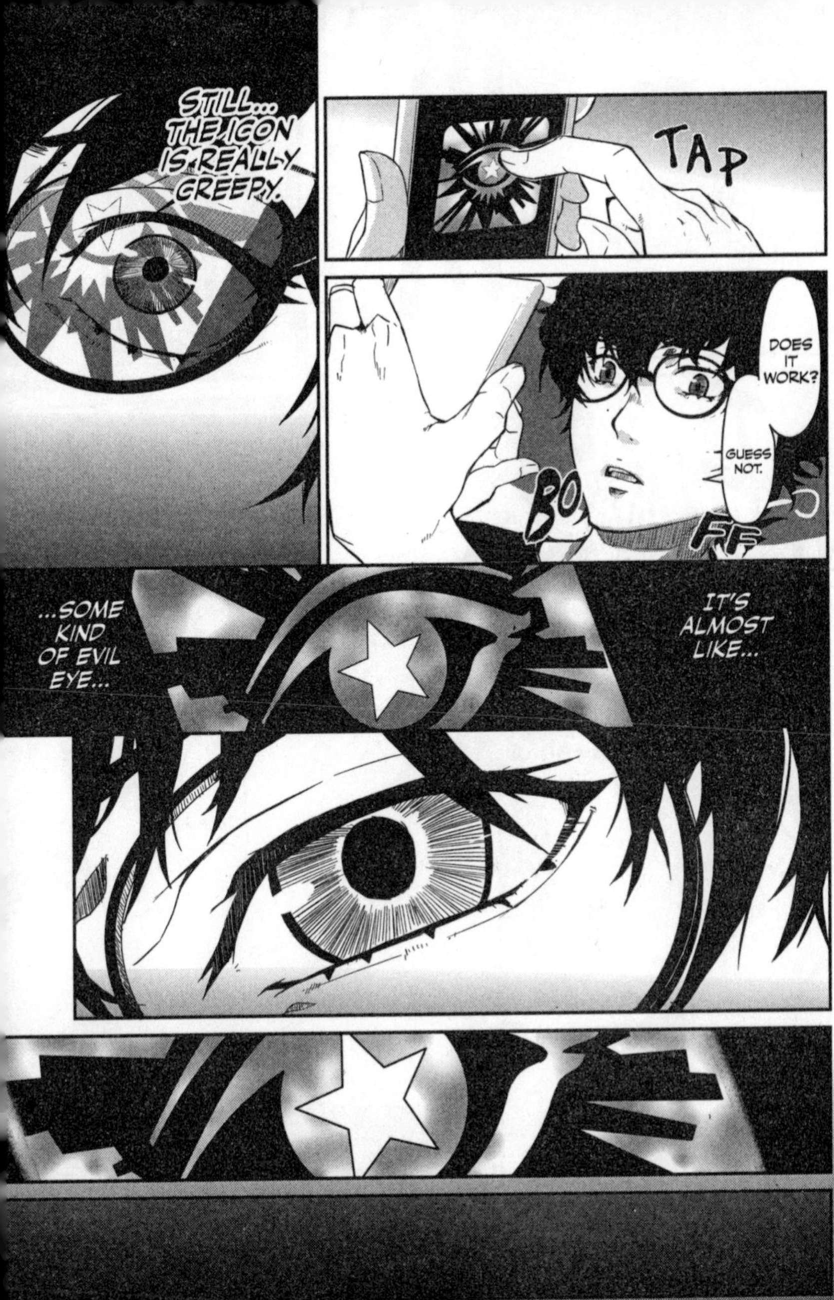
TAP
DOES IT WORK?
GUESS NOT.
BOFF
STILL... THE ICON IS REALLY CREEPY.
IT'S ALMOST LIKE...
...SOME KIND OF EVIL EYE...

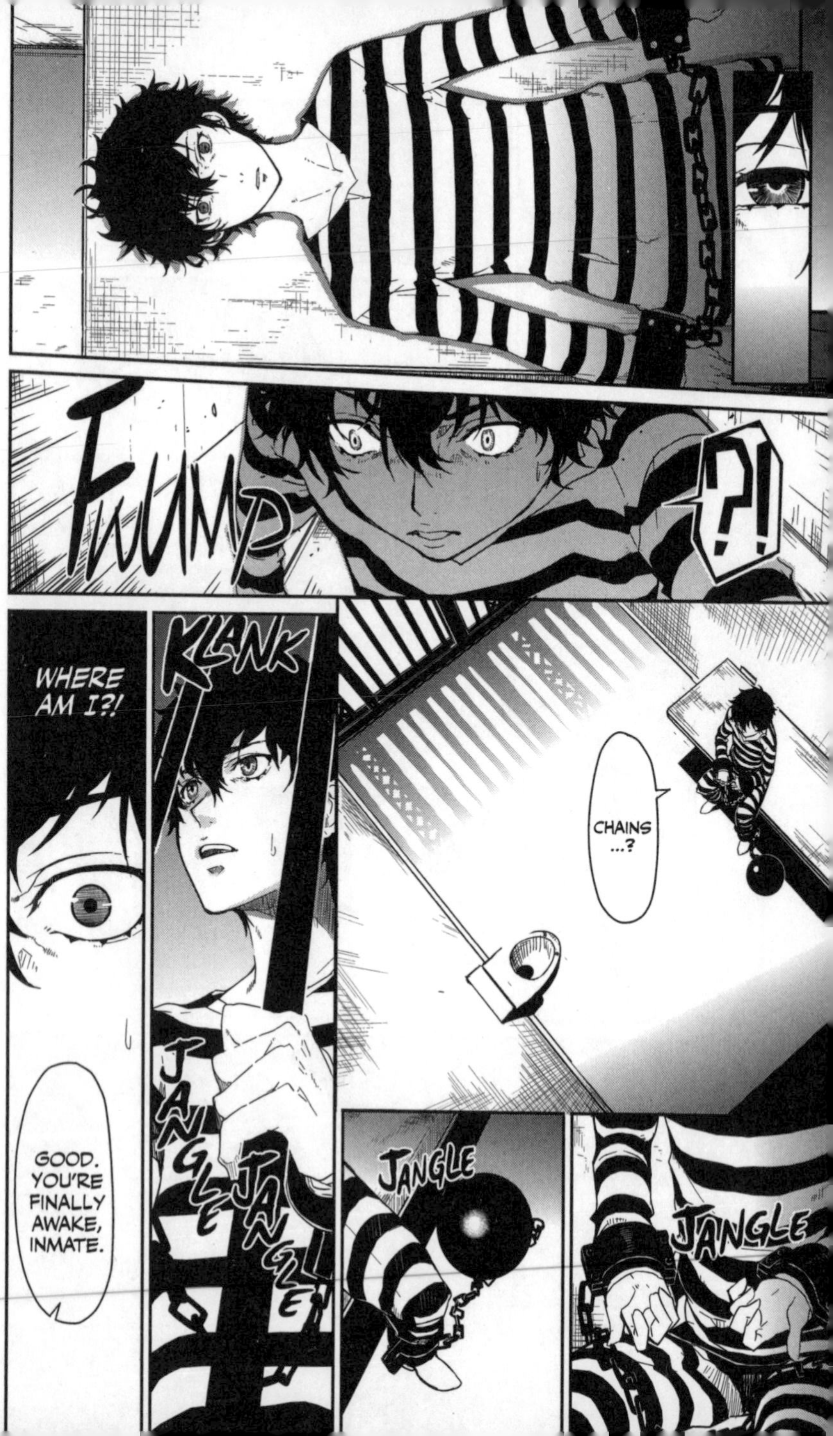
?!
FWUMP
CHAINS ...?
KLANK
WHERE AM I?!
JANGLE
JANGLE
JANGLE
JANGLE
GOOD. YOU'RE FINALLY AWAKE, INMATE.

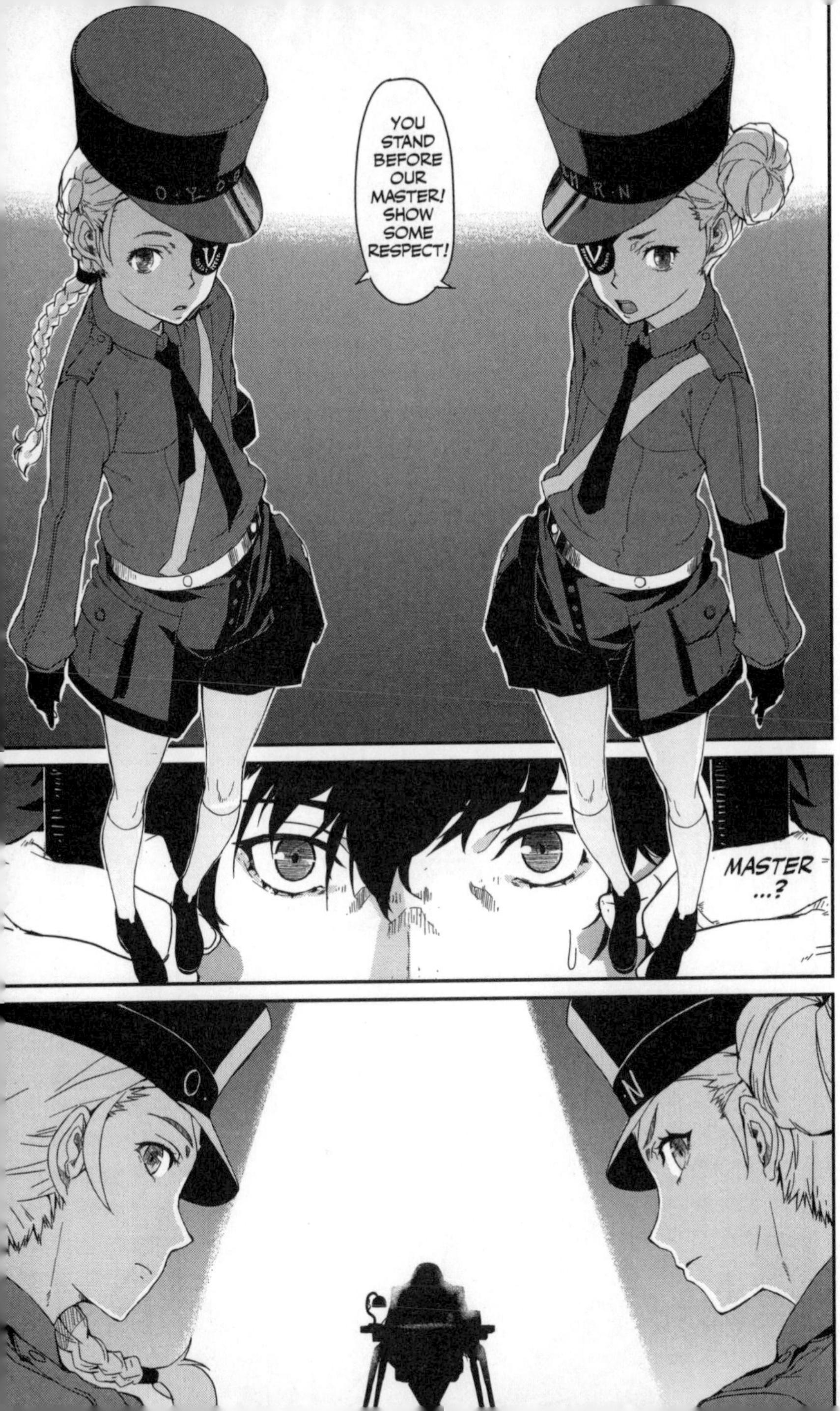
YOU STAND BEFORE OUR MASTER! SHOW SOME RESPECT!
MASTER ...?

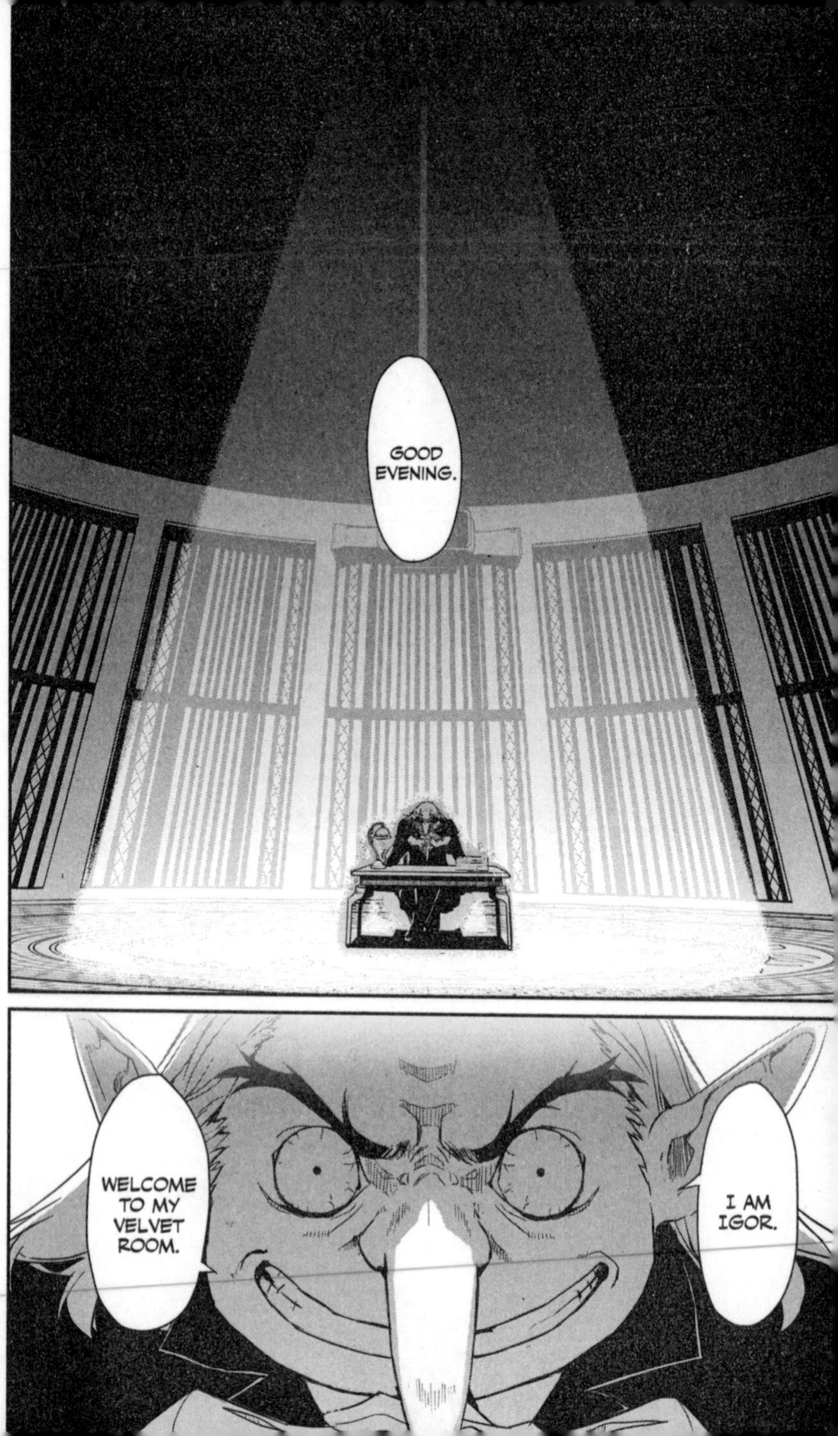
GOOD EVENING.
I AM IGOR.
WELCOME TO MY VELVET ROOM.

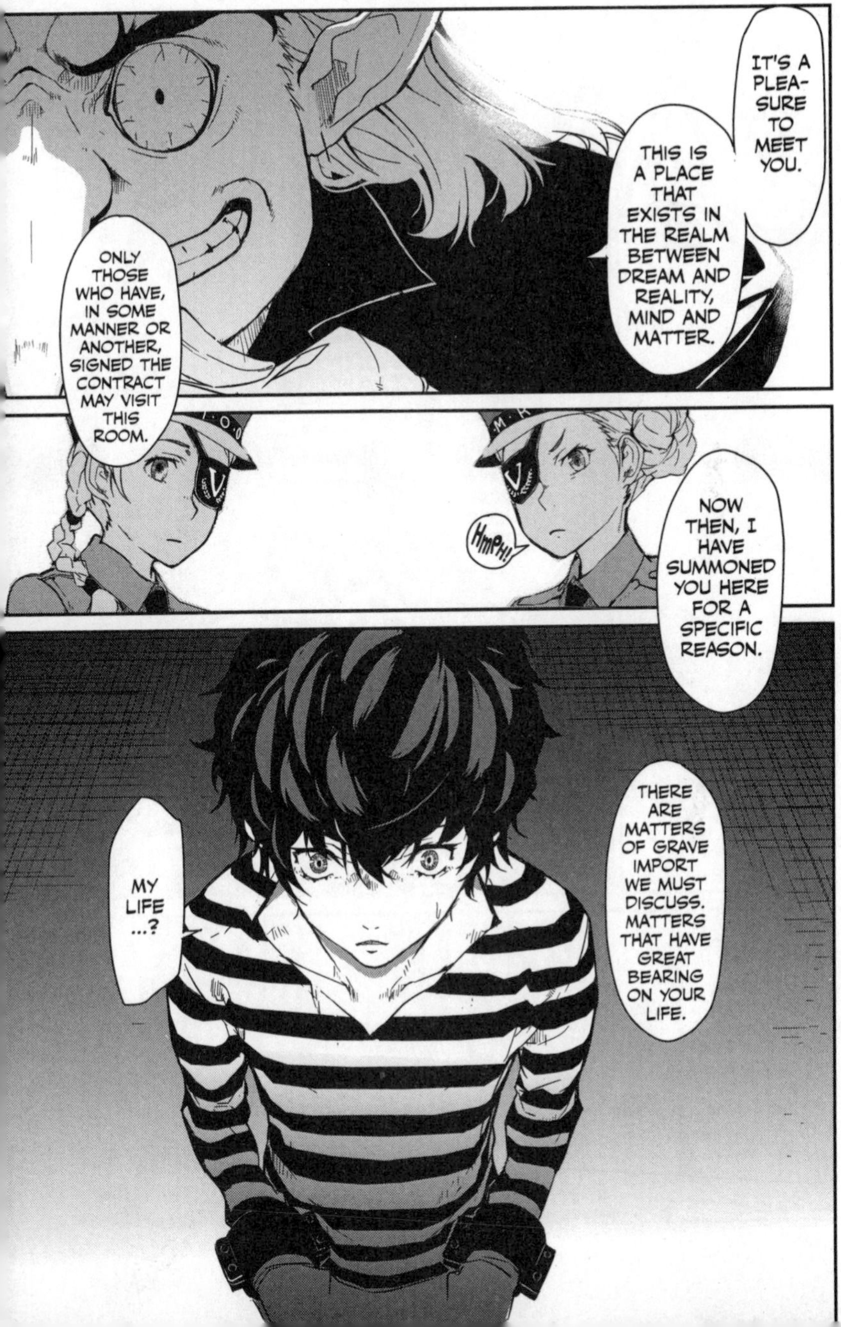
IT'S A PLEASURE TO MEET YOU.
THIS IS A PLACE THAT EXISTS IN THE REALM BETWEEN DREAM AND REALITY, MIND AND MATTER.
ONLY THOSE WHO HAVE, IN SOME MANNER OR ANOTHER, SIGNED THE CONTRACT MAY VISIT THIS ROOM.
NOW THEN, I HAVE SUMMONED YOU HERE FOR A SPECIFIC REASON.
HMPH!!
THERE ARE MATTERS OF GRAVE IMPORT WE MUST DISCUSS. MATTERS THAT HAVE GREAT BEARING ON YOUR LIFE.
MY LIFE ...?

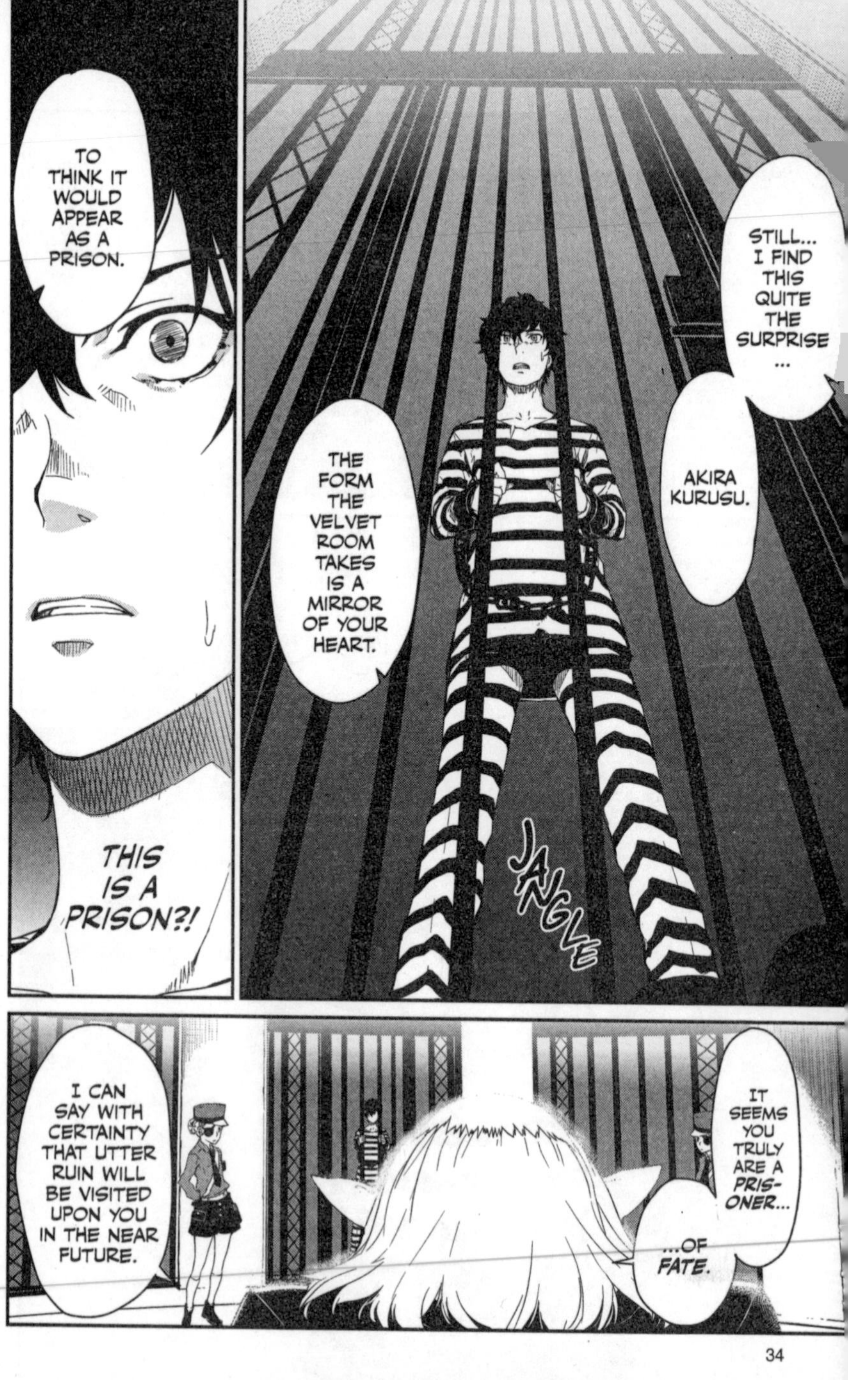
STILL... I FIND THIS QUITE THE SURPRISE...
AKIRA KURUSU.
THE FORM THE VELVET ROOM TAKES IS A MIRROR OF YOUR HEART.
JANGLE
TO THINK IT WOULD APPEAR AS A PRISON.
THIS IS A PRISON?!
IT SEEMS YOU TRULY ARE A PRIS-ONER...
...OF FATE.
I CAN SAY WITH CERTAINTY THAT UTTER RUIN WILL BE VISITED UPON YOU IN THE NEAR FUTURE.

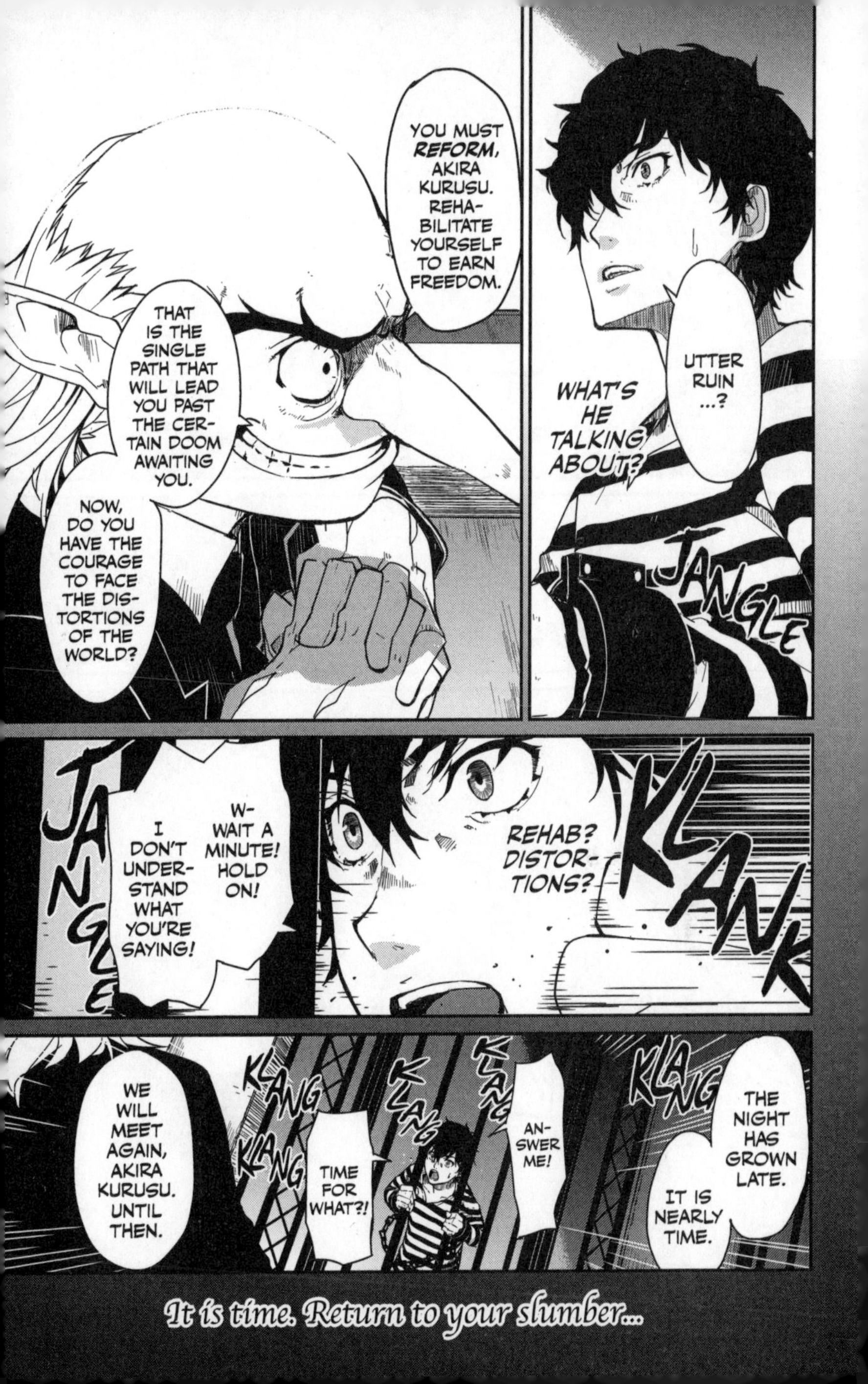

UTTER RUIN ...?
WHAT'S HE TALKING ABOUT?
JANGLE
YOU MUST REFORM, AKIRA KURUSU. REHABILITATE YOURSELF TO EARN FREEDOM.
THAT IS THE SINGLE PATH THAT WILL LEAD YOU PAST THE CERTAIN DOOM AWAITING YOU.
NOW, DO YOU HAVE THE COURAGE TO FACE THE DISTORTIONS OF THE WORLD?
KLANK
REHAB? DISTORTIONS?
W-WAIT A MINUTE! HOLD ON!
I DON'T UNDERSTAND WHAT YOU'RE SAYING!
JANGLE
THE NIGHT HAS GROWN LATE.
IT IS NEARLY TIME.
KLANG
KLANG
ANSWER ME!
KLANG
TIME FOR WHAT?!
KLANG
KLANG
WE WILL MEET AGAIN, AKIRA KURUSU. UNTIL THEN.
It is time. Return to your slumber...

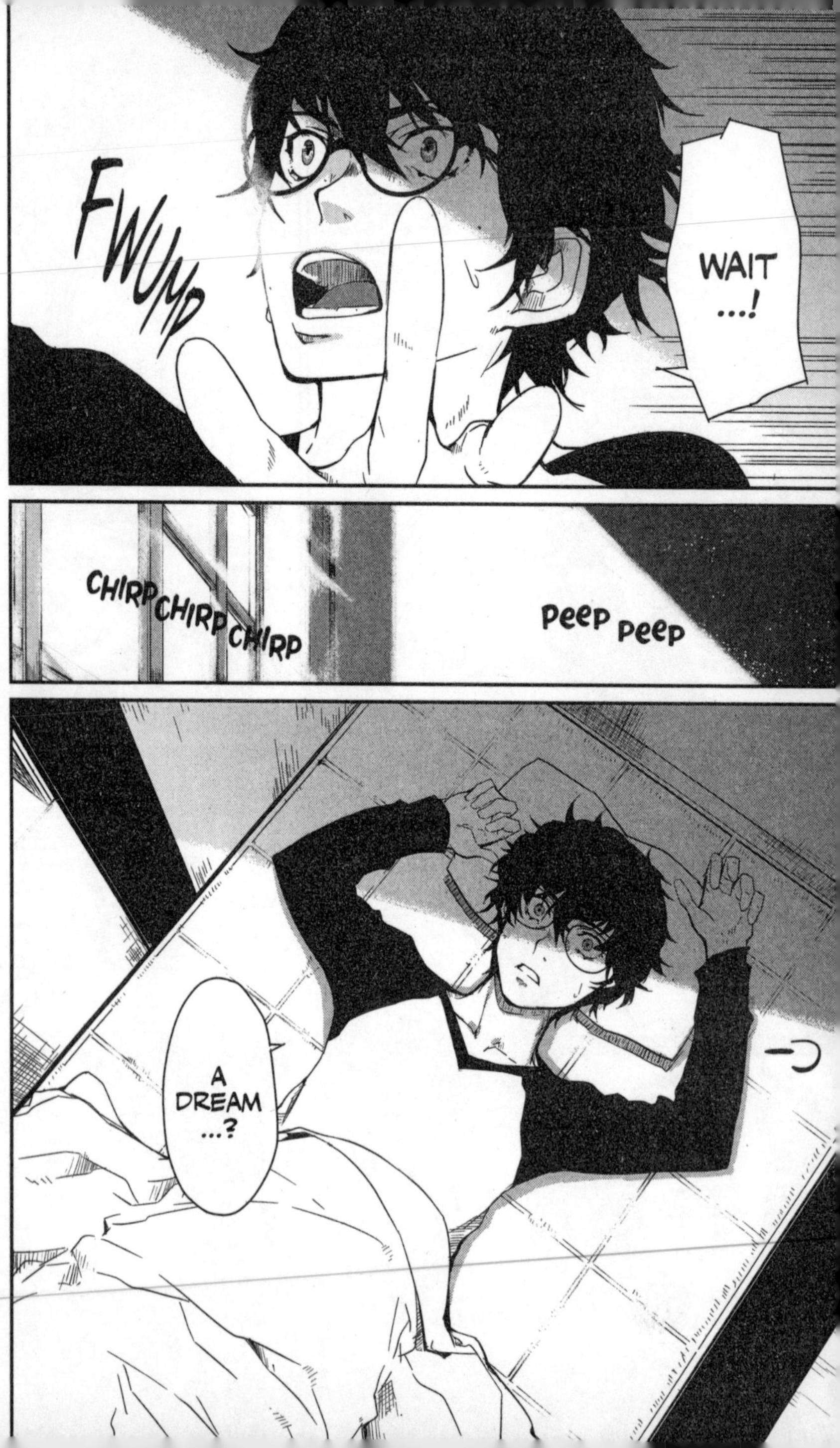
WAIT ...!
FWUMP
PEEP PEEP
CHIRP CHIRP CHIRP
A DREAM ...?

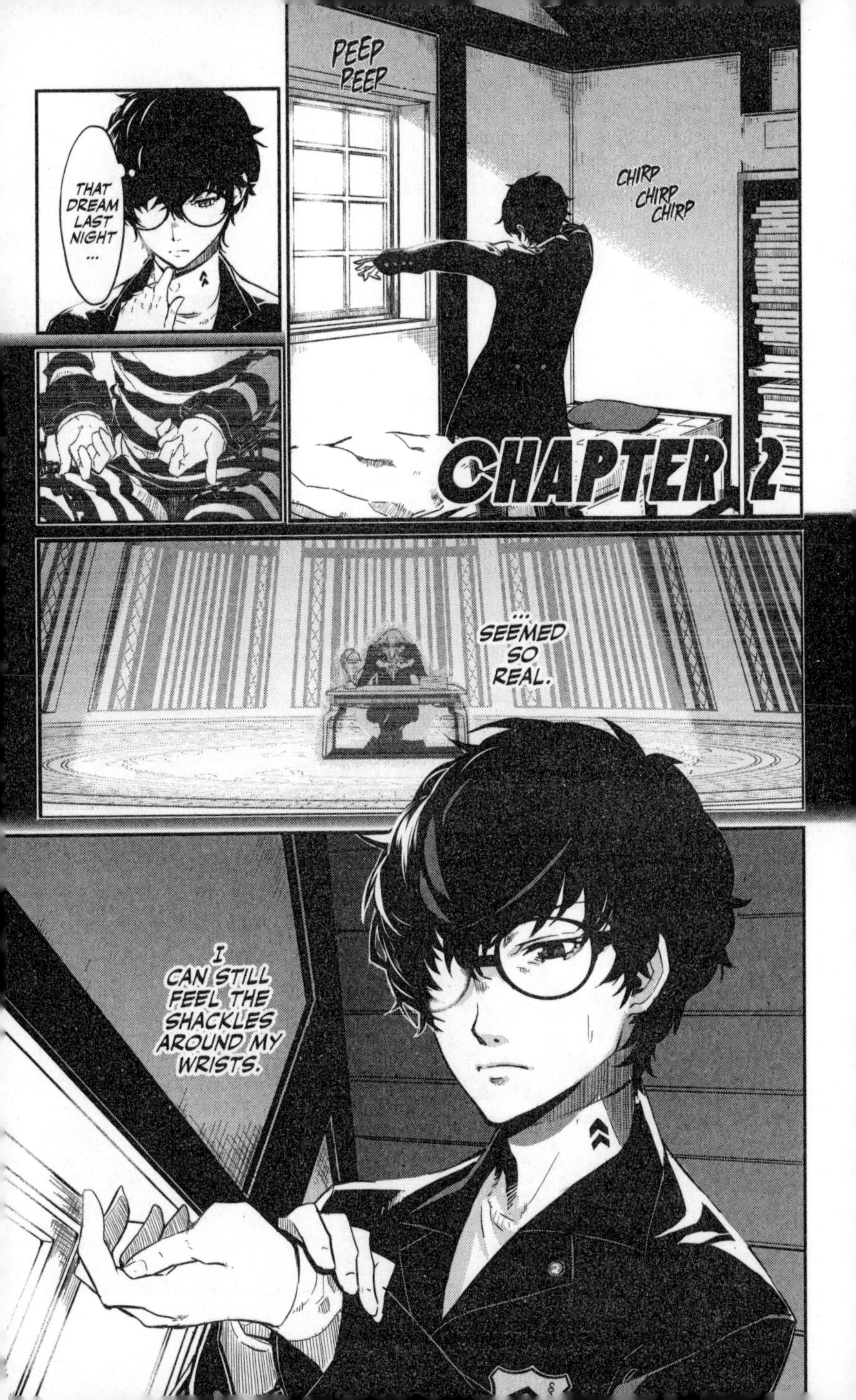
PEEP PEEP
CHIRP CHIRP CHIRP
CHAPTER 2
THAT DREAM LAST NIGHT ...
... SEEMED SO REAL.
I CAN STILL FEEL THE SHACKLES AROUND MY WRISTS.

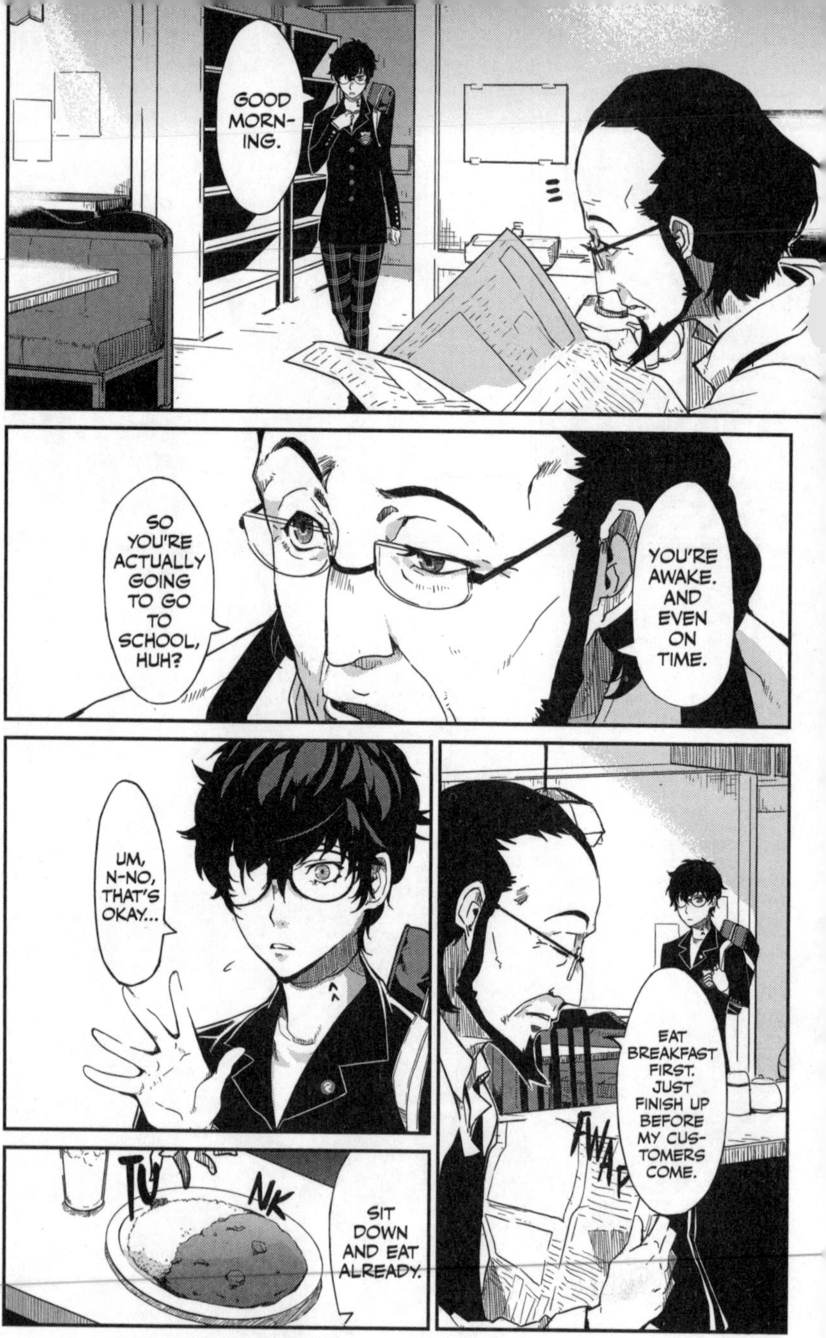
GOOD MORN-ING.
YOU'RE AWAKE. AND EVEN ON TIME.
SO YOU'RE ACTUALLY GOING TO GO TO SCHOOL, HUH?
EAT BREAKFAST FIRST. JUST FINISH UP BEFORE MY CUS-TOMERS COME.
FWAP
UM, N-NO, THAT'S OKAY...
TUNK
SIT DOWN AND EAT ALREADY.

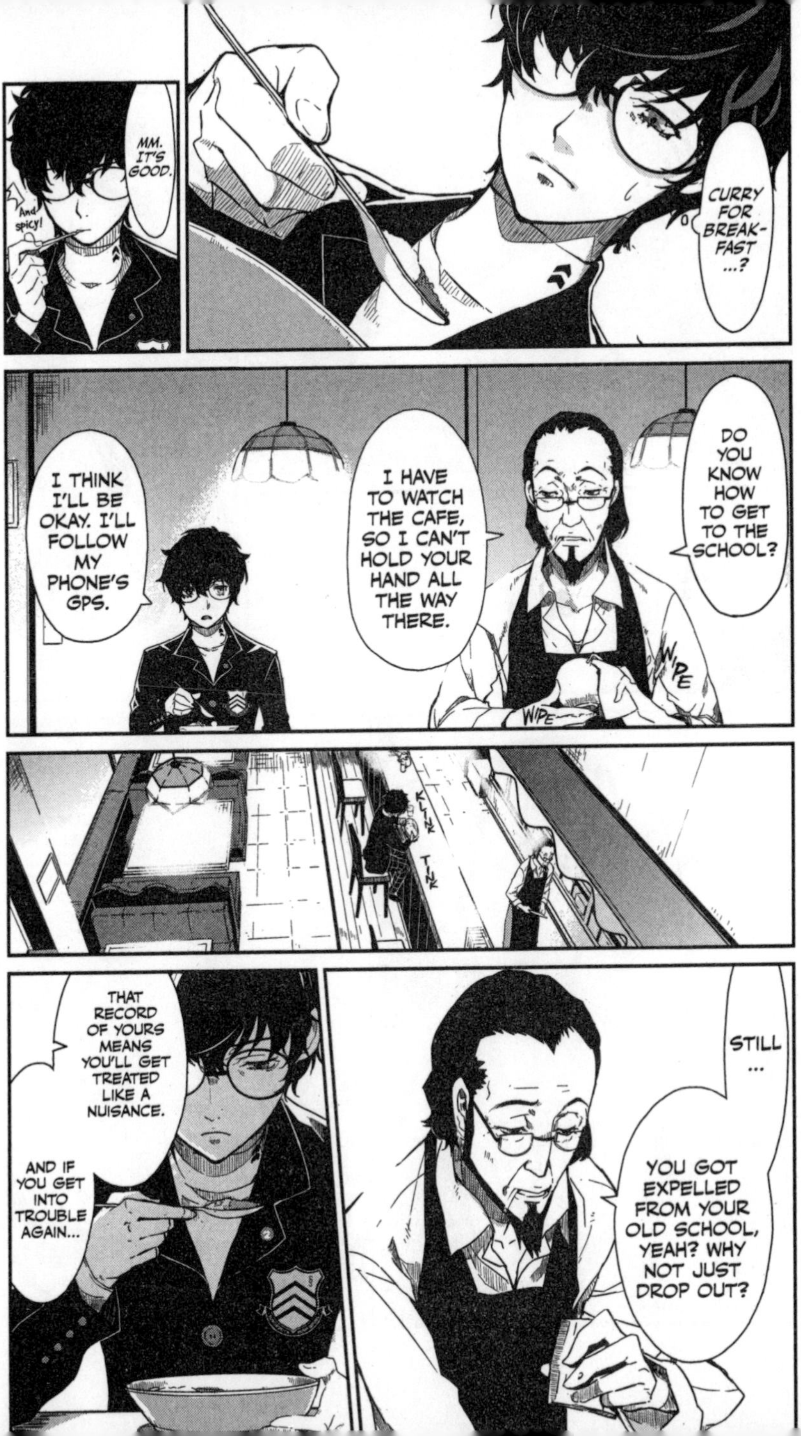
CURRY FOR BREAK-FAST ...?
MM. IT'S GOOD.
And spicy!
DO YOU KNOW HOW TO GET TO THE SCHOOL?
I HAVE TO WATCH THE CAFE, SO I CAN'T HOLD YOUR HAND ALL THE WAY THERE.
WIPE
WIPE
I THINK I'LL BE OKAY. I'LL FOLLOW MY PHONE'S GPS.
KLINK
TINK
STILL ...
YOU GOT EXPELLED FROM YOUR OLD SCHOOL, YEAH? WHY NOT JUST DROP OUT?
THAT RECORD OF YOURS MEANS YOU'LL GET TREATED LIKE A NUISANCE.
AND IF YOU GET INTO TROUBLE AGAIN...

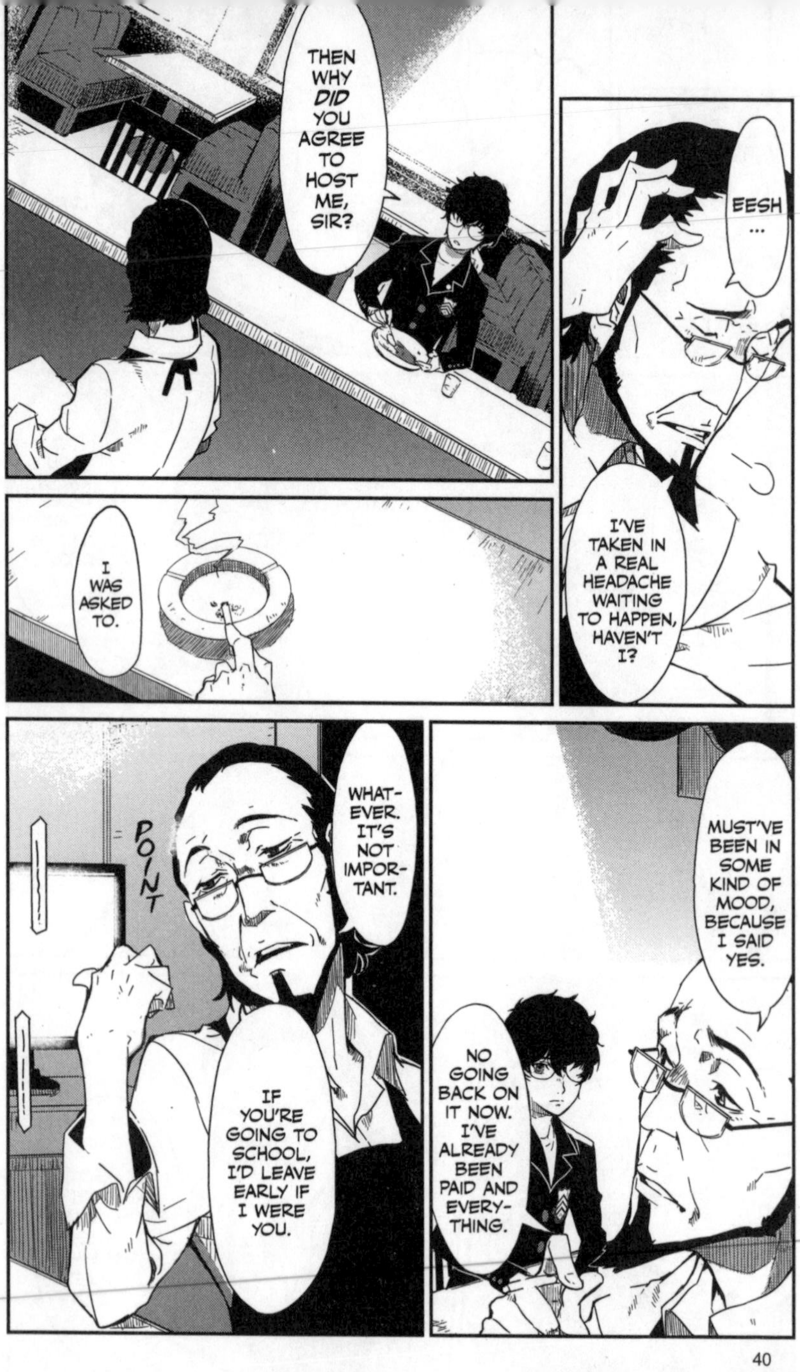
EESH...
I'VE TAKEN IN A REAL HEADACHE WAITING TO HAPPEN, HAVEN'T I?
THEN WHY *DID* YOU AGREE TO HOST ME, SIR?
I WAS ASKED TO.
MUST'VE BEEN IN SOME KIND OF MOOD, BECAUSE I SAID YES.
NO GOING BACK ON IT NOW. I'VE ALREADY BEEN PAID AND EVERYTHING.
WHATEVER. IT'S NOT IMPORTANT.
POINT
IF YOU'RE GOING TO SCHOOL, I'D LEAVE EARLY IF I WERE YOU.

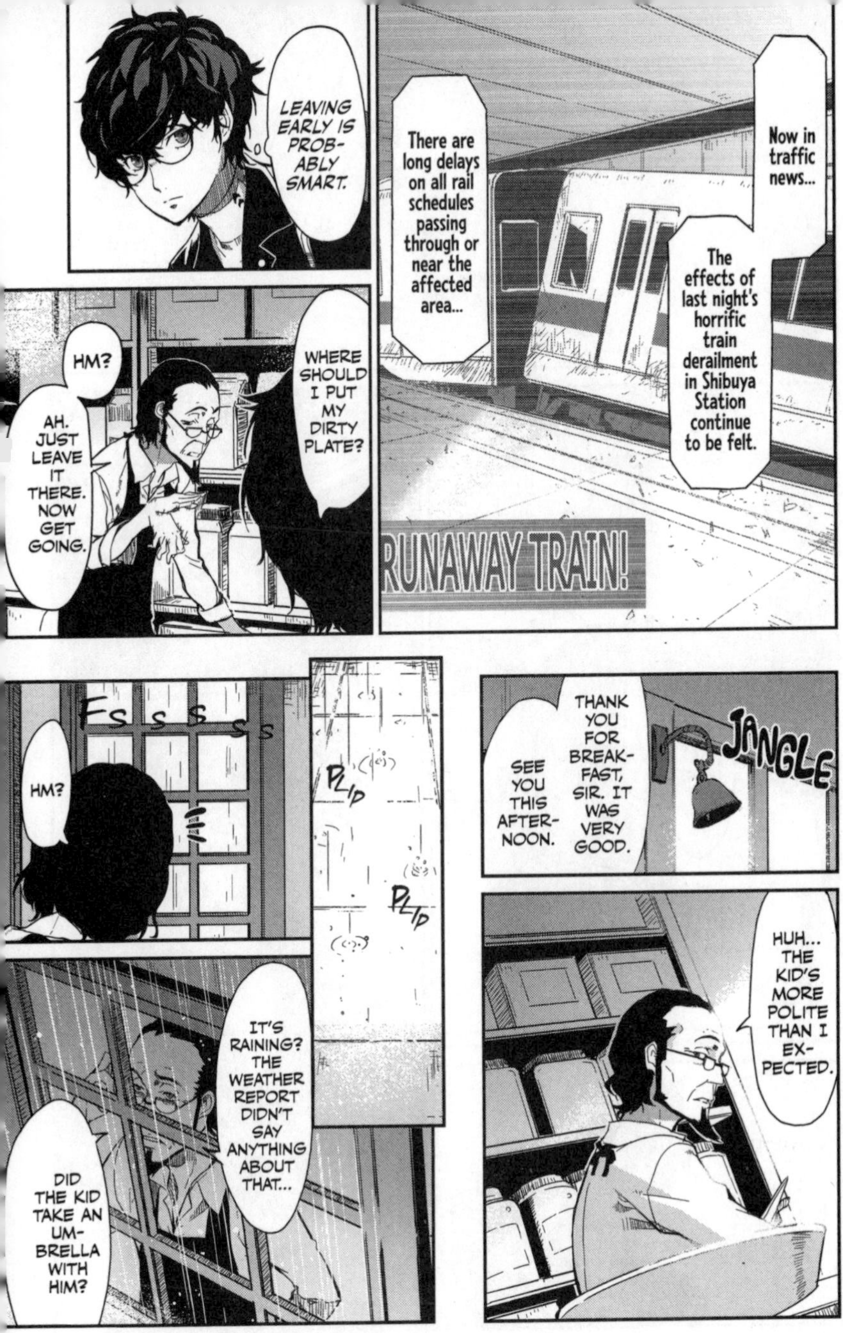
Now in traffic news...
The effects of last night's horrific train derailment in Shibuya Station continue to be felt.
There are long delays on all rail schedules passing through or near the affected area...
RUNAWAY TRAIN!
LEAVING EARLY IS PROBABLY SMART.
WHERE SHOULD I PUT MY DIRTY PLATE?
HM?
AH. JUST LEAVE IT THERE. NOW GET GOING.
JANGLE
THANK YOU FOR BREAKFAST, SIR. IT WAS VERY GOOD.
SEE YOU THIS AFTERNOON.
HUH... THE KID'S MORE POLITE THAN I EXPECTED.
PLIP
PLIP
FSSSSS
HM?
IT'S RAINING? THE WEATHER REPORT DIDN'T SAY ANYTHING ABOUT THAT...
DID THE KID TAKE AN UMBRELLA WITH HIM?

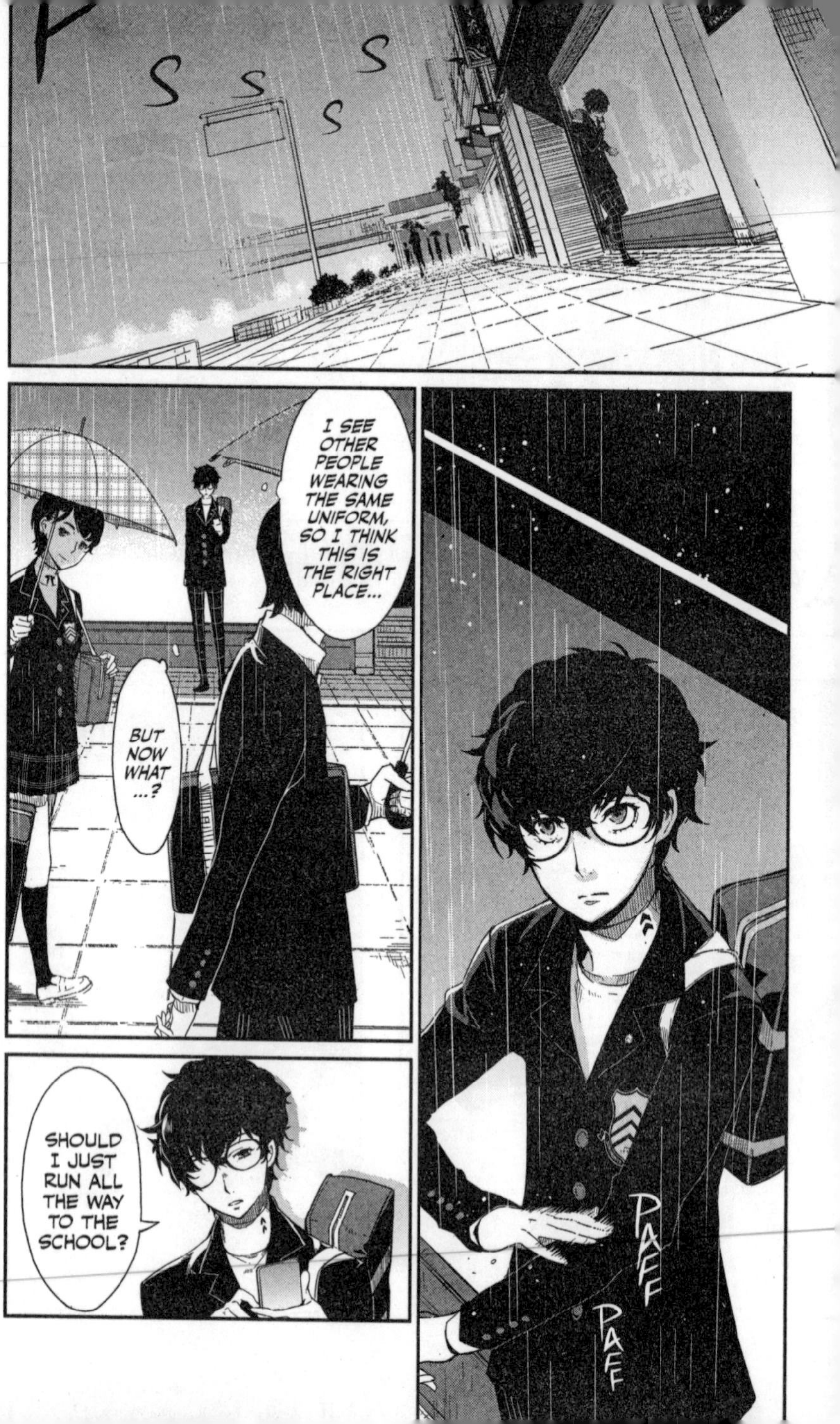
SSSSS
PAFF
PAFF
I SEE OTHER PEOPLE WEARING THE SAME UNIFORM, SO I THINK THIS IS THE RIGHT PLACE...
BUT NOW WHAT ...?
SHOULD I JUST RUN ALL THE WAY TO THE SCHOOL?

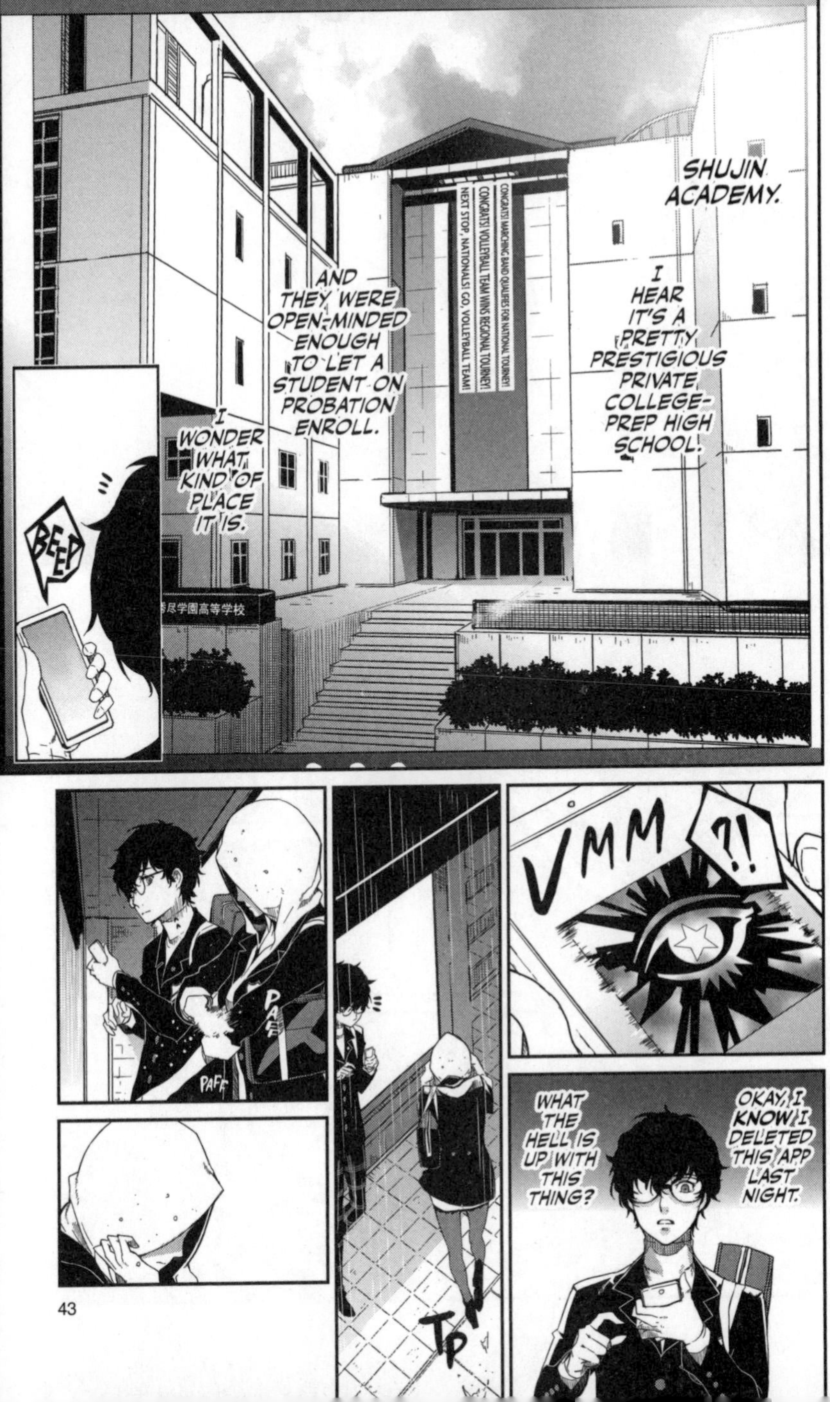
SHUJIN ACADEMY.
I HEAR IT'S A PRETTY PRESTIGIOUS PRIVATE COLLEGE-PREP HIGH SCHOOL.
CONGRATS! MARCHING BAND QUALIFIES FOR NATIONAL TOURNEY!
CONGRATS! VOLLEYBALL TEAM WINS REGIONAL TOURNEY!
NEXT STOP, NATIONALS! GO, VOLLEYBALL TEAM!
AND THEY WERE OPEN-MINDED ENOUGH TO LET A STUDENT ON PROBATION ENROLL.
I WONDER WHAT KIND OF PLACE IT IS.
秀尽学園高等学校
BEEP
?!
VMM
PAFF
PAFF
OKAY, I KNOW I DELETED THIS APP LAST NIGHT.
WHAT THE HELL IS UP WITH THIS THING?
TP

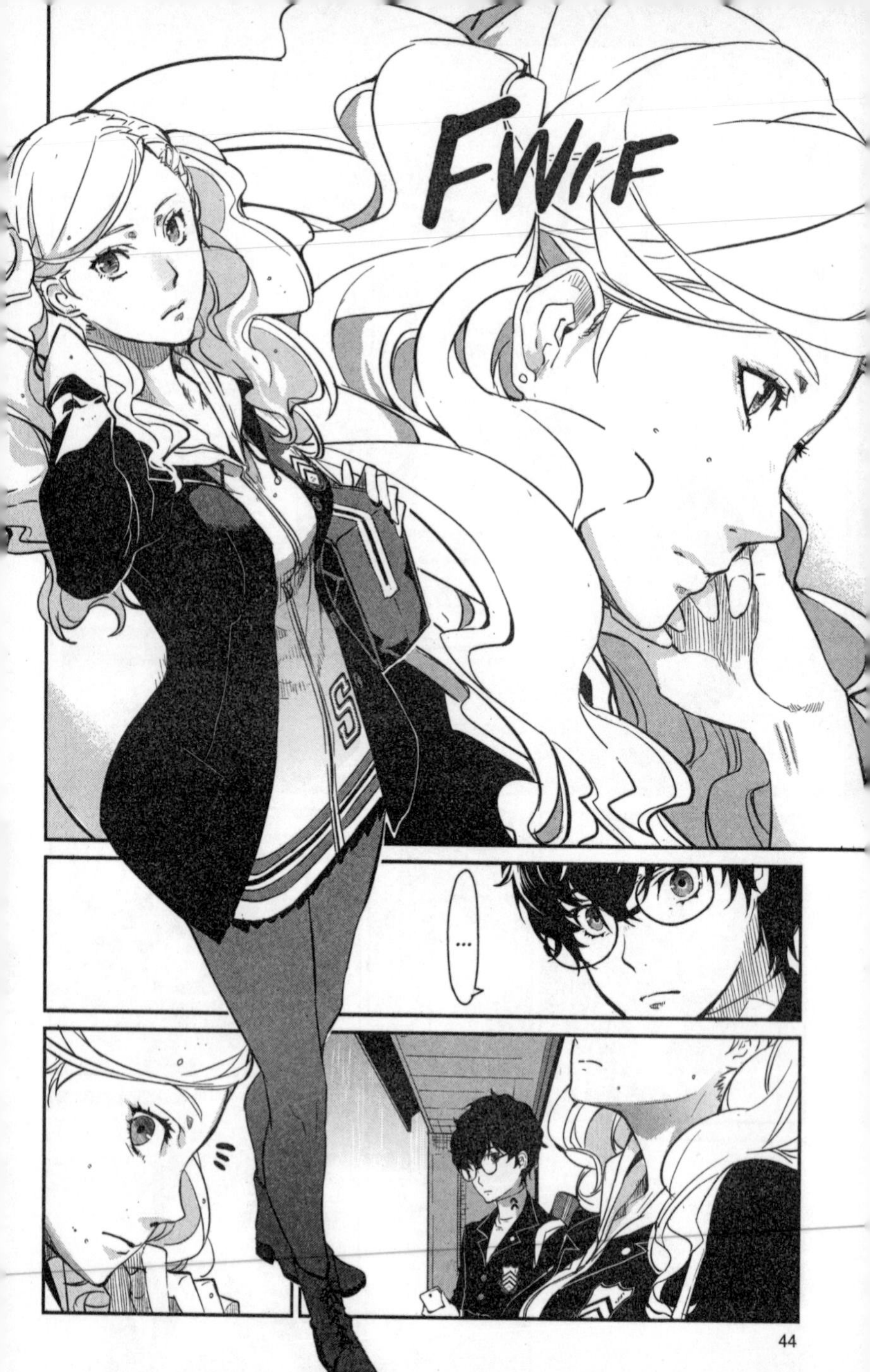
FWIF
...

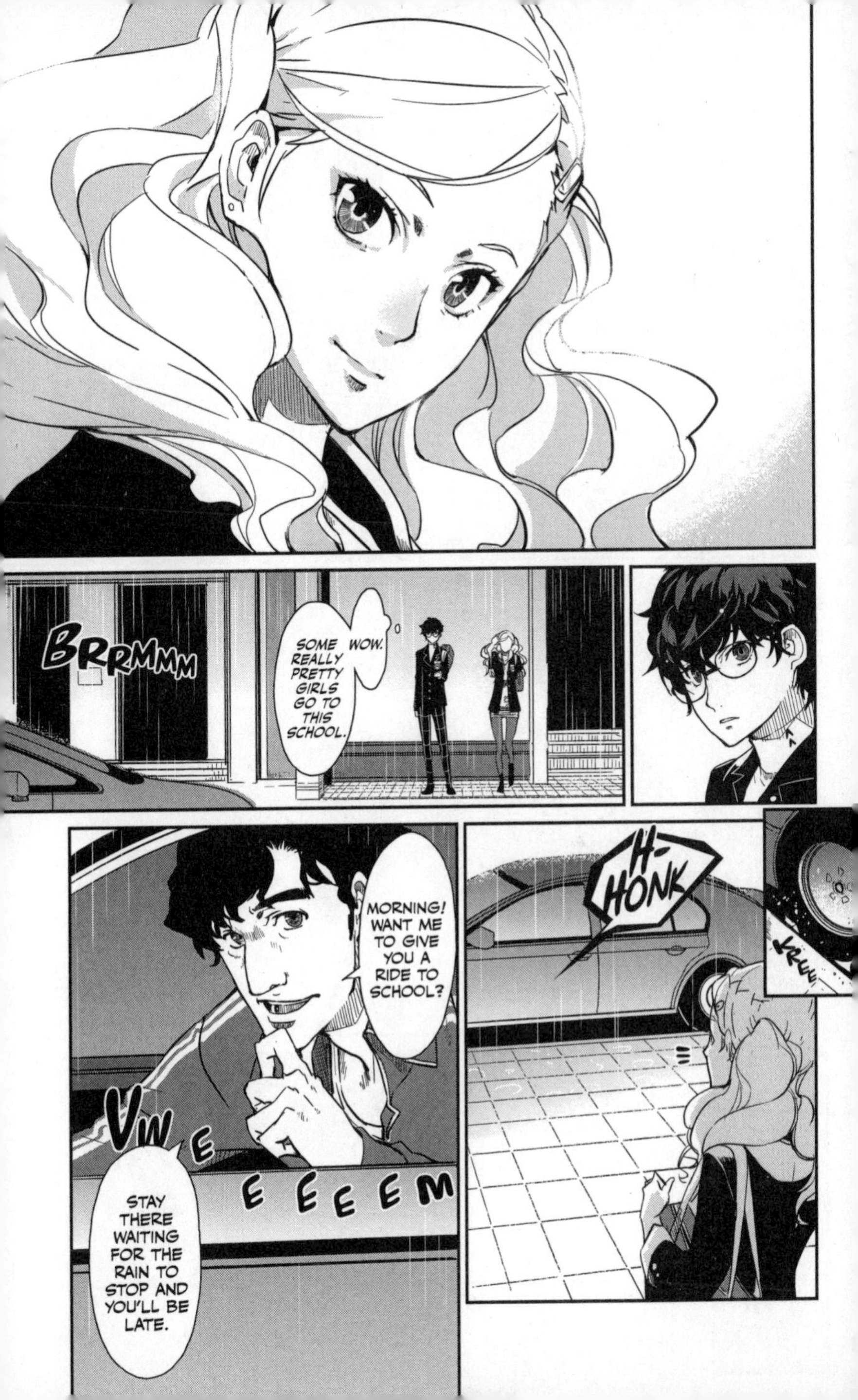
WOW.
SOME REALLY PRETTY GIRLS GO TO THIS SCHOOL.
BRRMMM
H-HONK
KREEE
MORNING! WANT ME TO GIVE YOU A RIDE TO SCHOOL?
VWEEEEEEM
STAY THERE WAITING FOR THE RAIN TO STOP AND YOU'LL BE LATE.

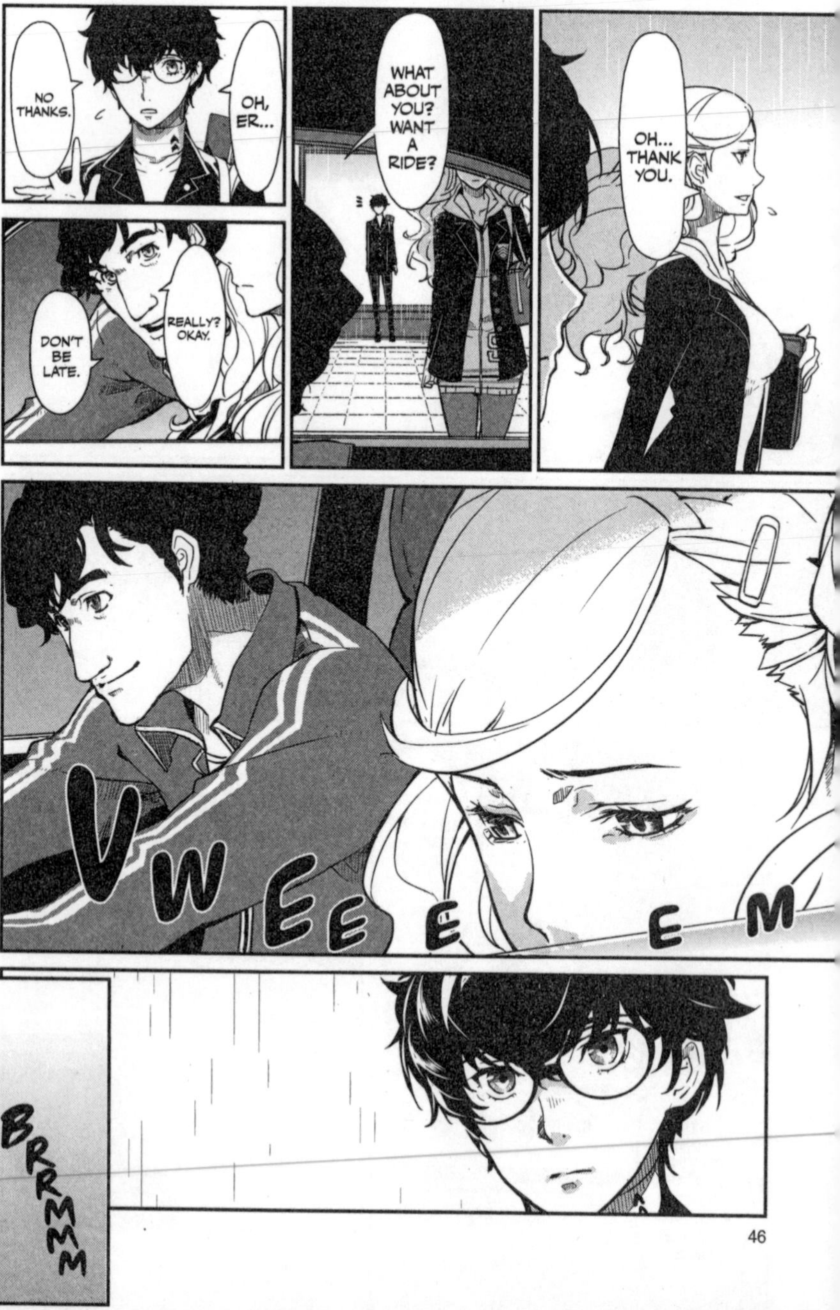
OH... THANK YOU.
WHAT ABOUT YOU? WANT A RIDE?
OH, ER...
NO THANKS.
REALLY? OKAY.
DON'T BE LATE.
VWEEEEEM
BRRMMM

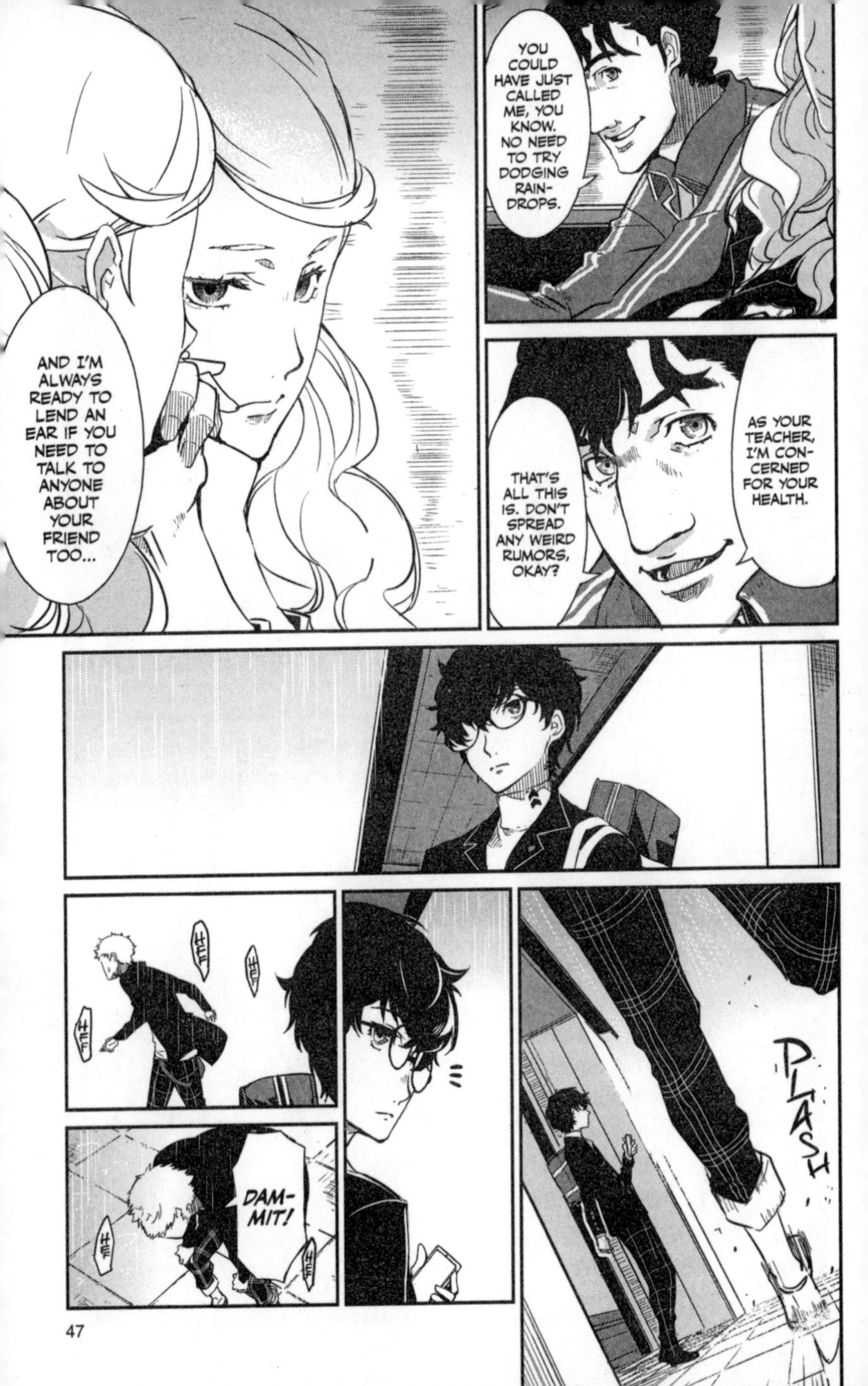
YOU COULD HAVE JUST CALLED ME, YOU KNOW. NO NEED TO TRY DODGING RAIN-DROPS.
AS YOUR TEACHER, I'M CON-CERNED FOR YOUR HEALTH.
THAT'S ALL THIS IS. DON'T SPREAD ANY WEIRD RUMORS, OKAY?
AND I'M ALWAYS READY TO LEND AN EAR IF YOU NEED TO TALK TO ANYONE ABOUT YOUR FRIEND TOO...
PLASH
HEF
HEF
HEF
DAM-MIT!
HEF
HEF

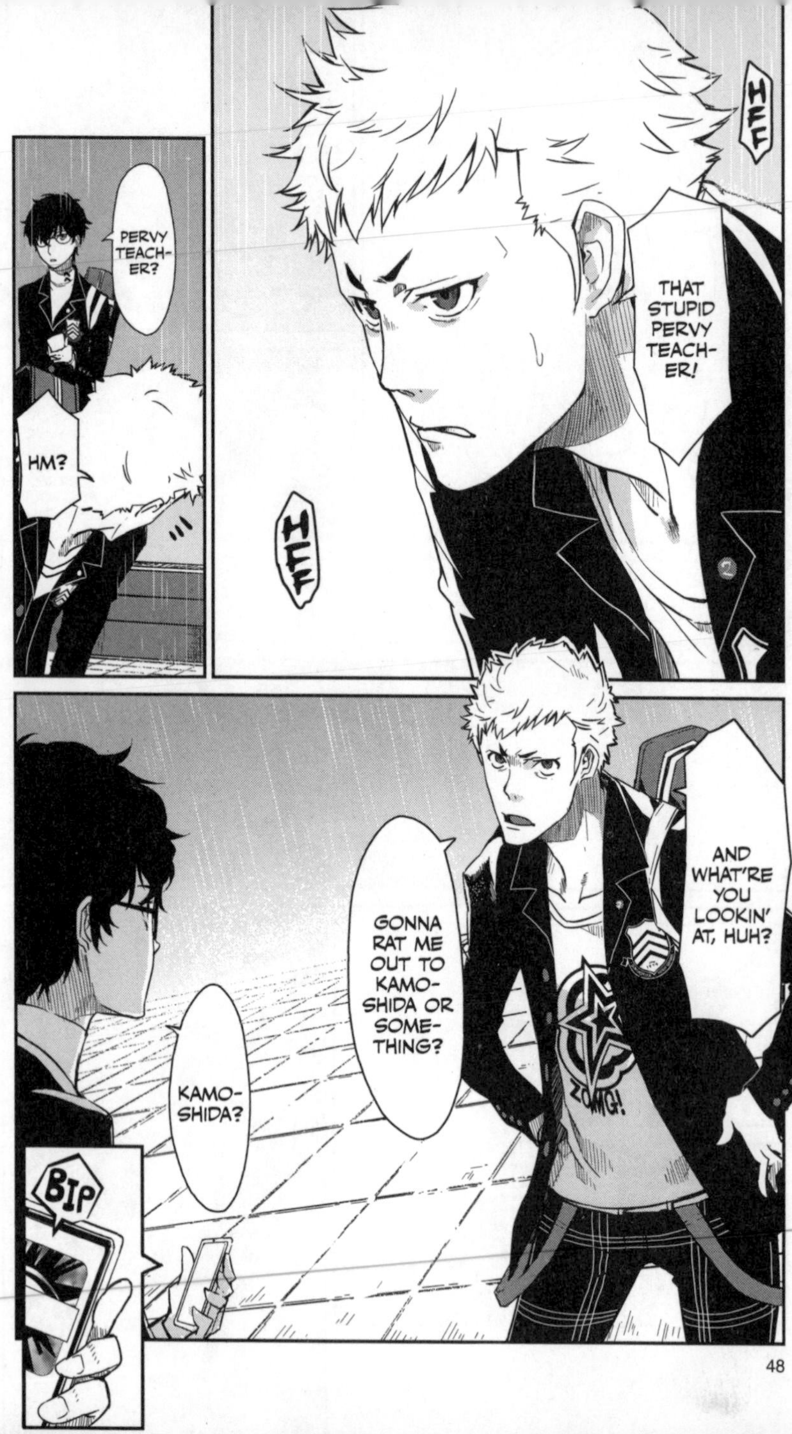
HFF
THAT STUPID PERVY TEACHER!
HFF
PERVY TEACHER?
HM?
AND WHAT'RE YOU LOOKIN' AT, HUH?
GONNA RAT ME OUT TO KAMOSHIDA OR SOMETHING?
ZOMG!
KAMOSHIDA?
BIP

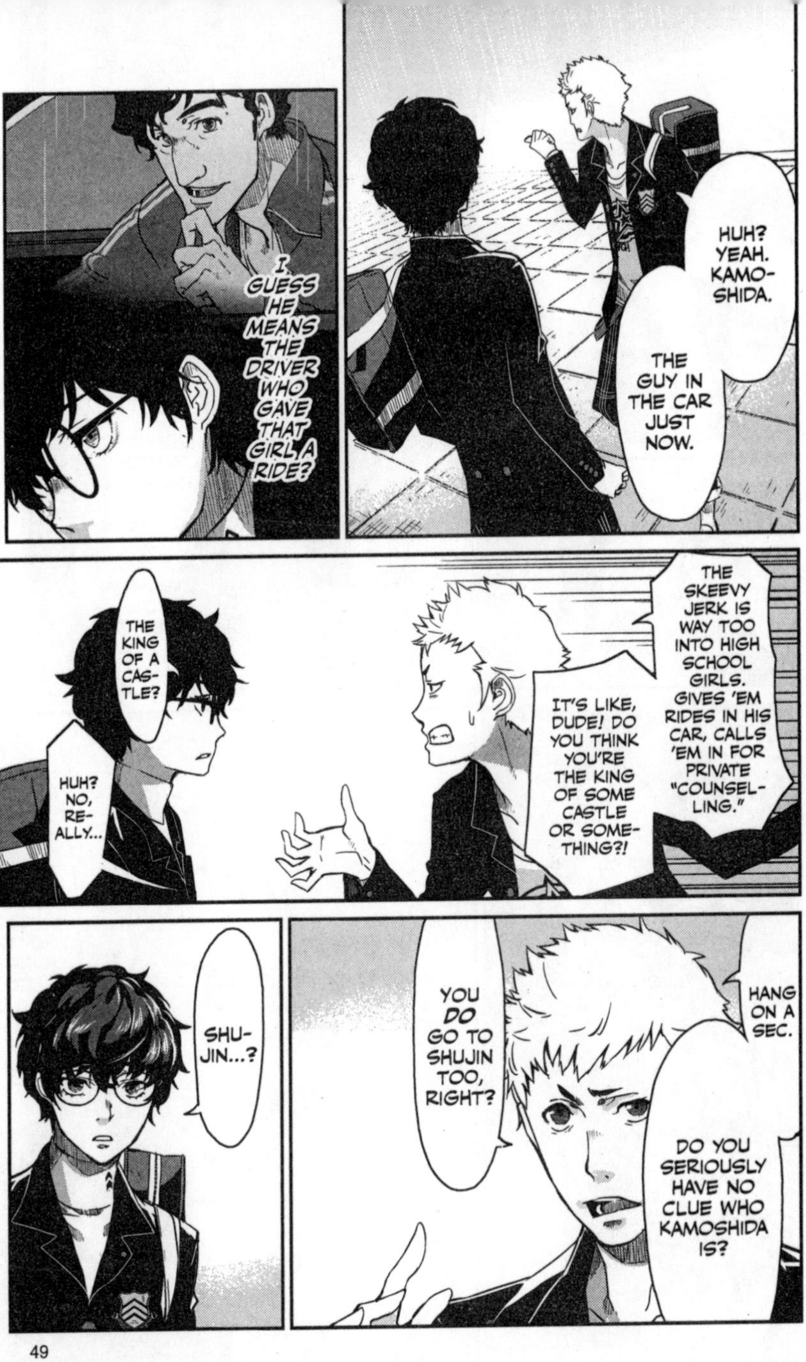
HUH? YEAH. KAMOSHIDA.
THE GUY IN THE CAR JUST NOW.
I GUESS HE MEANS THE DRIVER WHO GAVE THAT GIRL A RIDE?
THE SKEEVY JERK IS WAY TOO INTO HIGH SCHOOL GIRLS. GIVES 'EM RIDES IN HIS CAR, CALLS 'EM IN FOR PRIVATE "COUNSELLING."
IT'S LIKE, DUDE! DO YOU THINK YOU'RE THE KING OF SOME CASTLE OR SOMETHING?!
THE KING OF A CASTLE?
HUH? NO, REALLY...
HANG ON A SEC.
DO YOU SERIOUSLY HAVE NO CLUE WHO KAMOSHIDA IS?
YOU *DO* GO TO SHUJIN TOO, RIGHT?
SHUJIN...?

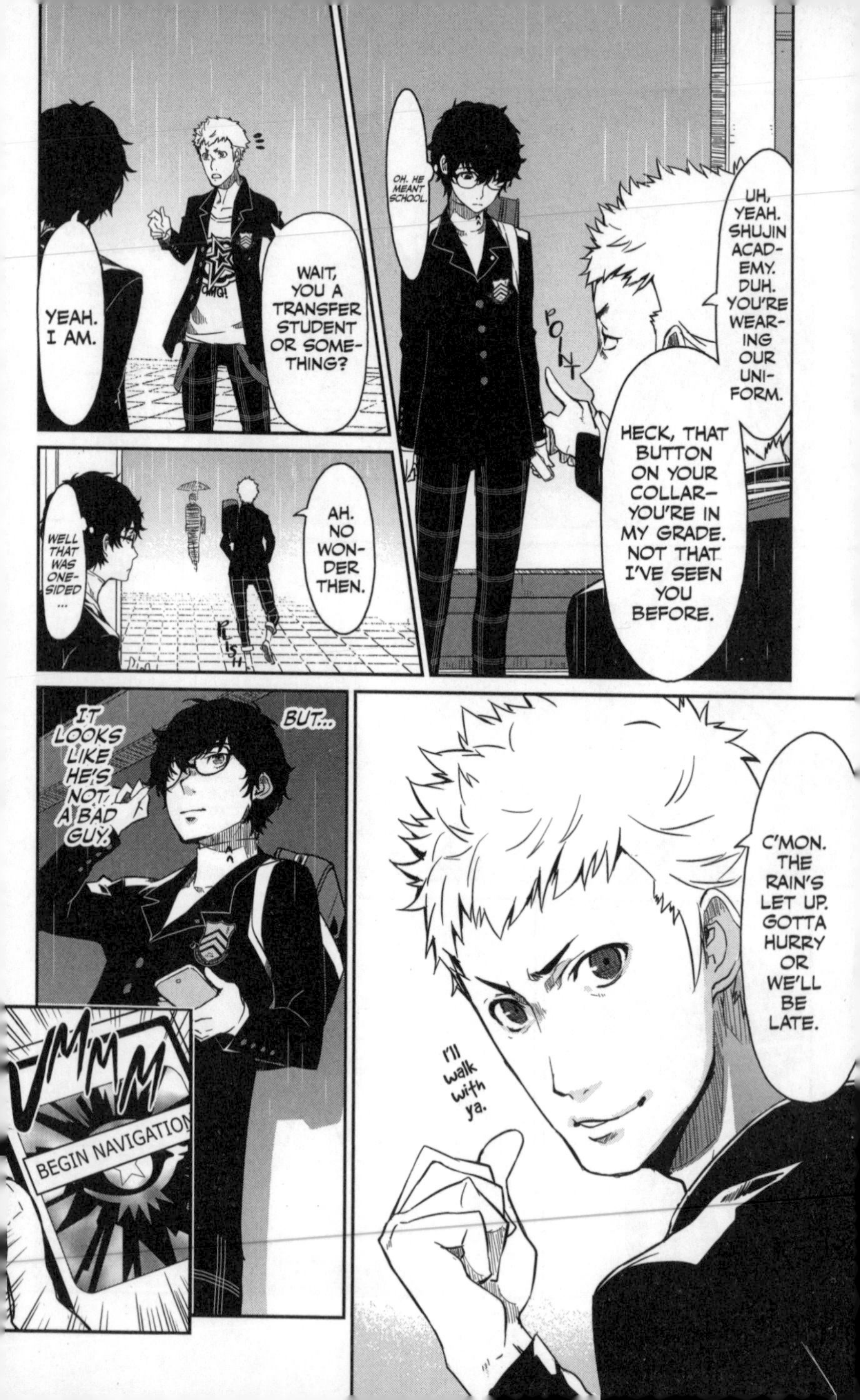
OH. HE MEANT SCHOOL.
UH, YEAH. SHUJIN ACADEMY. DUH. YOU'RE WEARING OUR UNIFORM.
POINT
HECK, THAT BUTTON ON YOUR COLLAR—YOU'RE IN MY GRADE. NOT THAT I'VE SEEN YOU BEFORE.
WAIT, YOU A TRANSFER STUDENT OR SOMETHING?
YEAH. I AM.
AH. NO WONDER THEN.
PLISH
WELL THAT WAS ONE-SIDED...
C'MON. THE RAIN'S LET UP. GOTTA HURRY OR WE'LL BE LATE.
I'll walk with ya.
BUT...
IT LOOKS LIKE HE'S NOT A BAD GUY.
VMMM
BEGIN NAVIGATION

UGH. MY HEAD HURTS.

I WANNA GO HOME...

Fsssss

?

?

ZONG!!

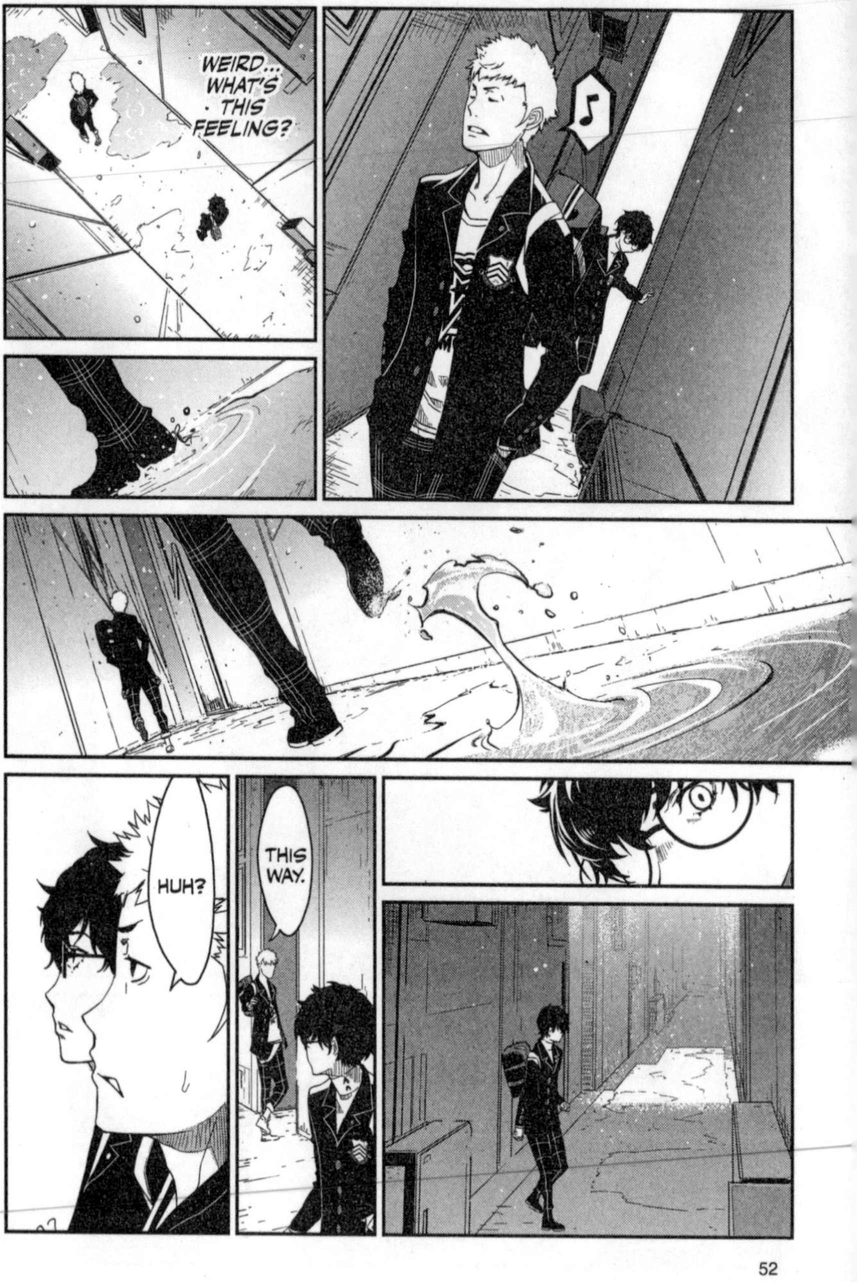
WEIRD... WHAT'S THIS FEELING?
THIS WAY.
HUH?

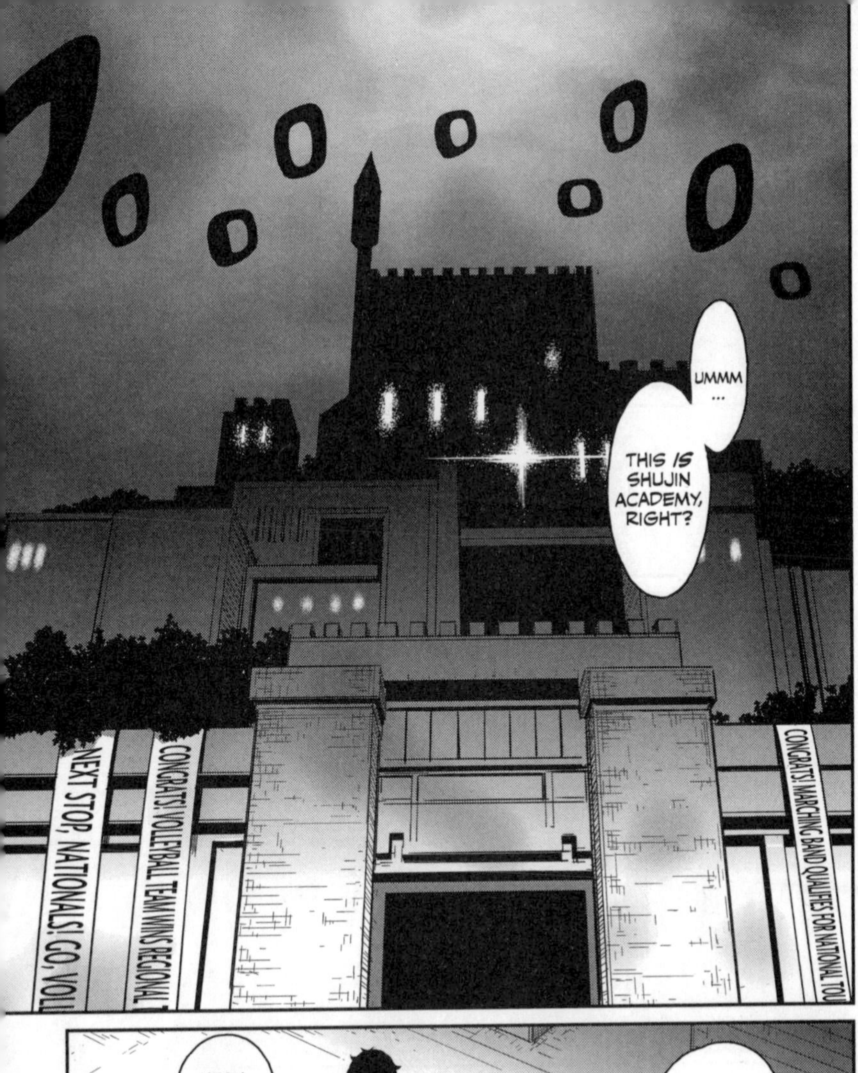
UMMM ...
THIS *IS* SHUJIN ACADEMY, RIGHT?
CONGRATS! MARCHING BAND QUALIFIES FOR NATIONAL TOU
CONGRATS! VOLLEYBALL TEAM WINS REGIONAL T
NEXT STOP, NATIONALS! GO, VOLL

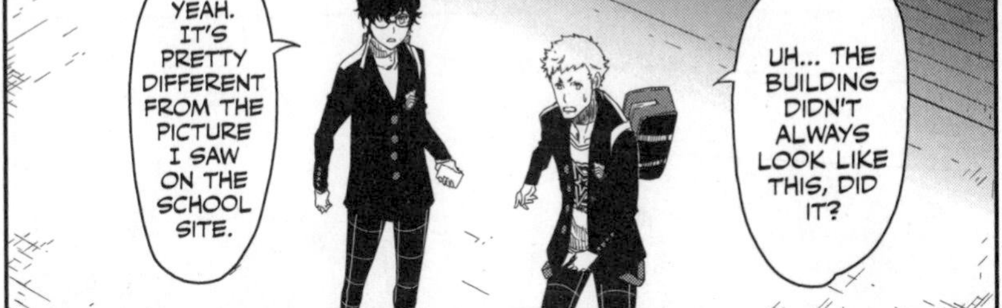
UH... THE BUILDING DIDN'T ALWAYS LOOK LIKE THIS, DID IT?
YEAH. IT'S PRETTY DIFFERENT FROM THE PICTURE I SAW ON THE SCHOOL SITE.

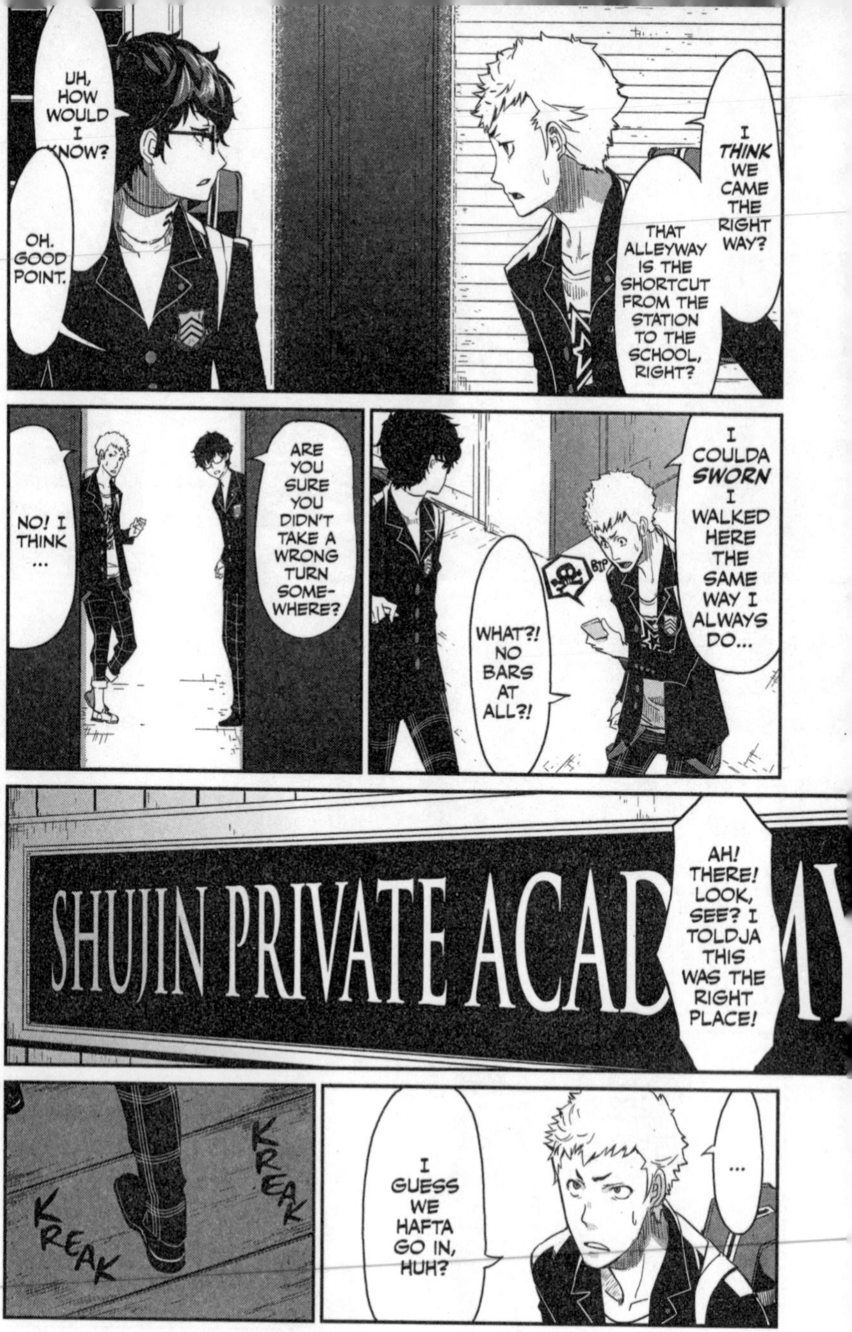
I *THINK* WE CAME THE RIGHT WAY?
THAT ALLEYWAY IS THE SHORTCUT FROM THE STATION TO THE SCHOOL, RIGHT?
UH, HOW WOULD I KNOW?
OH. GOOD POINT.
I COULDA *SWORN* I WALKED HERE THE SAME WAY I ALWAYS DO...
BIP
WHAT?! NO BARS AT ALL?!
ARE YOU SURE YOU DIDN'T TAKE A WRONG TURN SOME-WHERE?
NO! I THINK ...
SHUJIN PRIVATE ACAD
AH! THERE! LOOK, SEE? I TOLDJA THIS WAS THE RIGHT PLACE!
...
I GUESS WE HAFTA GO IN, HUH?
KREAK
KREAK

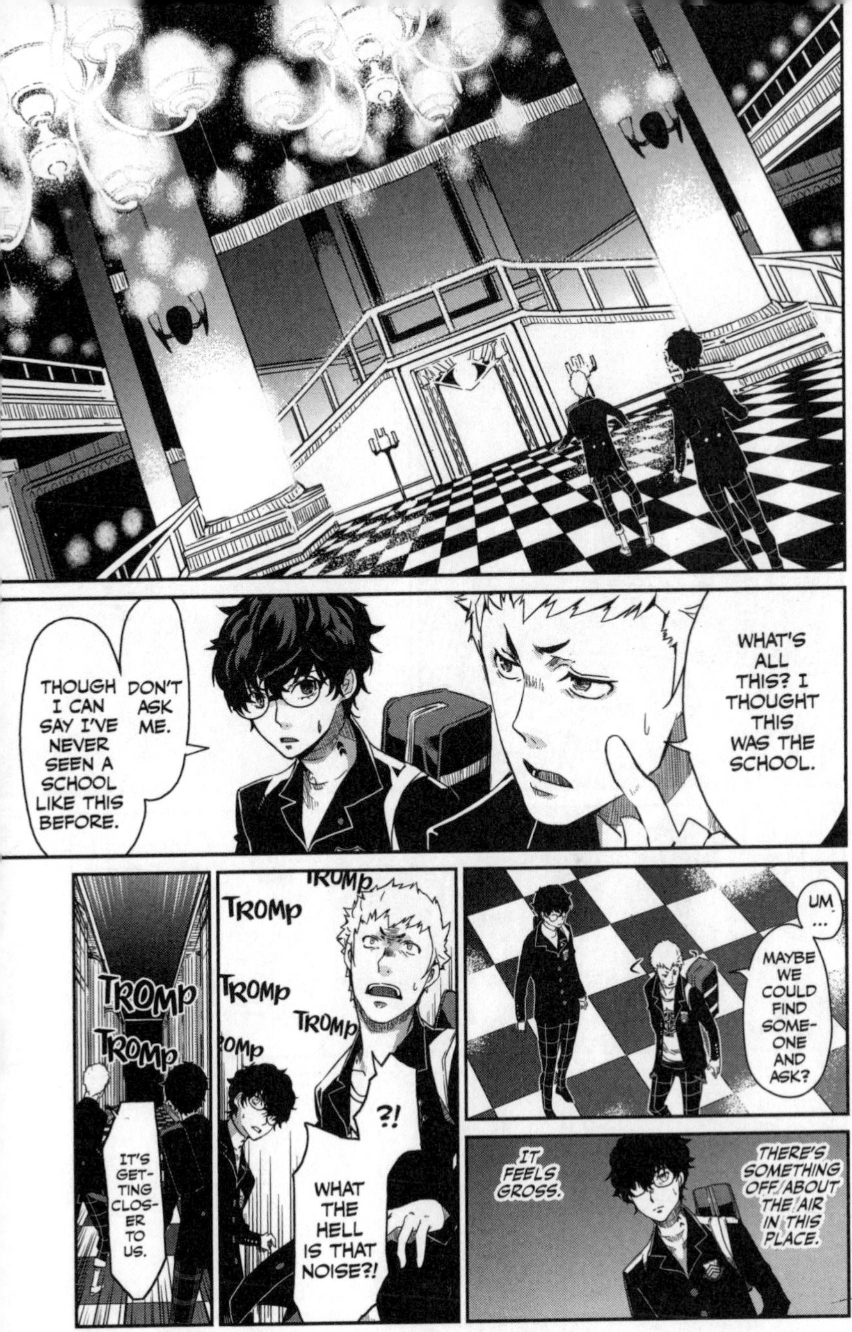

WHAT'S ALL THIS? I THOUGHT THIS WAS THE SCHOOL.
DON'T ASK ME.
THOUGH I CAN SAY I'VE NEVER SEEN A SCHOOL LIKE THIS BEFORE.
UM ...
MAYBE WE COULD FIND SOME-ONE AND ASK?
THERE'S SOMETHING OFF ABOUT THE AIR IN THIS PLACE.
IT FEELS GROSS.
TROMP
TROMP
TROMP
?!
WHAT THE HELL IS THAT NOISE?!
TROMP
TROMP
IT'S GET-TING CLOS-ER TO US.

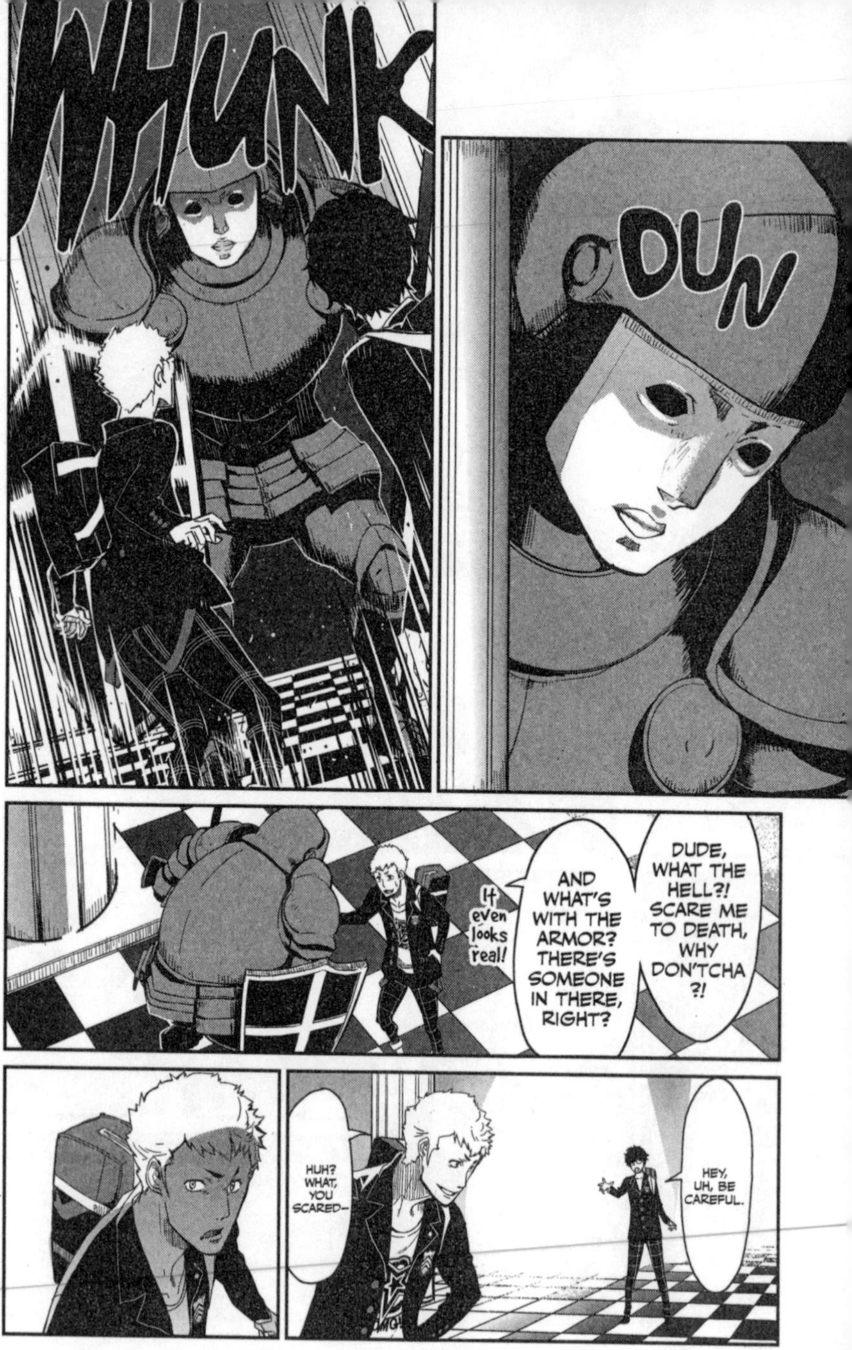
DUN
WHUNK
DUDE, WHAT THE HELL?! SCARE ME TO DEATH, WHY DON'TCHA?!
AND WHAT'S WITH THE ARMOR? THERE'S SOMEONE IN THERE, RIGHT?
It even looks real!
HEY, UH, BE CAREFUL.
HUH? WHAT, YOU SCARED—

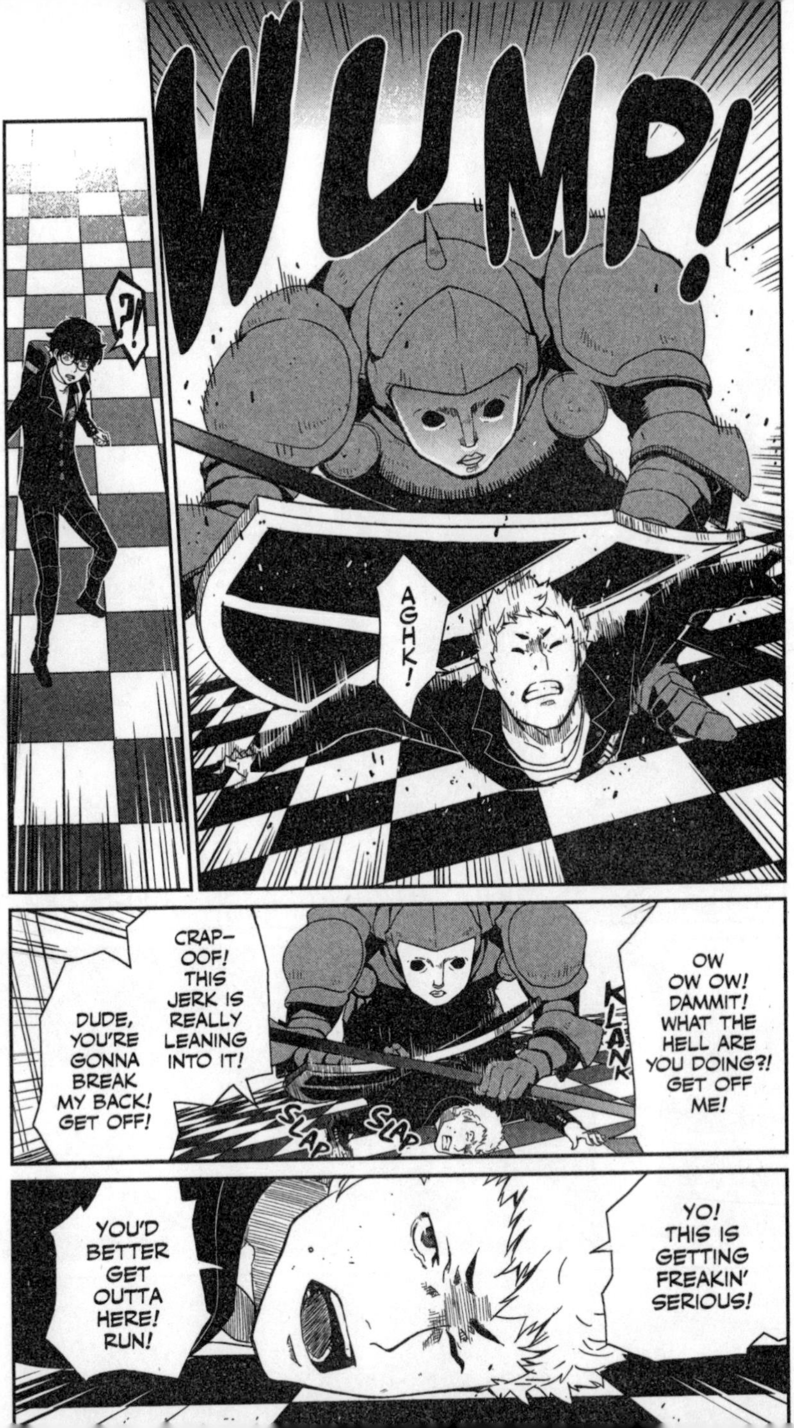
WUMP!
AGHK!
?!
OW OW OW! DAMMIT! WHAT THE HELL ARE YOU DOING?! GET OFF ME!
KLANK
CRAP—OOF! THIS JERK IS REALLY LEANING INTO IT!
DUDE, YOU'RE GONNA BREAK MY BACK! GET OFF!
SLAP
SLAP
YO! THIS IS GETTING FREAKIN' SERIOUS!
YOU'D BETTER GET OUTTA HERE! RUN!

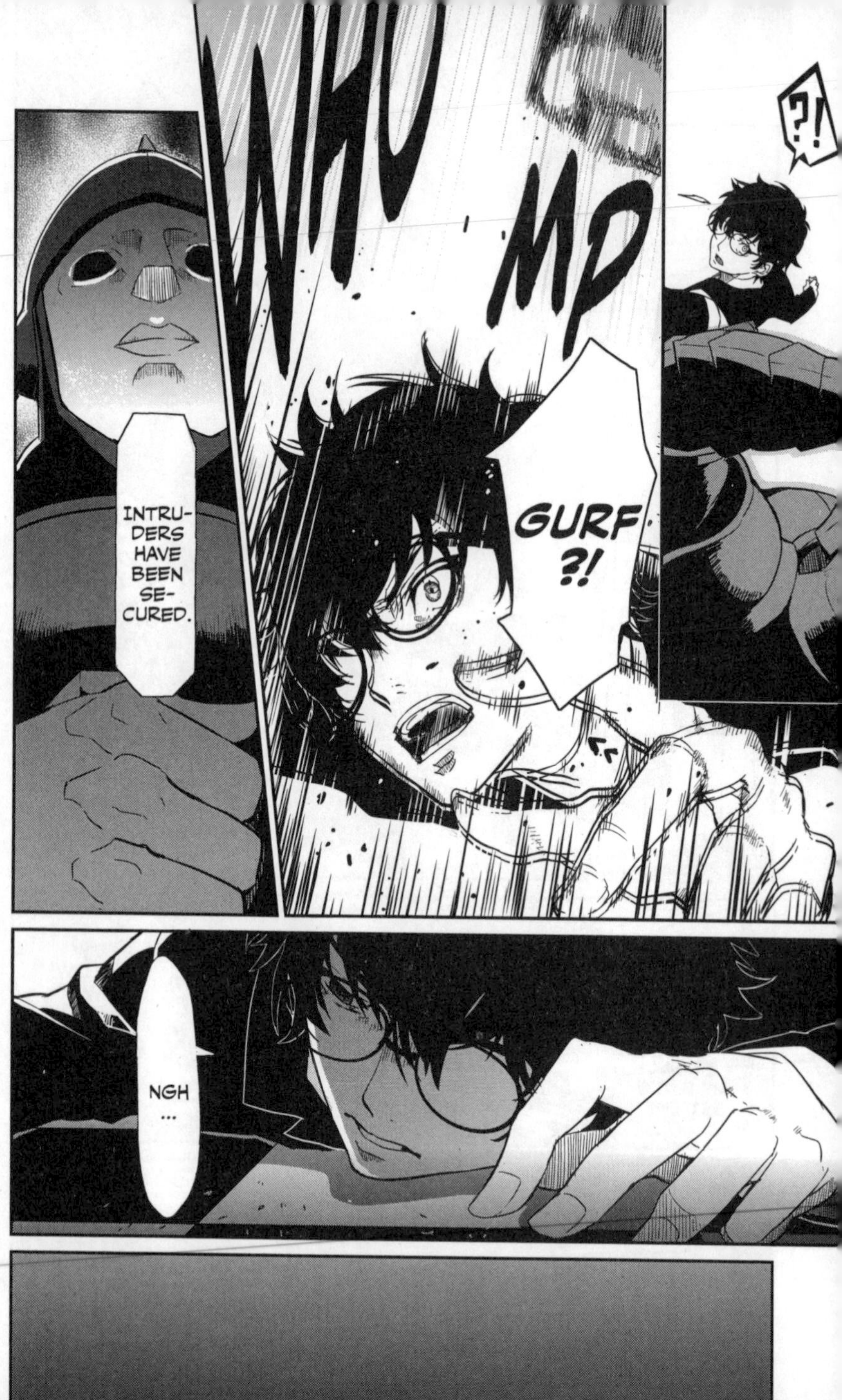
?!
WHUMP
GURF?!
INTRU-DERS HAVE BEEN SE-CURED.
NGH ...

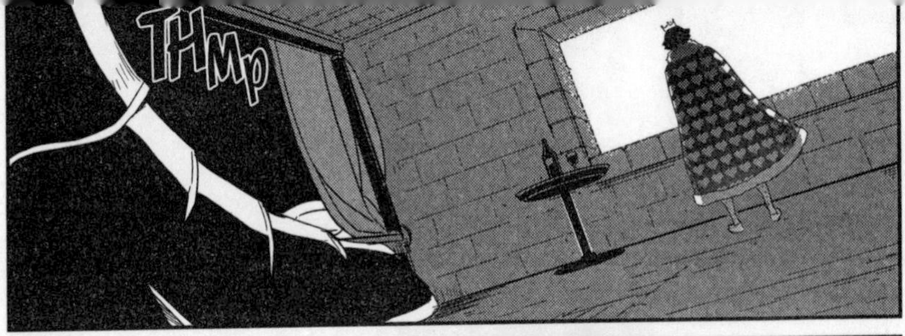
THMP
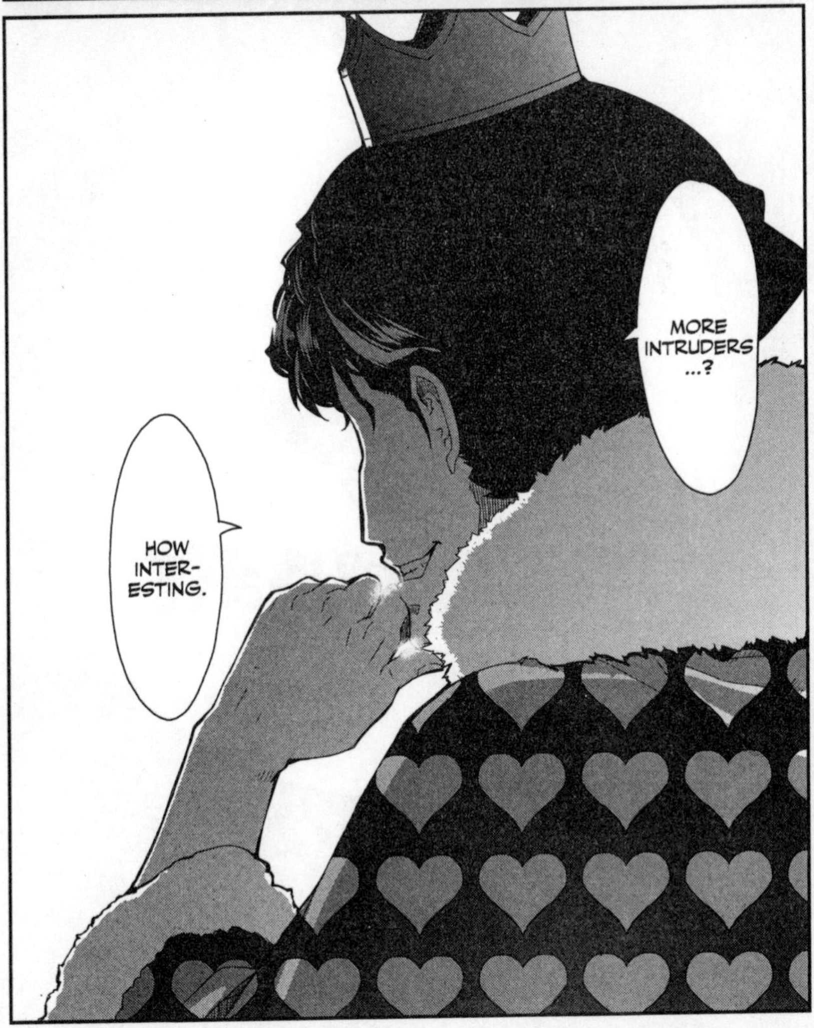
MORE INTRUDERS ...?
HOW INTER-ESTING.

TAKE YOUR HEART

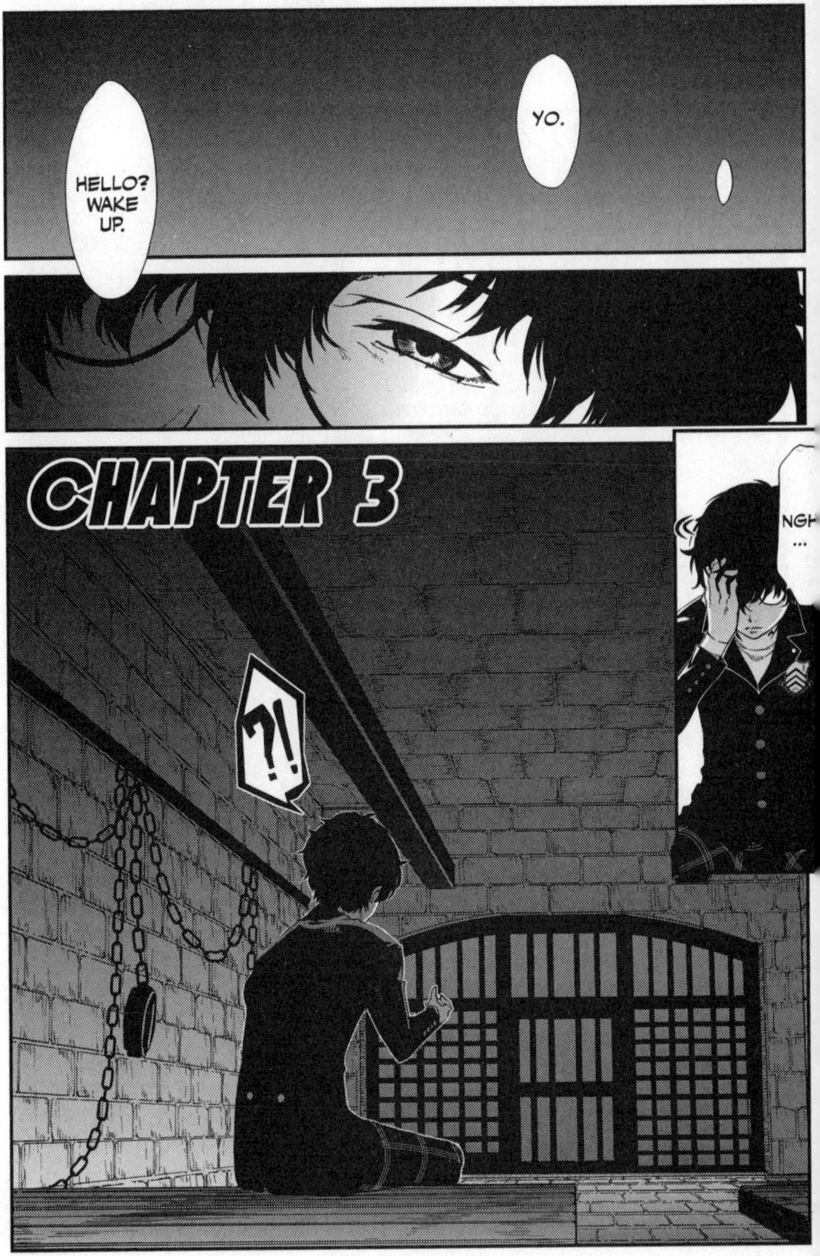
YO.
HELLO? WAKE UP.
NGH...
CHAPTER 3
?!

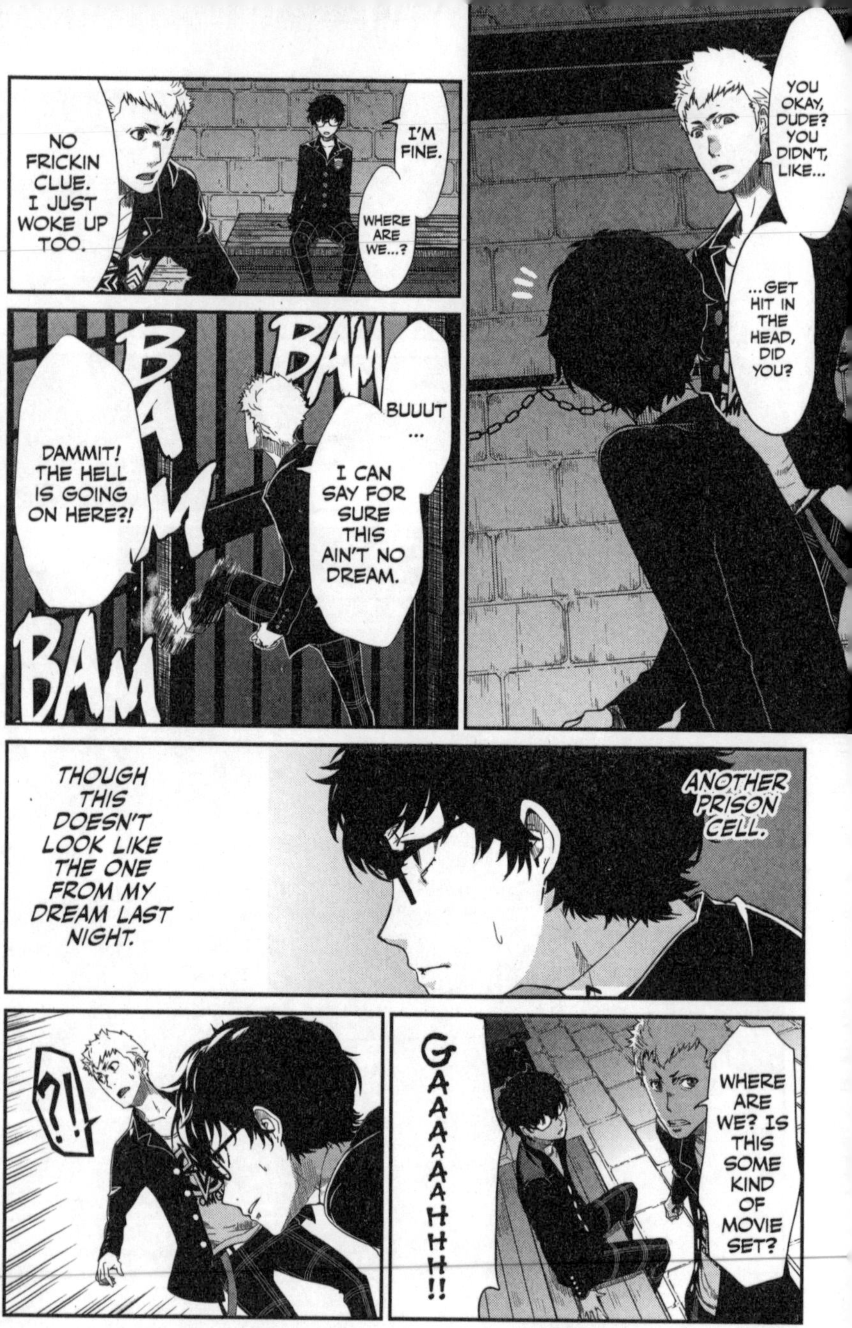
YOU OKAY, DUDE? YOU DIDN'T, LIKE...
...GET HIT IN THE HEAD, DID YOU?
I'M FINE.
WHERE ARE WE...?
NO FRICKIN CLUE. I JUST WOKE UP TOO.
BAM
BUUUT...
I CAN SAY FOR SURE THIS AIN'T NO DREAM.
BAM
DAMMIT! THE HELL IS GOING ON HERE?!
BAM
ANOTHER PRISON CELL.
THOUGH THIS DOESN'T LOOK LIKE THE ONE FROM MY DREAM LAST NIGHT.
WHERE ARE WE? IS THIS SOME KIND OF MOVIE SET?
GAAAAAAAHHHH!!
?!

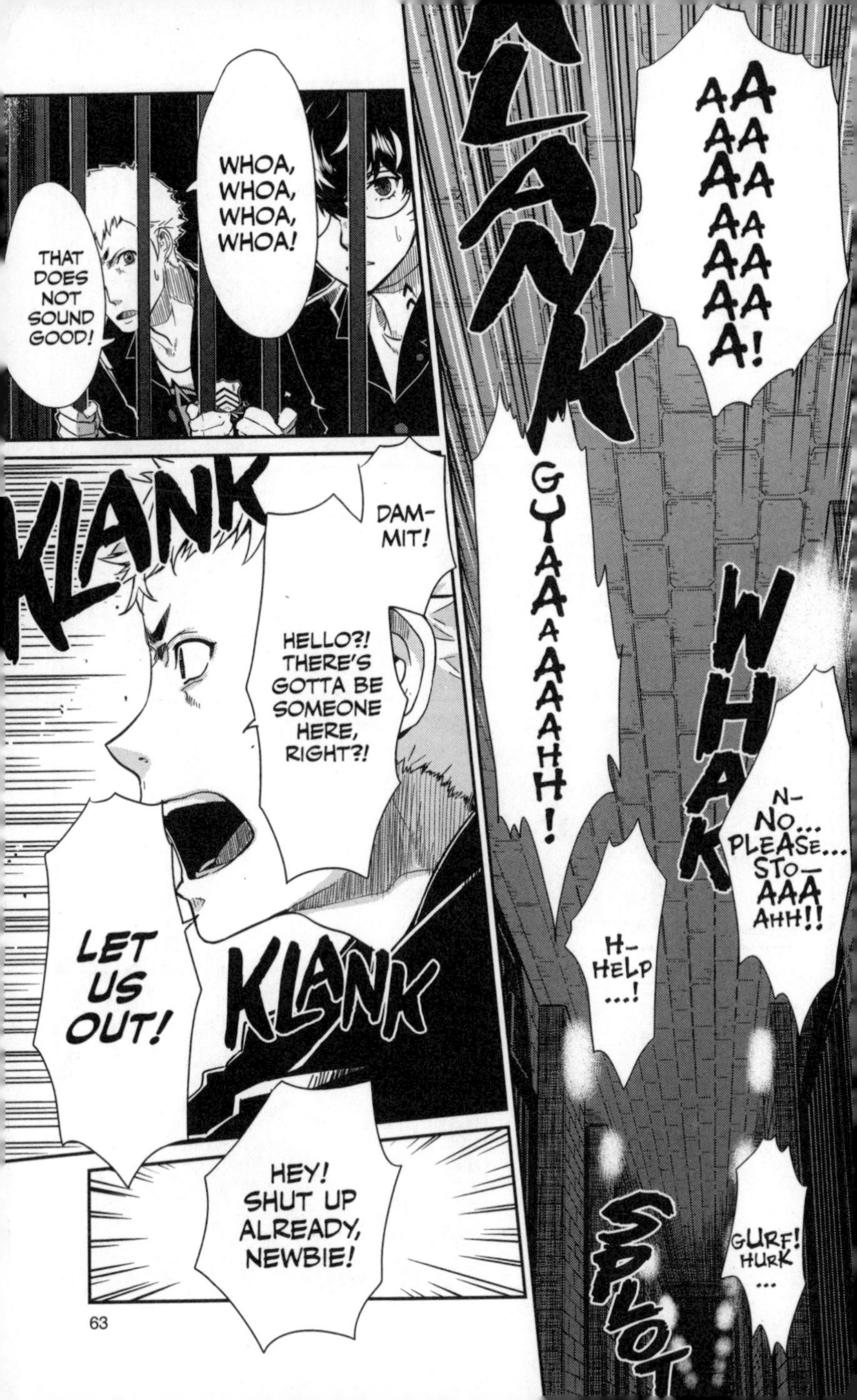
AAAAAAAAAAAAAA!
GYAAAAAAAAH!
WHAK
N-NO... PLEASE... STO—AAAAHH!!
H-HELP...!
GURF! HURK...
SPLOT
WHOA, WHOA, WHOA, WHOA!
THAT DOES NOT SOUND GOOD!
KLANK
DAM-MIT!
HELLO?! THERE'S GOTTA BE SOMEONE HERE, RIGHT?!
LET US OUT!
KLANK
HEY! SHUT UP ALREADY, NEWBIE!

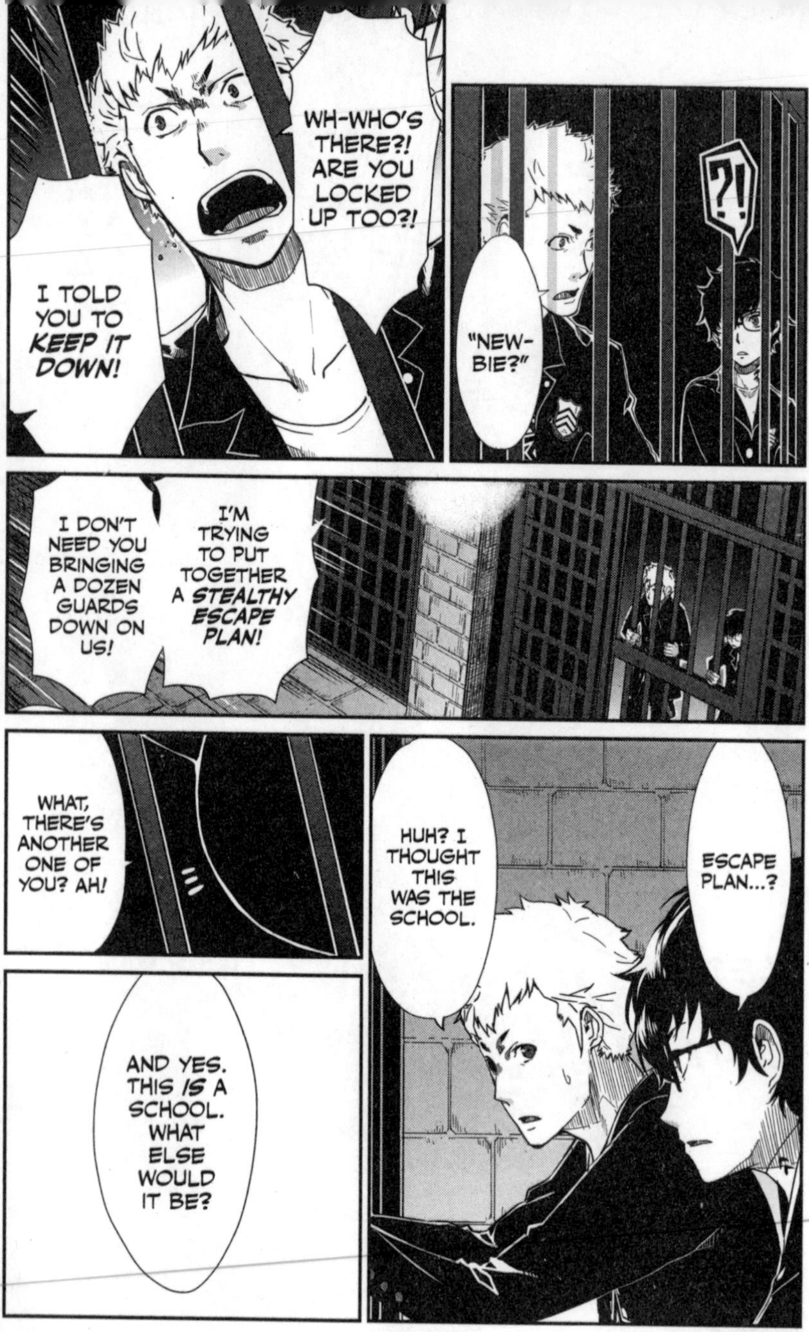
?!
"NEW-BIE?"
WH-WHO'S THERE?! ARE YOU LOCKED UP TOO?!
I TOLD YOU TO *KEEP IT DOWN!*
I'M TRYING TO PUT TOGETHER A *STEALTHY ESCAPE PLAN!*
I DON'T NEED YOU BRINGING A DOZEN GUARDS DOWN ON US!
ESCAPE PLAN...?
HUH? I THOUGHT THIS WAS THE SCHOOL.
WHAT, THERE'S ANOTHER ONE OF YOU? AH!
AND YES. THIS *IS* A SCHOOL. WHAT ELSE WOULD IT BE?

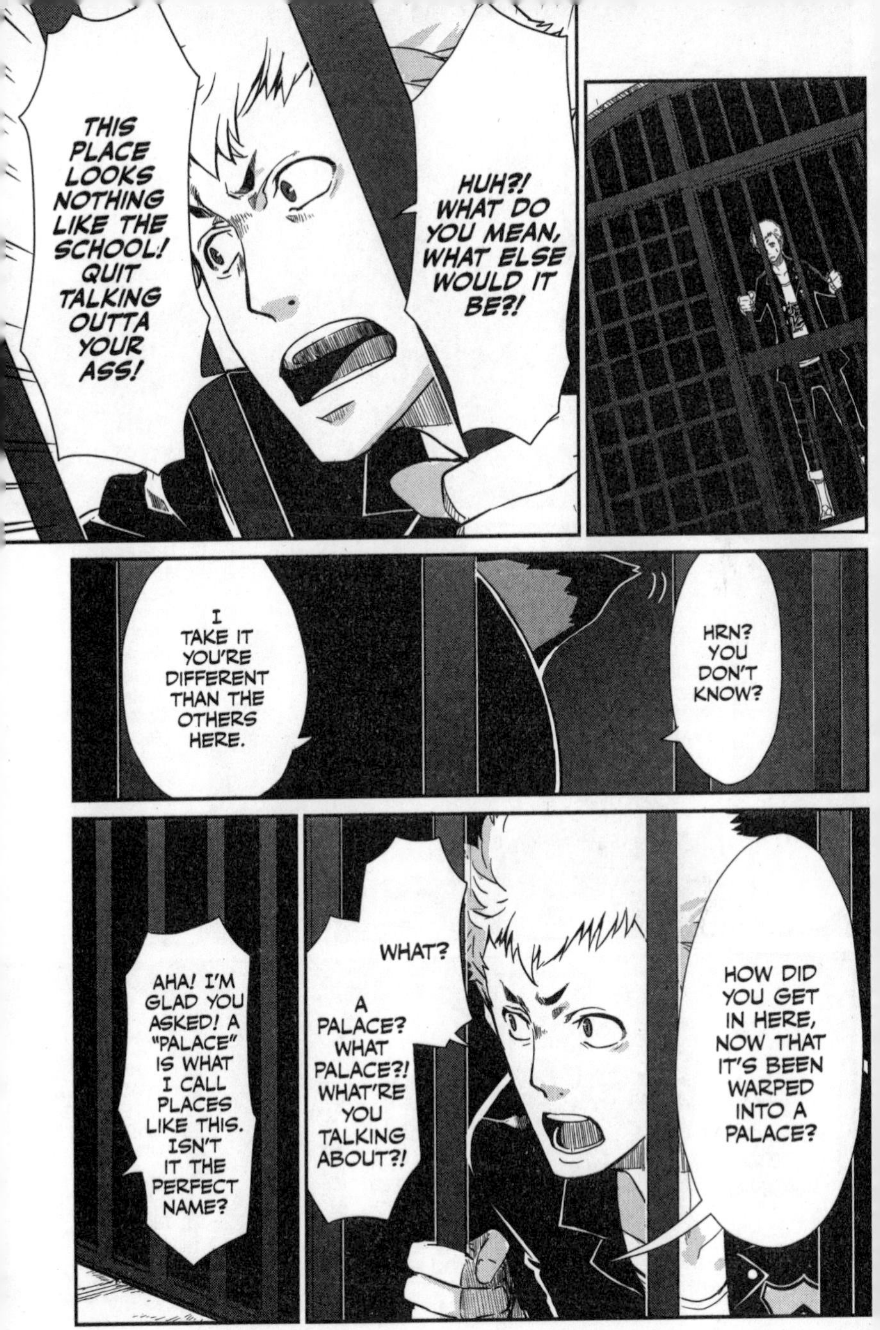
HUH?! WHAT DO YOU MEAN, WHAT ELSE WOULD IT BE?!
THIS PLACE LOOKS NOTHING LIKE THE SCHOOL! QUIT TALKING OUTTA YOUR ASS!
HRN? YOU DON'T KNOW?
I TAKE IT YOU'RE DIFFERENT THAN THE OTHERS HERE.
HOW DID YOU GET IN HERE, NOW THAT IT'S BEEN WARPED INTO A PALACE?
WHAT?
A PALACE? WHAT PALACE?! WHAT'RE YOU TALKING ABOUT?!
AHA! I'M GLAD YOU ASKED! A "PALACE" IS WHAT I CALL PLACES LIKE THIS. ISN'T IT THE PERFECT NAME?

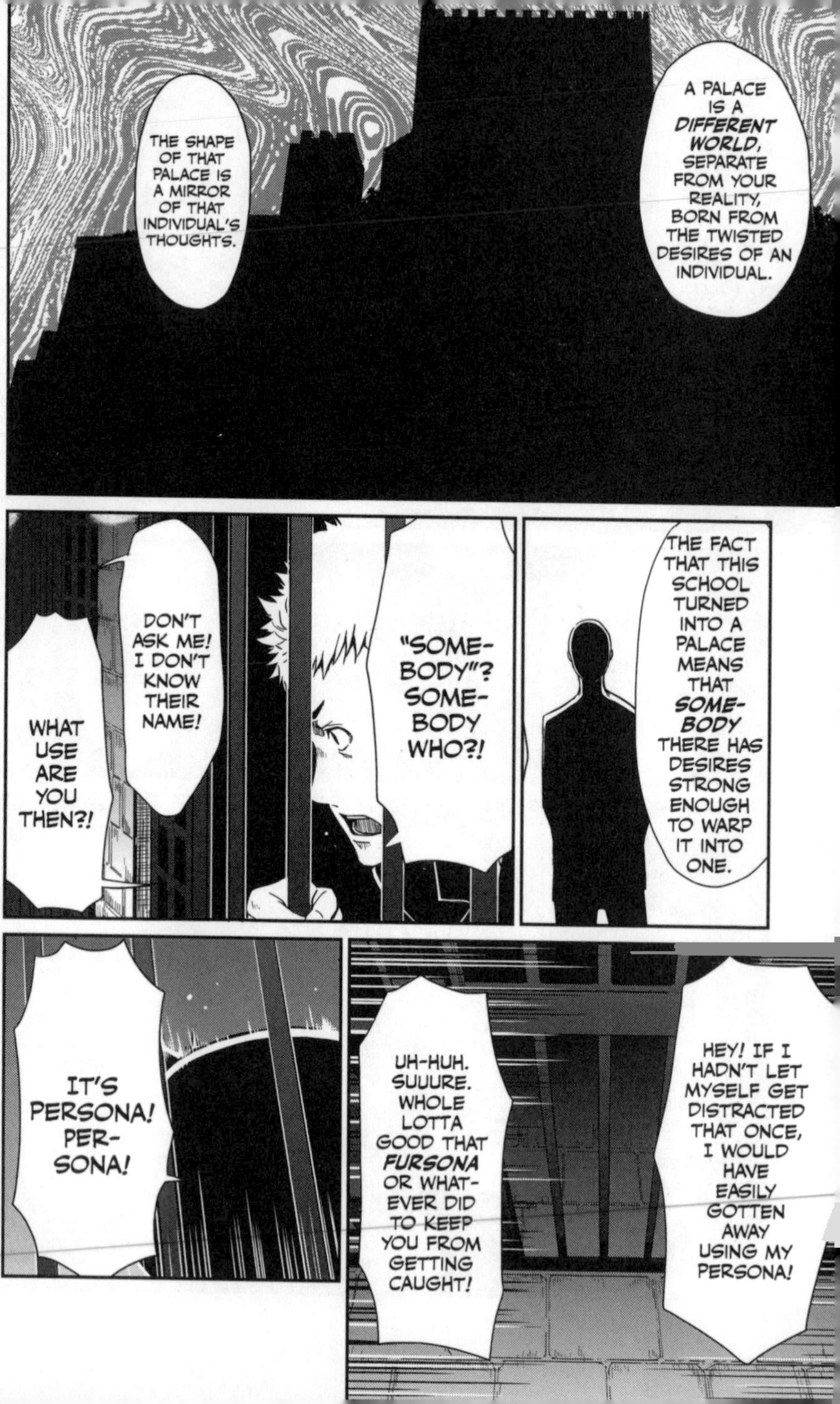
A PALACE IS A DIFFERENT WORLD, SEPARATE FROM YOUR REALITY, BORN FROM THE TWISTED DESIRES OF AN INDIVIDUAL.
THE SHAPE OF THAT PALACE IS A MIRROR OF THAT INDIVIDUAL'S THOUGHTS.
THE FACT THAT THIS SCHOOL TURNED INTO A PALACE MEANS THAT SOME-BODY THERE HAS DESIRES STRONG ENOUGH TO WARP IT INTO ONE.
"SOME-BODY"? SOME-BODY WHO?!
DON'T ASK ME! I DON'T KNOW THEIR NAME!
WHAT USE ARE YOU THEN?!
HEY! IF I HADN'T LET MYSELF GET DISTRACTED THAT ONCE, I WOULD HAVE EASILY GOTTEN AWAY USING MY PERSONA!
UH-HUH. SUUURE. WHOLE LOTTA GOOD THAT FURSONA OR WHAT-EVER DID TO KEEP YOU FROM GETTING CAUGHT!
IT'S PERSONA! PER-SONA!

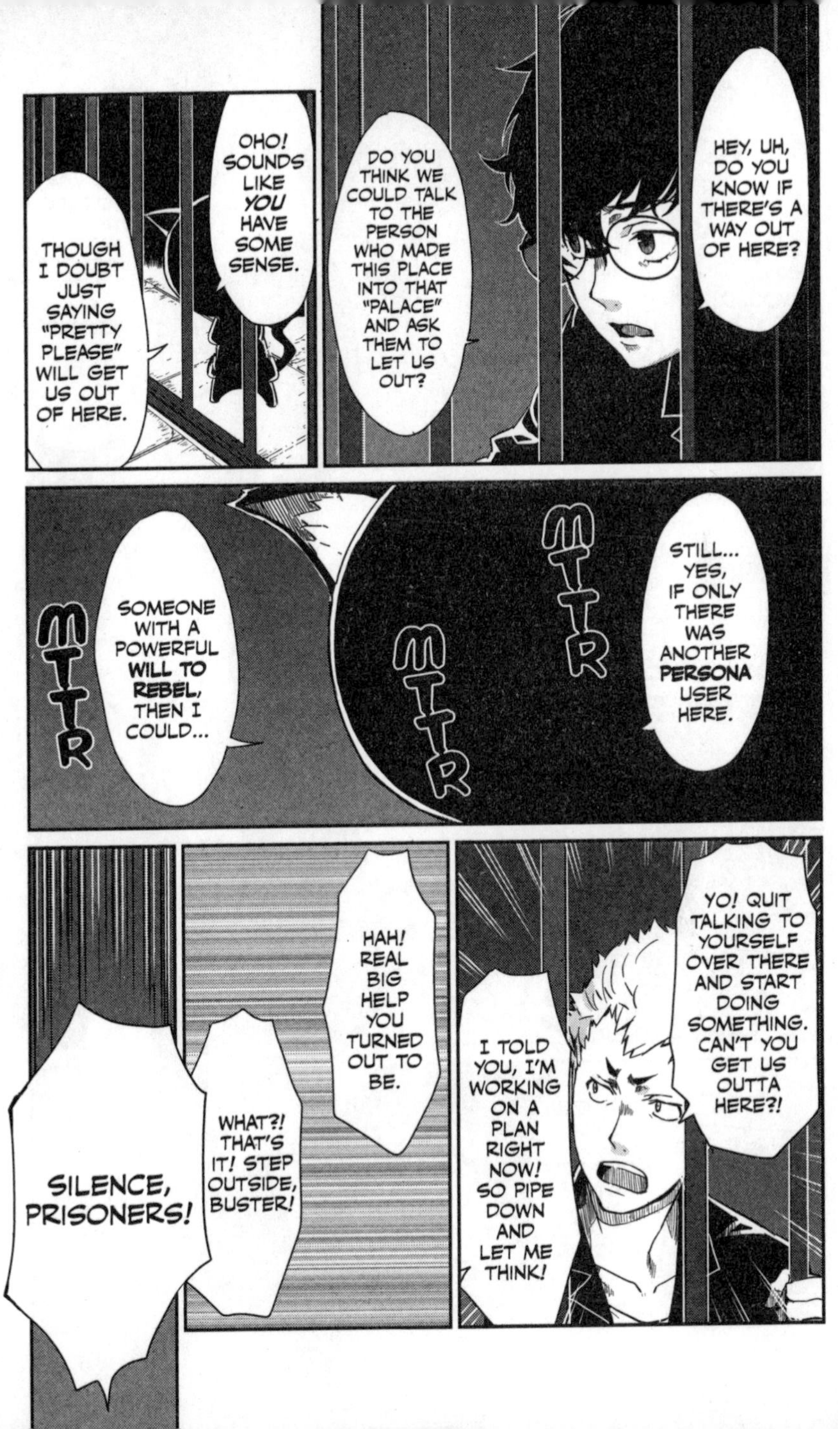
HEY, UH, DO YOU KNOW IF THERE'S A WAY OUT OF HERE?
DO YOU THINK WE COULD TALK TO THE PERSON WHO MADE THIS PLACE INTO THAT "PALACE" AND ASK THEM TO LET US OUT?
OHO! SOUNDS LIKE *YOU* HAVE SOME SENSE.
THOUGH I DOUBT JUST SAYING "PRETTY PLEASE" WILL GET US OUT OF HERE.
STILL... YES, IF ONLY THERE WAS ANOTHER **PERSONA** USER HERE.
MTTR
MTTR
SOMEONE WITH A POWERFUL **WILL TO REBEL**, THEN I COULD...
MTTR
YO! QUIT TALKING TO YOURSELF OVER THERE AND START DOING SOMETHING. CAN'T YOU GET US OUTTA HERE?!
I TOLD YOU, I'M WORKING ON A PLAN RIGHT NOW! SO PIPE DOWN AND LET ME THINK!
HAH! REAL BIG HELP YOU TURNED OUT TO BE.
WHAT?! THAT'S IT! STEP OUTSIDE, BUSTER!
SILENCE, PRISONERS!

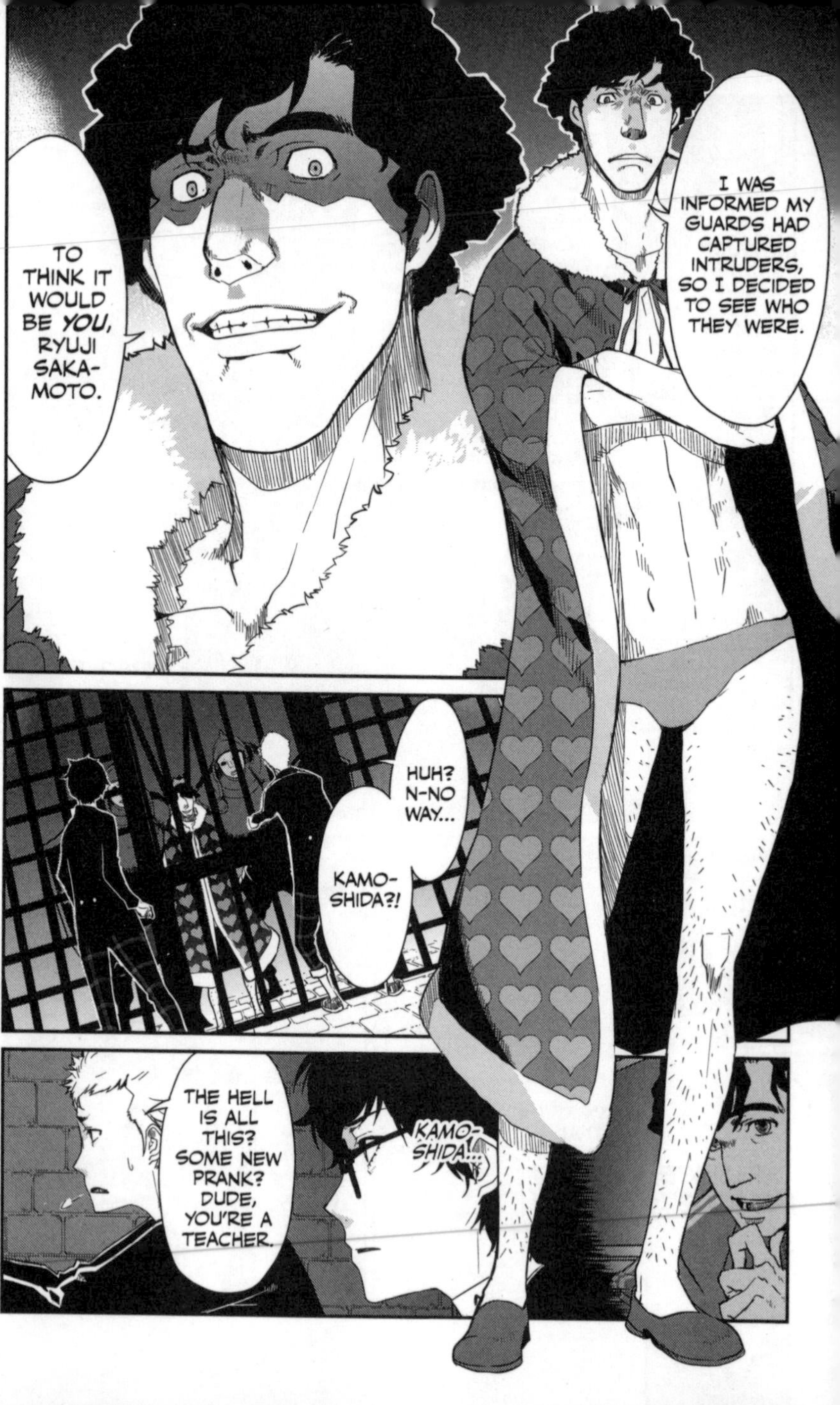
I WAS INFORMED MY GUARDS HAD CAPTURED INTRUDERS, SO I DECIDED TO SEE WHO THEY WERE.
TO THINK IT WOULD BE *YOU*, RYUJI SAKAMOTO.
HUH? N-NO WAY...
KAMOSHIDA?!
KAMOSHIDA...
THE HELL IS ALL THIS? SOME NEW PRANK? DUDE, YOU'RE A TEACHER.

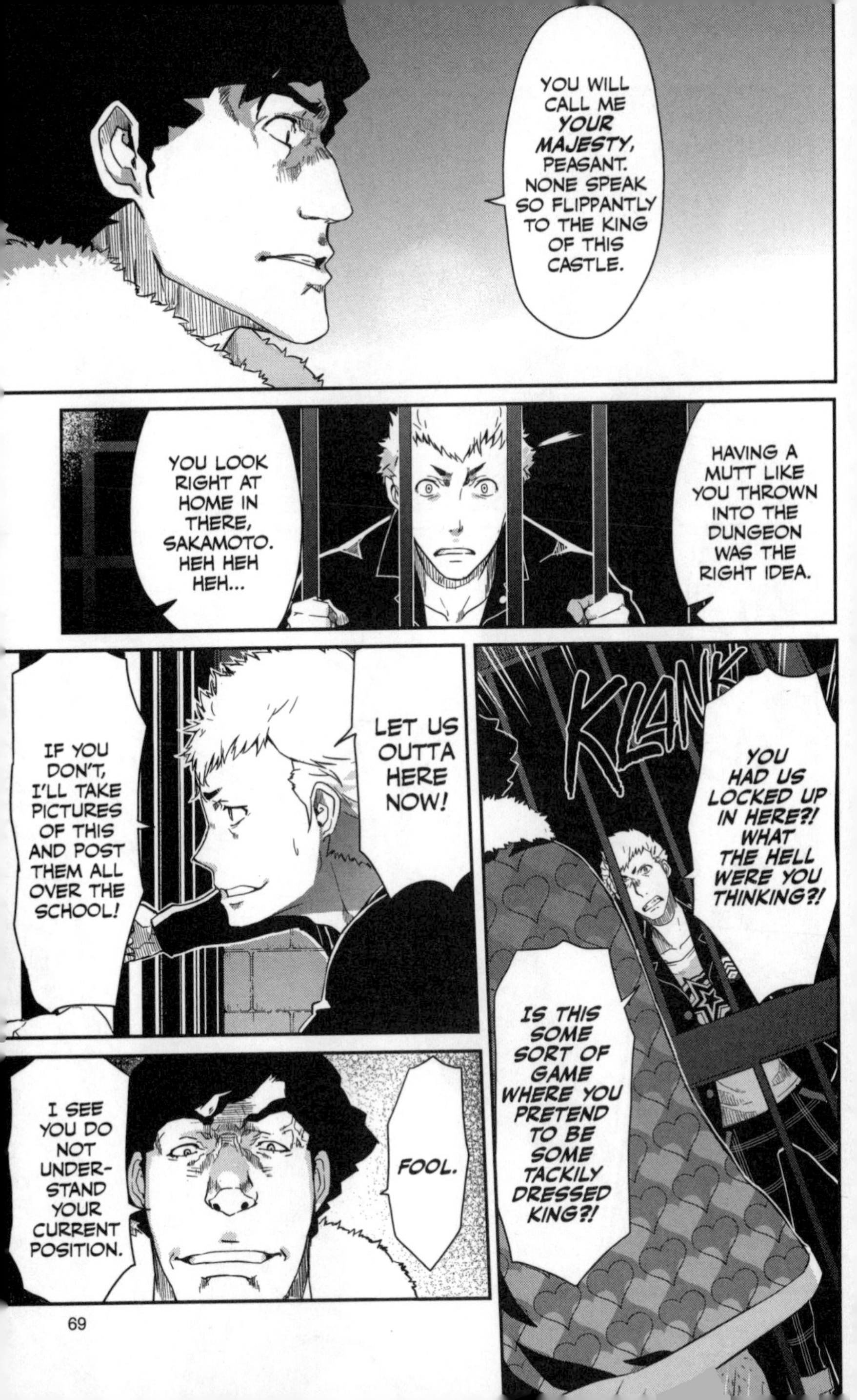
YOU WILL CALL ME *YOUR MAJESTY*, PEASANT. NONE SPEAK SO FLIPPANTLY TO THE KING OF THIS CASTLE.
HAVING A MUTT LIKE YOU THROWN INTO THE DUNGEON WAS THE RIGHT IDEA.
YOU LOOK RIGHT AT HOME IN THERE, SAKAMOTO. HEH HEH HEH...
KLANK
YOU HAD US LOCKED UP IN HERE?! WHAT THE HELL WERE YOU THINKING?!
IS THIS SOME SORT OF GAME WHERE YOU PRETEND TO BE SOME TACKILY DRESSED KING?!
LET US OUTTA HERE NOW!
IF YOU DON'T, I'LL TAKE PICTURES OF THIS AND POST THEM ALL OVER THE SCHOOL!
FOOL.
I SEE YOU DO NOT UNDER-STAND YOUR CURRENT POSITION.

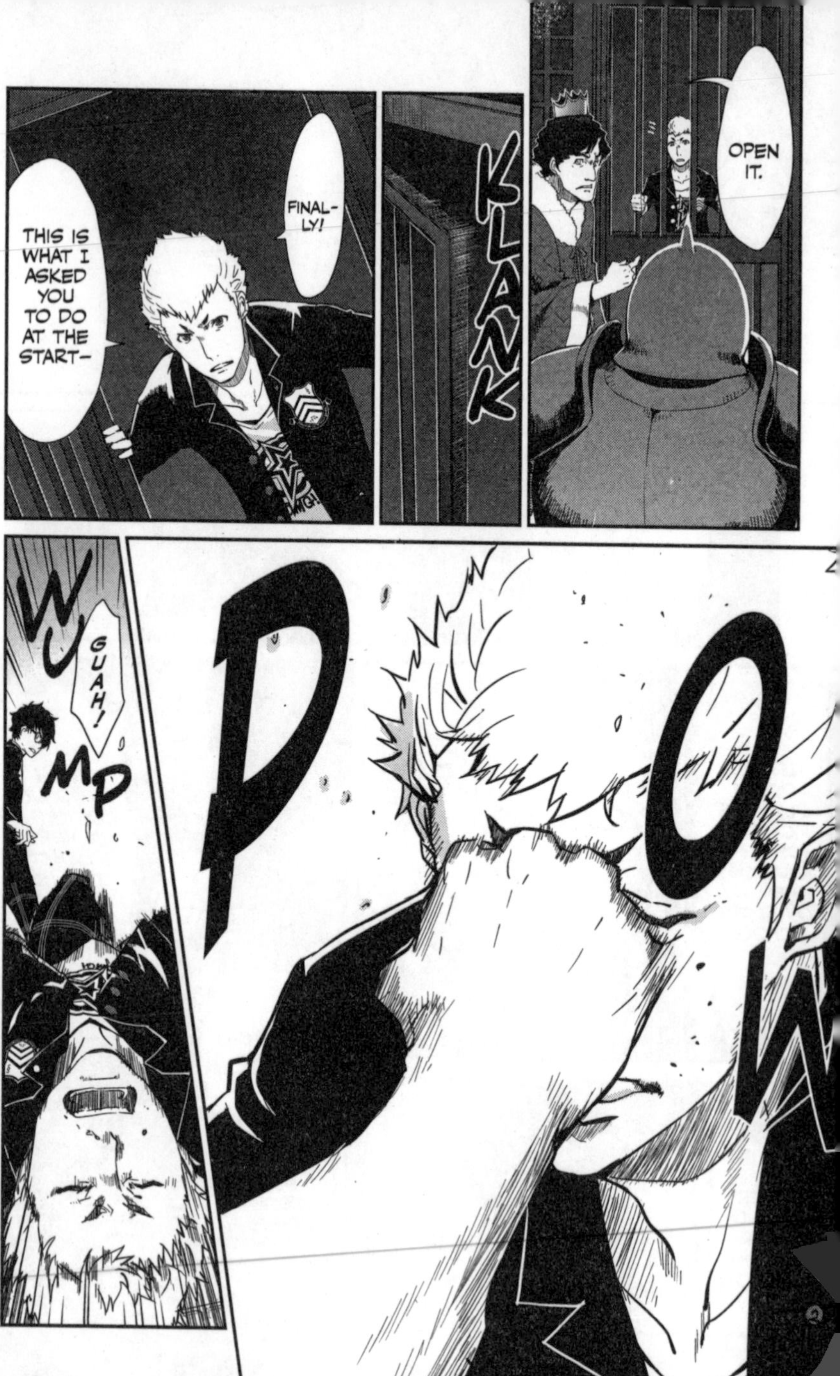
OPEN IT.
KLANK
FINAL-LY!
THIS IS WHAT I ASKED YOU TO DO AT THE START—
POW
WUMP
GUAH!

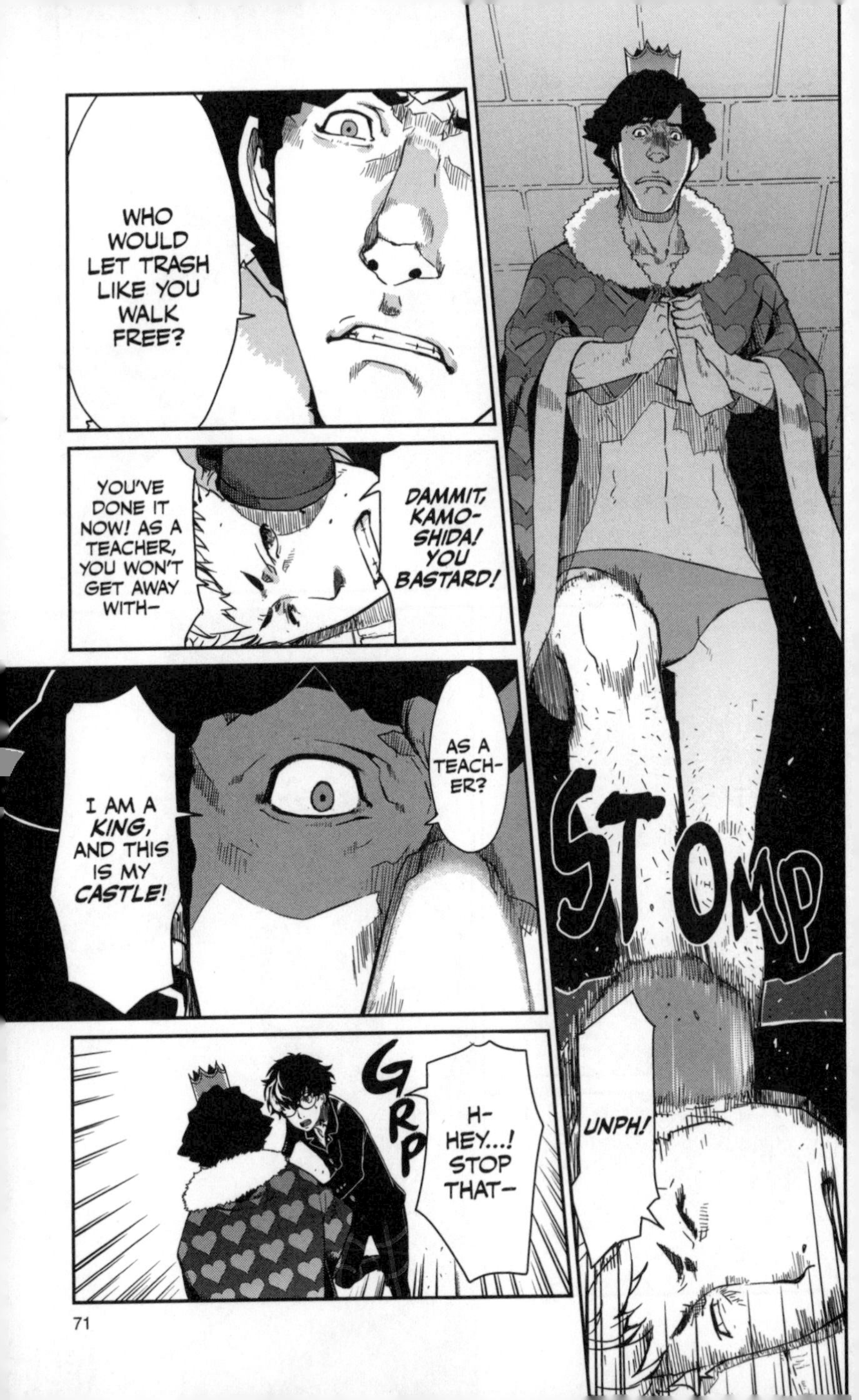
STOMP
UNPH!
WHO WOULD LET TRASH LIKE YOU WALK FREE?
DAMMIT, KAMO-SHIDA! YOU BASTARD!
YOU'VE DONE IT NOW! AS A TEACHER, YOU WON'T GET AWAY WITH—
AS A TEACH-ER?
I AM A KING, AND THIS IS MY CASTLE!
GRP
H-HEY...! STOP THAT—

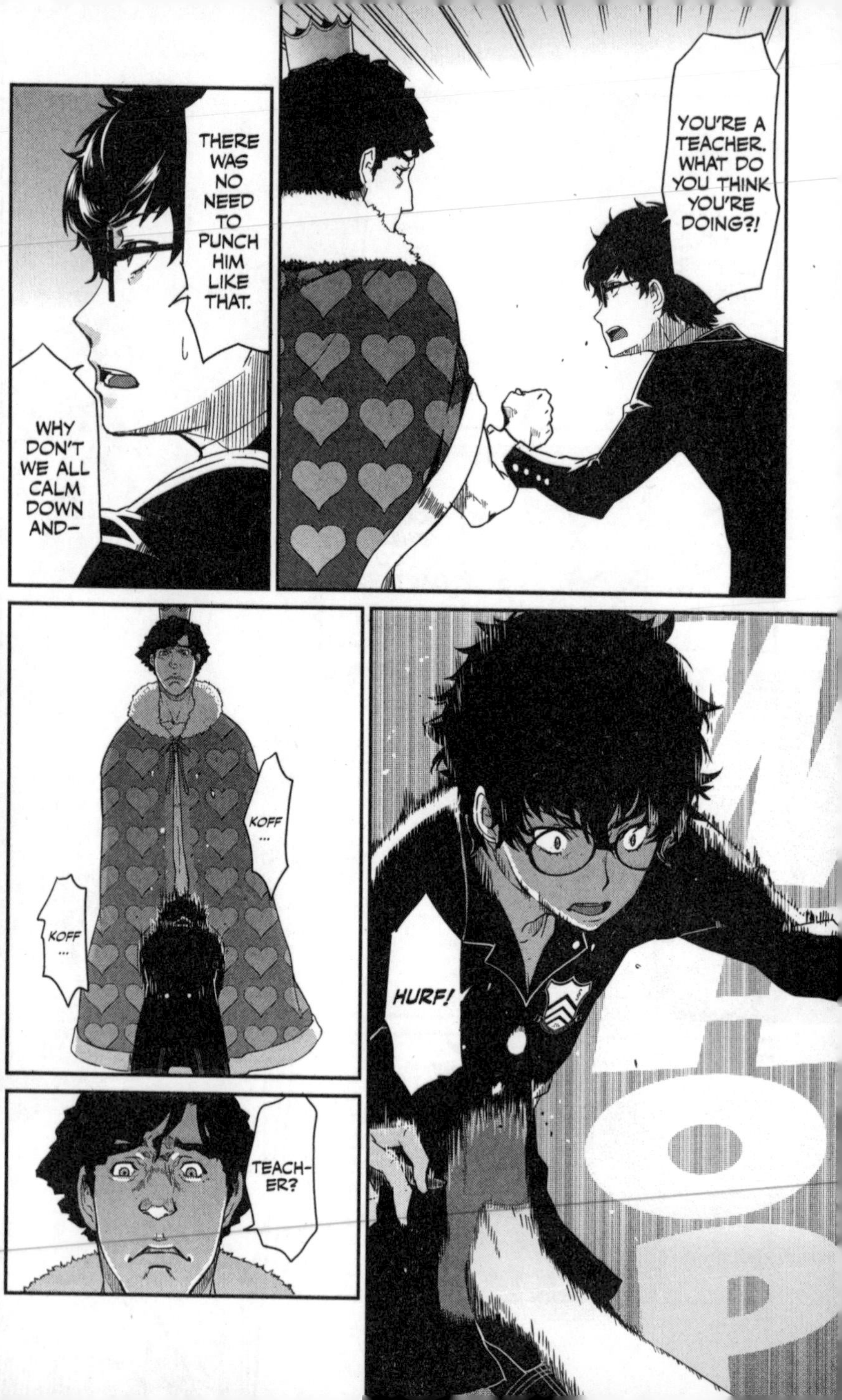
YOU'RE A TEACHER. WHAT DO YOU THINK YOU'RE DOING?!
THERE WAS NO NEED TO PUNCH HIM LIKE THAT.
WHY DON'T WE ALL CALM DOWN AND–
HURF!
KOFF ...
KOFF ...
TEACHER?

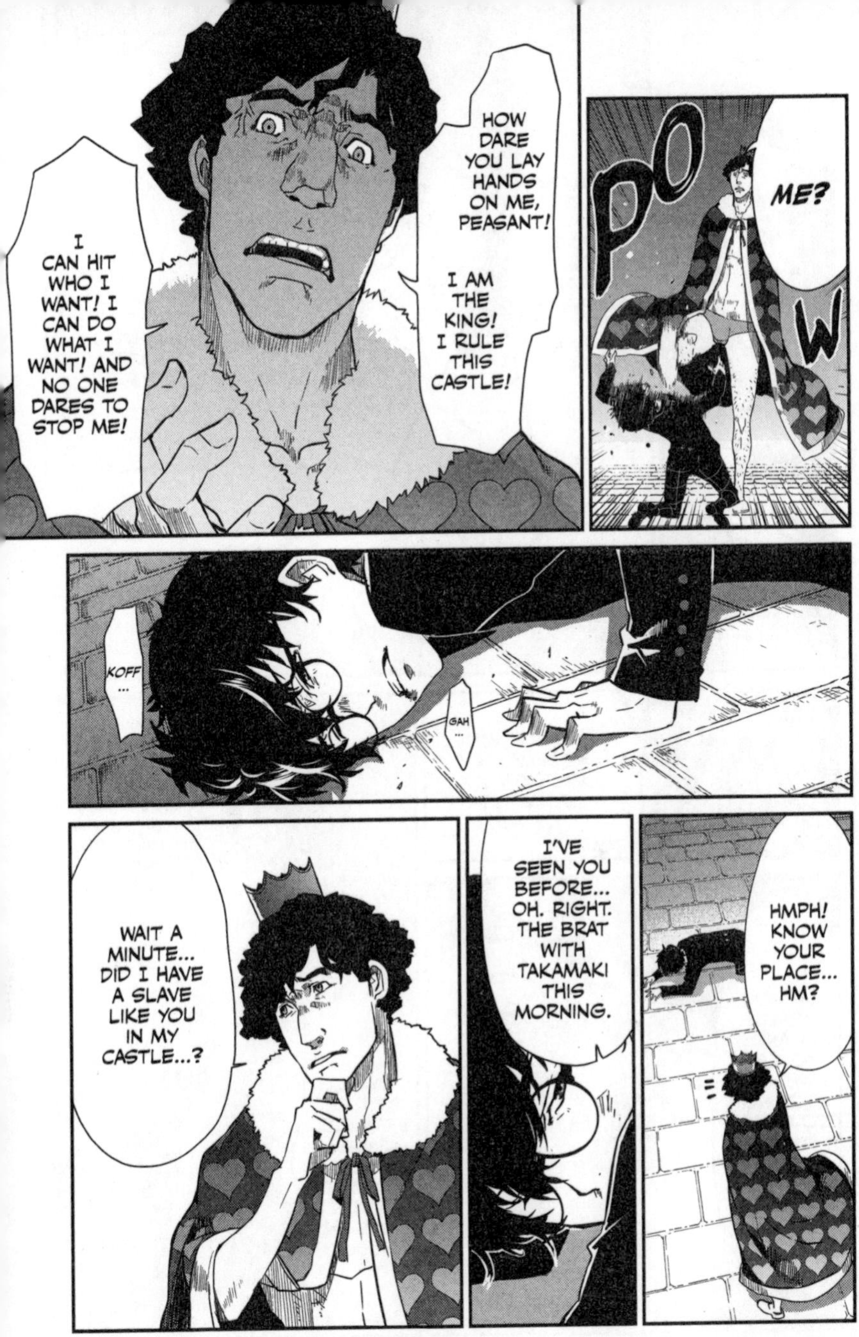
ME?
POW
HOW DARE YOU LAY HANDS ON ME, PEASANT!
I AM THE KING! I RULE THIS CASTLE!
I CAN HIT WHO I WANT! I CAN DO WHAT I WANT! AND NO ONE DARES TO STOP ME!
GAH...
KOFF...
HMPH! KNOW YOUR PLACE... HM?
I'VE SEEN YOU BEFORE... OH. RIGHT. THE BRAT WITH TAKAMAKI THIS MORNING.
WAIT A MINUTE... DID I HAVE A SLAVE LIKE YOU IN MY CASTLE...?

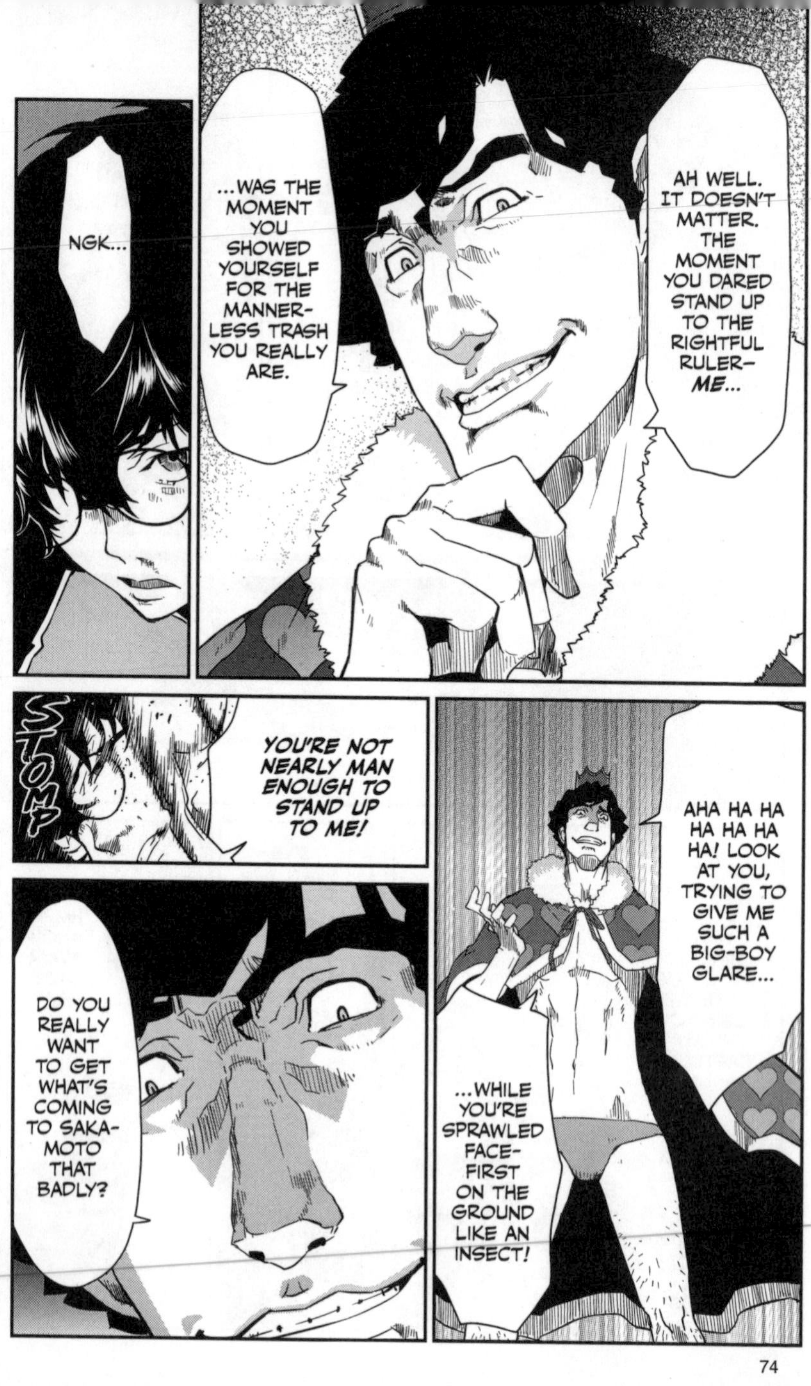
AH WELL. IT DOESN'T MATTER. THE MOMENT YOU DARED STAND UP TO THE RIGHTFUL RULER— *ME*...
...WAS THE MOMENT YOU SHOWED YOURSELF FOR THE MANNER-LESS TRASH YOU REALLY ARE.
NGK...
AHA HA HA HA HA HA HA! LOOK AT YOU, TRYING TO GIVE ME SUCH A BIG-BOY GLARE...
...WHILE YOU'RE SPRAWLED FACE-FIRST ON THE GROUND LIKE AN INSECT!
YOU'RE NOT NEARLY MAN ENOUGH TO STAND UP TO ME!
STOMP
DO YOU REALLY WANT TO GET WHAT'S COMING TO SAKA-MOTO THAT BADLY?

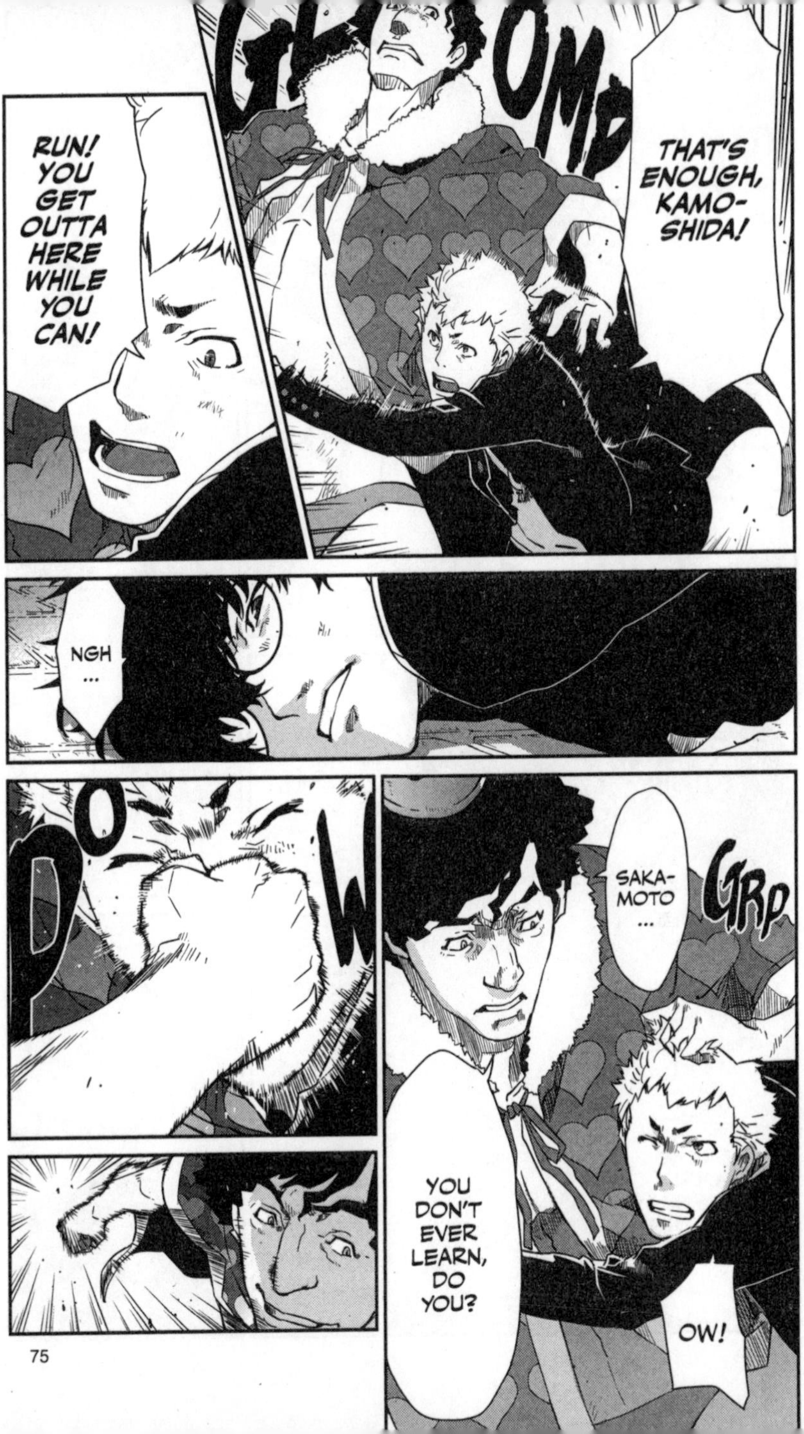
THAT'S ENOUGH, KAMOSHIDA!
RUN! YOU GET OUTTA HERE WHILE YOU CAN!
NGH ...
SAKAMOTO ...
GRP
YOU DON'T EVER LEARN, DO YOU?
OW!
DOW

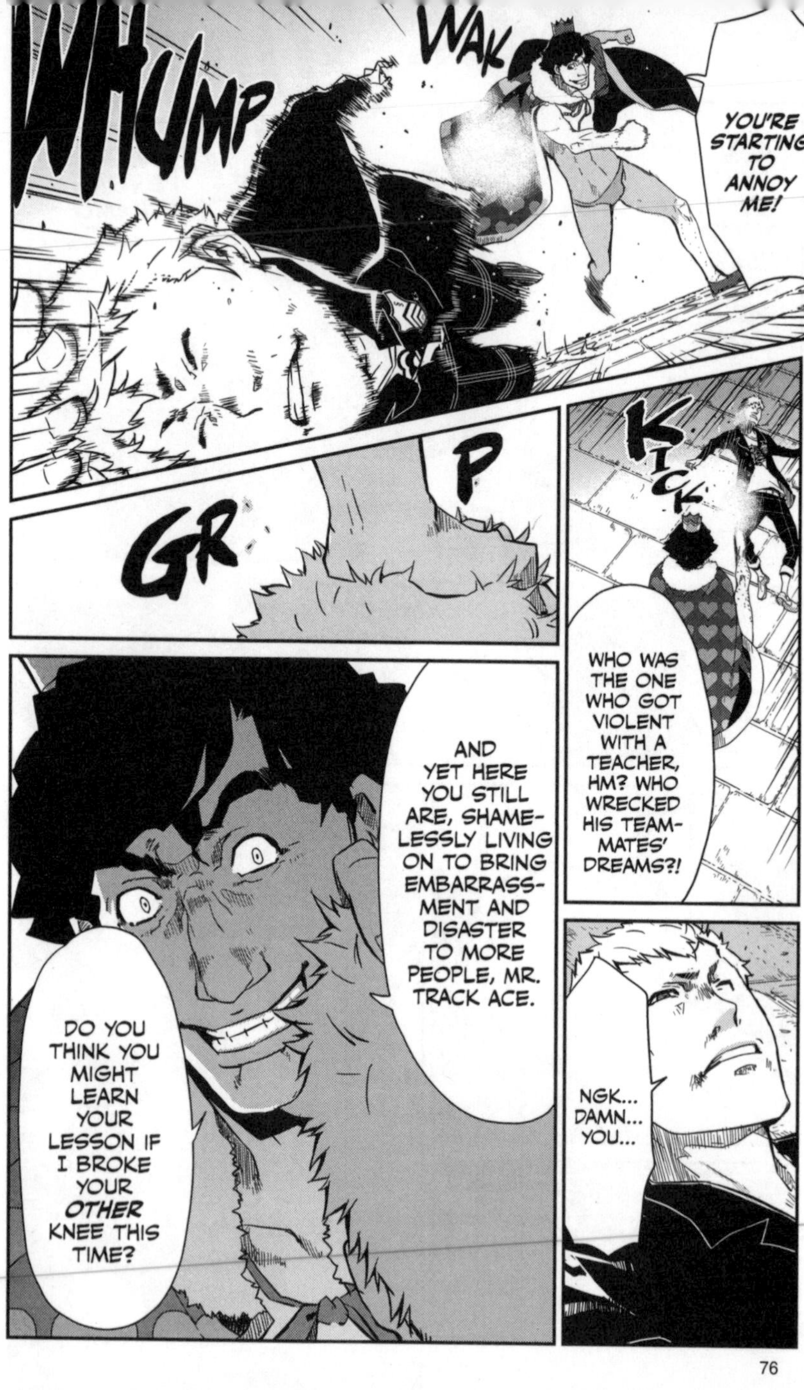
YOU'RE STARTING TO ANNOY ME!
WAK
WHUMP
KICK
WHO WAS THE ONE WHO GOT VIOLENT WITH A TEACHER, HM? WHO WRECKED HIS TEAM-MATES' DREAMS?!
NGK... DAMN... YOU...
GR
P
AND YET HERE YOU STILL ARE, SHAME-LESSLY LIVING ON TO BRING EMBARRASS-MENT AND DISASTER TO MORE PEOPLE, MR. TRACK ACE.
DO YOU THINK YOU MIGHT LEARN YOUR LESSON IF I BROKE YOUR *OTHER* KNEE THIS TIME?

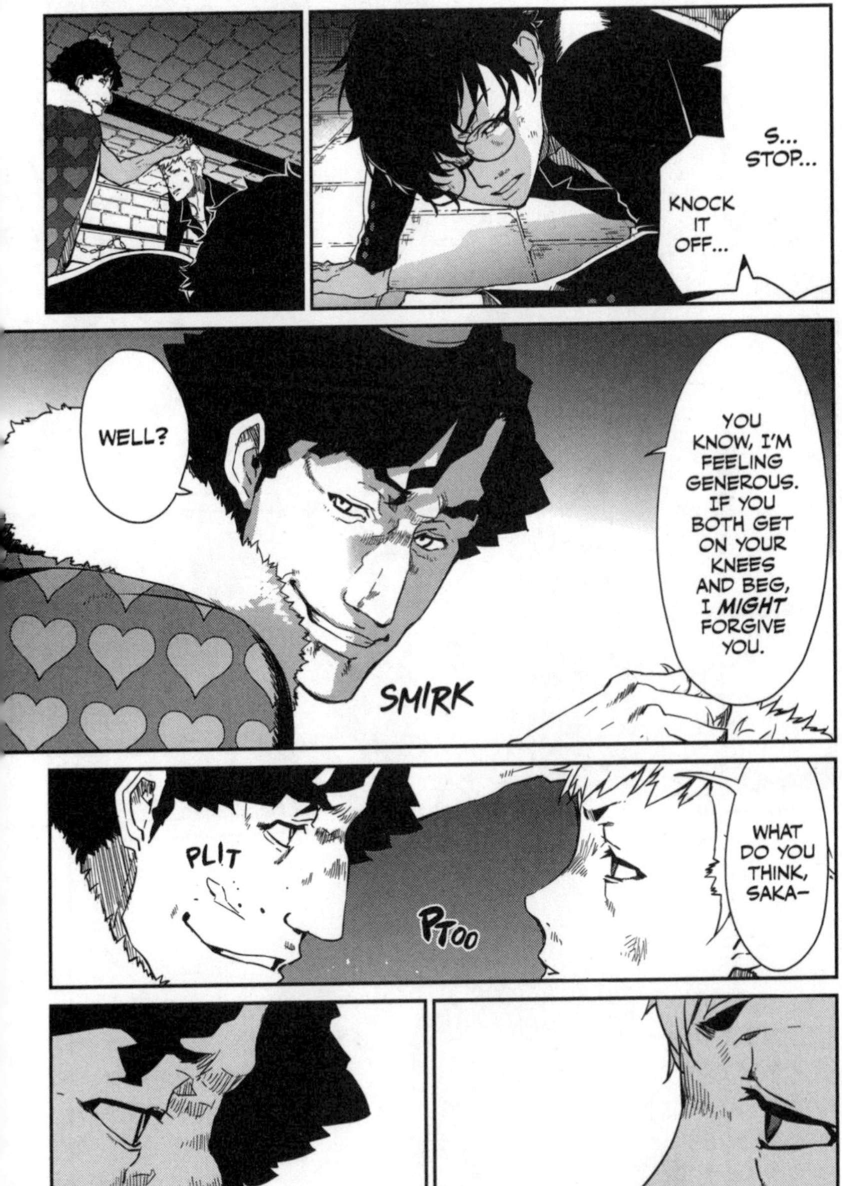
S... STOP...
KNOCK IT OFF...
YOU KNOW, I'M FEELING GENEROUS. IF YOU BOTH GET ON YOUR KNEES AND BEG, I *MIGHT* FORGIVE YOU.
WELL?
SMIRK
WHAT DO YOU THINK, SAKA-
PTOO
PLIT

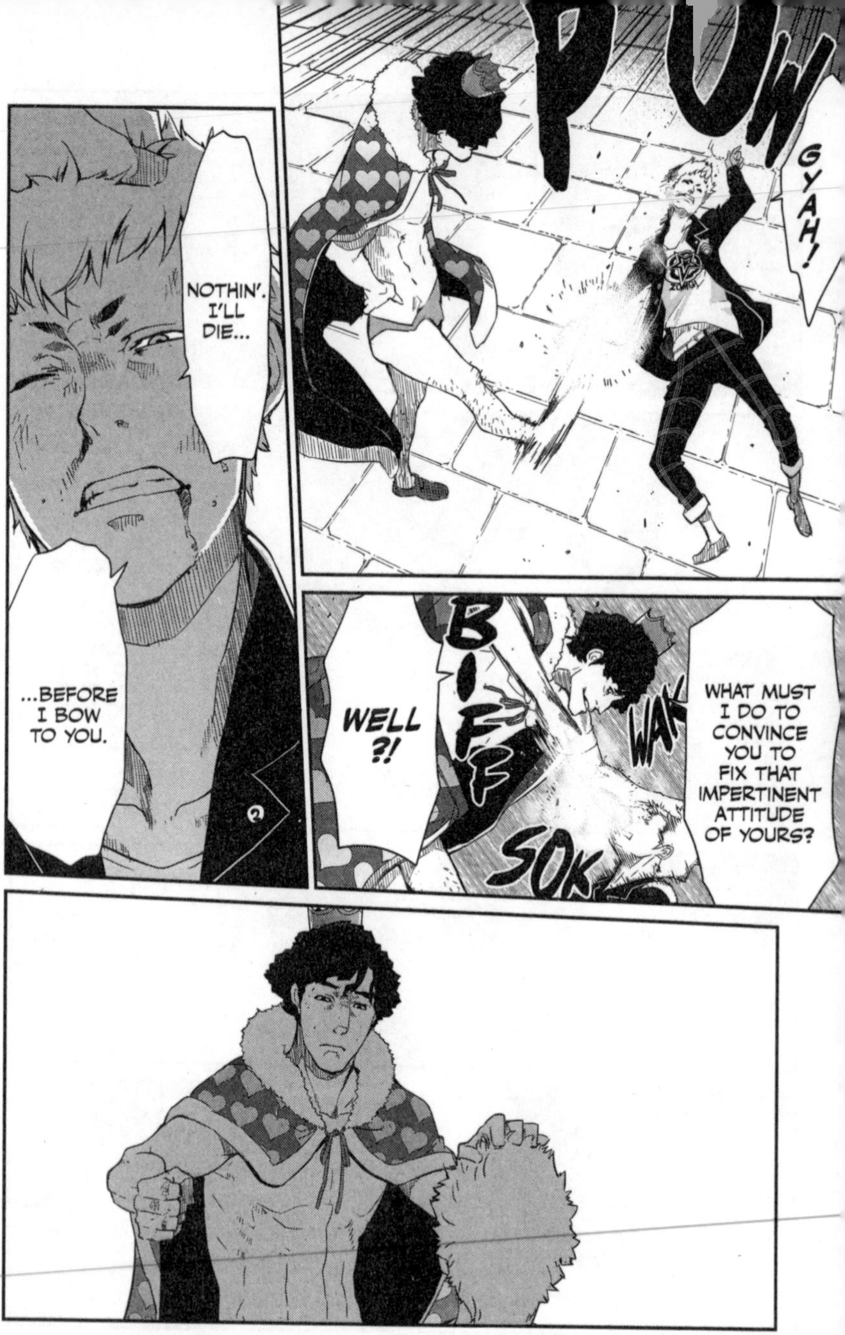
POW
GYAH!
WHAT MUST I DO TO CONVINCE YOU TO FIX THAT IMPERTINENT ATTITUDE OF YOURS?
WAK
BIFF
WELL?!
SOK
NOTHIN'. I'LL DIE...
...BEFORE I BOW TO YOU.

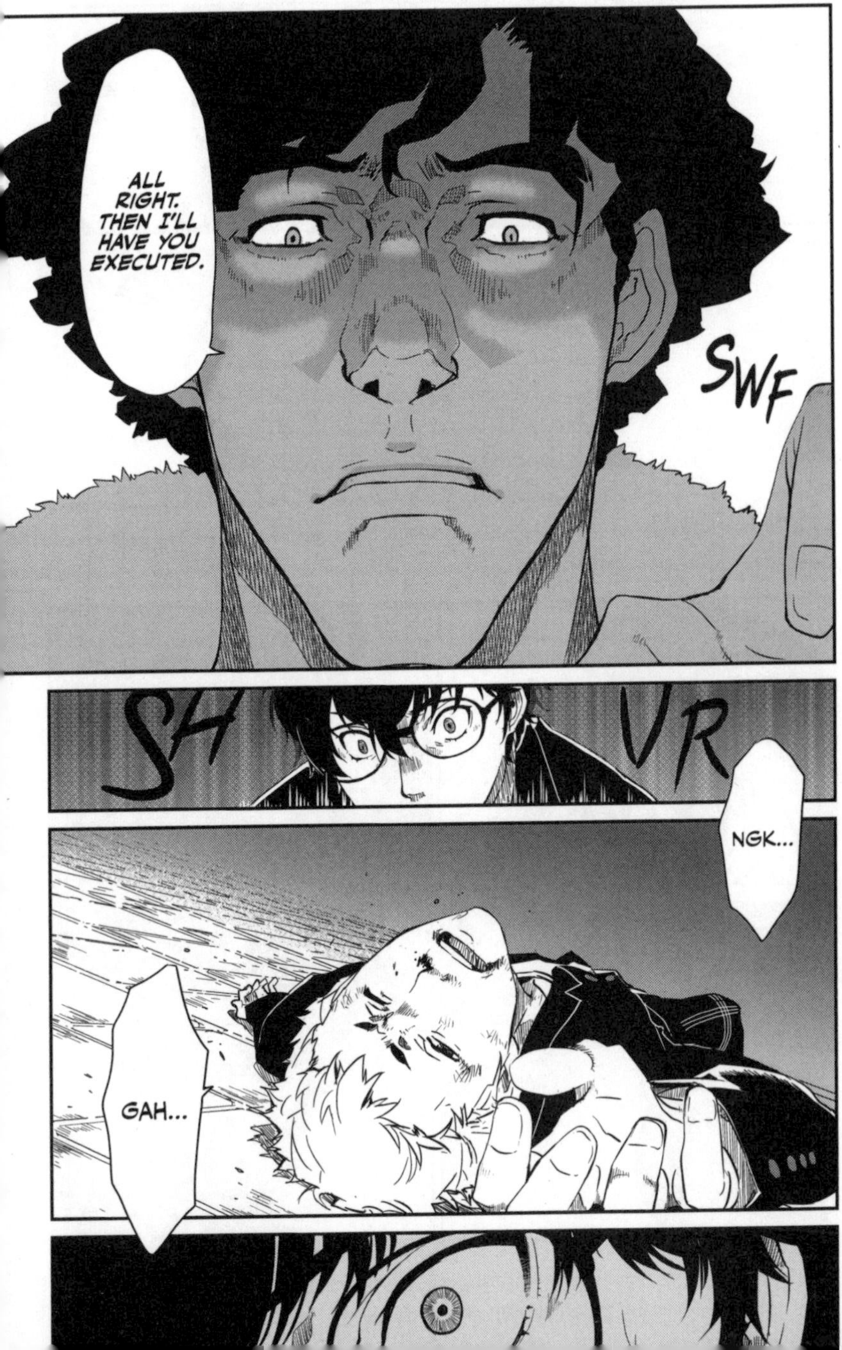
ALL RIGHT. THEN I'LL HAVE YOU EXECUTED.
SWF
SH
VR
NGK...
GAH...

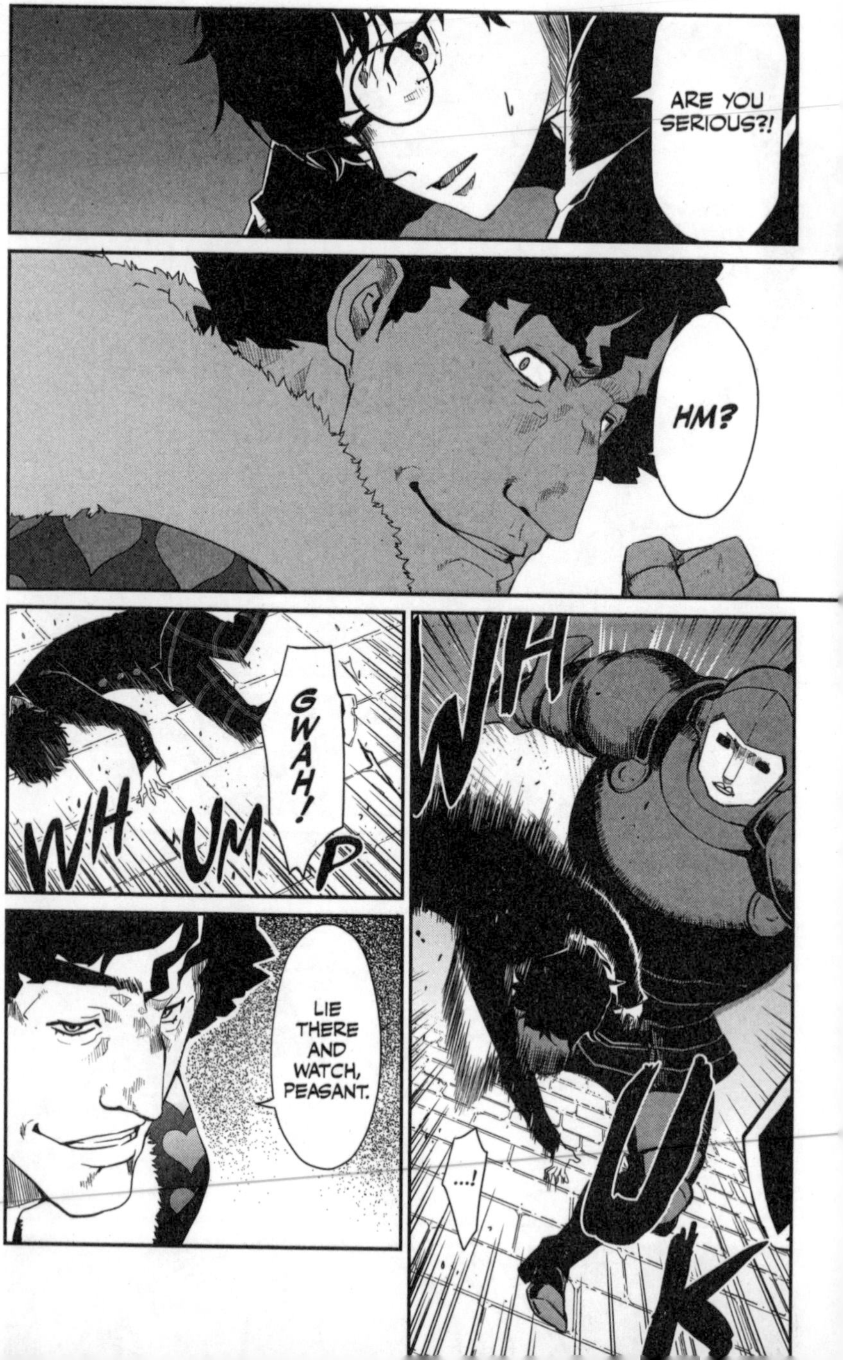
ARE YOU SERIOUS?!
HM?
WH UK
...!
GWAH!
WH UM P
LIE THERE AND WATCH, PEASANT.

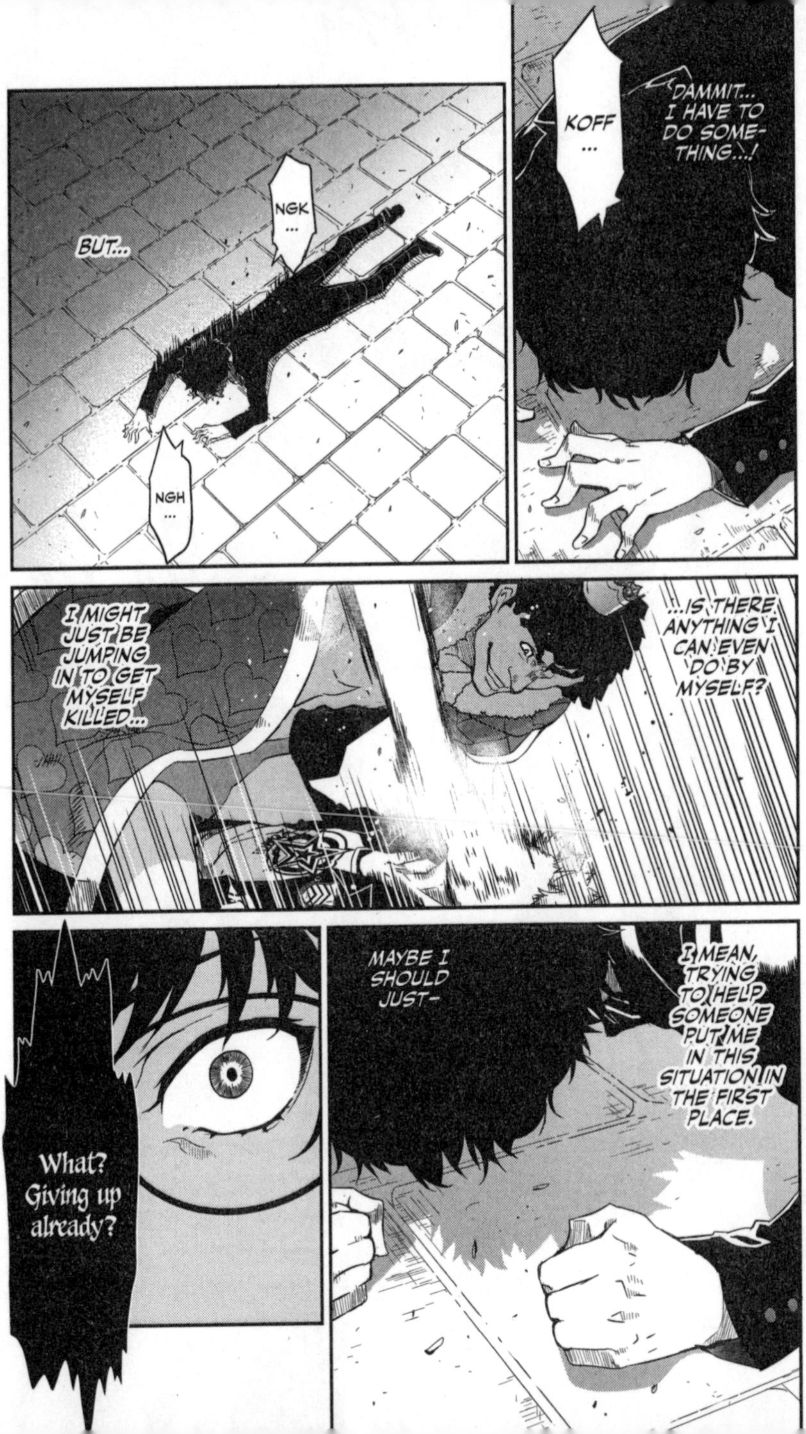
KOFF ...
DAMMIT... I HAVE TO DO SOME-THING...!
BUT...
NGK ...
NGH ...
...IS THERE ANYTHING I CAN EVEN DO BY MYSELF?
I MIGHT JUST BE JUMPING IN TO GET MYSELF KILLED...
I MEAN, TRYING TO HELP SOMEONE PUT ME IN THIS SITUATION IN THE FIRST PLACE.
MAYBE I SHOULD JUST-
What? Giving up already?

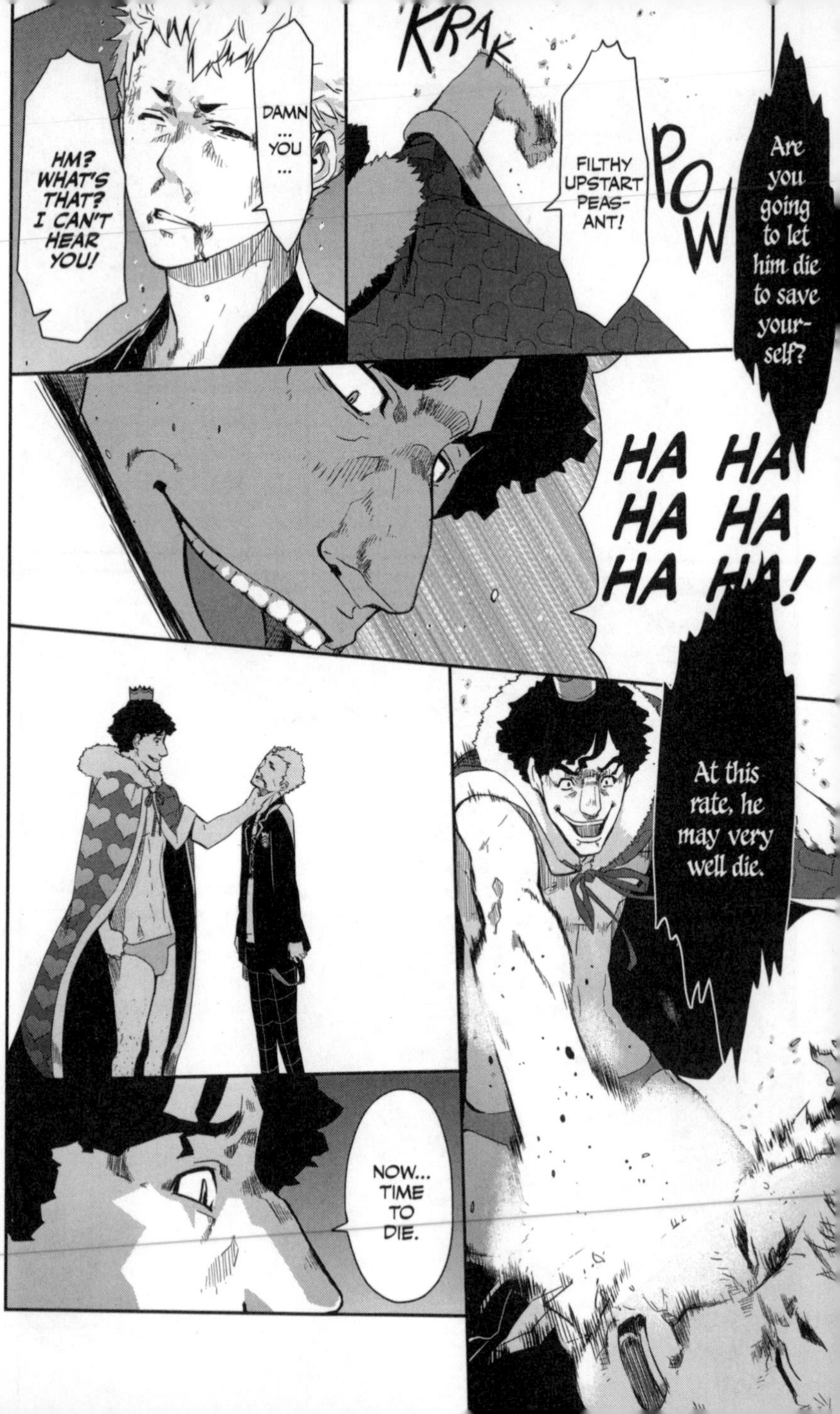

KRAK
FILTHY UPSTART PEAS-ANT!
POW
Are you going to let him die to save your-self?
DAMN ... YOU ...
HM? WHAT'S THAT? I CAN'T HEAR YOU!
HA HA HA HA HA HA!
At this rate, he may very well die.
NOW... TIME TO DIE.

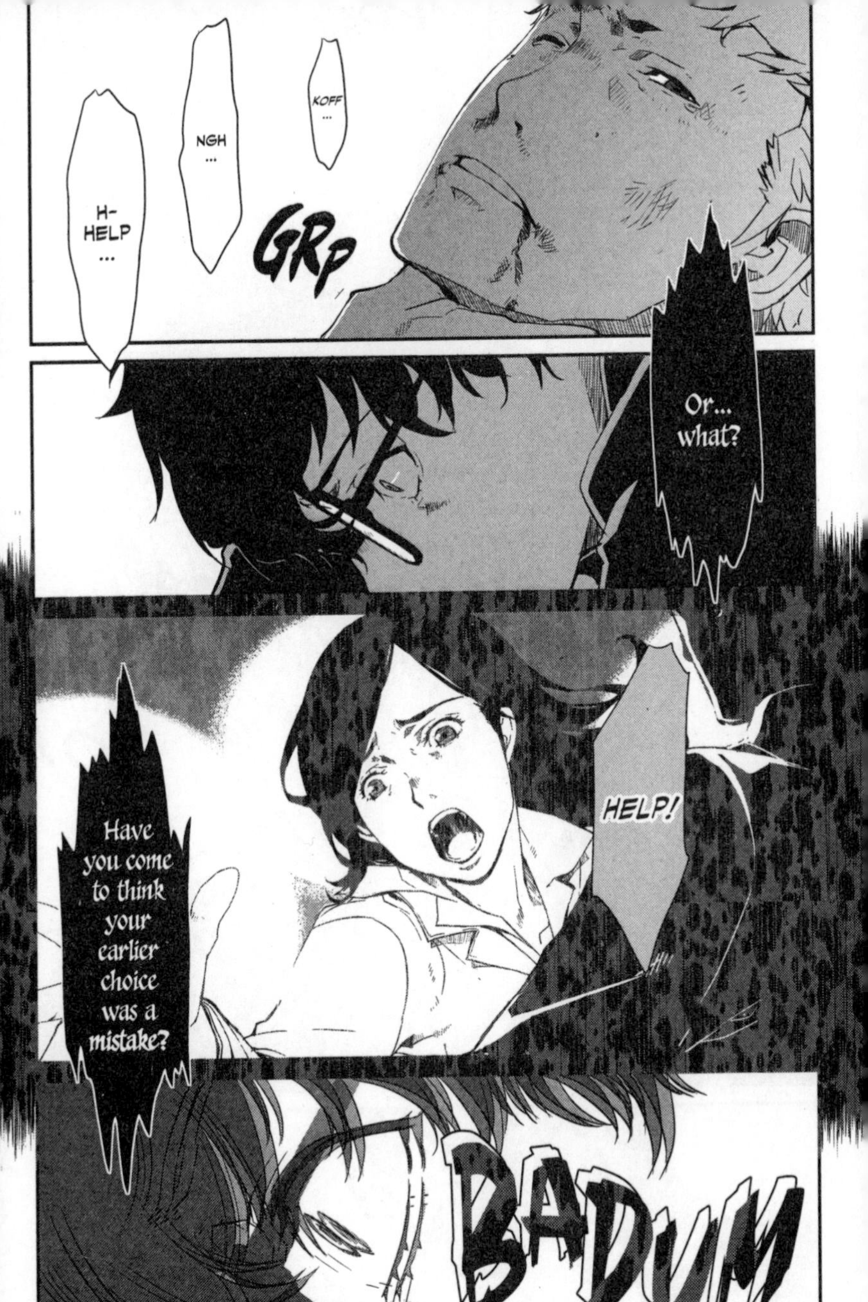
KOFF ...
NGH ...
H-HELP ...
GRP
Or... what?
HELP!
Have you come to think your earlier choice was a mistake?
BADUM

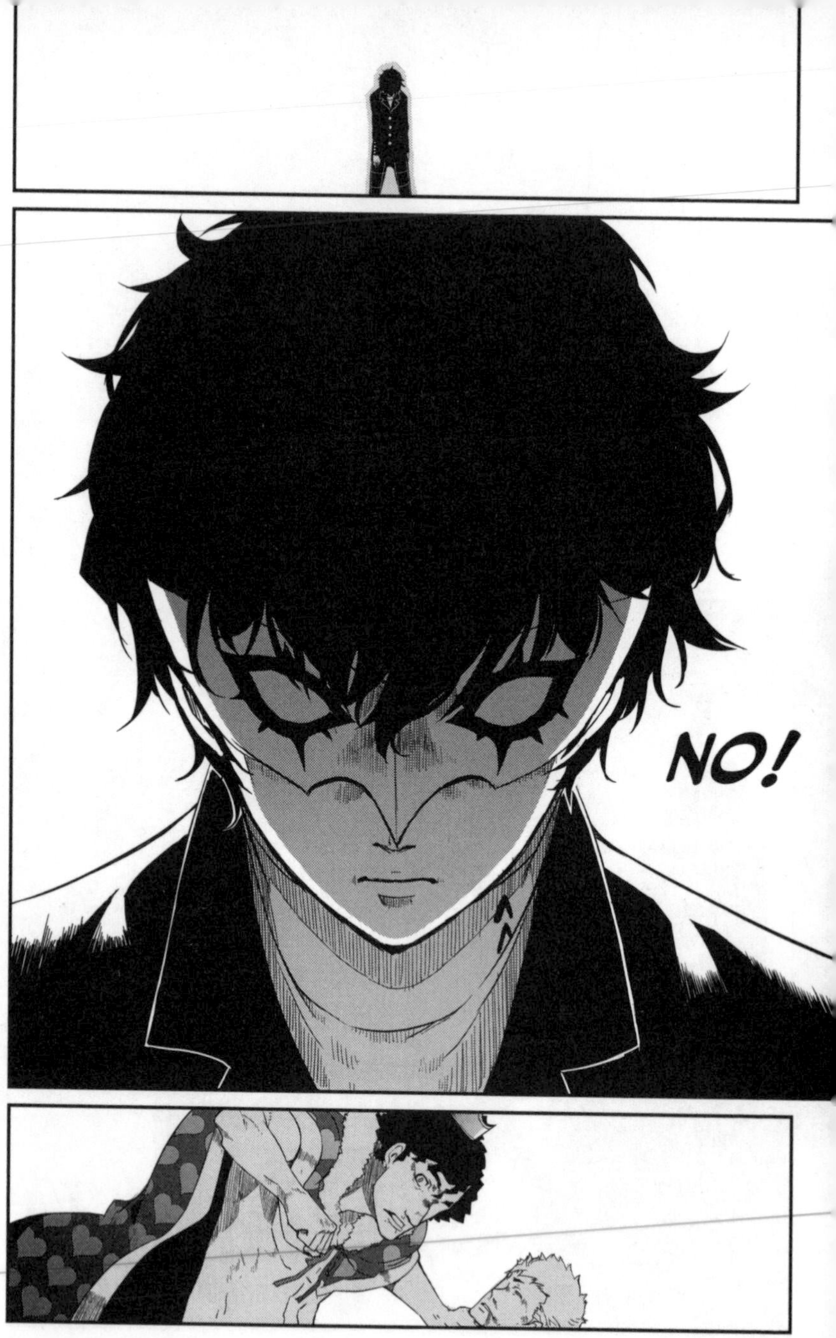
NO!

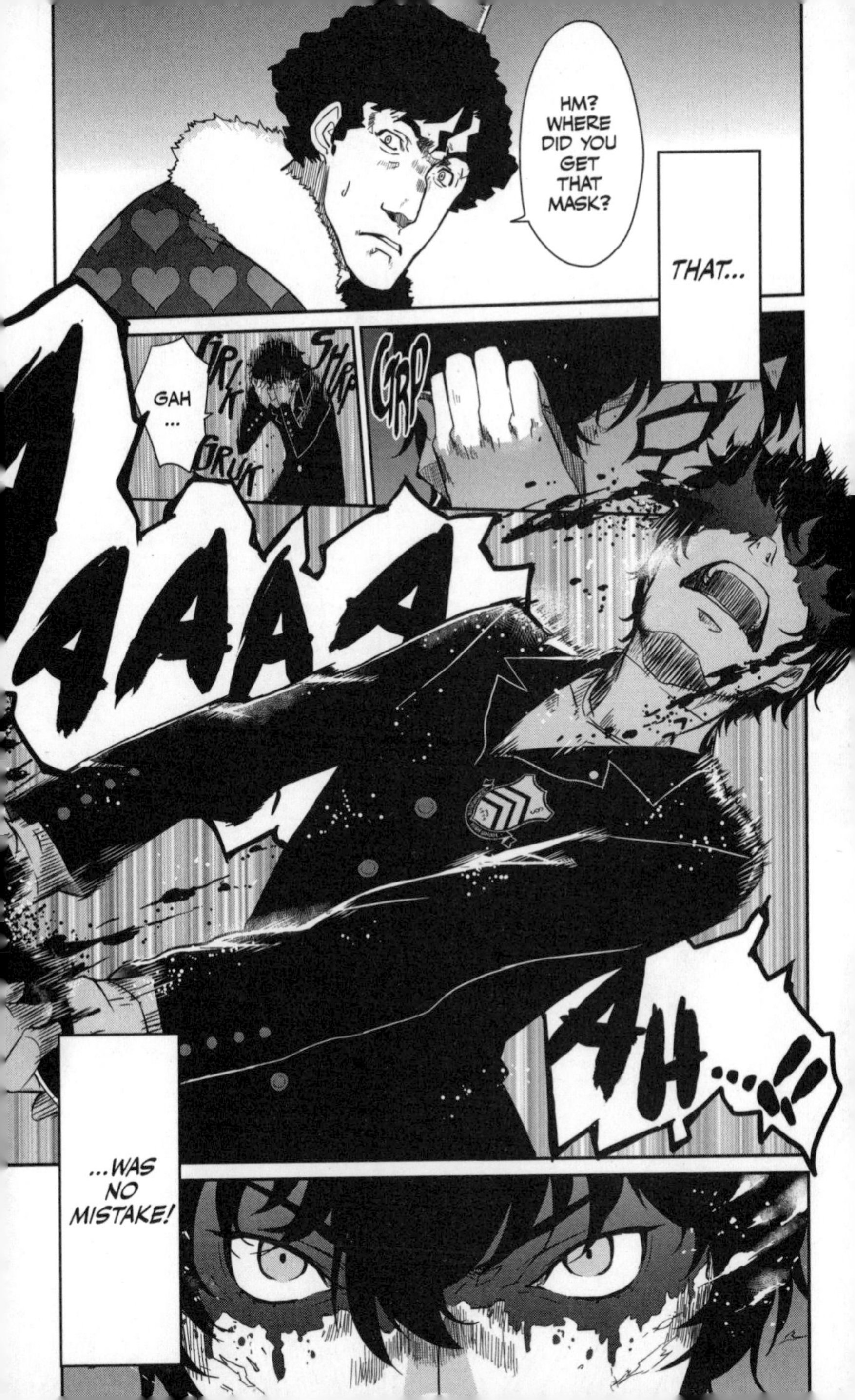
HM? WHERE DID YOU GET THAT MASK?
THAT...
GRP
SHRP
GRIK
GAH ...
GRUK
AAAAAH...!!
...WAS NO MISTAKE!

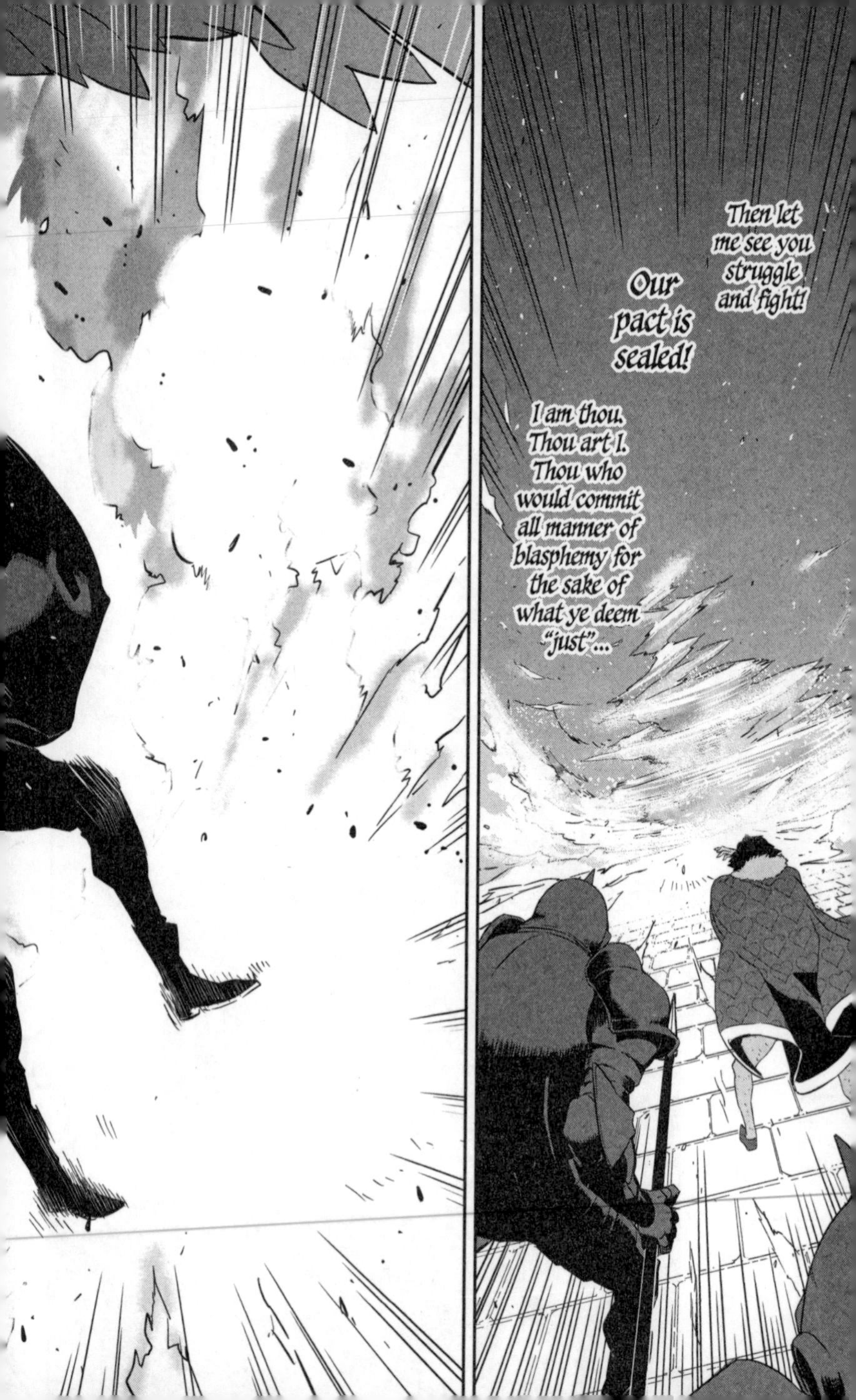
Then let me see you struggle and fight!
Our pact is sealed!
I am thou. Thou art I. Thou who would commit all manner of blasphemy for the sake of what ye deem "just"...

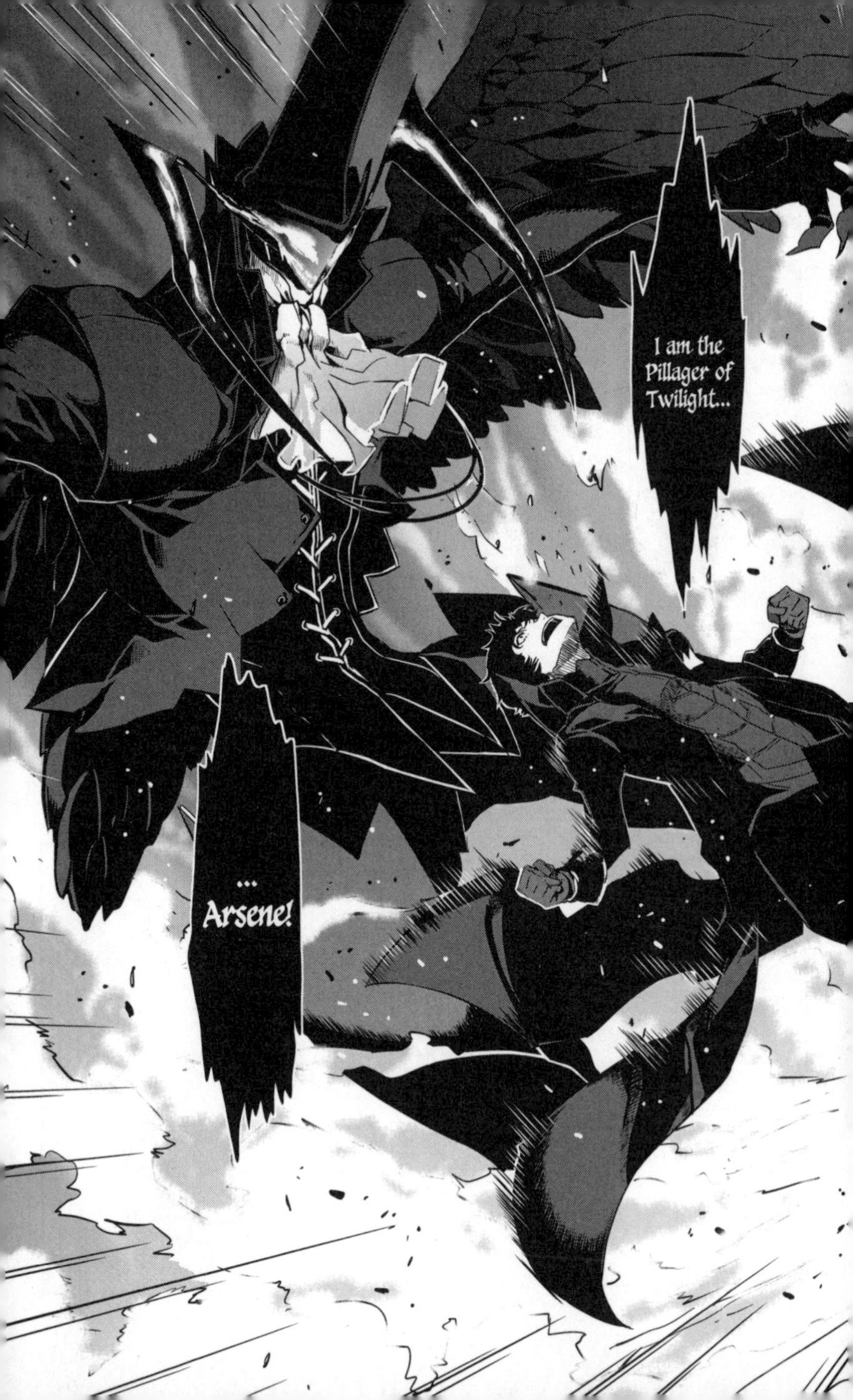
I am the Pillager of Twilight...
... Arsene!

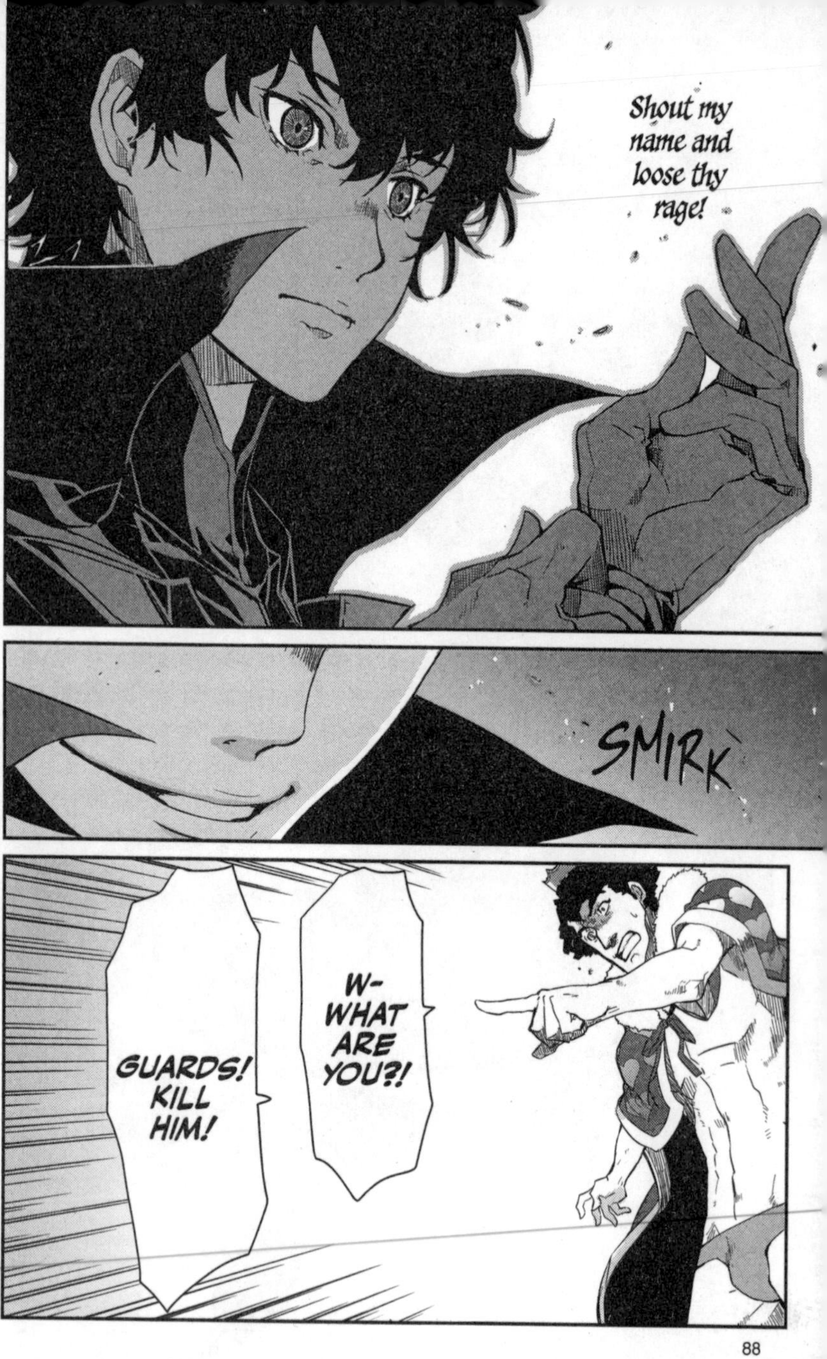
Shout my name and loose thy rage!
SMIRK
W-WHAT ARE YOU?!
GUARDS! KILL HIM!

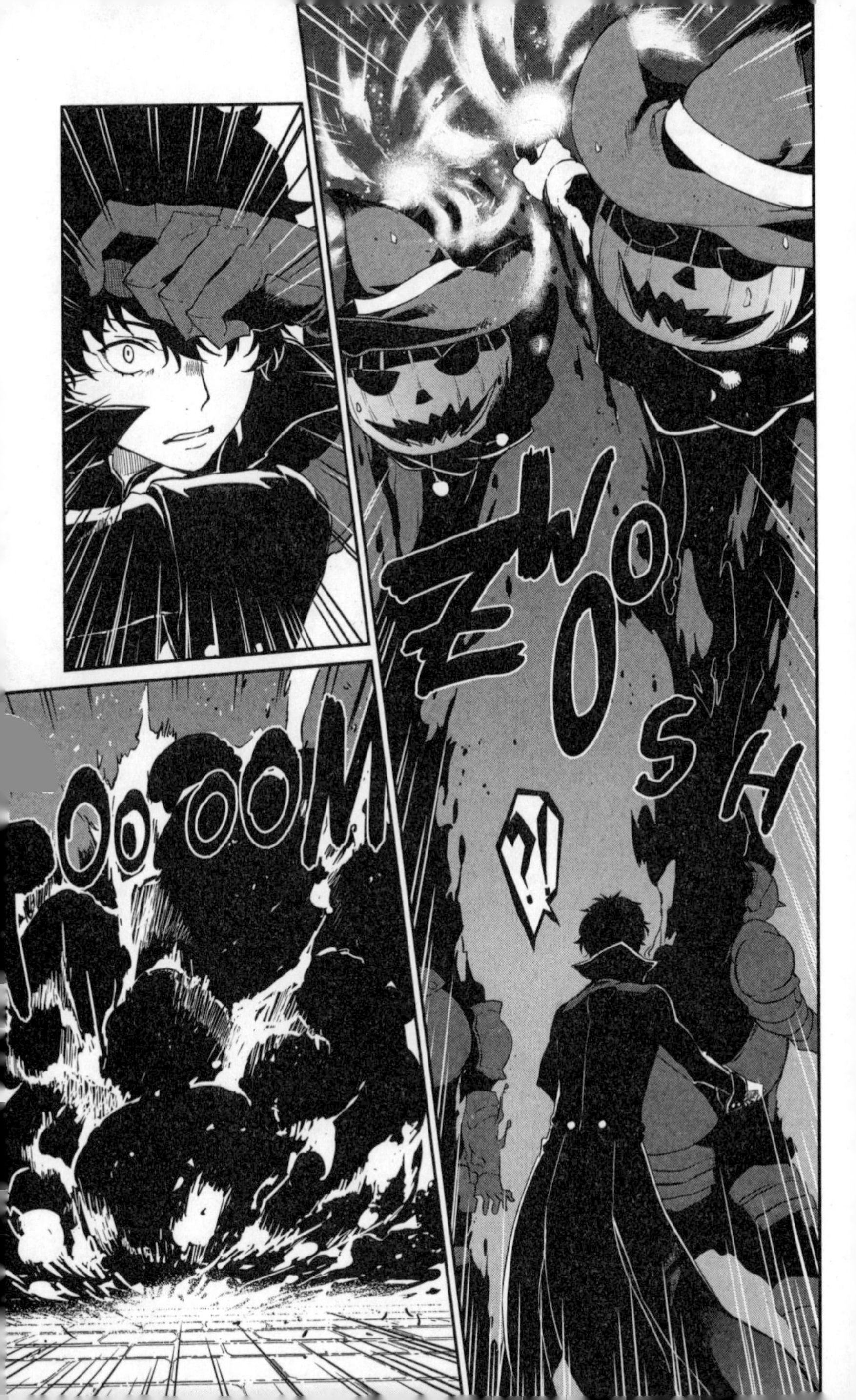
ZWOOSH
?!
OOOOOM

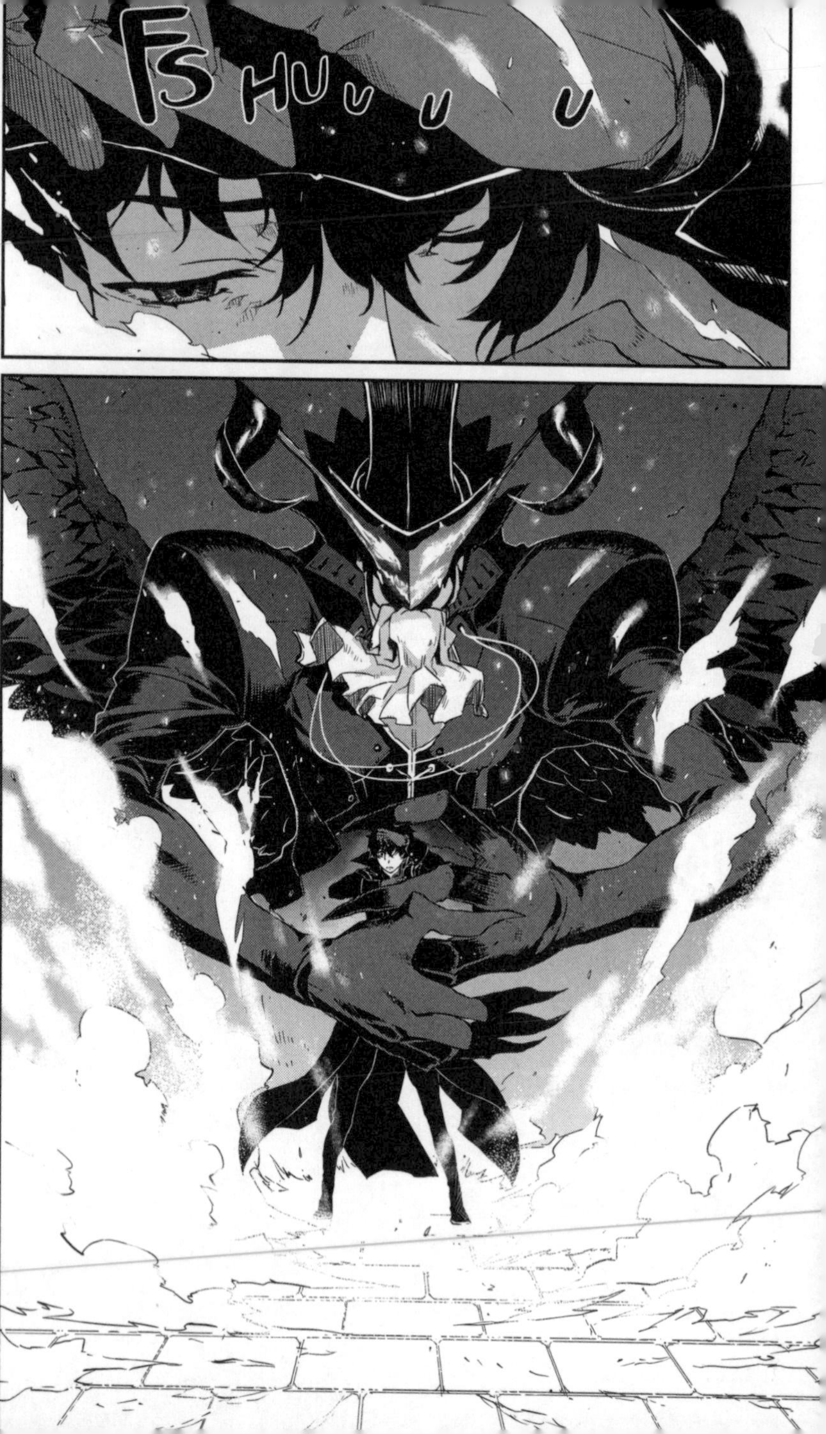
FSHUuuu

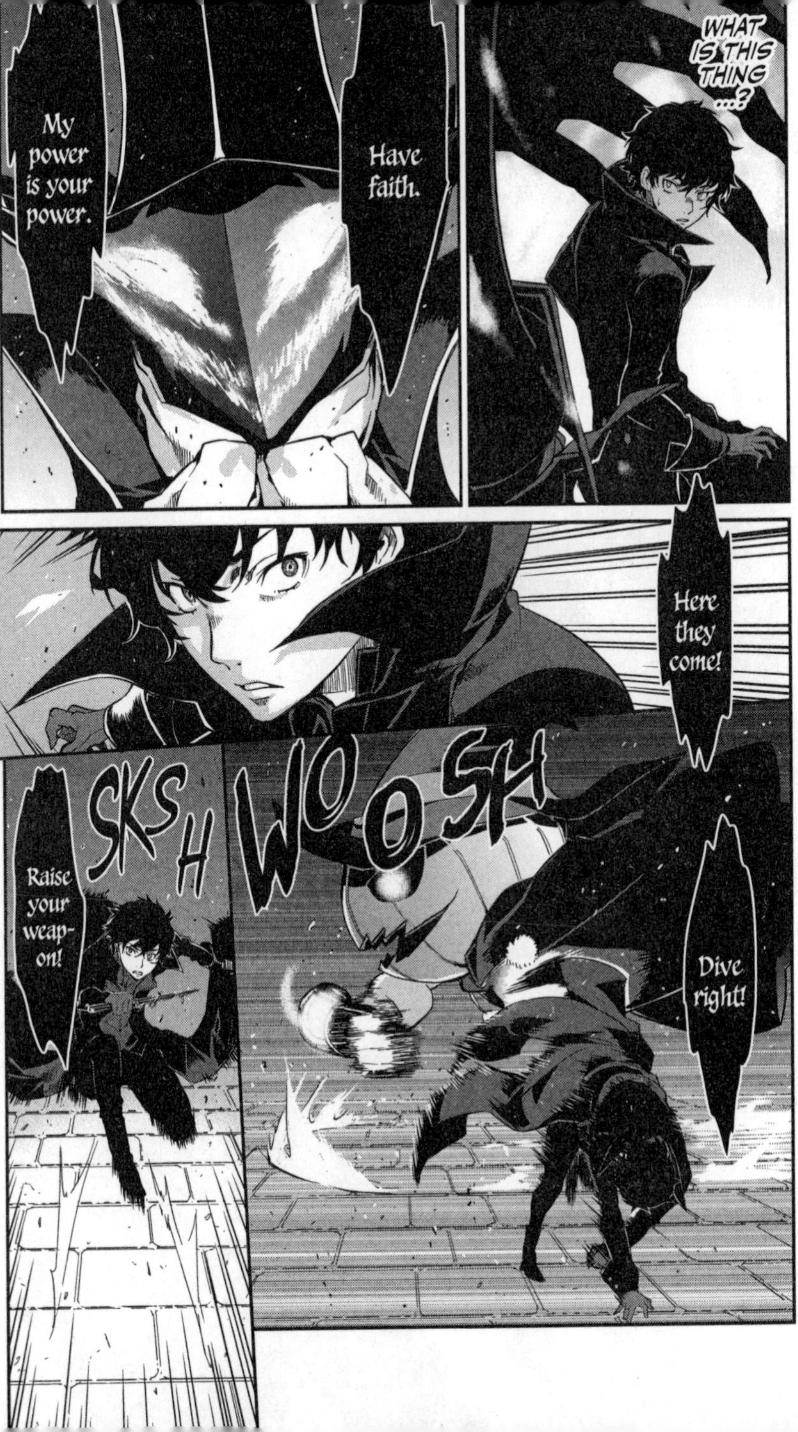
WHAT IS THIS THING ...?
Have faith.
My power is your power.
Here they come!
WOOSH
Dive right!
SKSH
Raise your weap-on!

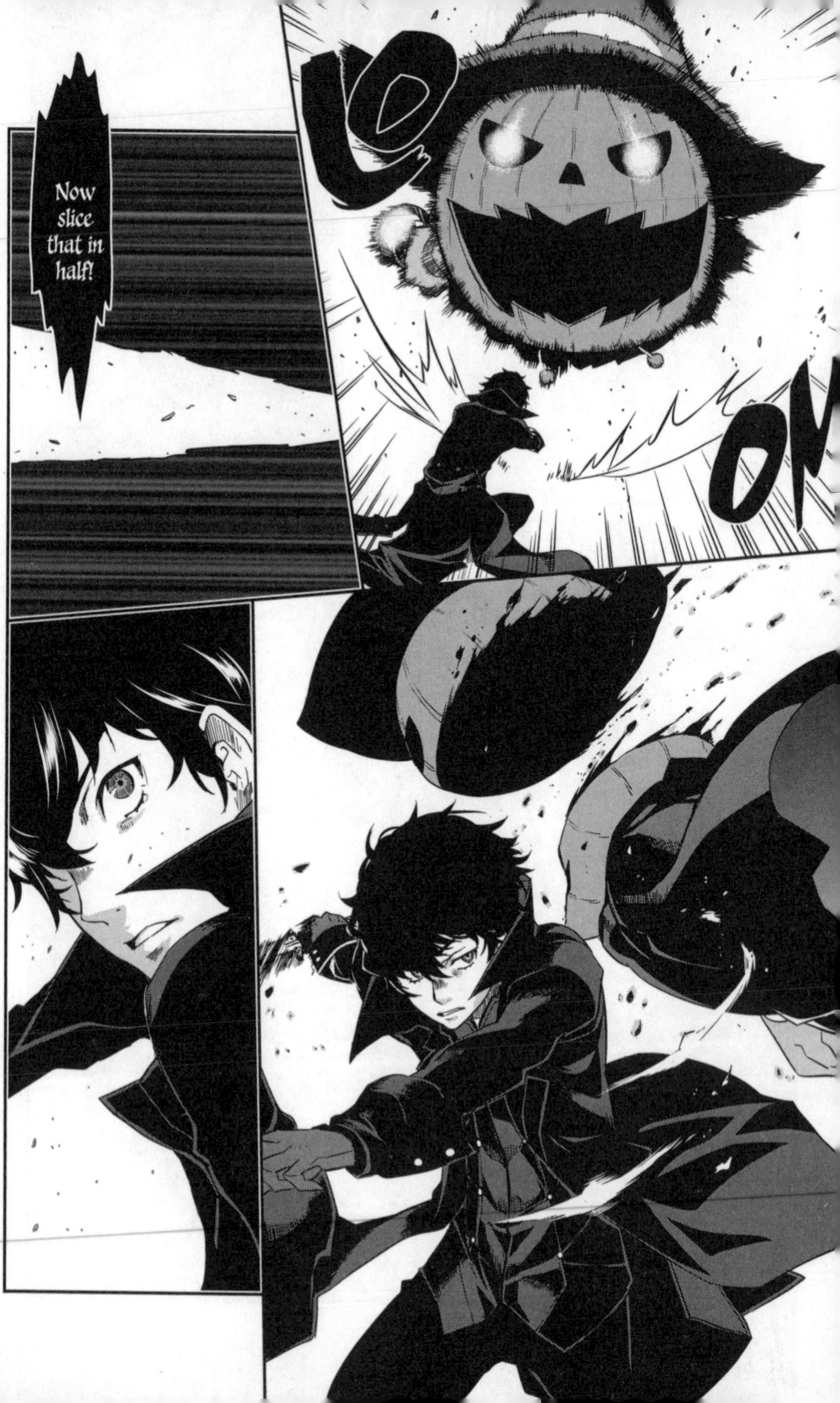
Now slice that in half!

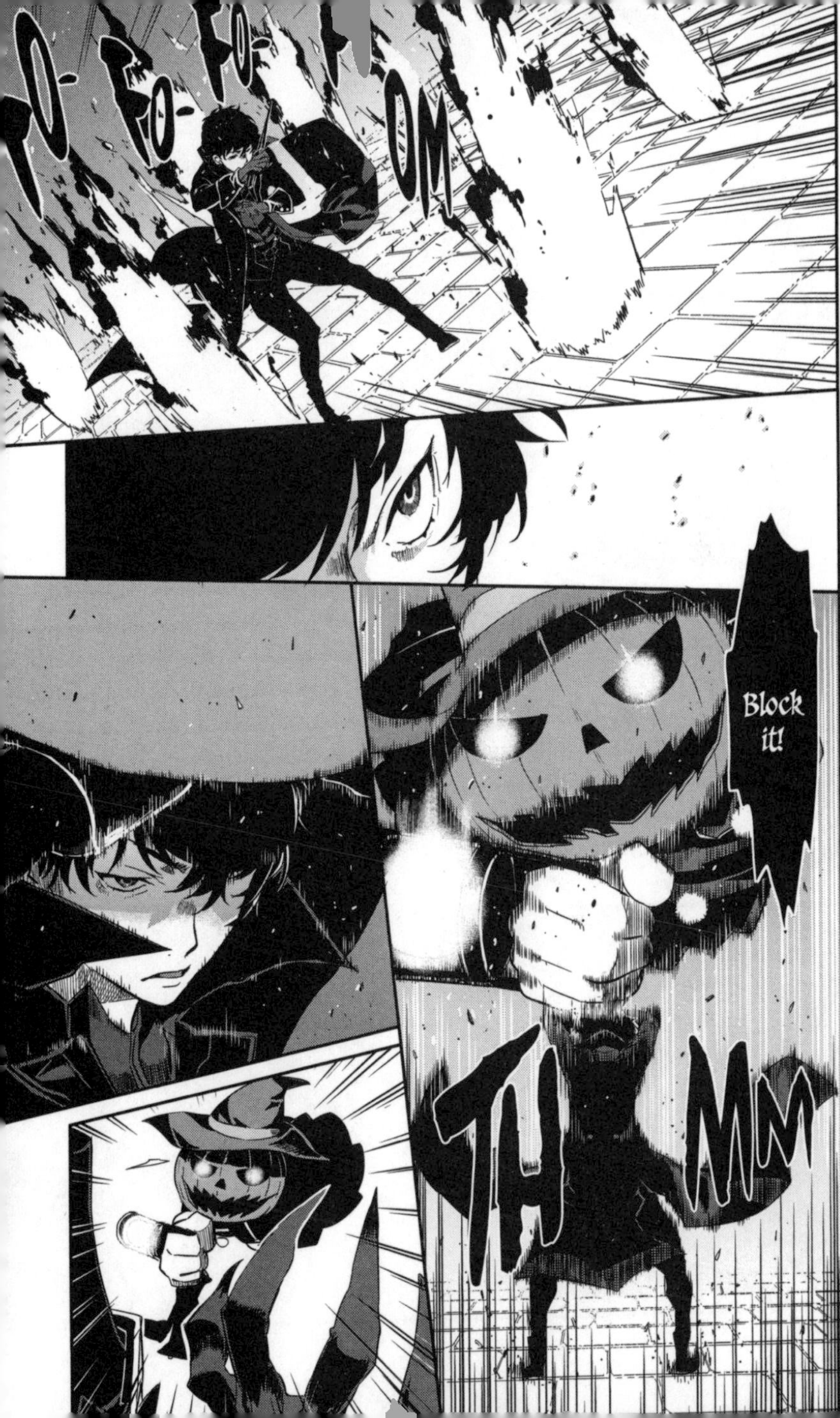
PO-PO-PO-POM
Block it!
THMM

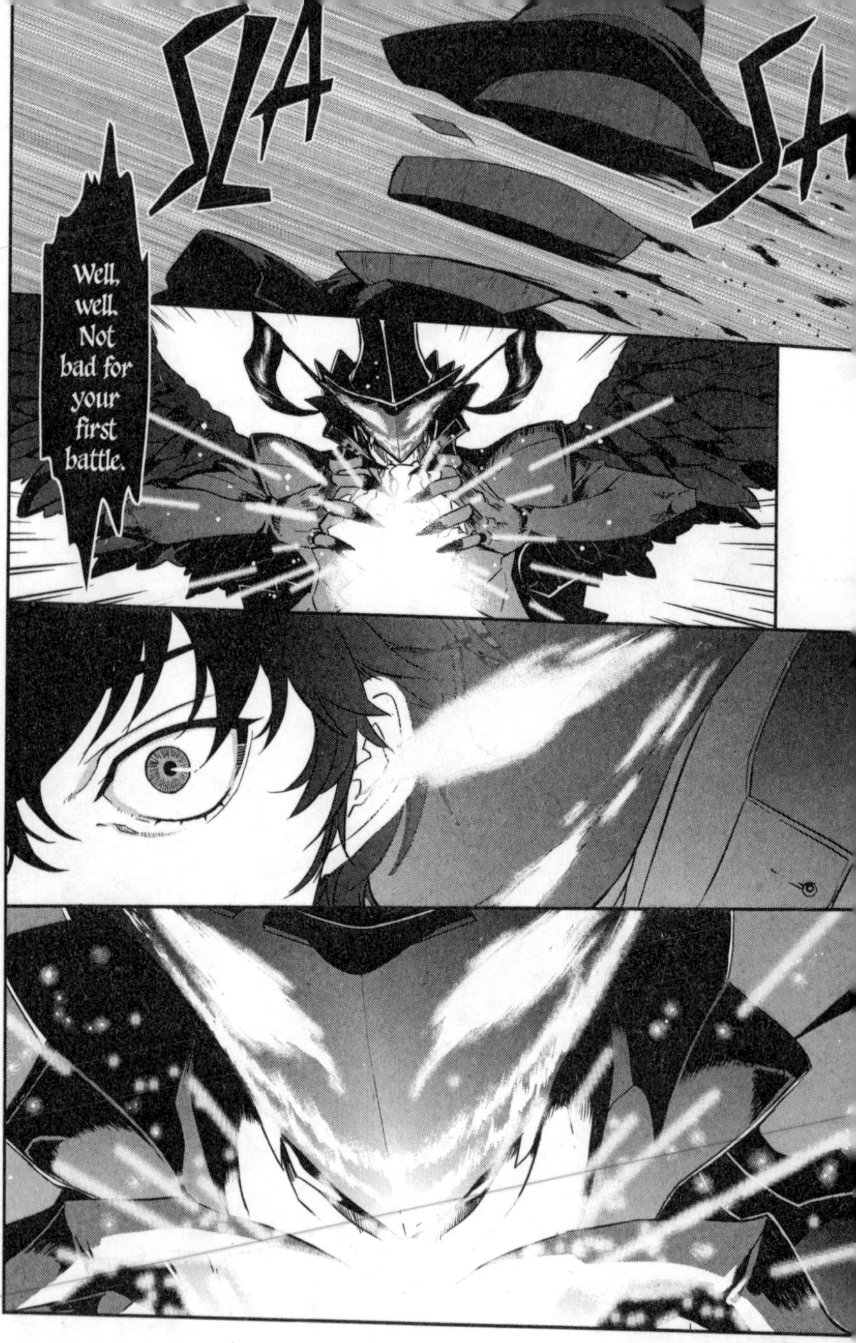
SLA SH
Well, well. Not bad for your first battle.

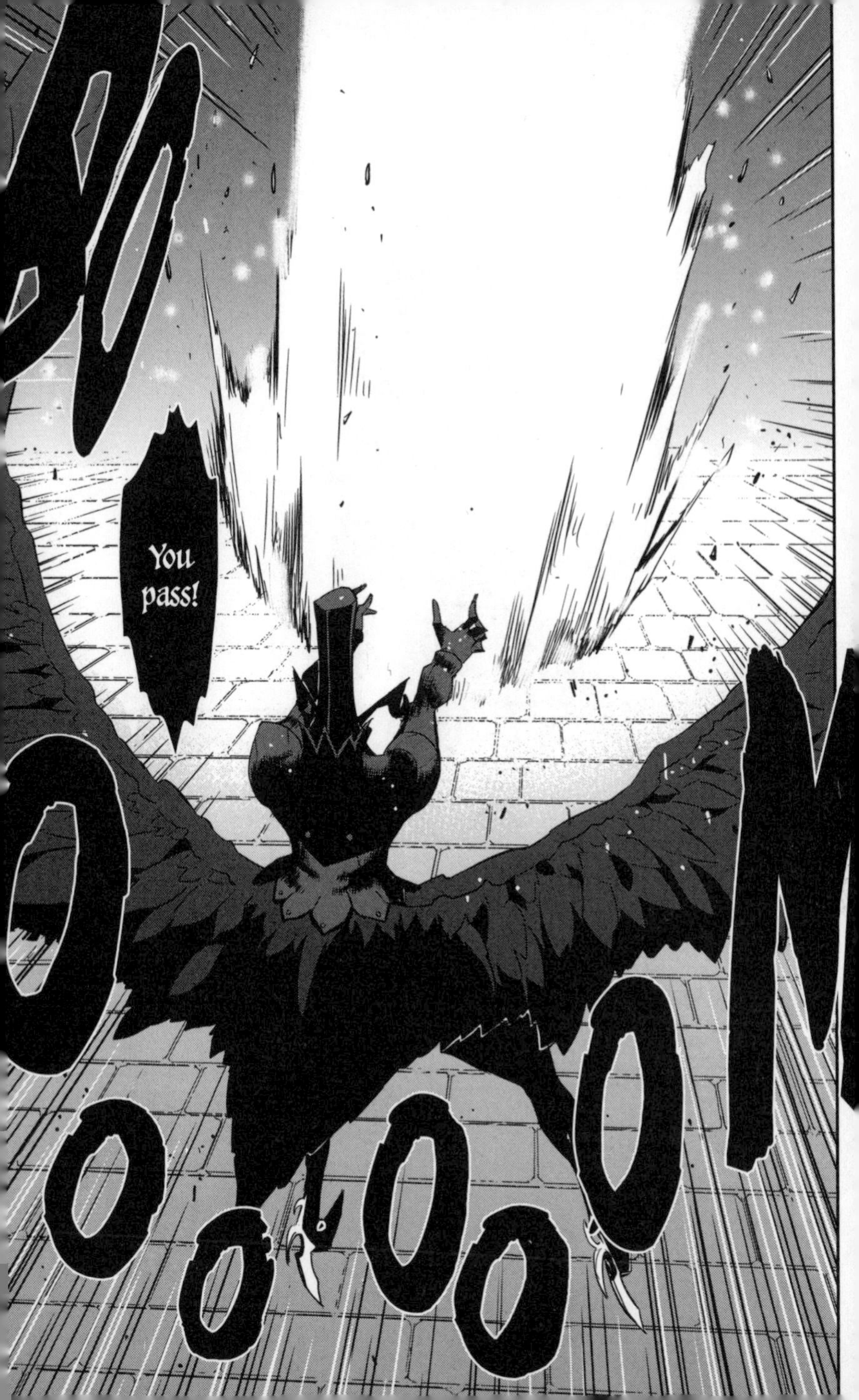
You pass!

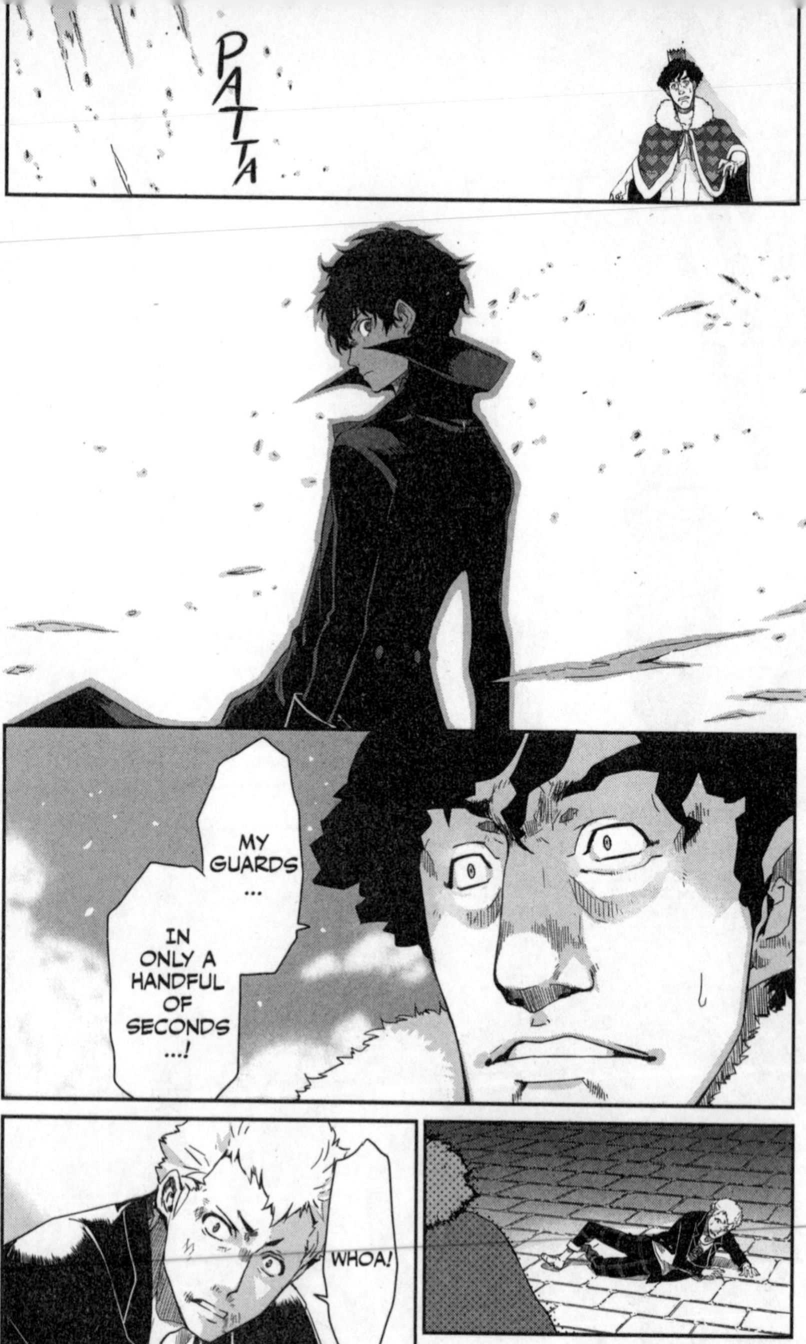
PATTA
MY GUARDS ...
IN ONLY A HANDFUL OF SECONDS ...!
WHOA!

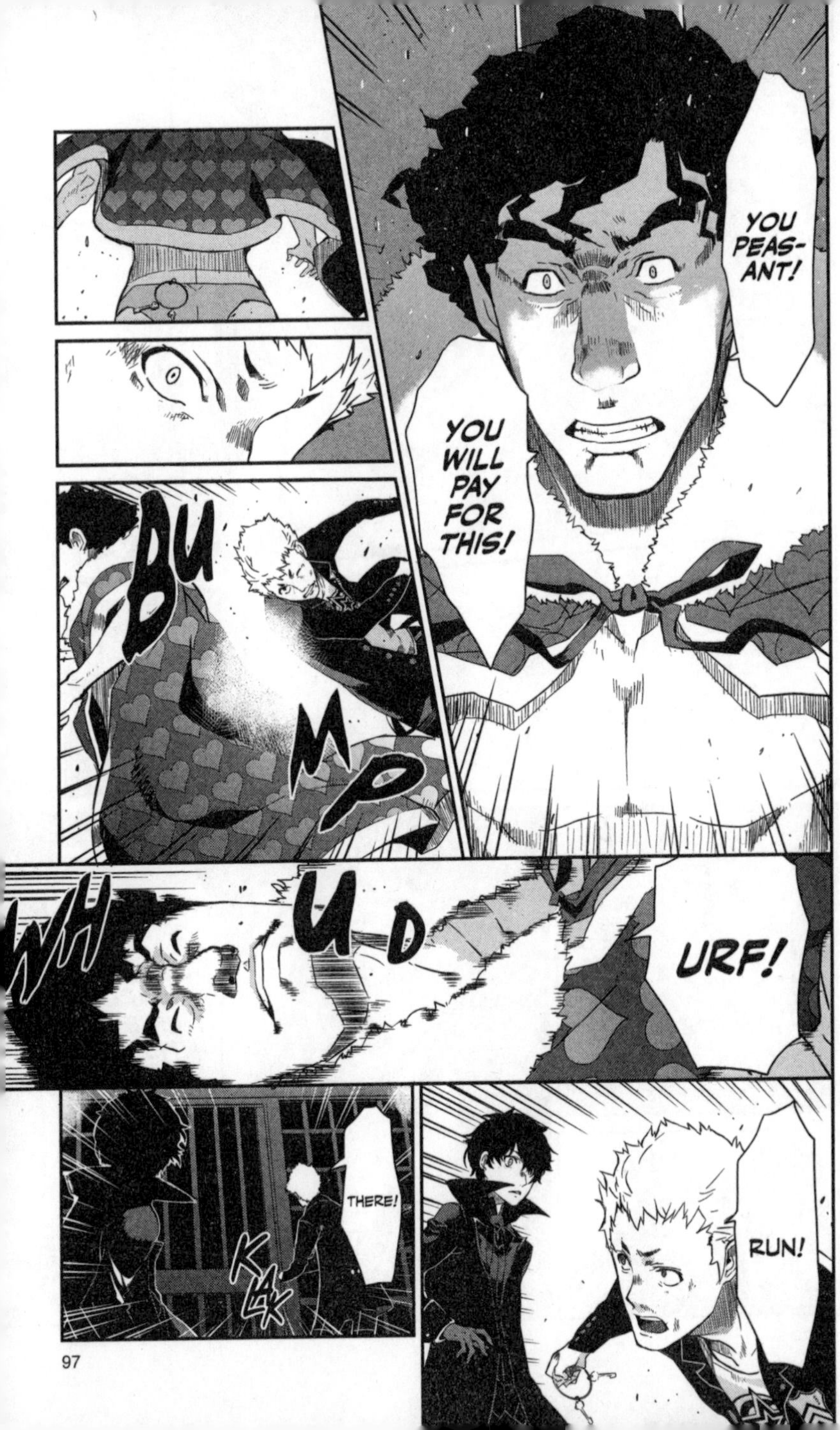
YOU PEAS-ANT!
YOU WILL PAY FOR THIS!
BUMP
URF!
WHUD
RUN!
THERE!
KLAK

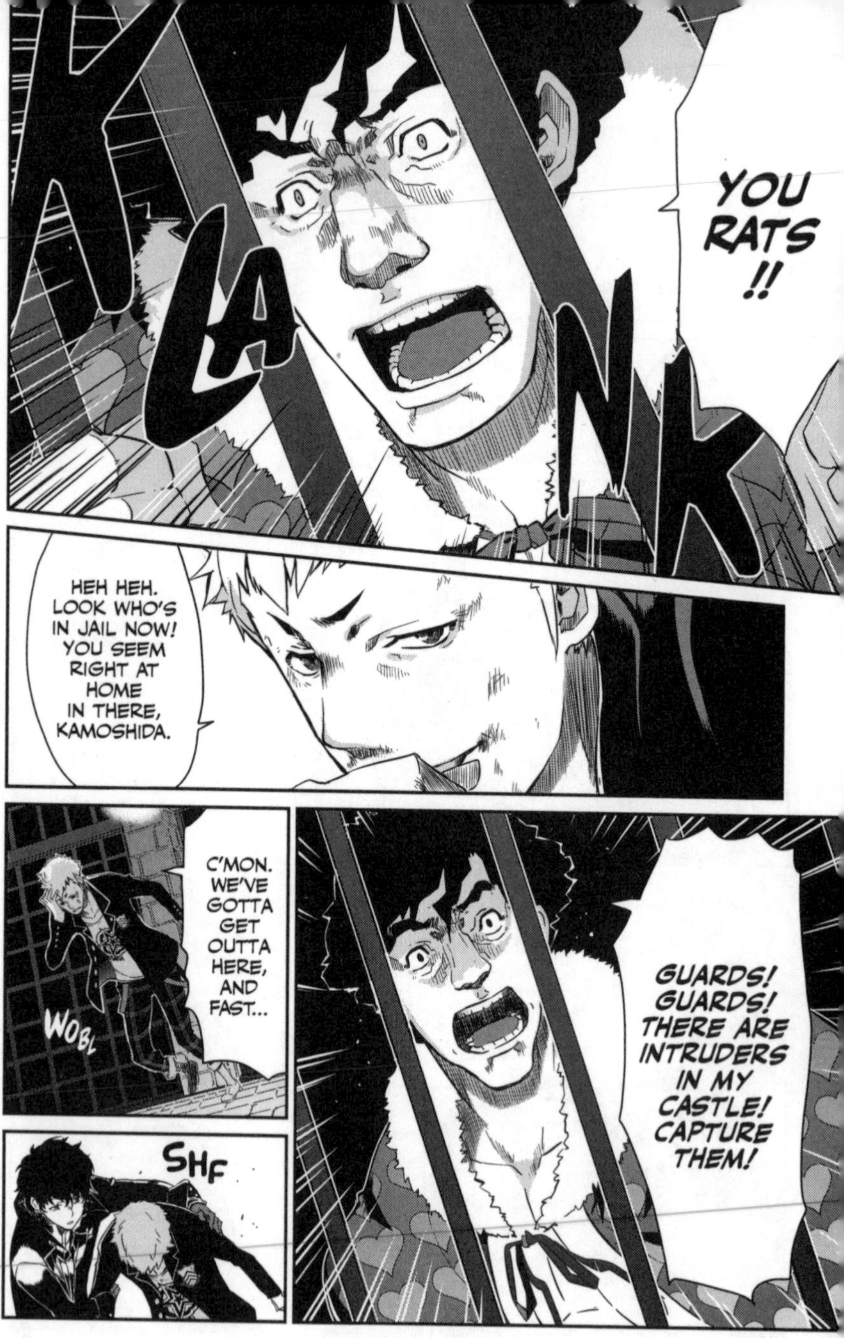
KLANK
YOU RATS!!
HEH HEH. LOOK WHO'S IN JAIL NOW! YOU SEEM RIGHT AT HOME IN THERE, KAMOSHIDA.
GUARDS! GUARDS! THERE ARE INTRUDERS IN MY CASTLE! CAPTURE THEM!
C'MON. WE'VE GOTTA GET OUTTA HERE, AND FAST...
WOBL
SHF

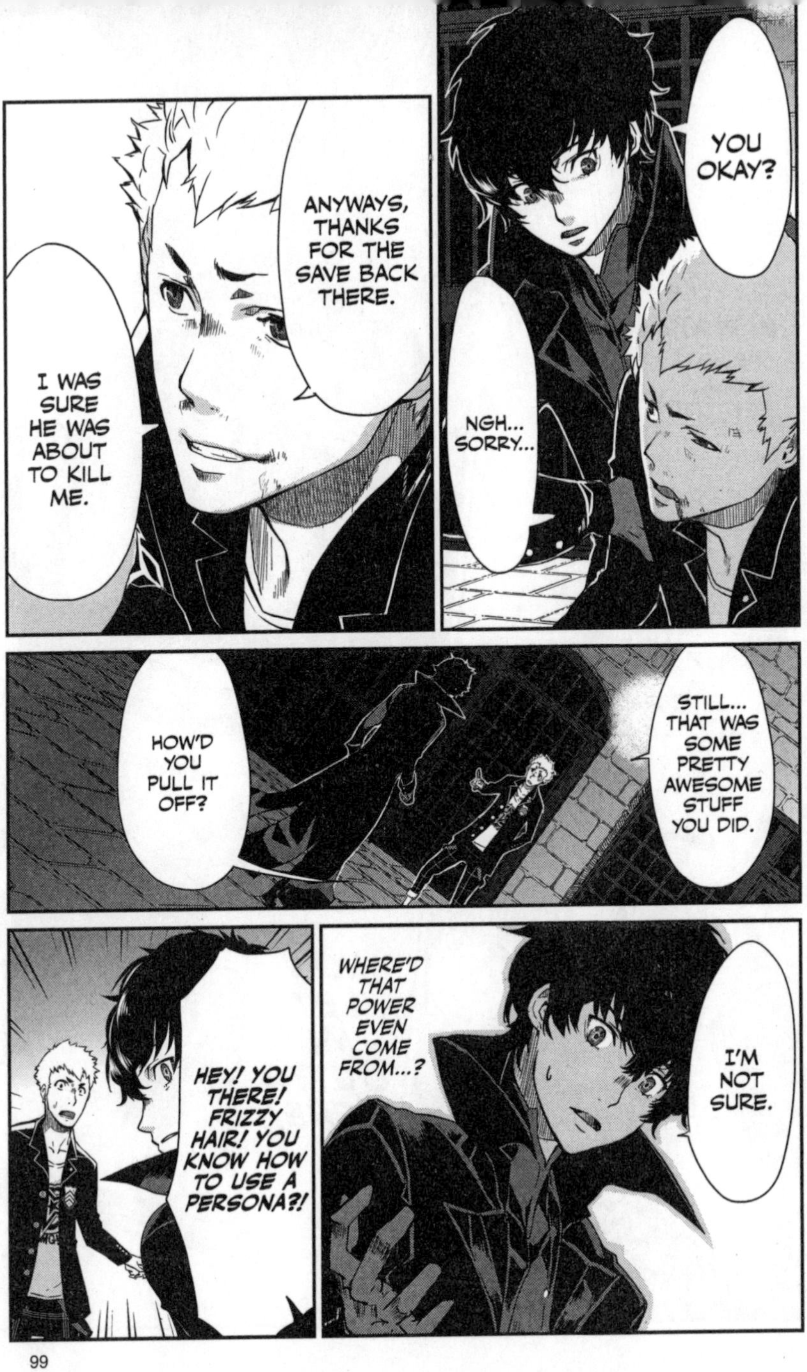
YOU OKAY?
NGH... SORRY...
ANYWAYS, THANKS FOR THE SAVE BACK THERE.
I WAS SURE HE WAS ABOUT TO KILL ME.
STILL... THAT WAS SOME PRETTY AWESOME STUFF YOU DID.
HOW'D YOU PULL IT OFF?
I'M NOT SURE.
WHERE'D THAT POWER EVEN COME FROM...?
HEY! YOU THERE! FRIZZY HAIR! YOU KNOW HOW TO USE A PERSONA?!

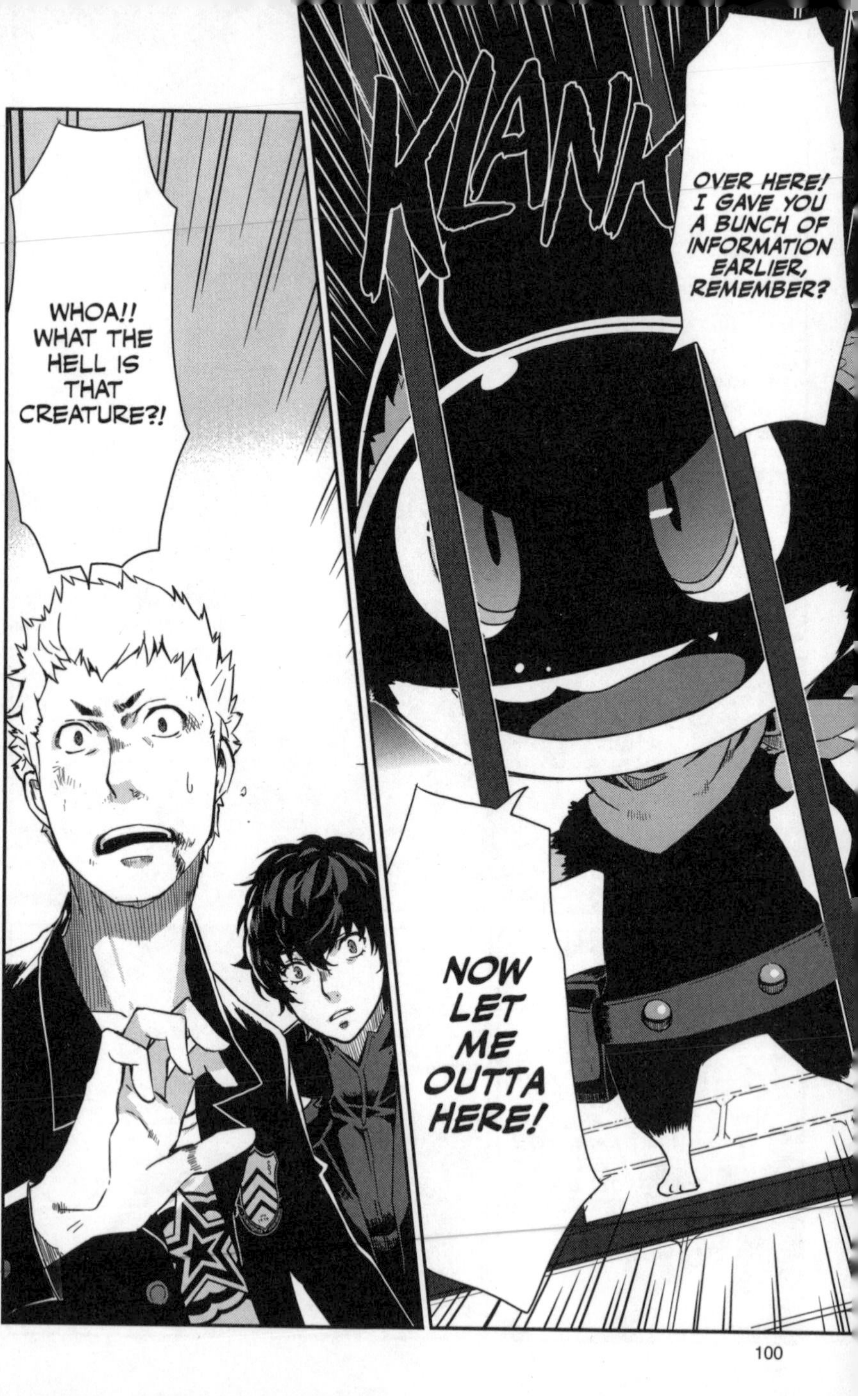
KLANK
OVER HERE! I GAVE YOU A BUNCH OF INFORMATION EARLIER, REMEMBER?
NOW LET ME OUTTA HERE!
WHOA!! WHAT THE HELL IS THAT CREATURE?!

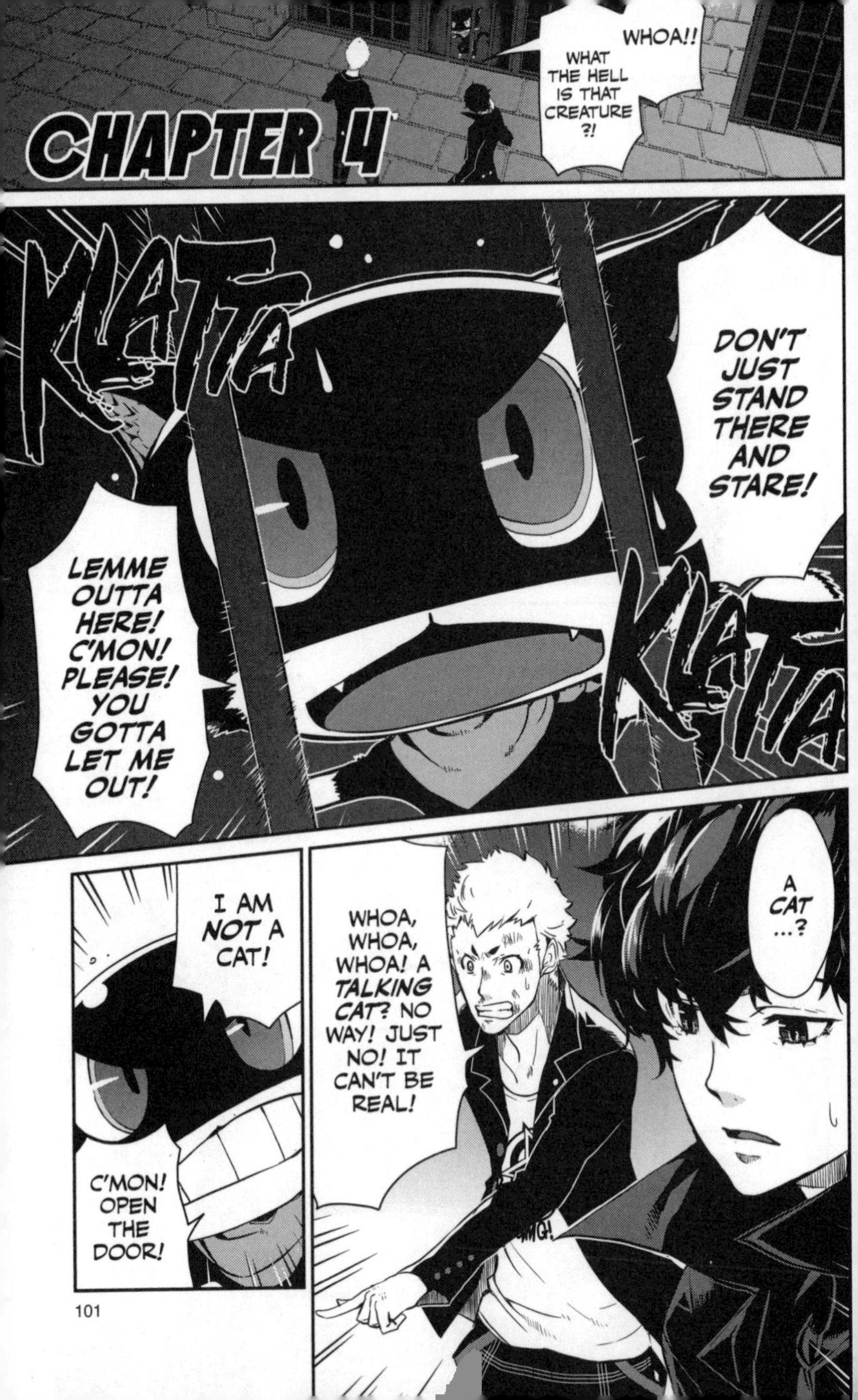
CHAPTER 4
WHOA!!
WHAT THE HELL IS THAT CREATURE ?!
DON'T JUST STAND THERE AND STARE!
KLATA
LEMME OUTTA HERE! C'MON! PLEASE! YOU GOTTA LET ME OUT!
KLATA
A CAT ...?
WHOA, WHOA, WHOA! A *TALKING CAT?* NO WAY! JUST NO! IT CAN'T BE REAL!
I AM *NOT* A CAT!
C'MON! OPEN THE DOOR!

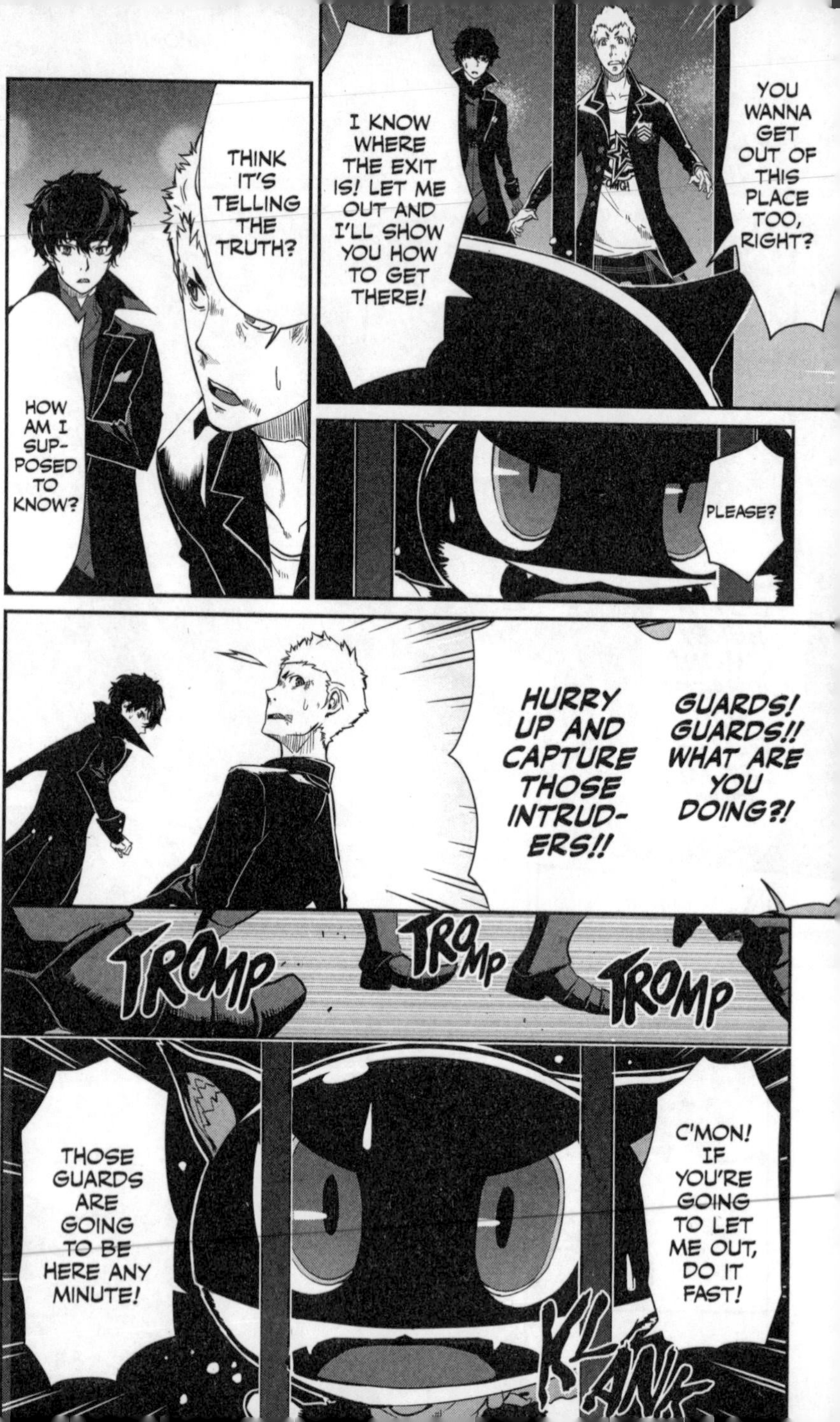
YOU WANNA GET OUT OF THIS PLACE TOO, RIGHT?
I KNOW WHERE THE EXIT IS! LET ME OUT AND I'LL SHOW YOU HOW TO GET THERE!
PLEASE?
THINK IT'S TELLING THE TRUTH?
HOW AM I SUP-POSED TO KNOW?
GUARDS! GUARDS!! WHAT ARE YOU DOING?!
HURRY UP AND CAPTURE THOSE INTRUD-ERS!!
TROMP
TROMP
TROMP
C'MON! IF YOU'RE GOING TO LET ME OUT, DO IT FAST!
THOSE GUARDS ARE GOING TO BE HERE ANY MINUTE!
KLANK

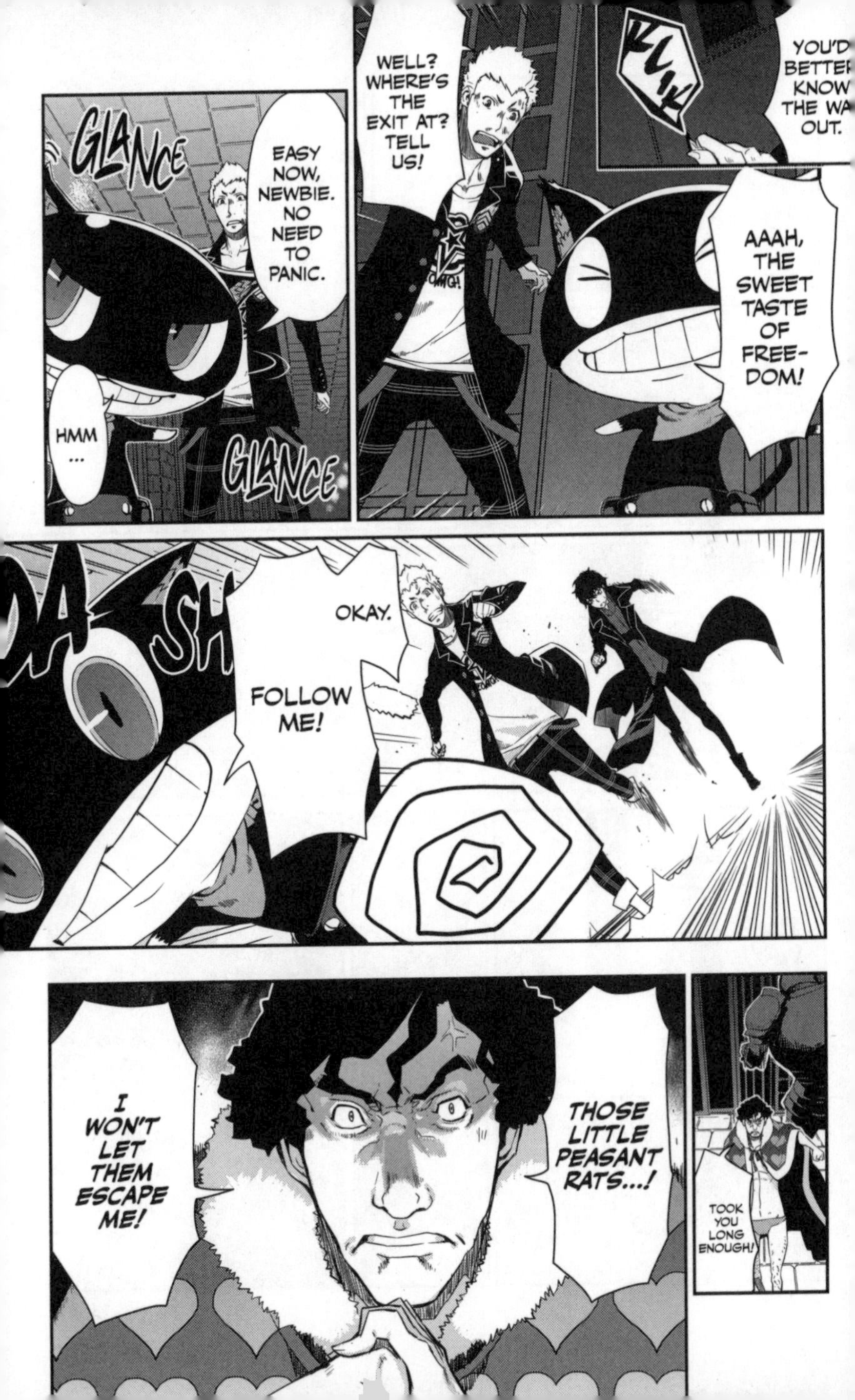
KLIK
YOU'D BETTER KNOW THE WA OUT.
AAAH, THE SWEET TASTE OF FREE-DOM!
WELL? WHERE'S THE EXIT AT? TELL US!
GLANCE
EASY NOW, NEWBIE. NO NEED TO PANIC.
HMM ...
GLANCE
DASH
OKAY.
FOLLOW ME!
TOOK YOU LONG ENOUGH!
THOSE LITTLE PEASANT RATS...!
I WON'T LET THEM ESCAPE ME!

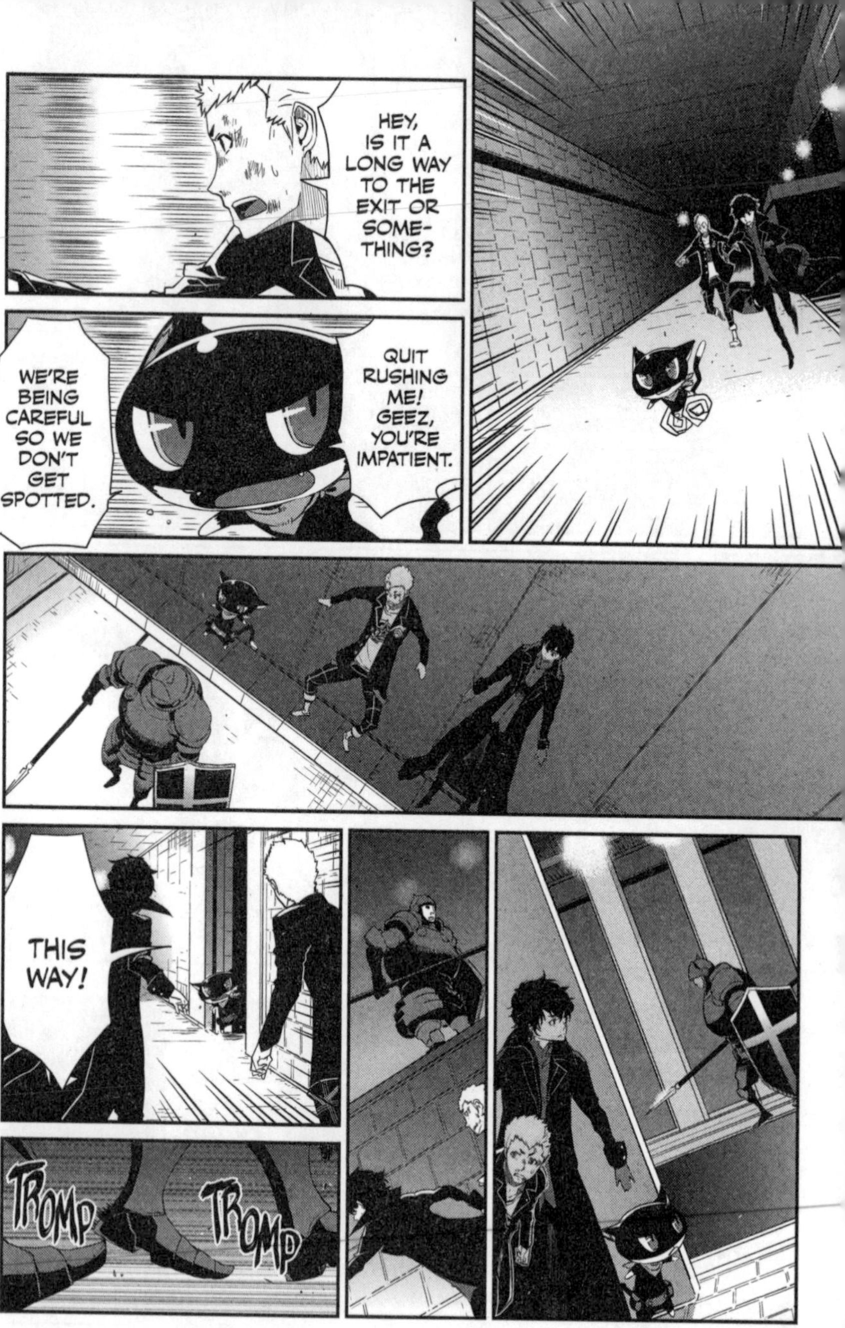

HEY, IS IT A LONG WAY TO THE EXIT OR SOME-THING?
QUIT RUSHING ME! GEEZ, YOU'RE IMPATIENT.
WE'RE BEING CAREFUL SO WE DON'T GET SPOTTED.
THIS WAY!
TROMP
TROMP

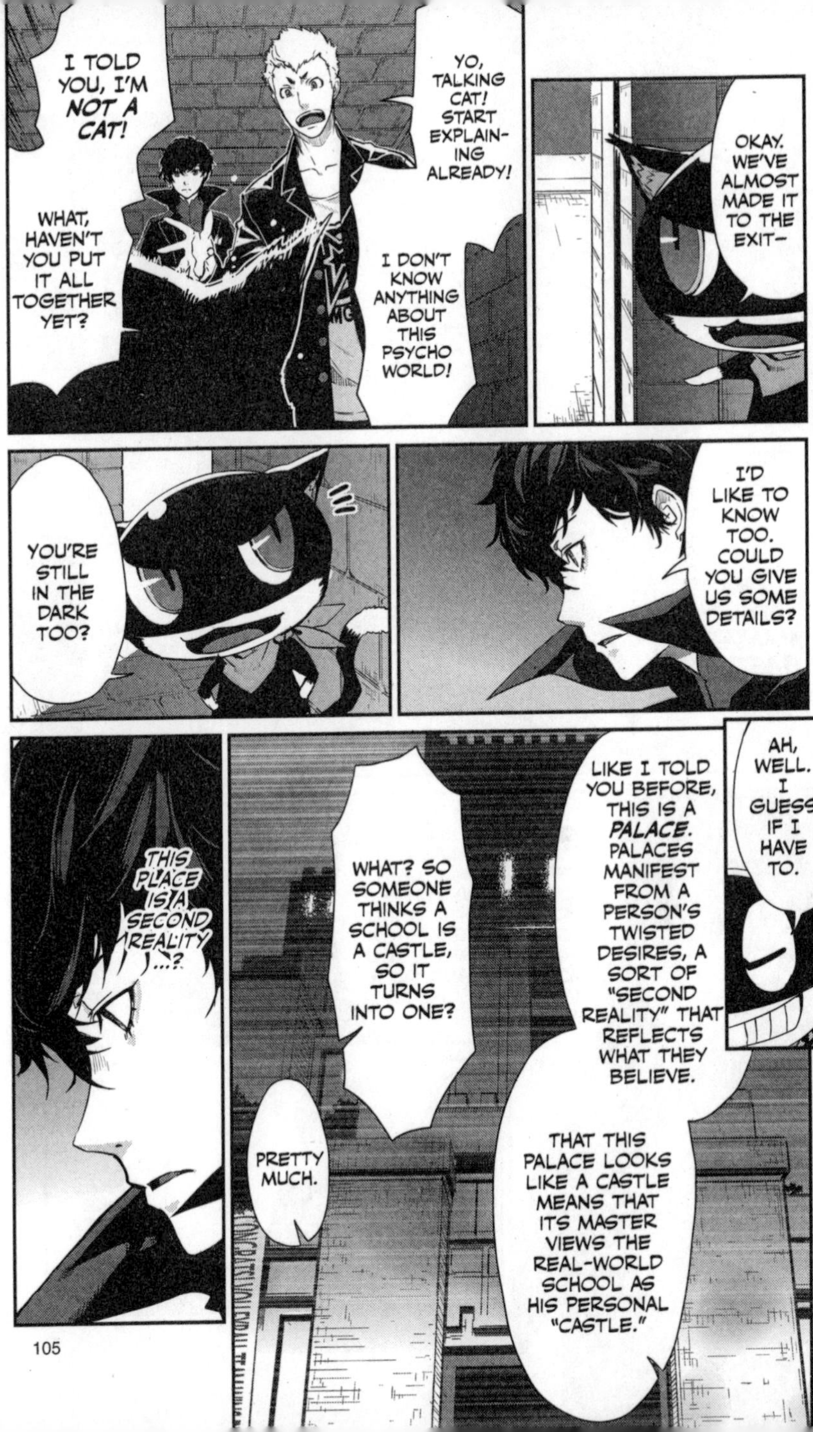
OKAY. WE'VE ALMOST MADE IT TO THE EXIT–
YO, TALKING CAT! START EXPLAINING ALREADY!
I TOLD YOU, I'M *NOT A CAT!*
I DON'T KNOW ANYTHING ABOUT THIS PSYCHO WORLD!
WHAT, HAVEN'T YOU PUT IT ALL TOGETHER YET?
I'D LIKE TO KNOW TOO. COULD YOU GIVE US SOME DETAILS?
YOU'RE STILL IN THE DARK TOO?
AH, WELL. I GUESS IF I HAVE TO.
LIKE I TOLD YOU BEFORE, THIS IS A *PALACE*. PALACES MANIFEST FROM A PERSON'S TWISTED DESIRES, A SORT OF "SECOND REALITY" THAT REFLECTS WHAT THEY BELIEVE.
WHAT? SO SOMEONE THINKS A SCHOOL IS A CASTLE, SO IT TURNS INTO ONE?
THAT THIS PALACE LOOKS LIKE A CASTLE MEANS THAT ITS MASTER VIEWS THE REAL-WORLD SCHOOL AS HIS PERSONAL "CASTLE."
PRETTY MUCH.
THIS PLACE IS A SECOND REALITY ...?

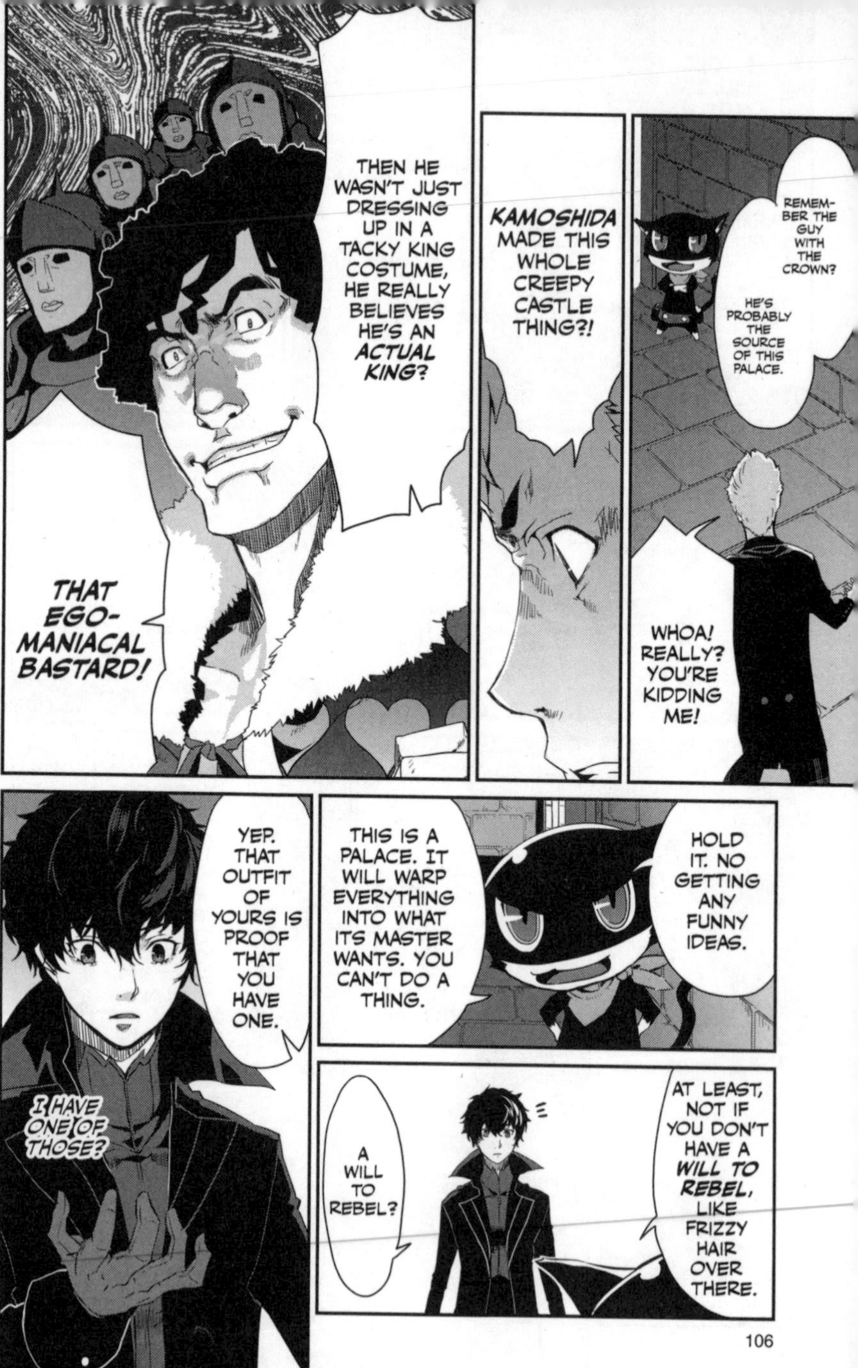
REMEMBER THE GUY WITH THE CROWN?
HE'S PROBABLY THE SOURCE OF THIS PALACE.
WHOA! REALLY? YOU'RE KIDDING ME!
KAMOSHIDA MADE THIS WHOLE CREEPY CASTLE THING?!
THEN HE WASN'T JUST DRESSING UP IN A TACKY KING COSTUME, HE REALLY BELIEVES HE'S AN ACTUAL KING?
THAT EGO-MANIACAL BASTARD!
HOLD IT. NO GETTING ANY FUNNY IDEAS.
THIS IS A PALACE. IT WILL WARP EVERYTHING INTO WHAT ITS MASTER WANTS. YOU CAN'T DO A THING.
AT LEAST, NOT IF YOU DON'T HAVE A WILL TO REBEL, LIKE FRIZZY HAIR OVER THERE.
A WILL TO REBEL?
YEP. THAT OUTFIT OF YOURS IS PROOF THAT YOU HAVE ONE.
I HAVE ONE OF THOSE?

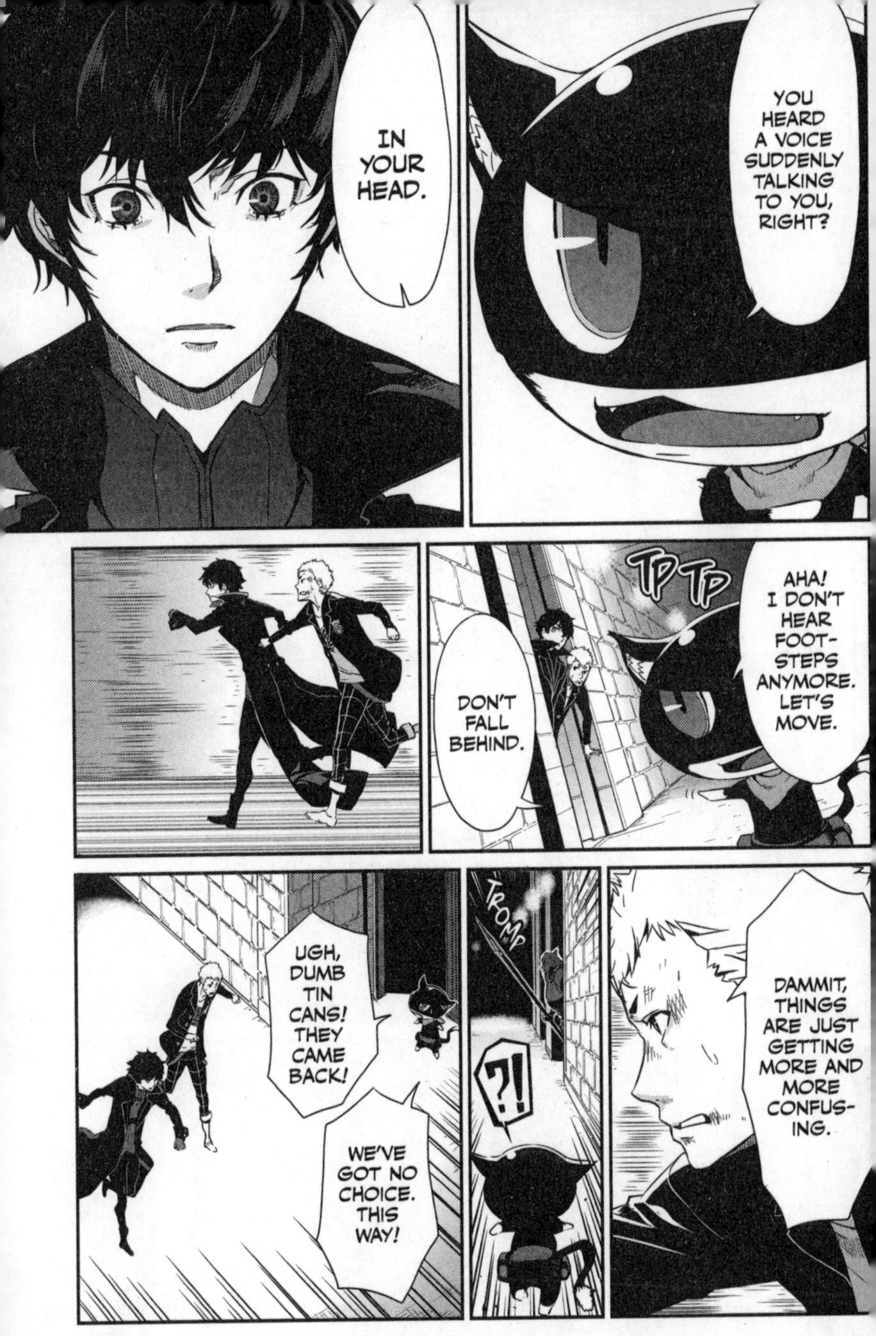
YOU HEARD A VOICE SUDDENLY TALKING TO YOU, RIGHT?
IN YOUR HEAD.
TP TP
AHA! I DON'T HEAR FOOT-STEPS ANYMORE. LET'S MOVE.
DON'T FALL BEHIND.
DAMMIT, THINGS ARE JUST GETTING MORE AND MORE CONFUS-ING.
TROMP
?!
UGH, DUMB TIN CANS! THEY CAME BACK!
WE'VE GOT NO CHOICE. THIS WAY!

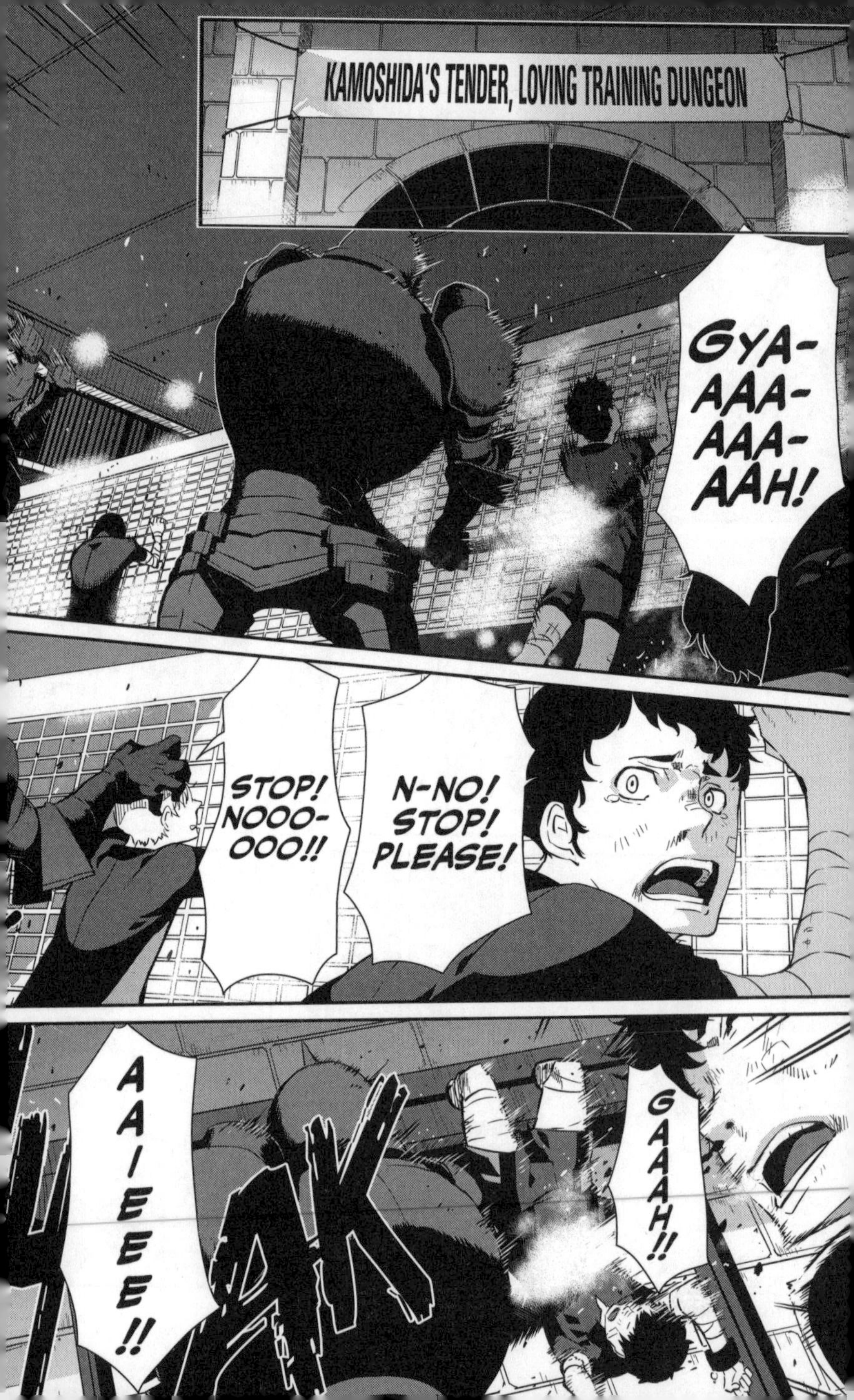
KAMOSHIDA'S TENDER, LOVING TRAINING DUNGEON
GYA-AAA-AAA-AAH!
N-NO! STOP! PLEASE!
STOP! NOOO-OOO!!
GAAAH!!
AAIEEEE!!

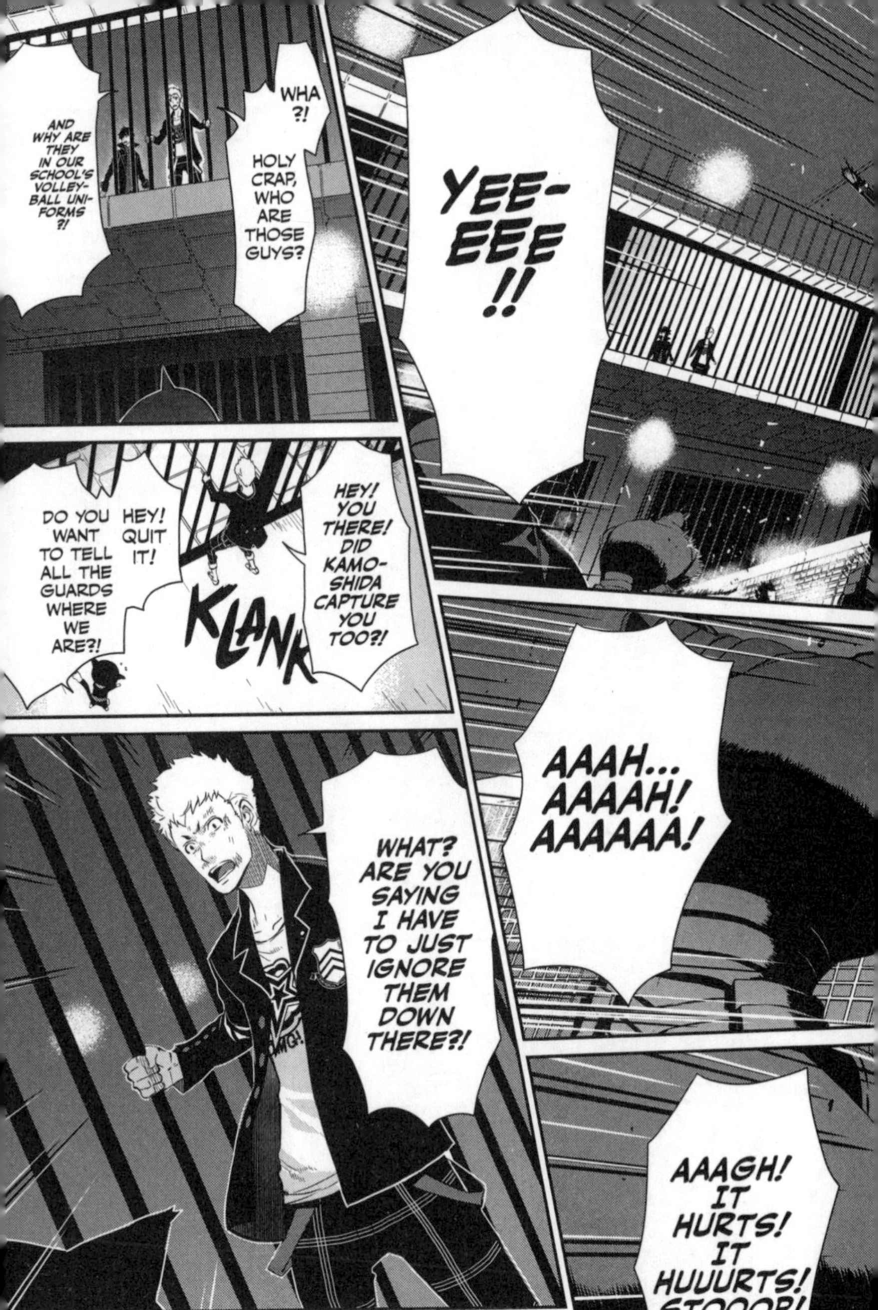
YEE-EEEE!!
WHA?!
HOLY CRAP, WHO ARE THOSE GUYS?
AND WHY ARE THEY IN OUR SCHOOL'S VOLLEY-BALL UNI-FORMS?!
AAAH... AAAAH! AAAAAA!
HEY! YOU THERE! DID KAMO-SHIDA CAPTURE YOU TOO?!
KLANK
HEY! QUIT IT!
DO YOU WANT TO TELL ALL THE GUARDS WHERE WE ARE?!
AAAGH! IT HURTS! IT HUUURTS! STOOOP!
WHAT? ARE YOU SAYING I HAVE TO JUST IGNORE THEM DOWN THERE?!

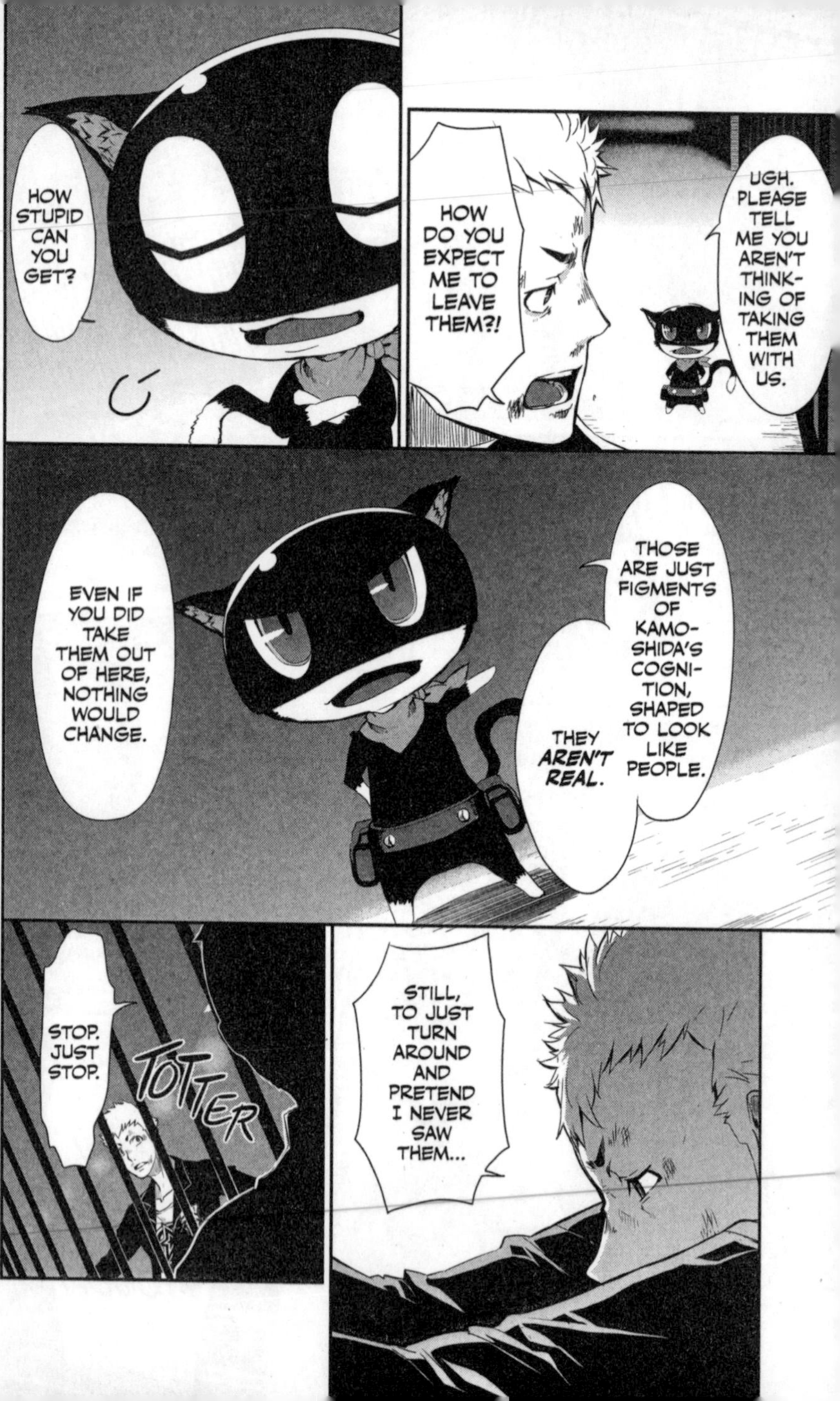
UGH. PLEASE TELL ME YOU AREN'T THINKING OF TAKING THEM WITH US.
HOW DO YOU EXPECT ME TO LEAVE THEM?!
HOW STUPID CAN YOU GET?
THOSE ARE JUST FIGMENTS OF KAMOSHIDA'S COGNITION, SHAPED TO LOOK LIKE PEOPLE.
THEY *AREN'T REAL*.
EVEN IF YOU DID TAKE THEM OUT OF HERE, NOTHING WOULD CHANGE.
STILL, TO JUST TURN AROUND AND PRETEND I NEVER SAW THEM...
STOP. JUST STOP.
TOTTER

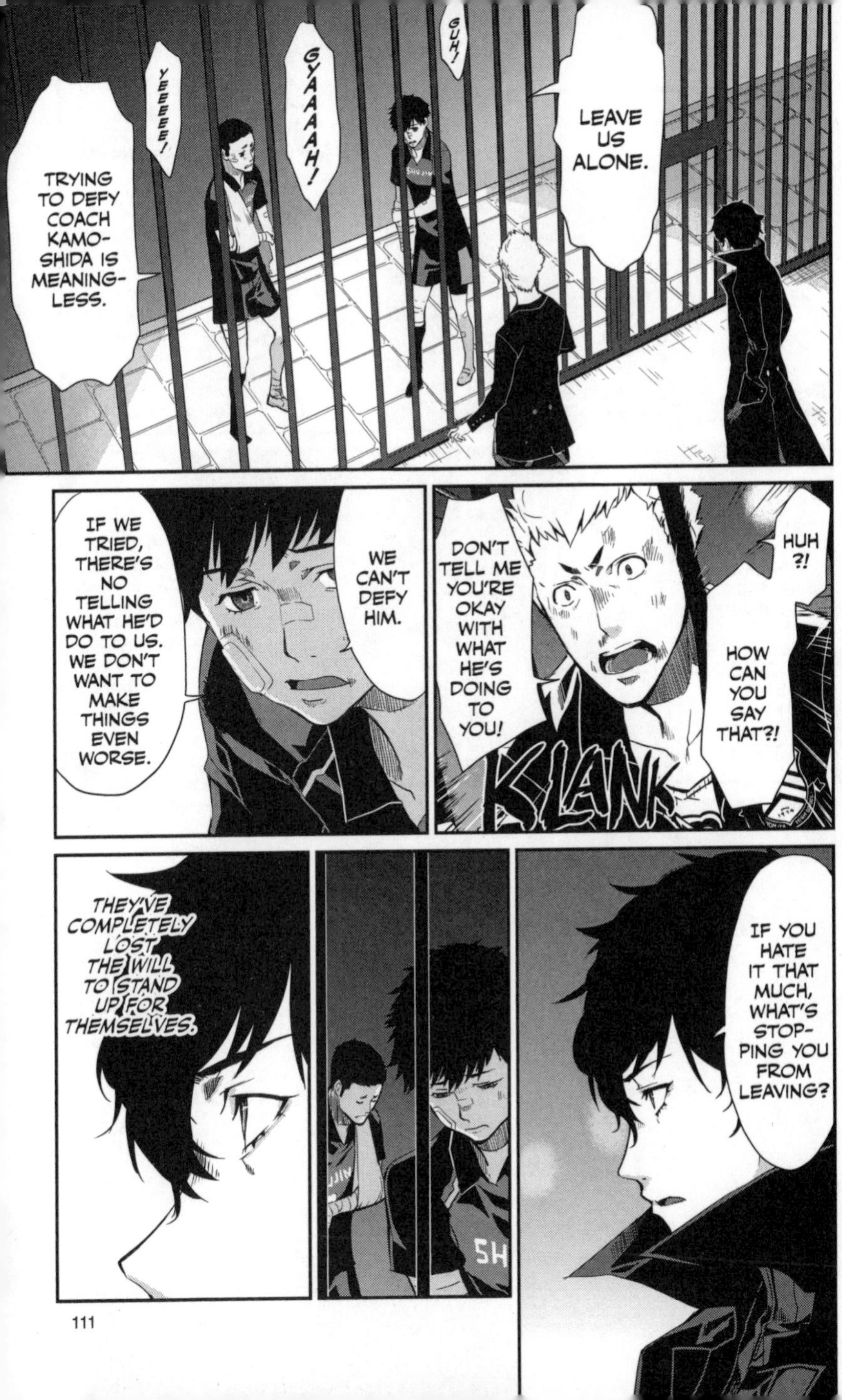
LEAVE US ALONE.
GUH!
GYAAAAAH!
YEEEEE!
TRYING TO DEFY COACH KAMO-SHIDA IS MEANING-LESS.
HUH?!
HOW CAN YOU SAY THAT?!
DON'T TELL ME YOU'RE OKAY WITH WHAT HE'S DOING TO YOU!
KLANK
WE CAN'T DEFY HIM.
IF WE TRIED, THERE'S NO TELLING WHAT HE'D DO TO US. WE DON'T WANT TO MAKE THINGS EVEN WORSE.
IF YOU HATE IT THAT MUCH, WHAT'S STOP-PING YOU FROM LEAVING?
THEY'VE COMPLETELY LOST THE WILL TO STAND UP FOR THEMSELVES.

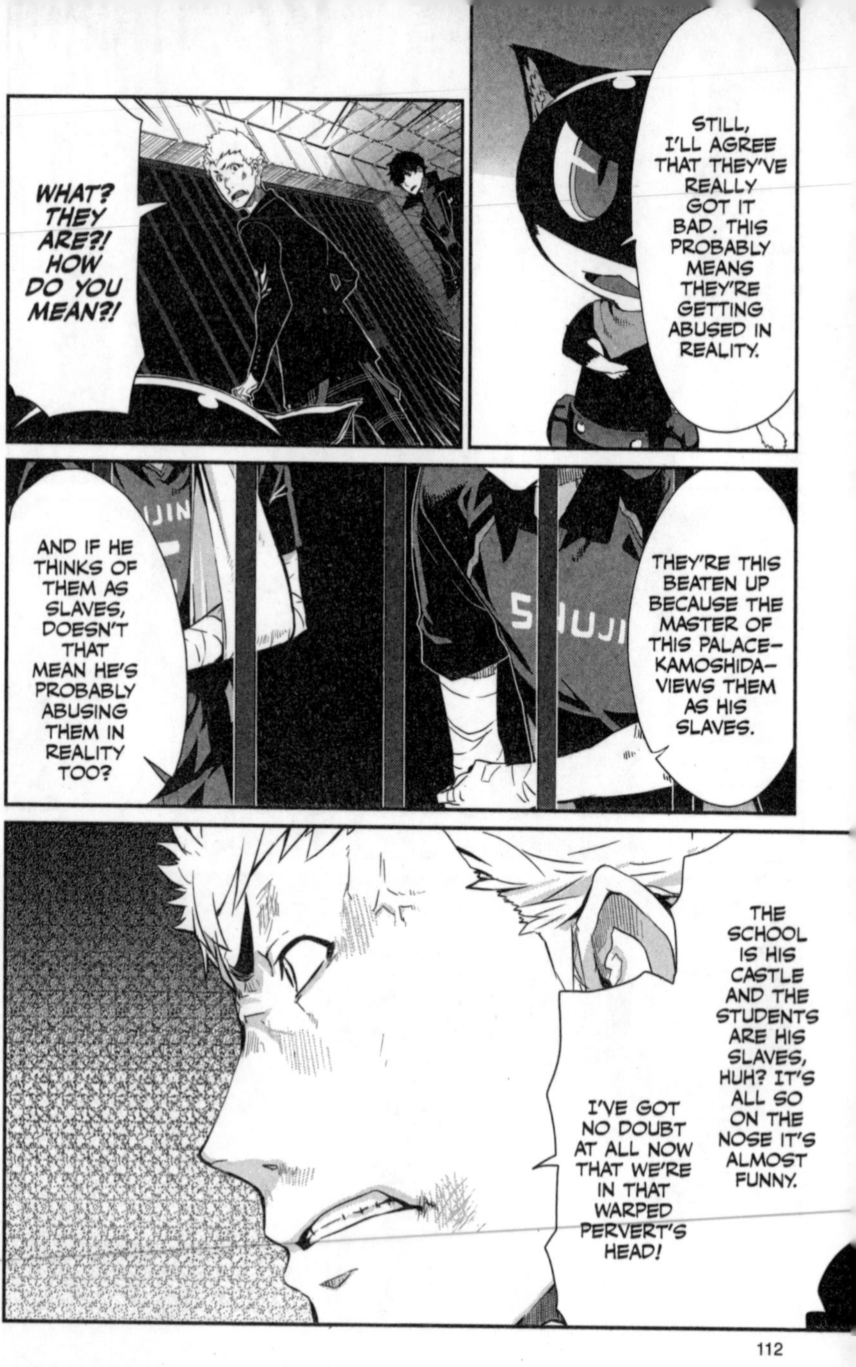
STILL, I'LL AGREE THAT THEY'VE REALLY GOT IT BAD. THIS PROBABLY MEANS THEY'RE GETTING ABUSED IN REALITY.
WHAT? THEY ARE?! HOW DO YOU MEAN?!
THEY'RE THIS BEATEN UP BECAUSE THE MASTER OF THIS PALACE- KAMOSHIDA- VIEWS THEM AS HIS SLAVES.
AND IF HE THINKS OF THEM AS SLAVES, DOESN'T THAT MEAN HE'S PROBABLY ABUSING THEM IN REALITY TOO?
THE SCHOOL IS HIS CASTLE AND THE STUDENTS ARE HIS SLAVES, HUH? IT'S ALL SO ON THE NOSE IT'S ALMOST FUNNY.
I'VE GOT NO DOUBT AT ALL NOW THAT WE'RE IN THAT WARPED PERVERT'S HEAD!

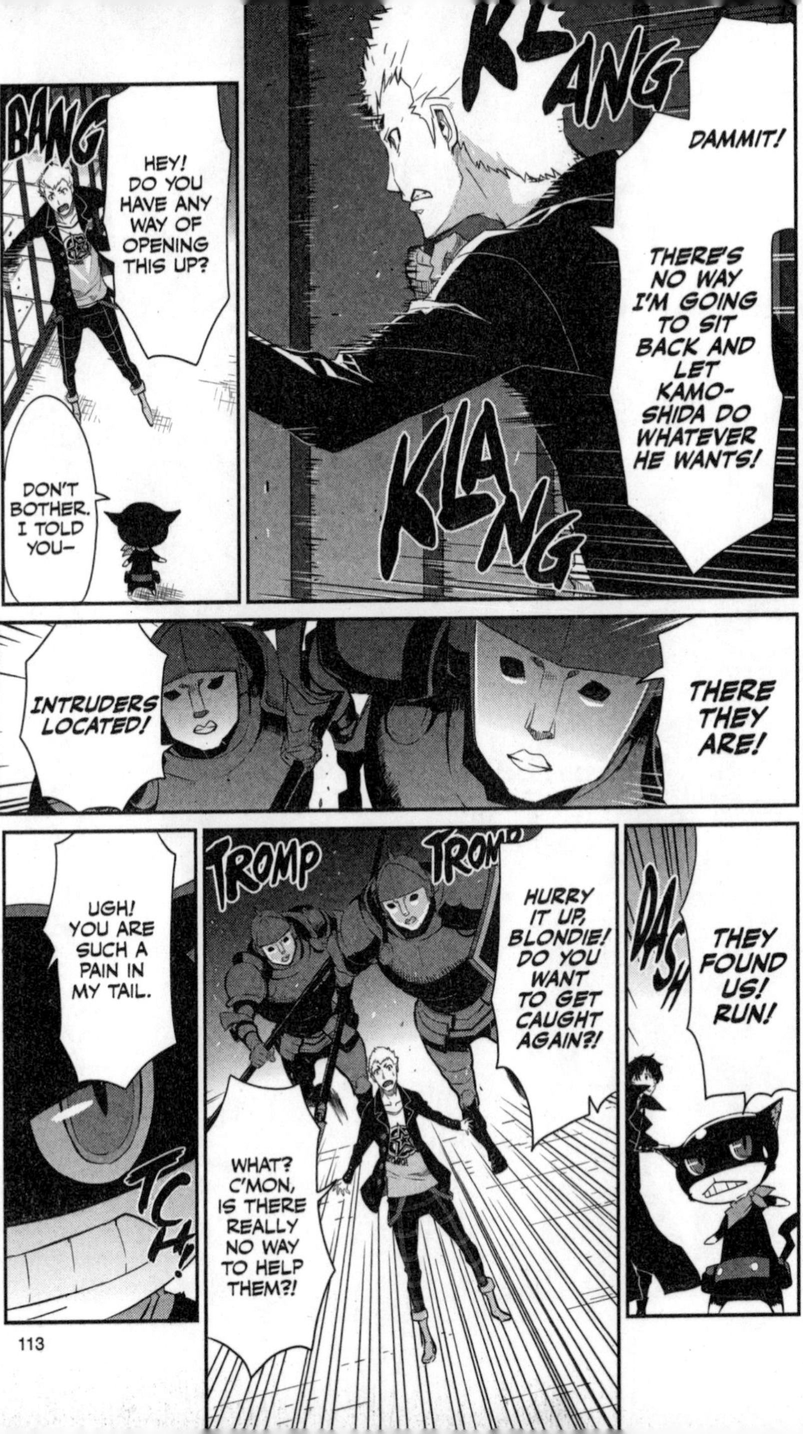
KLANG
DAMMIT!
THERE'S NO WAY I'M GOING TO SIT BACK AND LET KAMOSHIDA DO WHATEVER HE WANTS!
KLANG
BANG
HEY! DO YOU HAVE ANY WAY OF OPENING THIS UP?
DON'T BOTHER. I TOLD YOU–
THERE THEY ARE!
INTRUDERS LOCATED!
DASH
THEY FOUND US! RUN!
TROM
TROMP
HURRY IT UP, BLONDIE! DO YOU WANT TO GET CAUGHT AGAIN?!
WHAT? C'MON, IS THERE REALLY NO WAY TO HELP THEM?!
UGH! YOU ARE SUCH A PAIN IN MY TAIL.
TCH!

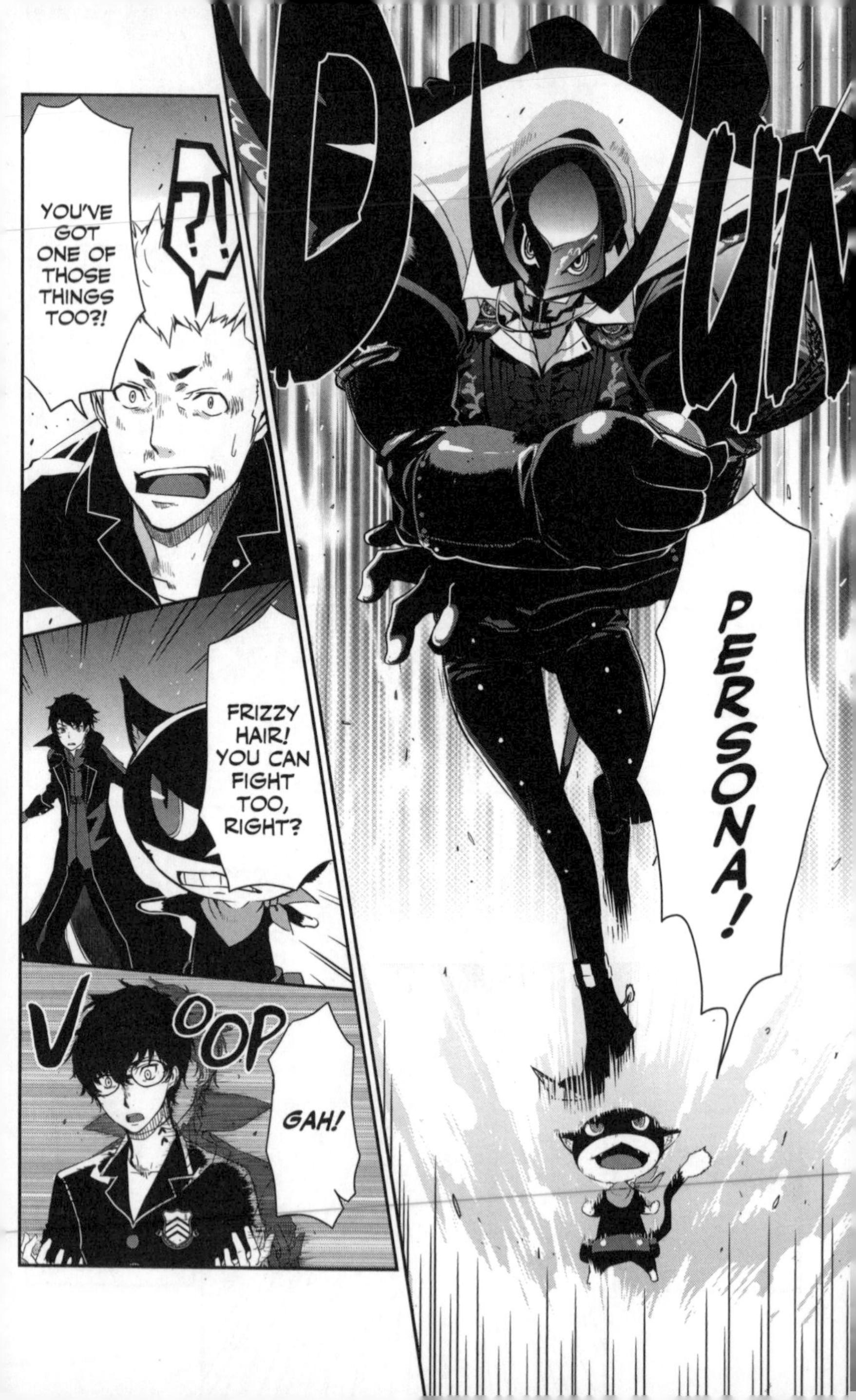
PERSONA!
?!
YOU'VE GOT ONE OF THOSE THINGS TOO?!
FRIZZY HAIR! YOU CAN FIGHT TOO, RIGHT?
VOOP
GAH!

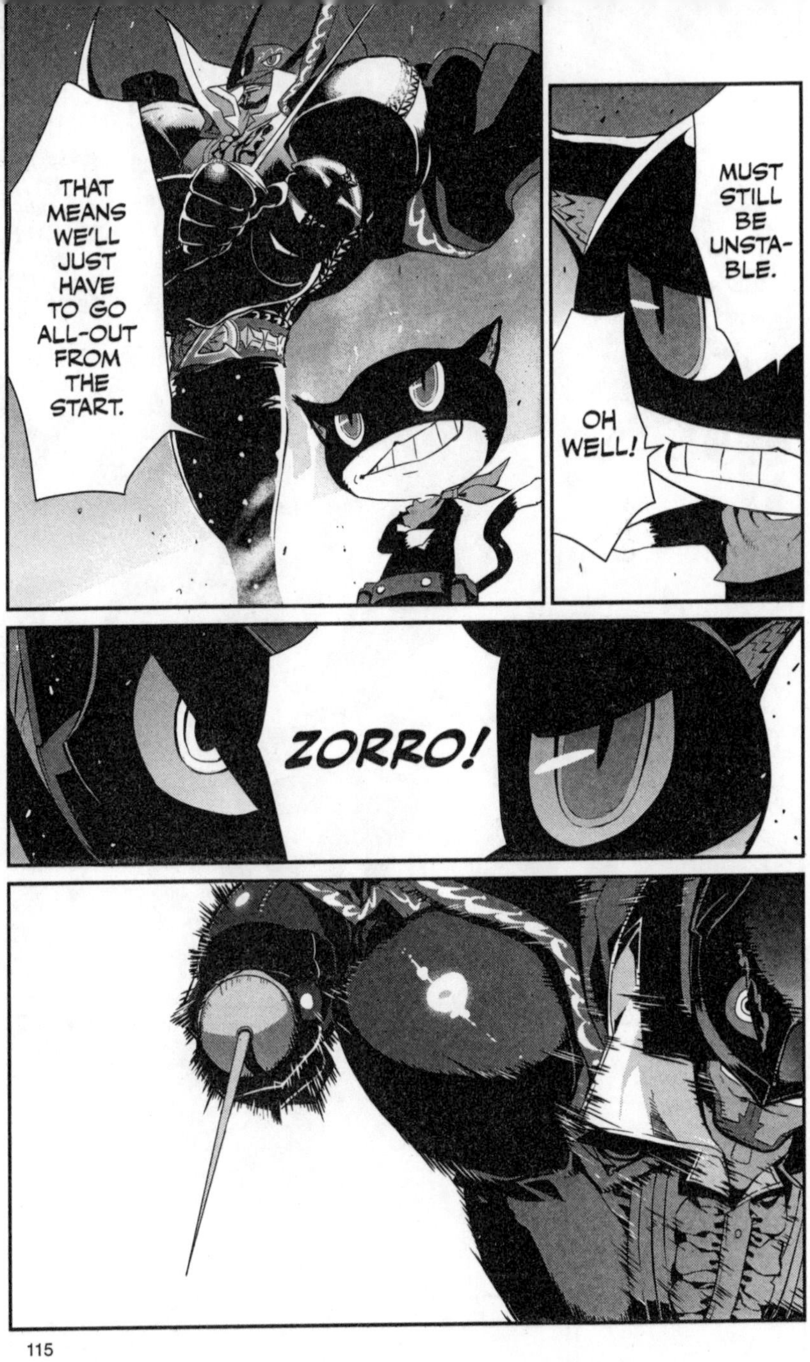
MUST STILL BE UNSTA-BLE.
OH WELL!
THAT MEANS WE'LL JUST HAVE TO GO ALL-OUT FROM THE START.
ZORRO!

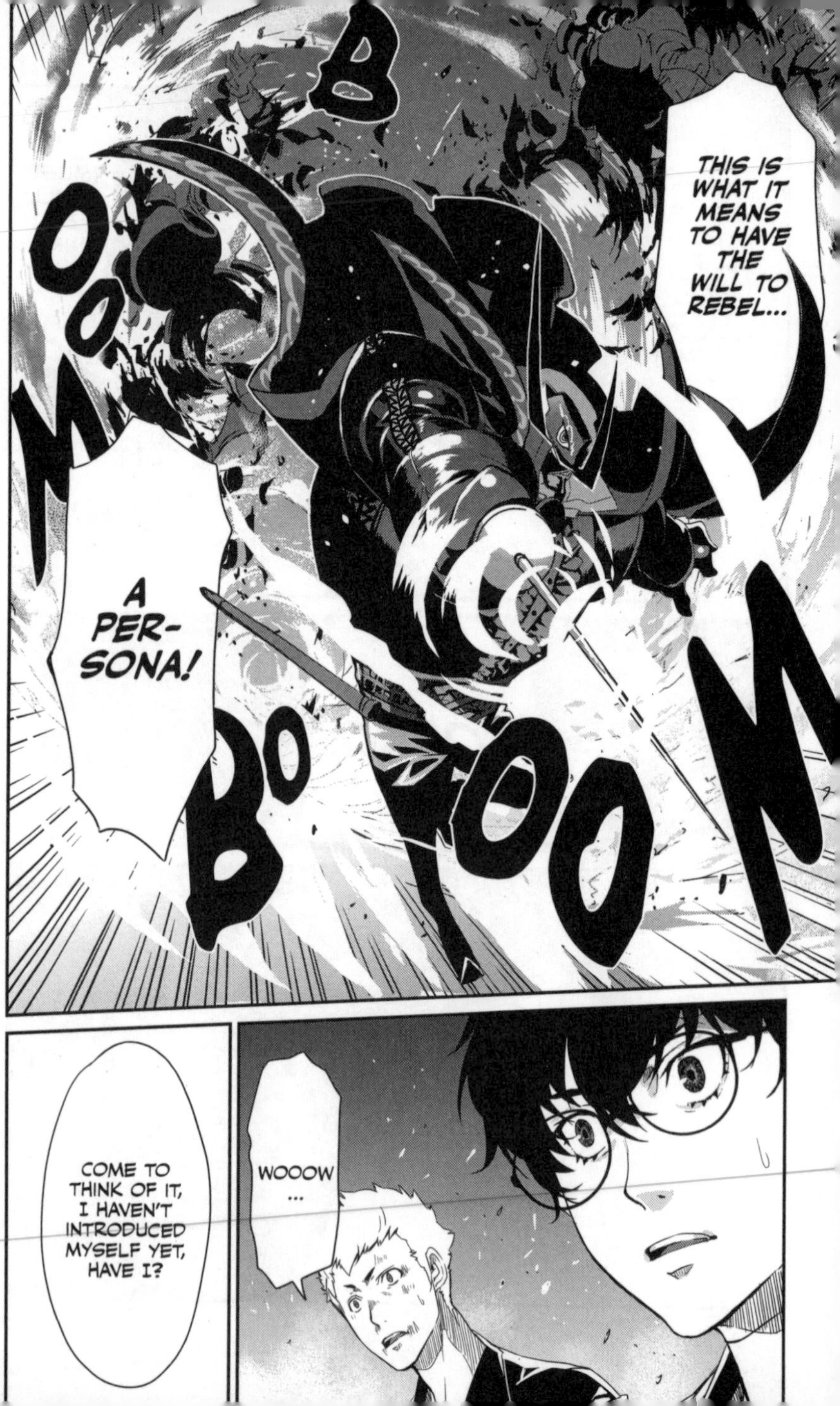
THIS IS WHAT IT MEANS TO HAVE THE WILL TO REBEL...
BOOM
A PER-SONA!
BOOOM
WOOOW ...
COME TO THINK OF IT, I HAVEN'T INTRODUCED MYSELF YET, HAVE I?

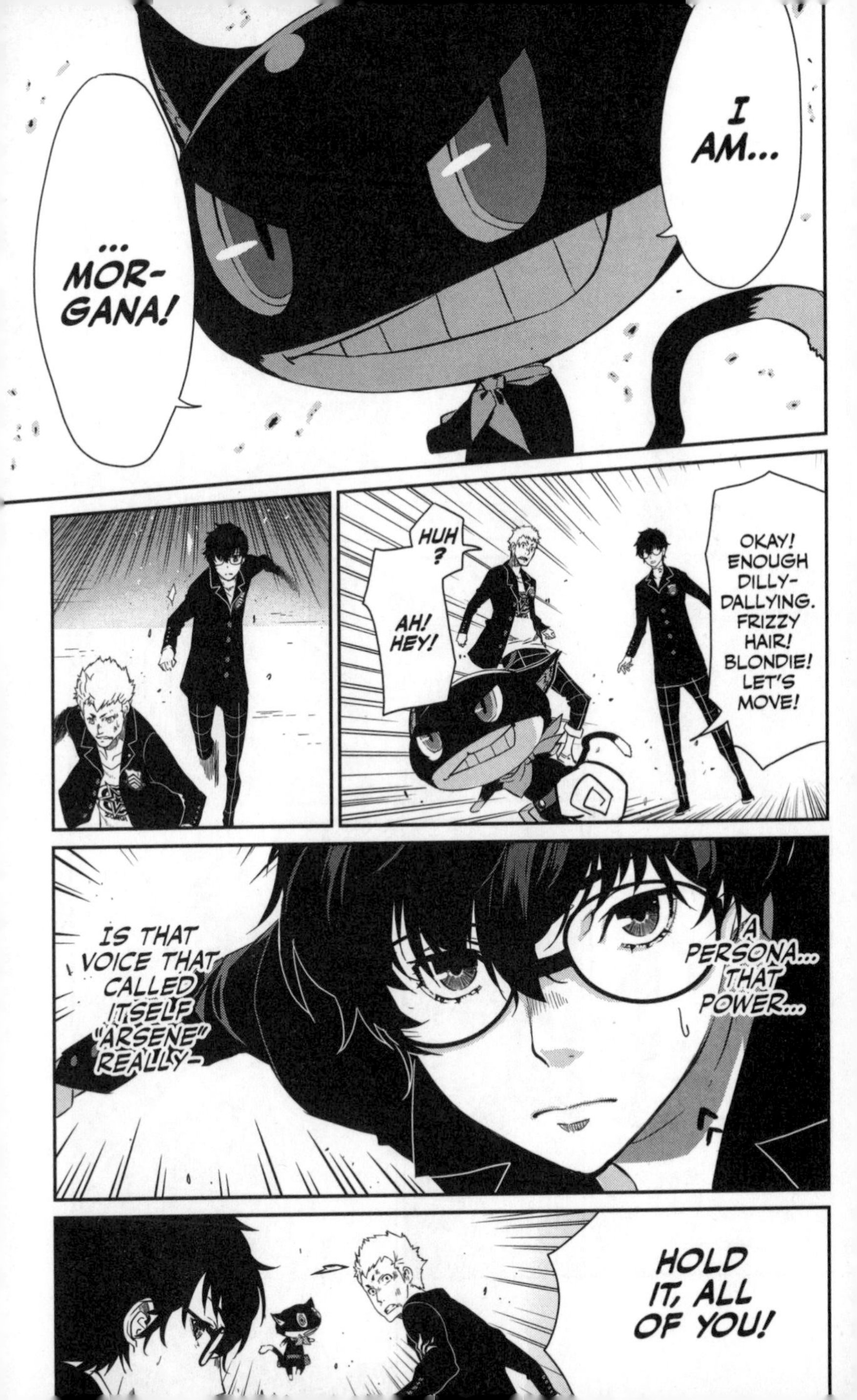
I AM...
...MÖRGANA!
OKAY! ENOUGH DILLY-DALLYING. FRIZZY HAIR! BLONDIE! LET'S MOVE!
HUH?
AH! HEY!
A PERSONA... THAT POWER...
IS THAT VOICE THAT CALLED ITSELF "ARSENE" REALLY–
HOLD IT, ALL OF YOU!

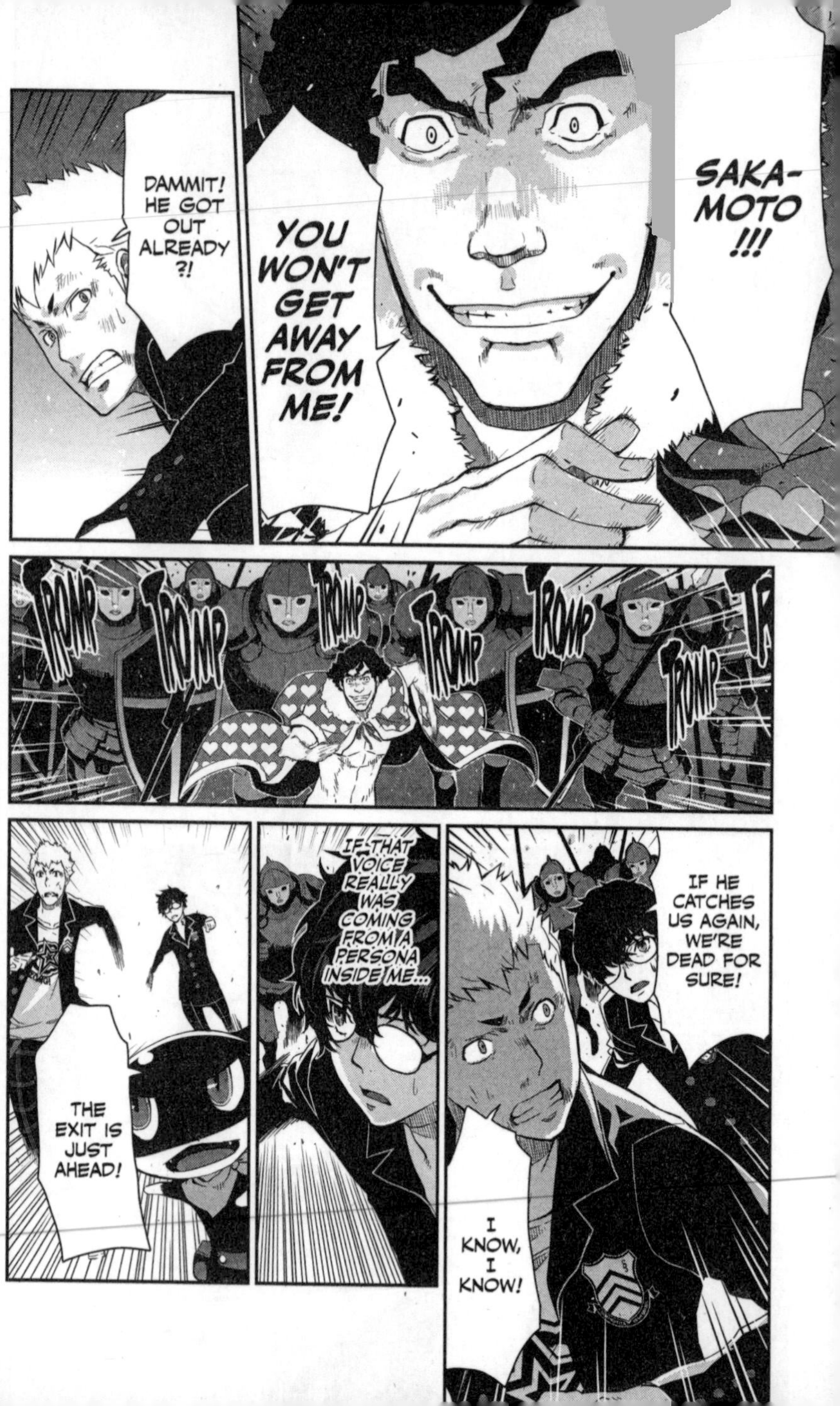
SAKA-MOTO!!!
YOU WON'T GET AWAY FROM ME!
DAMMIT! HE GOT OUT ALREADY?!
TROMP
TROMP
TROMP
TROMP
TROMP
TROMP
TROMP
IF HE CATCHES US AGAIN, WE'RE DEAD FOR SURE!
I KNOW, I KNOW!
IF THAT VOICE REALLY WAS COMING FROM A PERSONA INSIDE ME...
THE EXIT IS JUST AHEAD!

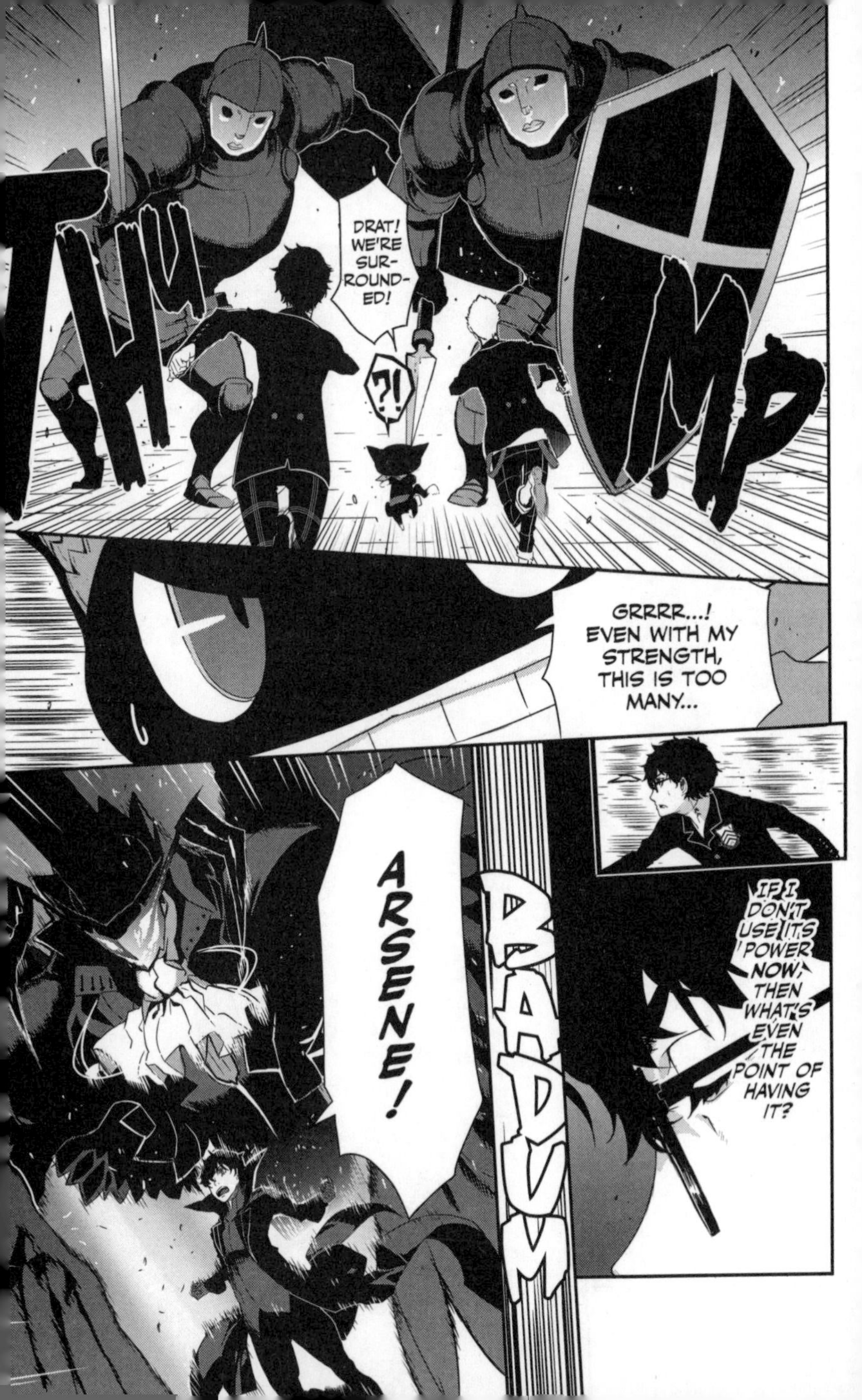

THUMP
DRAT! WE'RE SUR-ROUNDED!
?!
GRRRR...! EVEN WITH MY STRENGTH, THIS IS TOO MANY...
IF I DON'T USE ITS POWER NOW, THEN WHAT'S EVEN THE POINT OF HAVING IT?
BADUM
ARSENE!

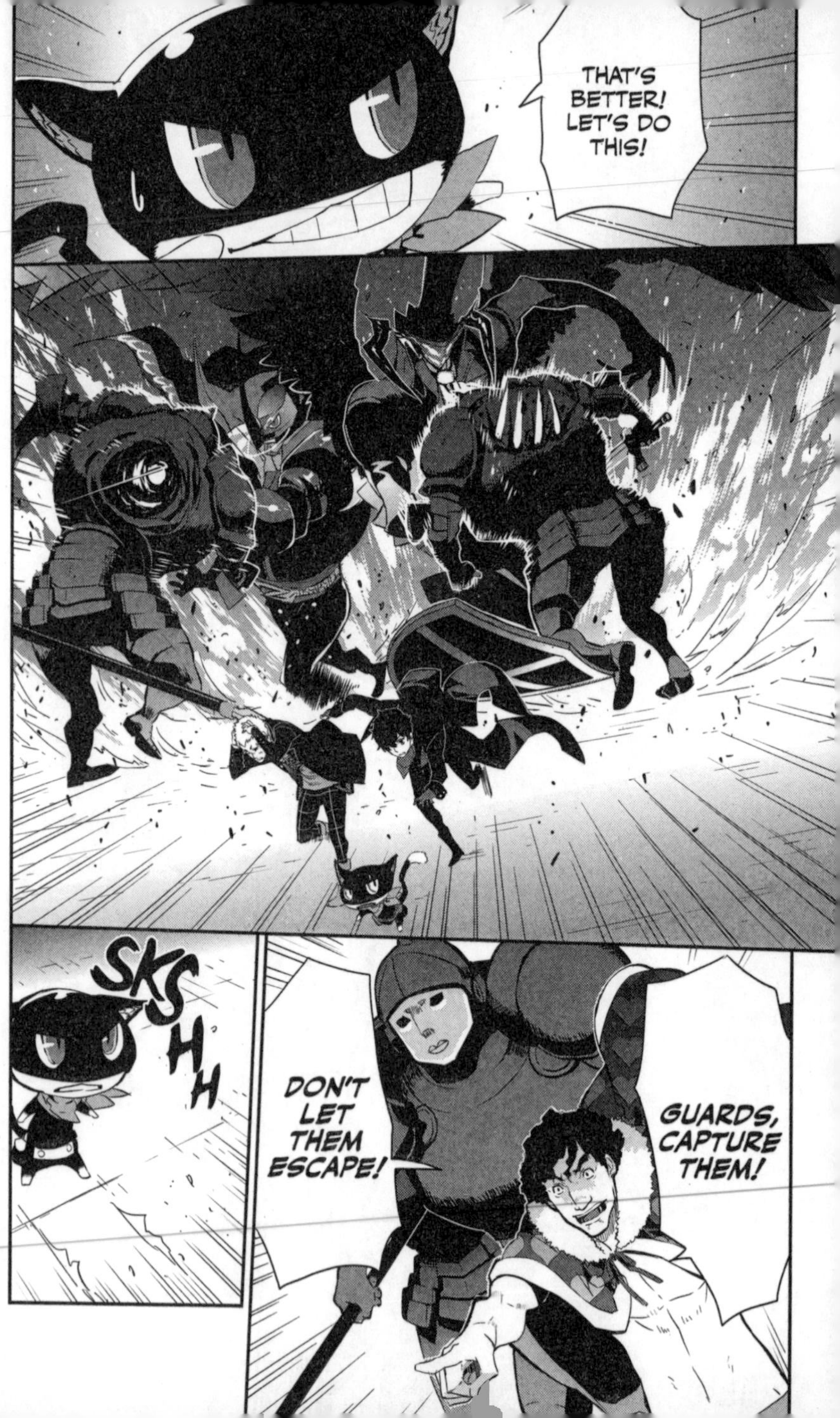
THAT'S BETTER! LET'S DO THIS!
GUARDS, CAPTURE THEM!
DON'T LET THEM ESCAPE!
SKSHH

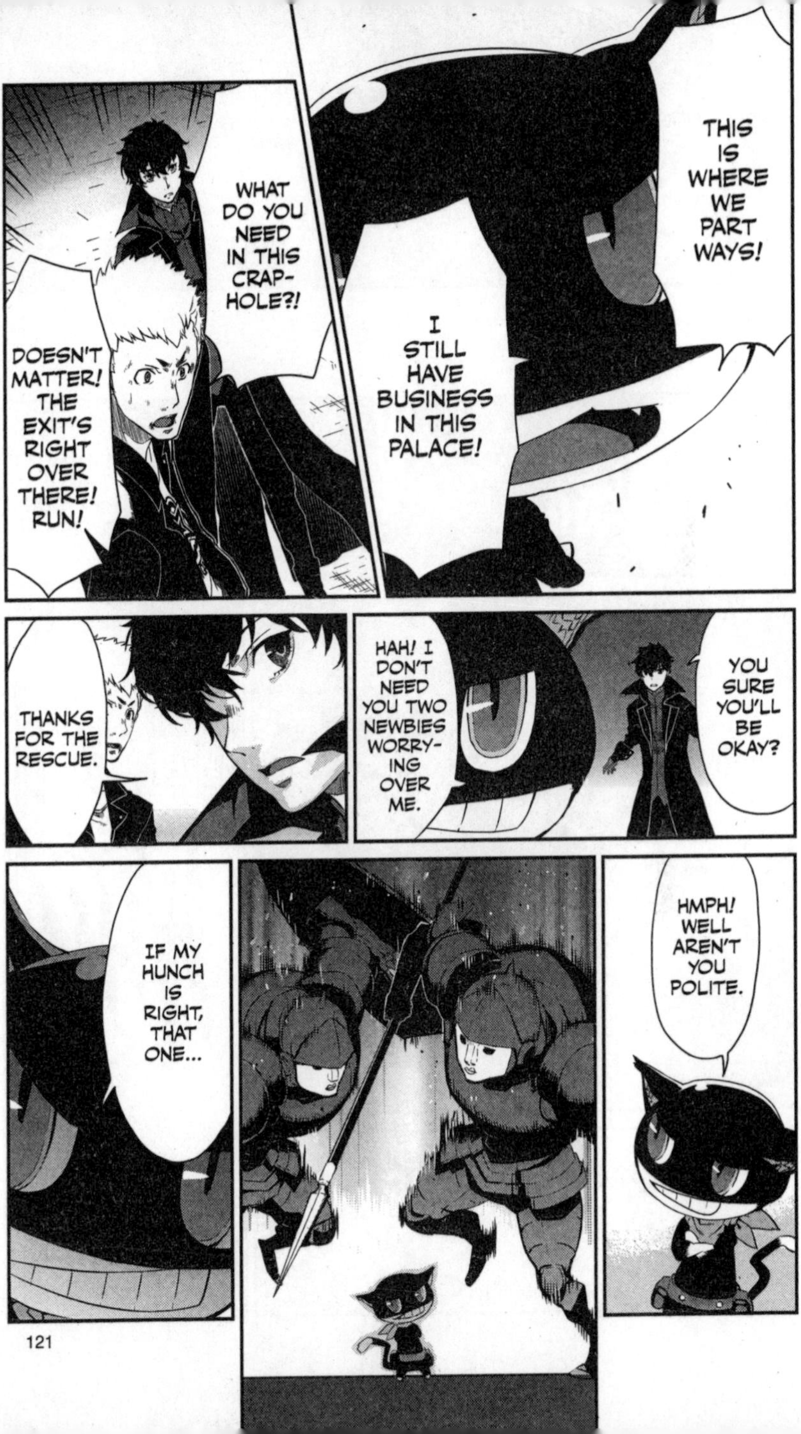
THIS IS WHERE WE PART WAYS!
I STILL HAVE BUSINESS IN THIS PALACE!
WHAT DO YOU NEED IN THIS CRAP-HOLE?!
DOESN'T MATTER! THE EXIT'S RIGHT OVER THERE! RUN!
YOU SURE YOU'LL BE OKAY?
HAH! I DON'T NEED YOU TWO NEWBIES WORRYING OVER ME.
THANKS FOR THE RESCUE.
HMPH! WELL AREN'T YOU POLITE.
IF MY HUNCH IS RIGHT, THAT ONE...

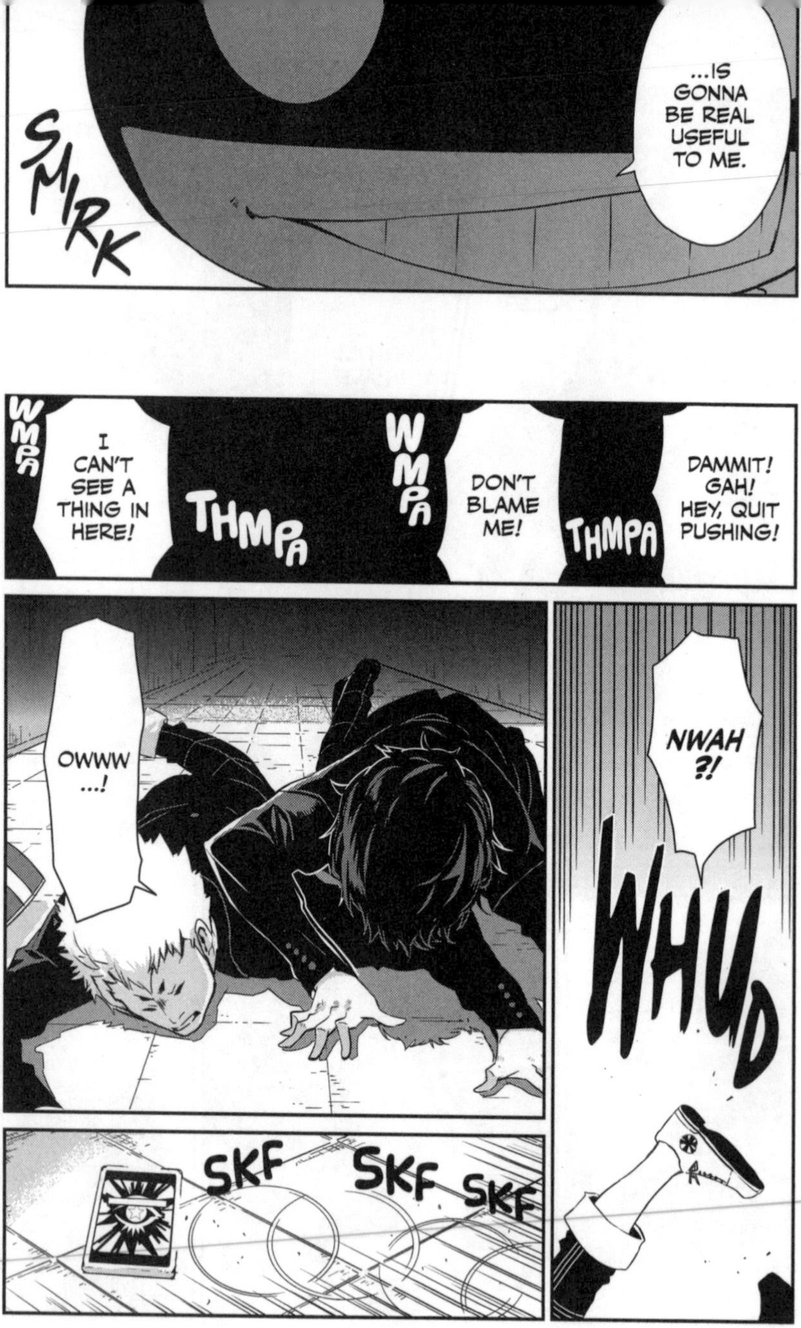
...IS GONNA BE REAL USEFUL TO ME.
SMIRK
DAMMIT! GAH! HEY, QUIT PUSHING!
THMPA
DON'T BLAME ME!
WMPA
THMPA
I CAN'T SEE A THING IN HERE!
WMPA
NWAH ?!
WHUD
OWWW ...!
SKF
SKF
SKF

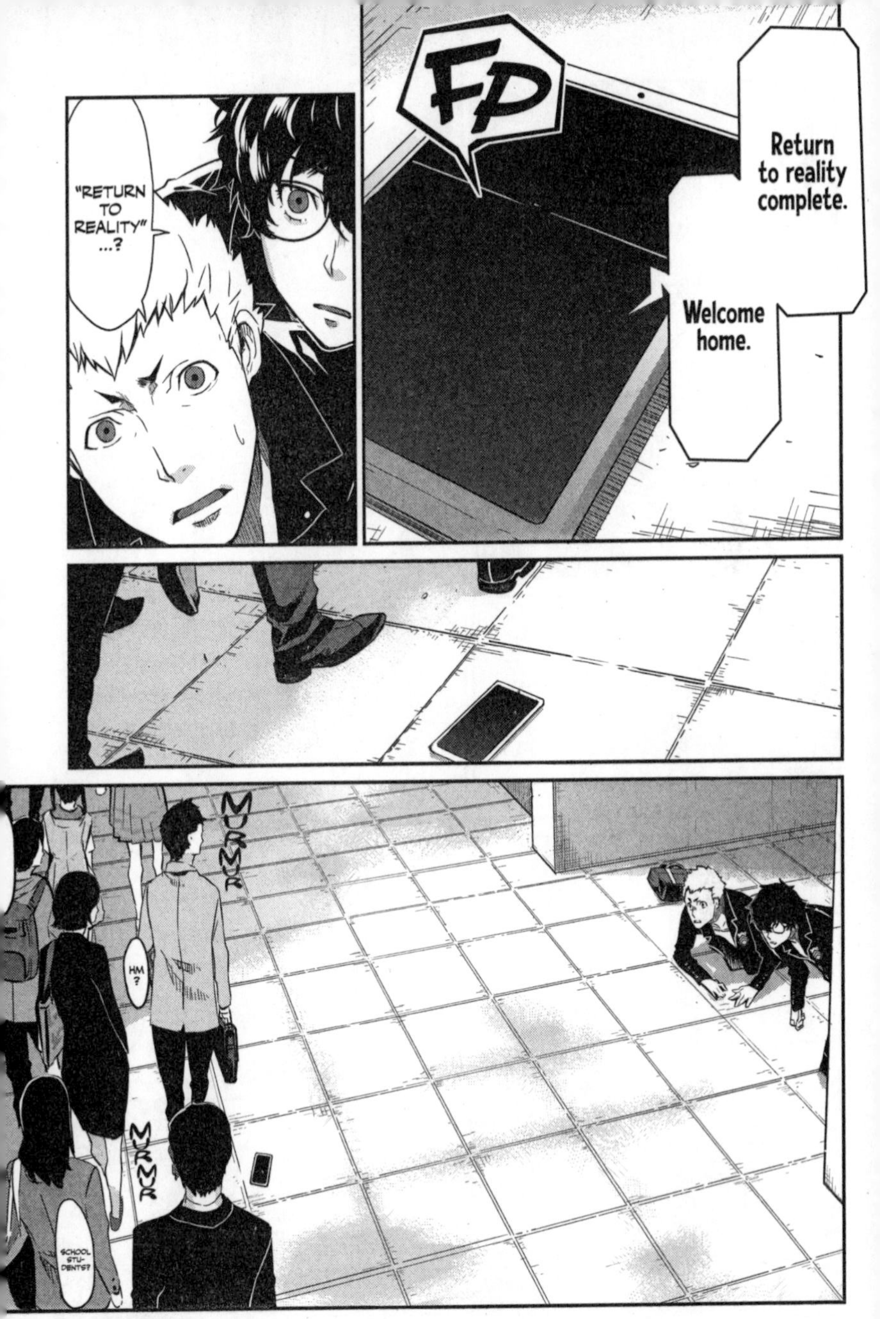
FD
Return to reality complete.
Welcome home.
"RETURN TO REALITY" ...?
MURMUR
HM?
MURMUR
SCHOOL STU-DENTS?

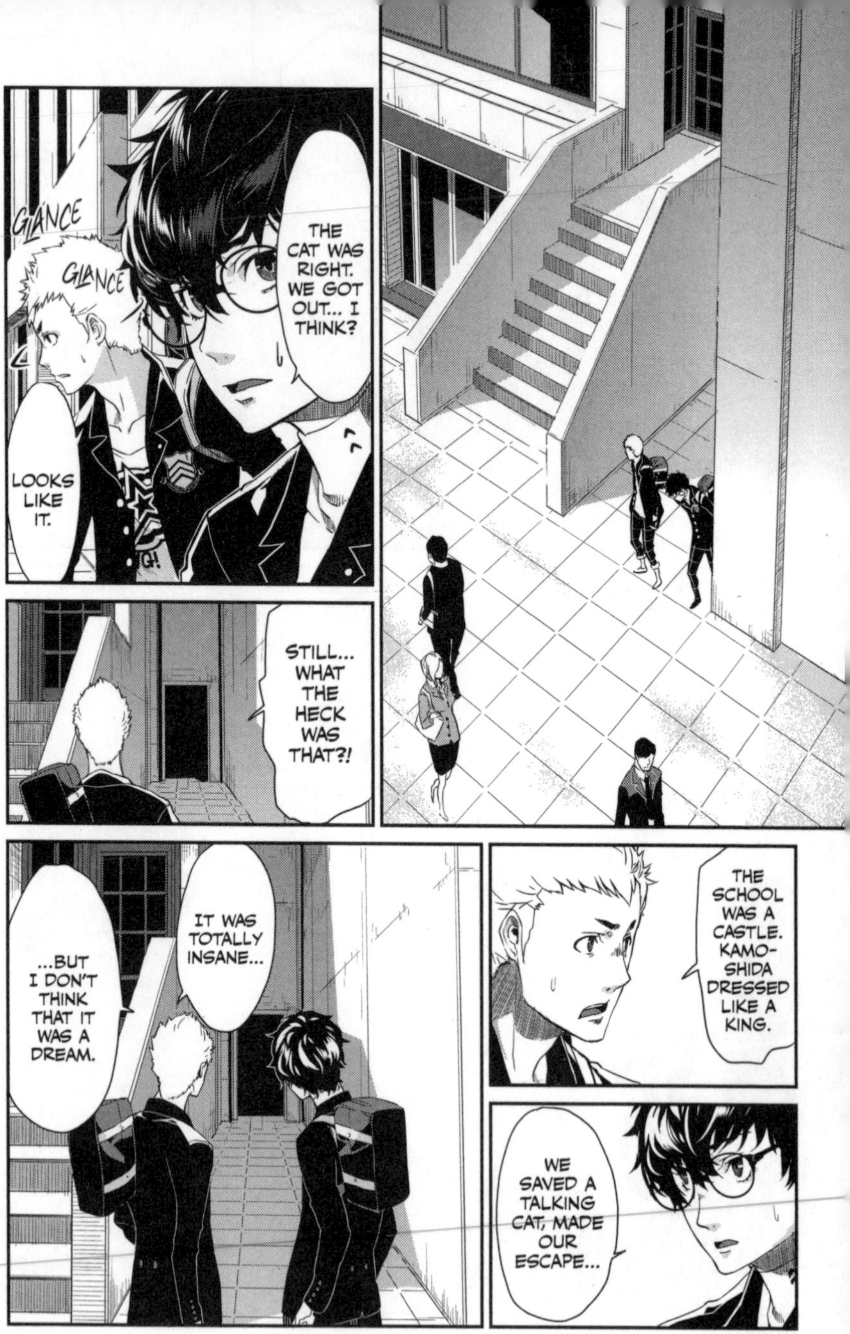
GLANCE
GLANCE
THE CAT WAS RIGHT. WE GOT OUT... I THINK?
LOOKS LIKE IT.
STILL... WHAT THE HECK WAS THAT?!
THE SCHOOL WAS A CASTLE. KAMO-SHIDA DRESSED LIKE A KING.
WE SAVED A TALKING CAT, MADE OUR ESCAPE...
IT WAS TOTALLY INSANE...
...BUT I DON'T THINK THAT IT WAS A DREAM.

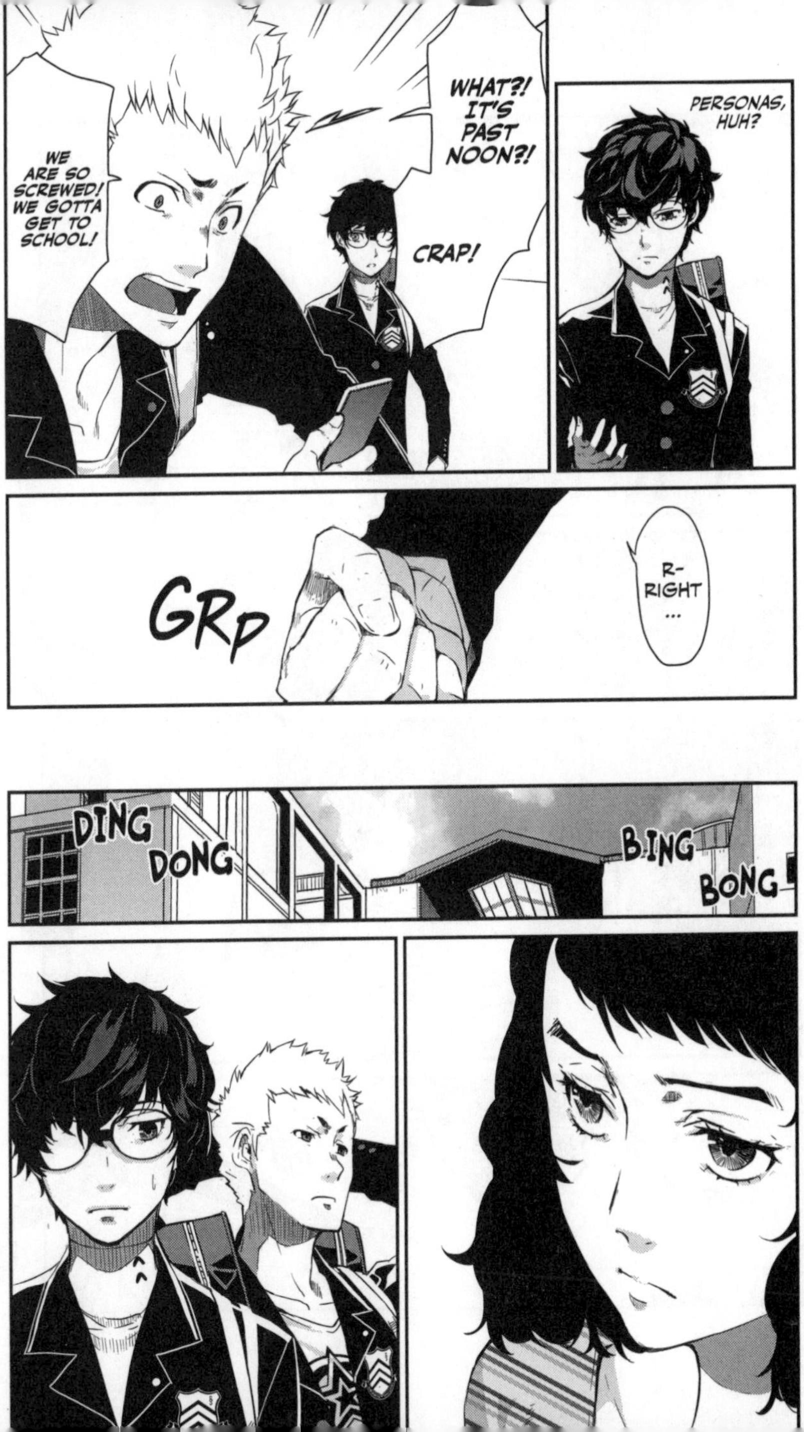
PERSONAS, HUH?
WHAT?! IT'S PAST NOON?!
CRAP!
WE ARE SO SCREWED! WE GOTTA GET TO SCHOOL!
R-RIGHT ...
GRp
BING BONG
DING DONG

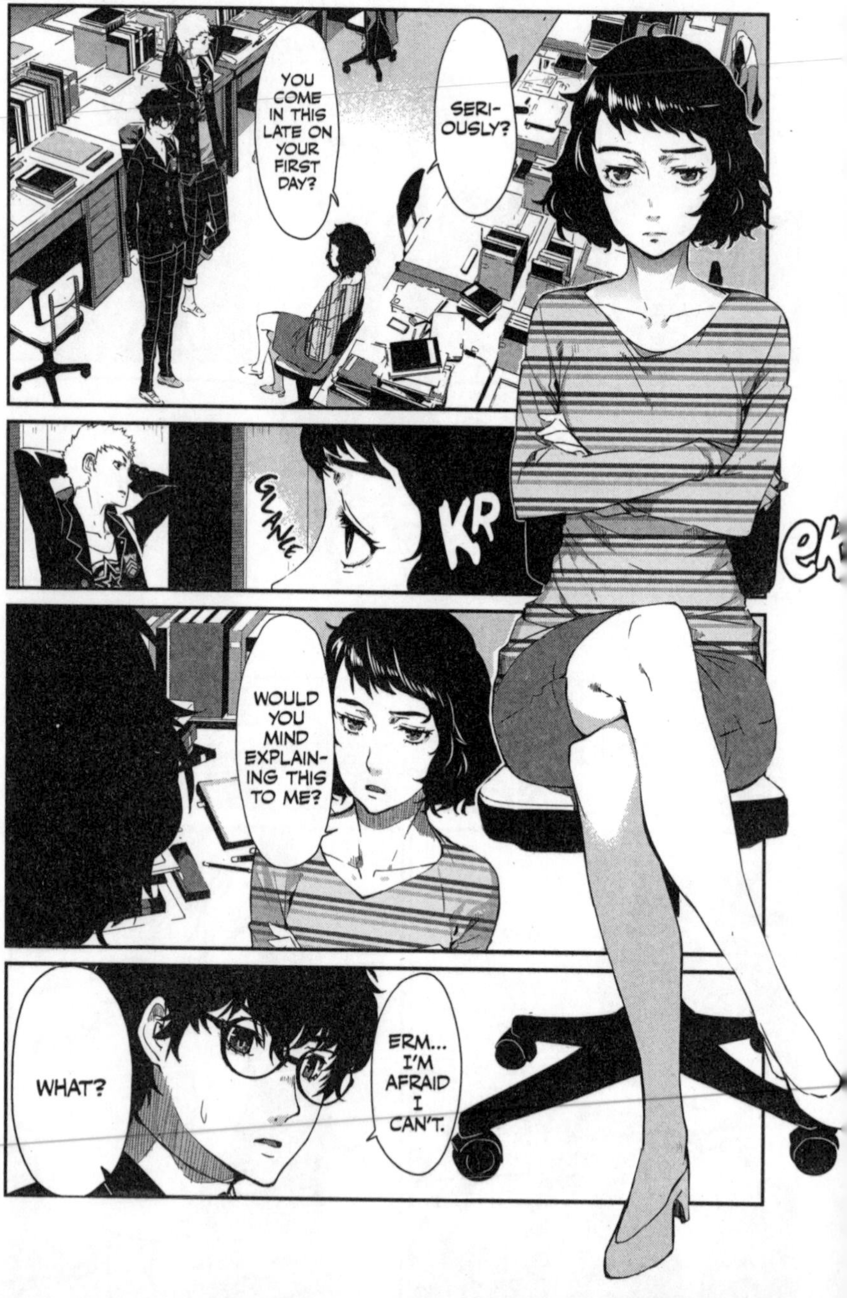
SERI-OUSLY?
YOU COME IN THIS LATE ON YOUR FIRST DAY?
KR
ek
GLANCE
WOULD YOU MIND EXPLAIN-ING THIS TO ME?
ERM... I'M AFRAID I CAN'T.
WHAT?

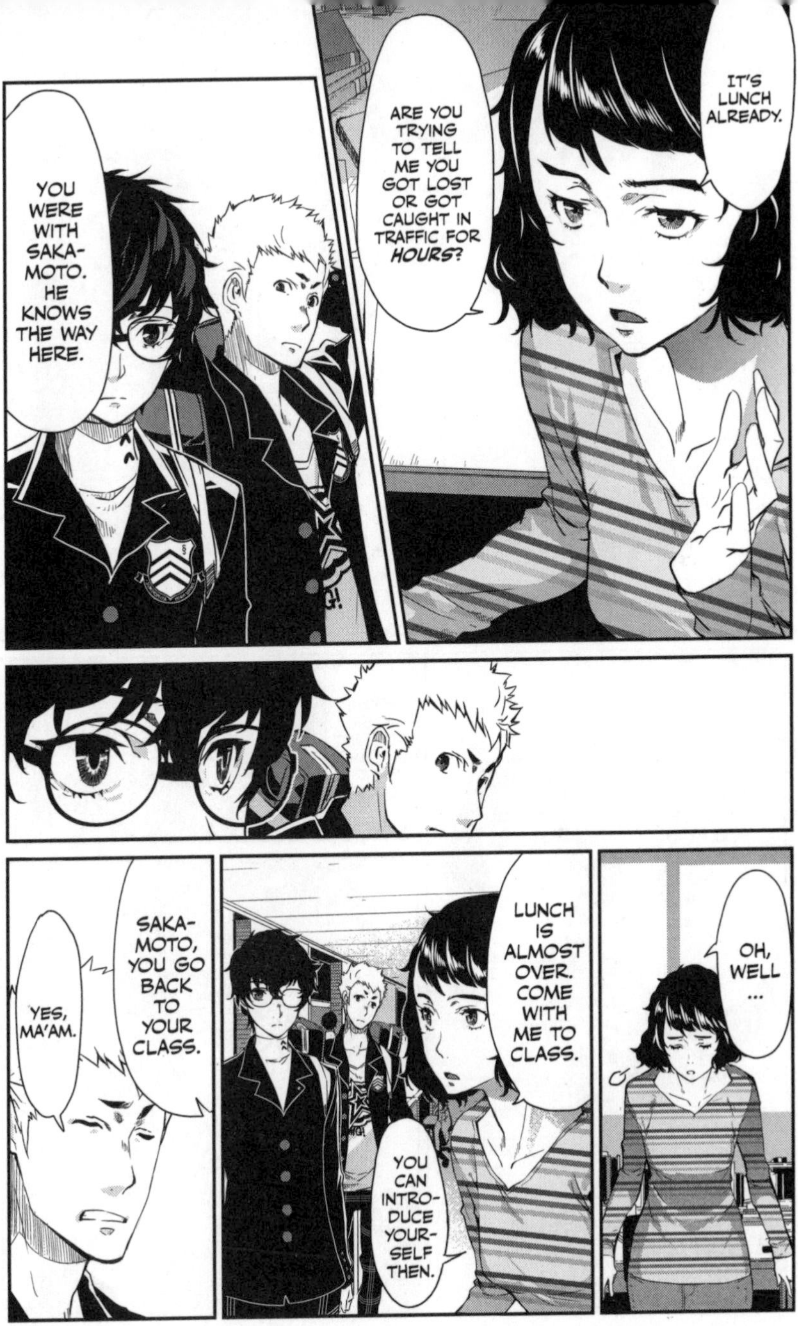
IT'S LUNCH ALREADY.
ARE YOU TRYING TO TELL ME YOU GOT LOST OR GOT CAUGHT IN TRAFFIC FOR ***HOURS***?
YOU WERE WITH SAKA-MOTO. HE KNOWS THE WAY HERE.
OH, WELL ...
LUNCH IS ALMOST OVER. COME WITH ME TO CLASS.
YOU CAN INTRO-DUCE YOUR-SELF THEN.
SAKA-MOTO, YOU GO BACK TO YOUR CLASS.
YES, MA'AM.

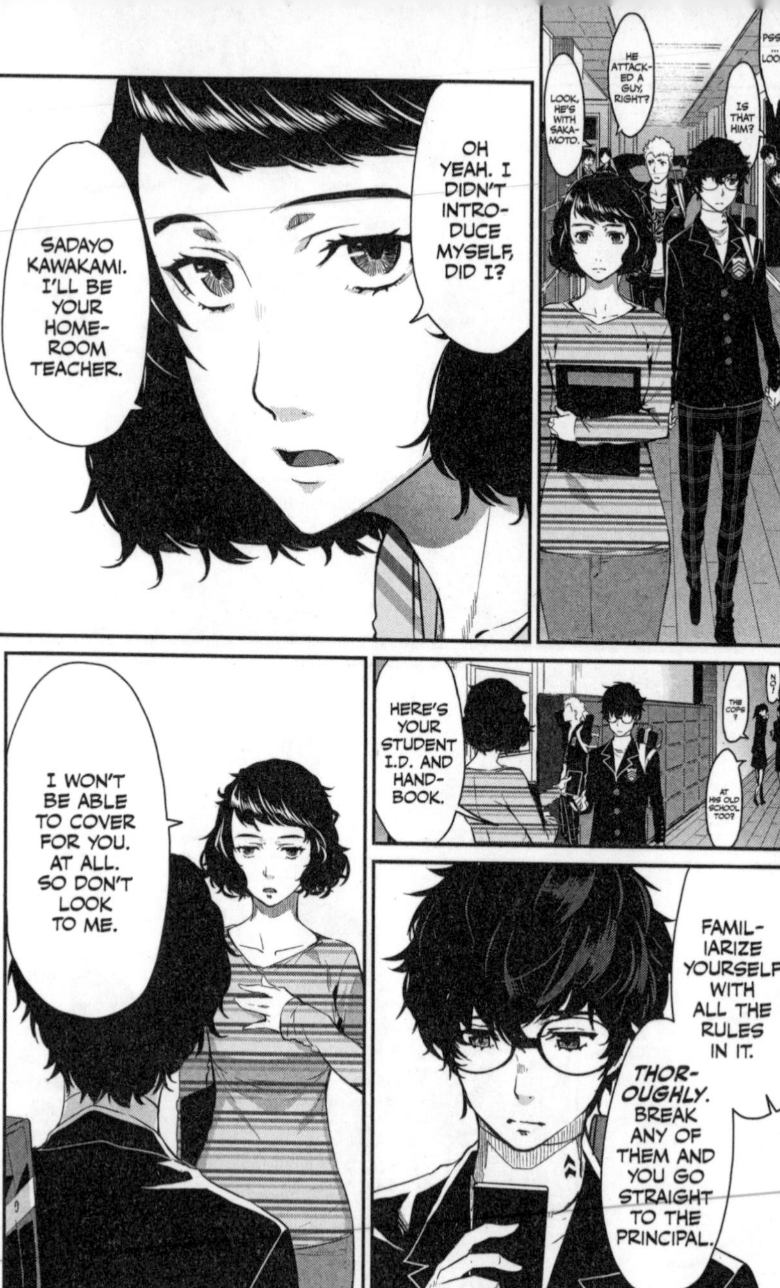
PSST ... LOOK.
IS THAT HIM?
HE ATTACKED A GUY, RIGHT?
LOOK, HE'S WITH SAKAMOTO.
OH YEAH. I DIDN'T INTRODUCE MYSELF, DID I?
SADAYO KAWAKAMI. I'LL BE YOUR HOMEROOM TEACHER.
NO?
THE COPS?
AT HIS OLD SCHOOL TOO?
HERE'S YOUR STUDENT I.D. AND HANDBOOK.
FAMILIARIZE YOURSELF WITH ALL THE RULES IN IT.
THOROUGHLY. BREAK ANY OF THEM AND YOU GO STRAIGHT TO THE PRINCIPAL.
I WON'T BE ABLE TO COVER FOR YOU. AT ALL. SO DON'T LOOK TO ME.

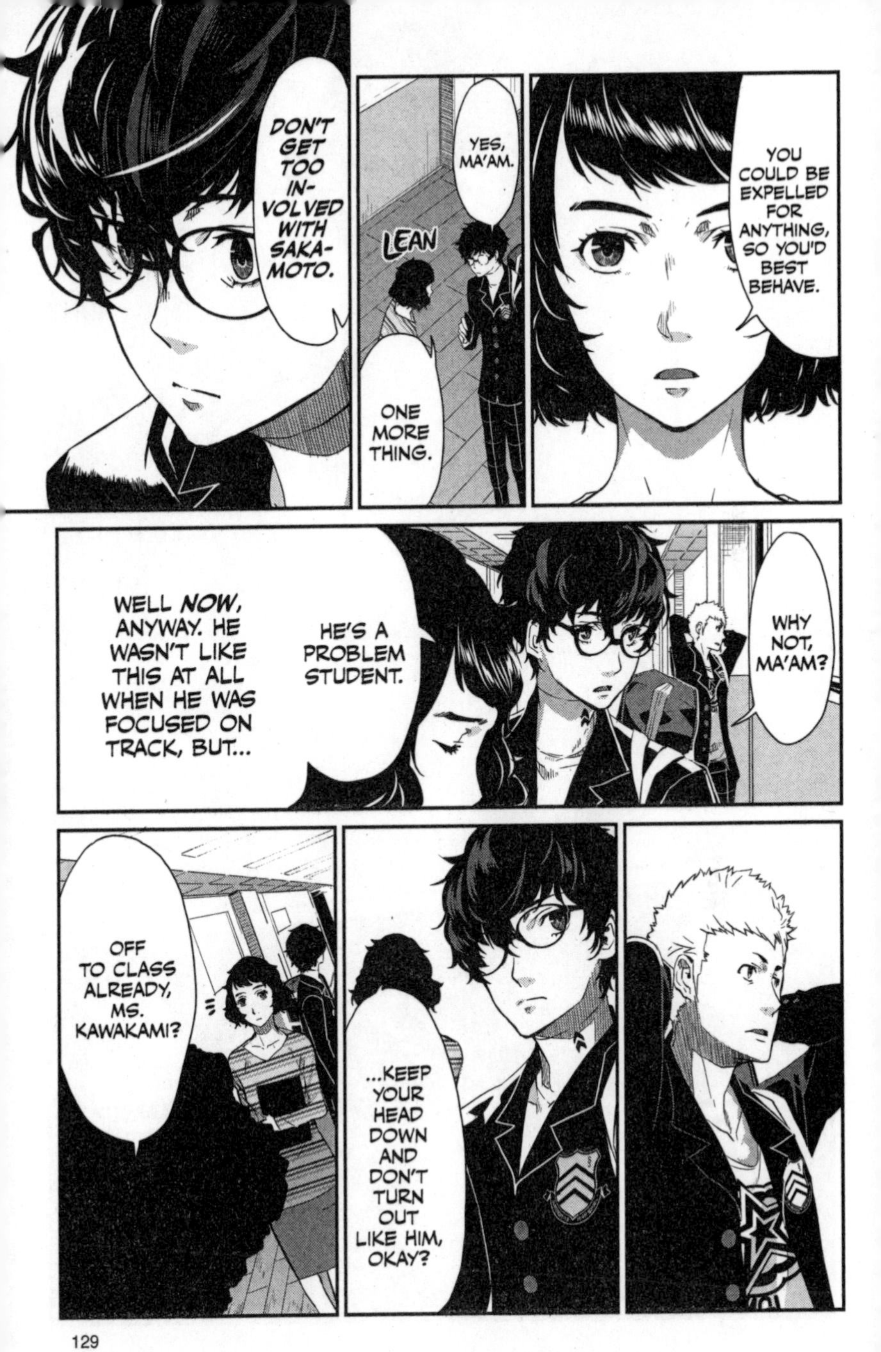
YOU COULD BE EXPELLED FOR ANYTHING, SO YOU'D BEST BEHAVE.
YES, MA'AM.
LEAN
ONE MORE THING.
DON'T GET TOO INVOLVED WITH SAKAMOTO.
WHY NOT, MA'AM?
HE'S A PROBLEM STUDENT.
WELL *NOW*, ANYWAY. HE WASN'T LIKE THIS AT ALL WHEN HE WAS FOCUSED ON TRACK, BUT...
...KEEP YOUR HEAD DOWN AND DON'T TURN OUT LIKE HIM, OKAY?
OFF TO CLASS ALREADY, MS. KAWAKAMI?

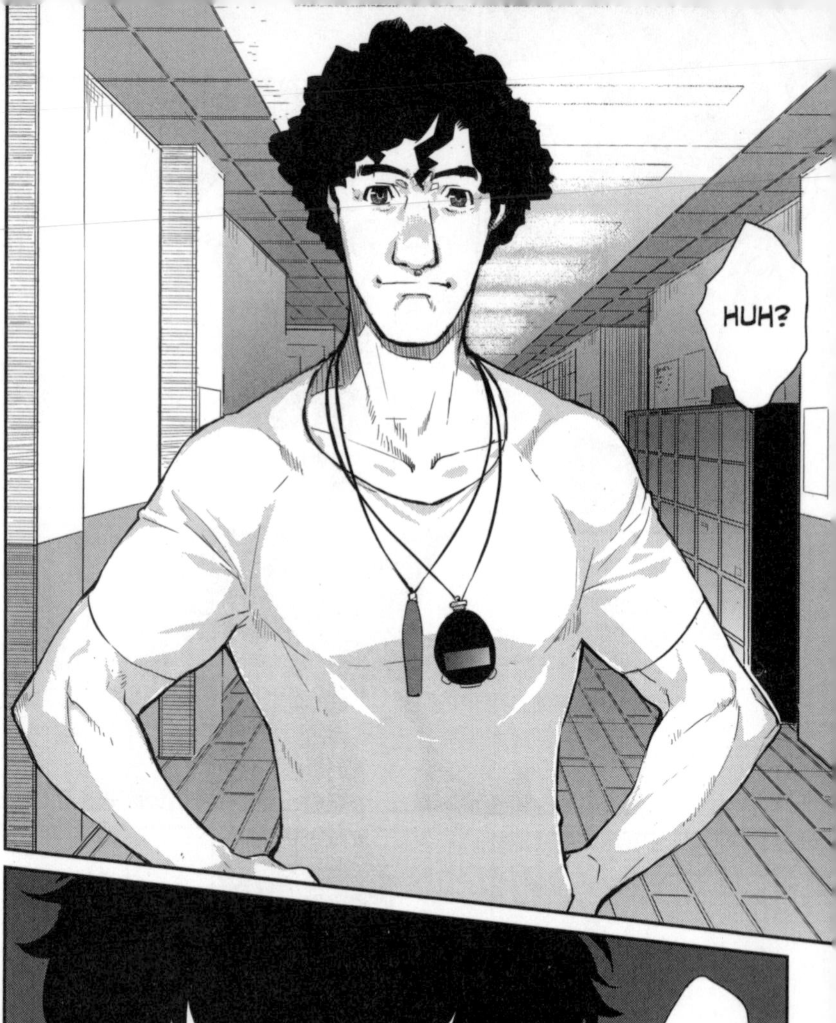
HUH?
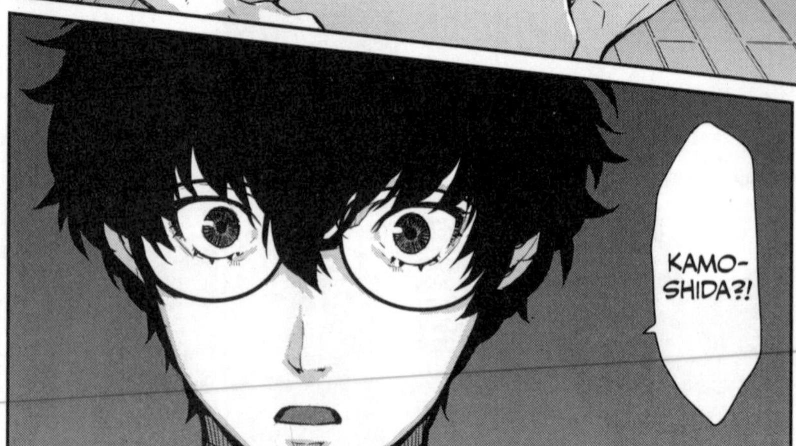
KAMO-
SHIDA?!

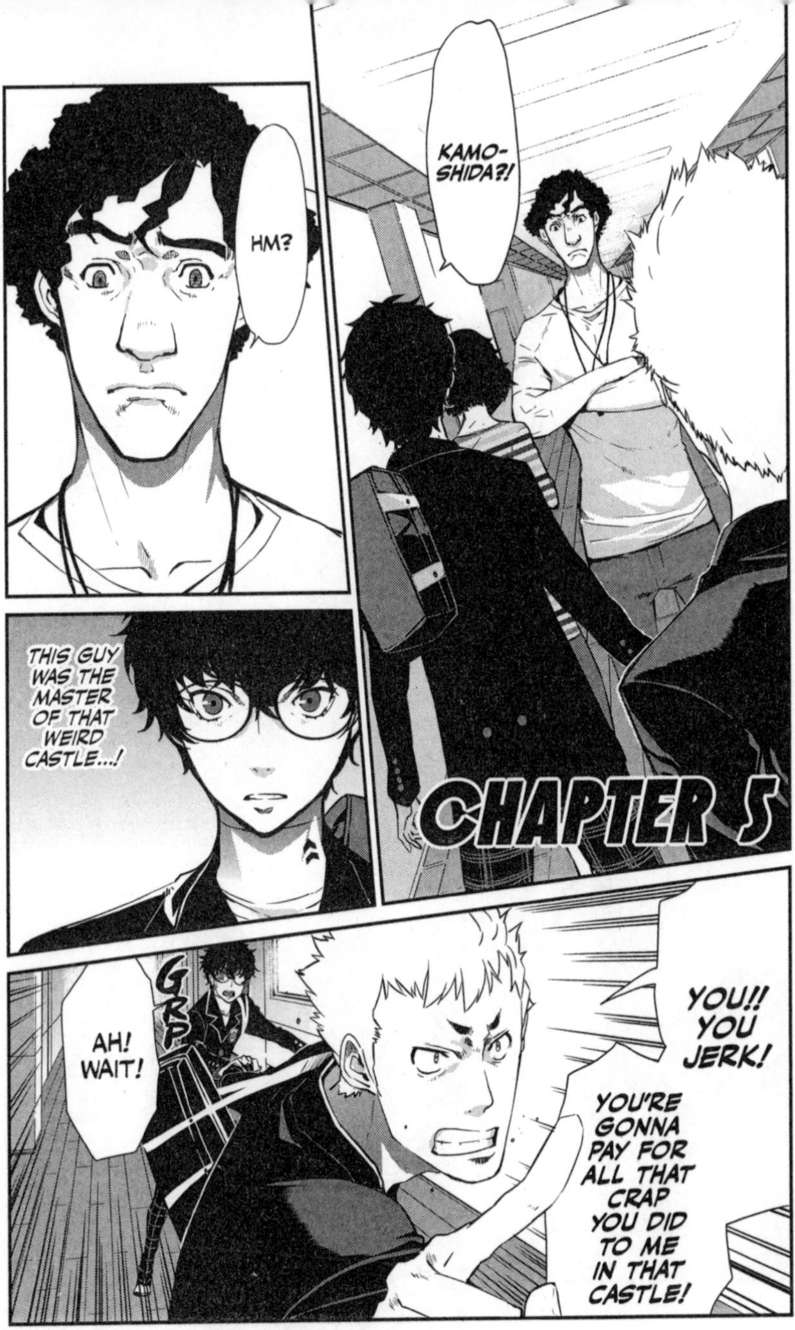
KAMO-SHIDA?!
CHAPTER 5
HM?
THIS GUY WAS THE MASTER OF THAT WEIRD CASTLE...!
YOU!! YOU JERK!
YOU'RE GONNA PAY FOR ALL THAT CRAP YOU DID TO ME IN THAT CASTLE!
GRP
AH! WAIT!

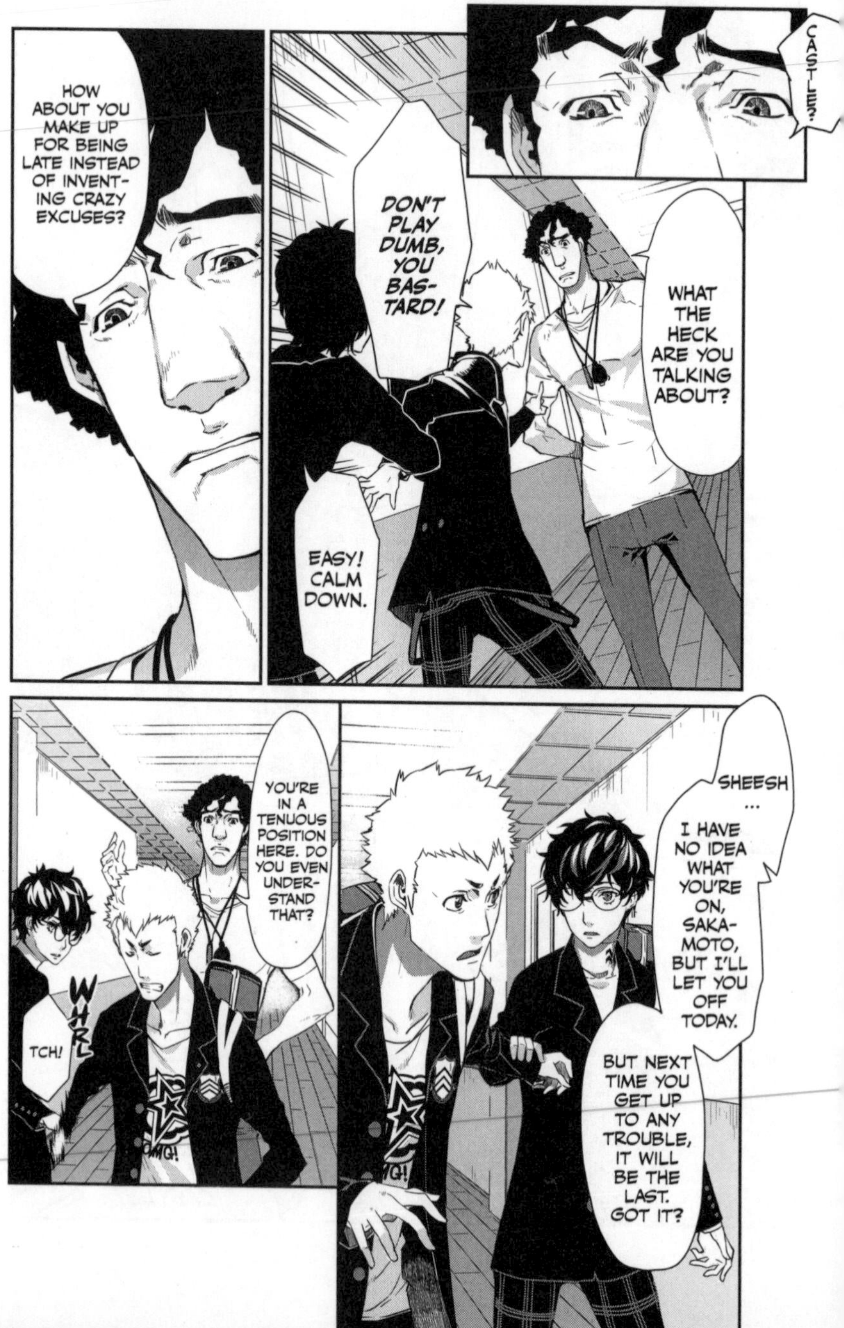
CASTLE?
DON'T PLAY DUMB, YOU BASTARD!
WHAT THE HECK ARE YOU TALKING ABOUT?
EASY! CALM DOWN.
HOW ABOUT YOU MAKE UP FOR BEING LATE INSTEAD OF INVENTING CRAZY EXCUSES?
SHEESH...
I HAVE NO IDEA WHAT YOU'RE ON, SAKAMOTO, BUT I'LL LET YOU OFF TODAY.
BUT NEXT TIME YOU GET UP TO ANY TROUBLE, IT WILL BE THE LAST. GOT IT?
YOU'RE IN A TENUOUS POSITION HERE. DO YOU EVEN UNDERSTAND THAT?
WHIRL
TCH!

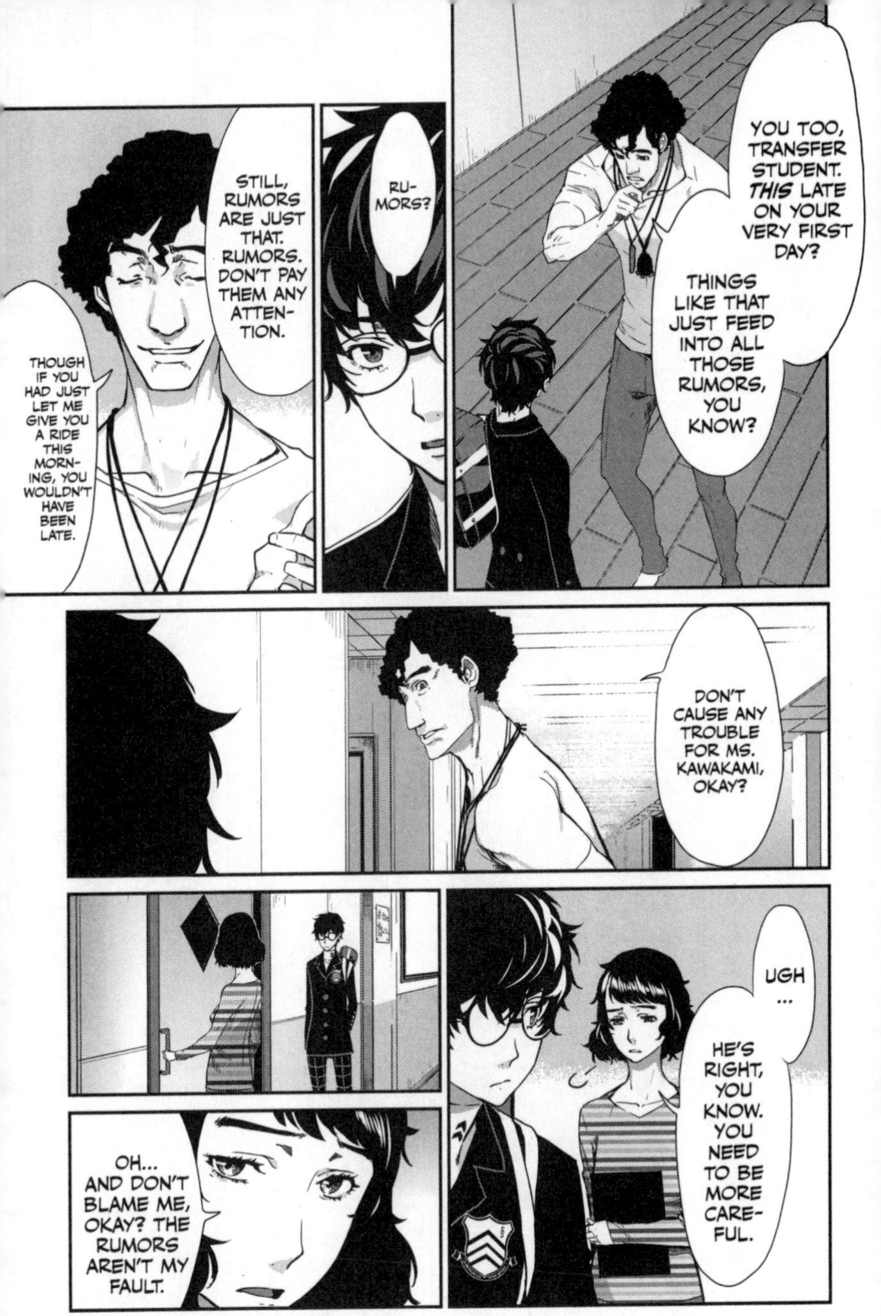
YOU TOO, TRANSFER STUDENT. *THIS* LATE ON YOUR VERY FIRST DAY?
THINGS LIKE THAT JUST FEED INTO ALL THOSE RUMORS, YOU KNOW?
RU-MORS?
STILL, RUMORS ARE JUST THAT. RUMORS. DON'T PAY THEM ANY ATTEN-TION.
THOUGH IF YOU HAD JUST LET ME GIVE YOU A RIDE THIS MORN-ING, YOU WOULDN'T HAVE BEEN LATE.
DON'T CAUSE ANY TROUBLE FOR MS. KAWAKAMI, OKAY?
UGH...
HE'S RIGHT, YOU KNOW. YOU NEED TO BE MORE CARE-FUL.
OH... AND DON'T BLAME ME, OKAY? THE RUMORS AREN'T MY FAULT.

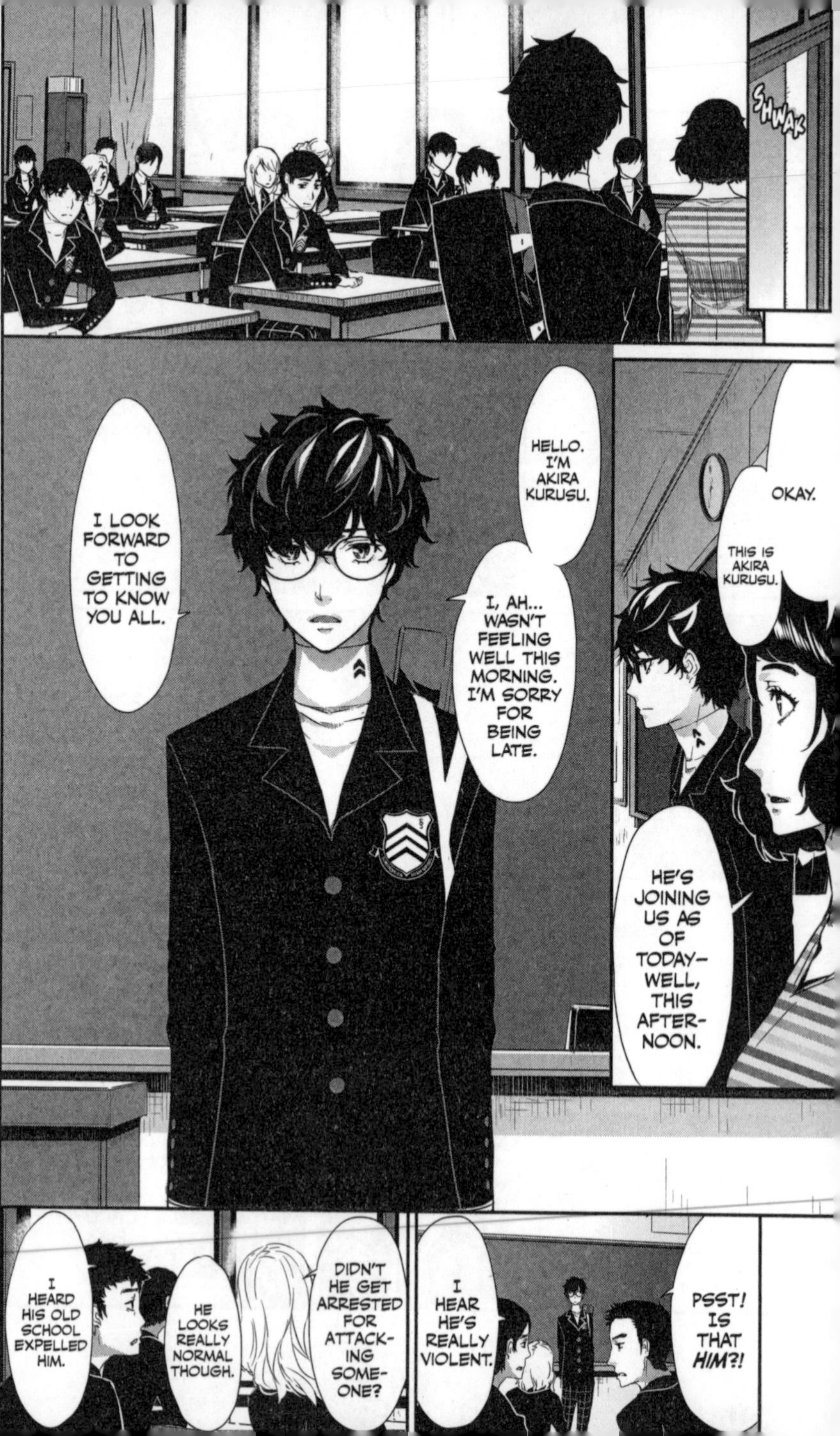
SHWAK
OKAY.
THIS IS AKIRA KURUSU.
HE'S JOINING US AS OF TODAY—WELL, THIS AFTERNOON.
HELLO. I'M AKIRA KURUSU.
I, AH... WASN'T FEELING WELL THIS MORNING. I'M SORRY FOR BEING LATE.
I LOOK FORWARD TO GETTING TO KNOW YOU ALL.
PSST! IS THAT *HIM*?!
I HEAR HE'S REALLY VIOLENT.
DIDN'T HE GET ARRESTED FOR ATTACKING SOMEONE?
HE LOOKS REALLY NORMAL THOUGH.
I HEARD HIS OLD SCHOOL EXPELLED HIM.

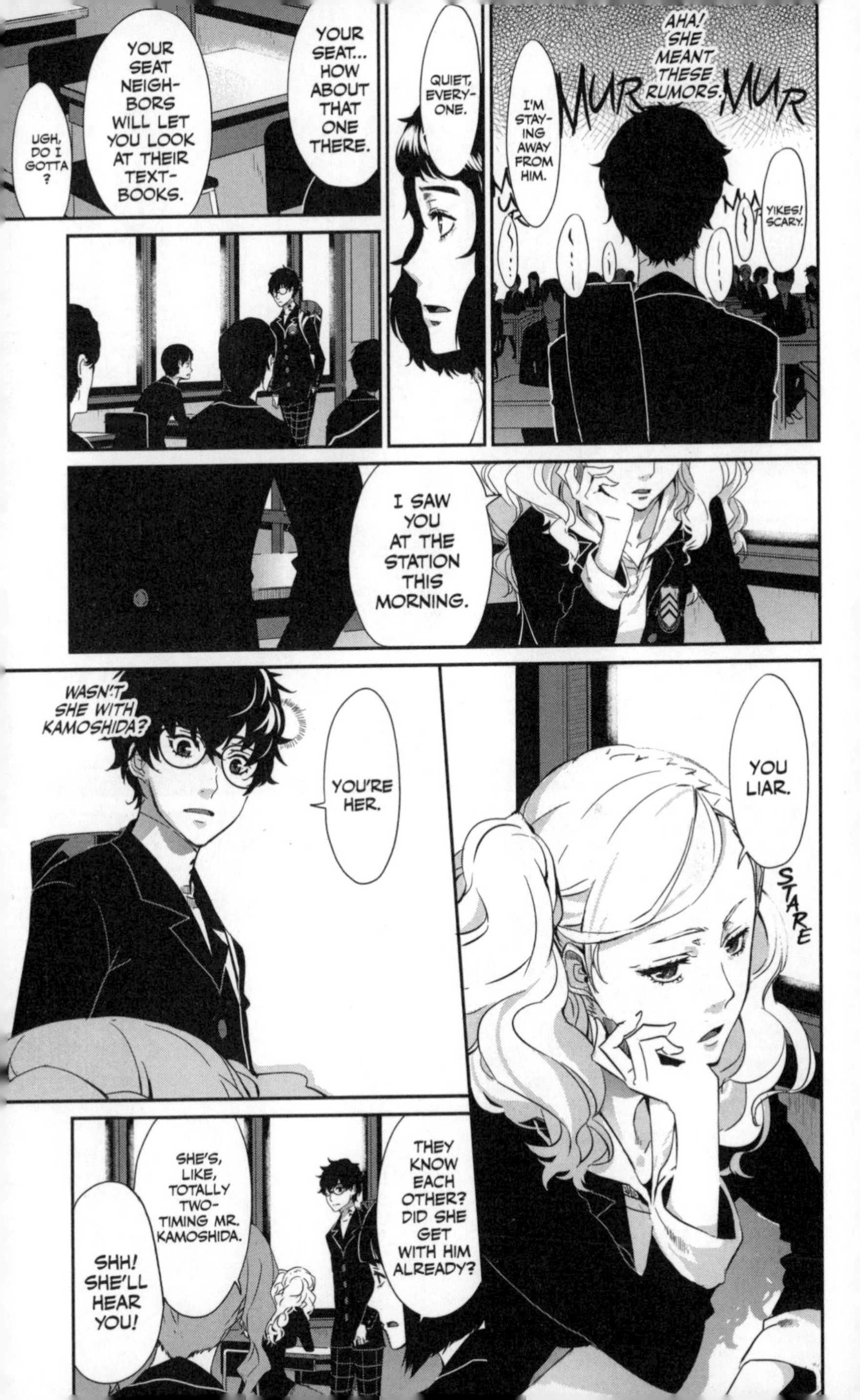
AHA! SHE MEANT THESE RUMORS.
MUR MUR
YIKES! SCARY.
I'M STAYING AWAY FROM HIM.
QUIET, EVERYONE.
YOUR SEAT... HOW ABOUT THAT ONE THERE.
YOUR SEAT NEIGHBORS WILL LET YOU LOOK AT THEIR TEXTBOOKS.
UGH, DO I GOTTA?
I SAW YOU AT THE STATION THIS MORNING.
YOU LIAR.
STARE
YOU'RE HER.
WASN'T SHE WITH KAMOSHIDA?
THEY KNOW EACH OTHER? DID SHE GET WITH HIM ALREADY?
SHE'S, LIKE, TOTALLY TWO-TIMING MR. KAMOSHIDA.
SHH! SHE'LL HEAR YOU!

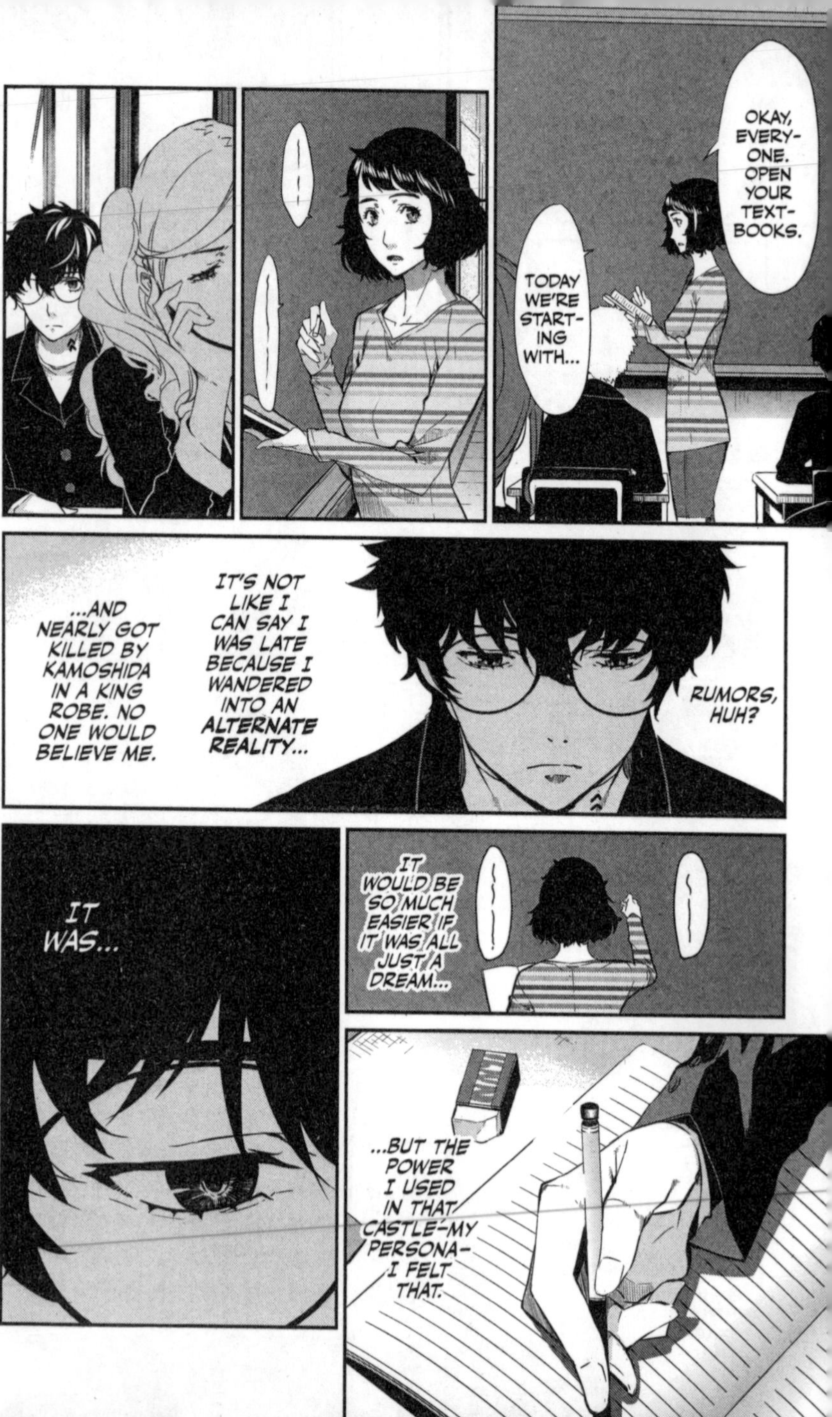
OKAY, EVERYONE. OPEN YOUR TEXTBOOKS.
TODAY WE'RE STARTING WITH...
...
...
RUMORS, HUH?
IT'S NOT LIKE I CAN SAY I WAS LATE BECAUSE I WANDERED INTO AN ALTERNATE REALITY...
...AND NEARLY GOT KILLED BY KAMOSHIDA IN A KING ROBE. NO ONE WOULD BELIEVE ME.
...
IT WOULD BE SO MUCH EASIER IF IT WAS ALL JUST A DREAM...
...
...BUT THE POWER I USED IN THAT CASTLE—MY PERSONA—I FELT THAT.
IT WAS...

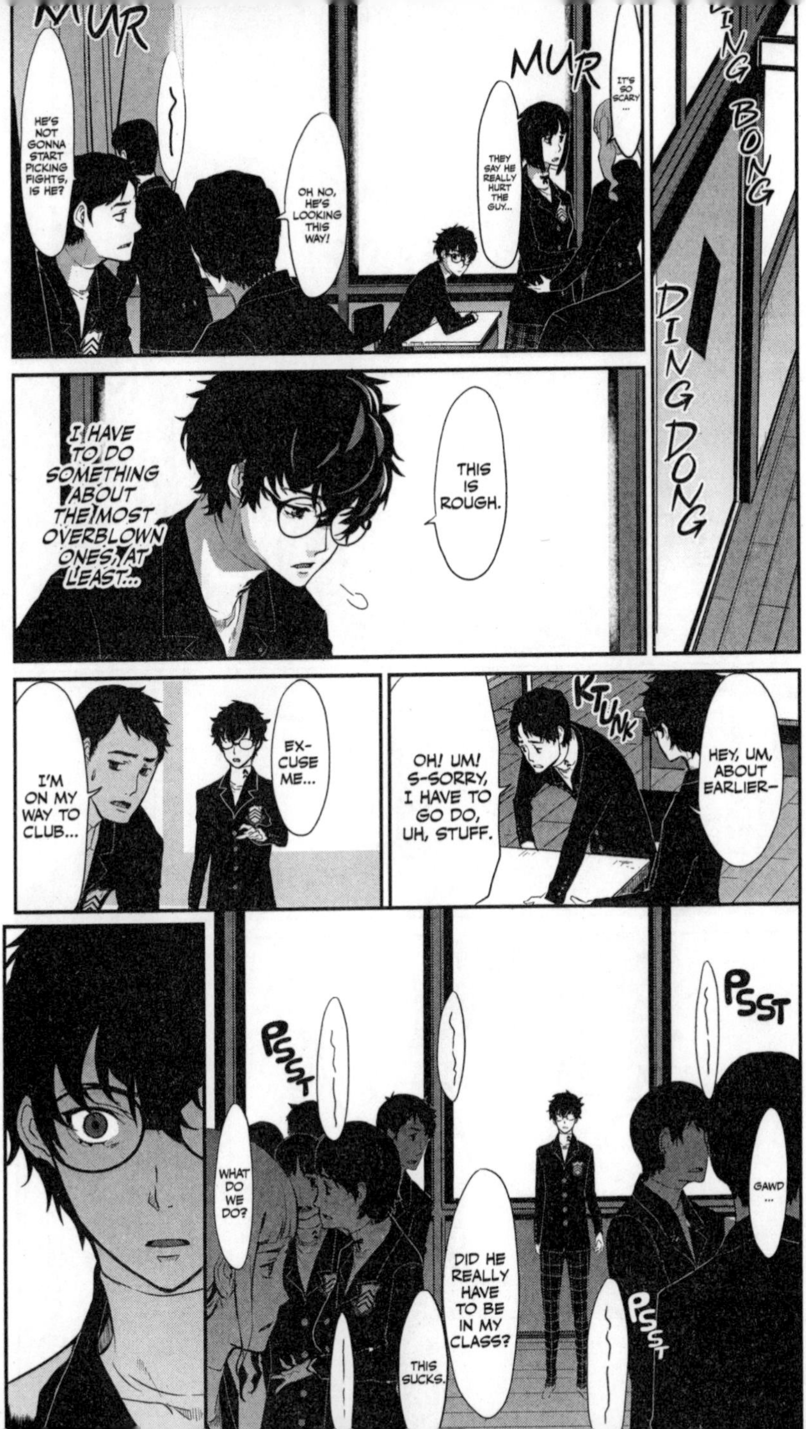
ING BONG
DING DONG
IT'S SO SCARY...
MUR
THEY SAY HE REALLY HURT THE GUY...
OH NO, HE'S LOOKING THIS WAY!
MUR
HE'S NOT GONNA START PICKING FIGHTS, IS HE?
THIS IS ROUGH.
I HAVE TO DO SOMETHING ABOUT THE MOST OVERBLOWN ONES, AT LEAST...
HEY, UM, ABOUT EARLIER—
KTUNK
OH! UM! S-SORRY, I HAVE TO GO DO, UH, STUFF.
EX-CUSE ME...
I'M ON MY WAY TO CLUB...
PSST
GAWD...
PSST
DID HE REALLY HAVE TO BE IN MY CLASS?
THIS SUCKS.
PSST
WHAT DO WE DO?

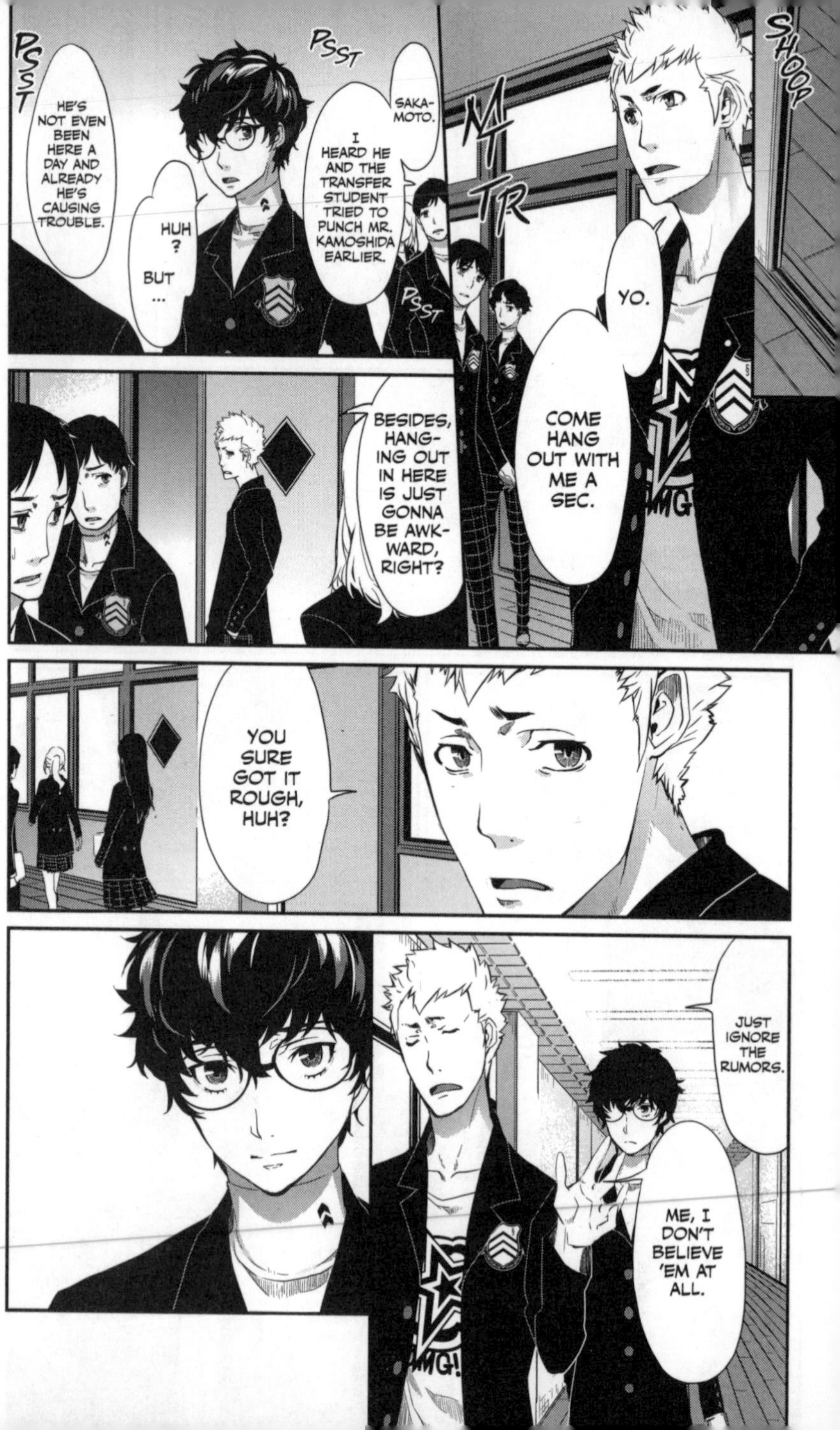
SHOOP
MTTR
YO.
COME HANG OUT WITH ME A SEC.
PSST
SAKAMOTO.
I HEARD HE AND THE TRANSFER STUDENT TRIED TO PUNCH MR. KAMOSHIDA EARLIER.
PSST
HE'S NOT EVEN BEEN HERE A DAY AND ALREADY HE'S CAUSING TROUBLE.
HUH? BUT...
PSST
BESIDES, HANGING OUT IN HERE IS JUST GONNA BE AWKWARD, RIGHT?
YOU SURE GOT IT ROUGH, HUH?
JUST IGNORE THE RUMORS.
ME, I DON'T BELIEVE 'EM AT ALL.

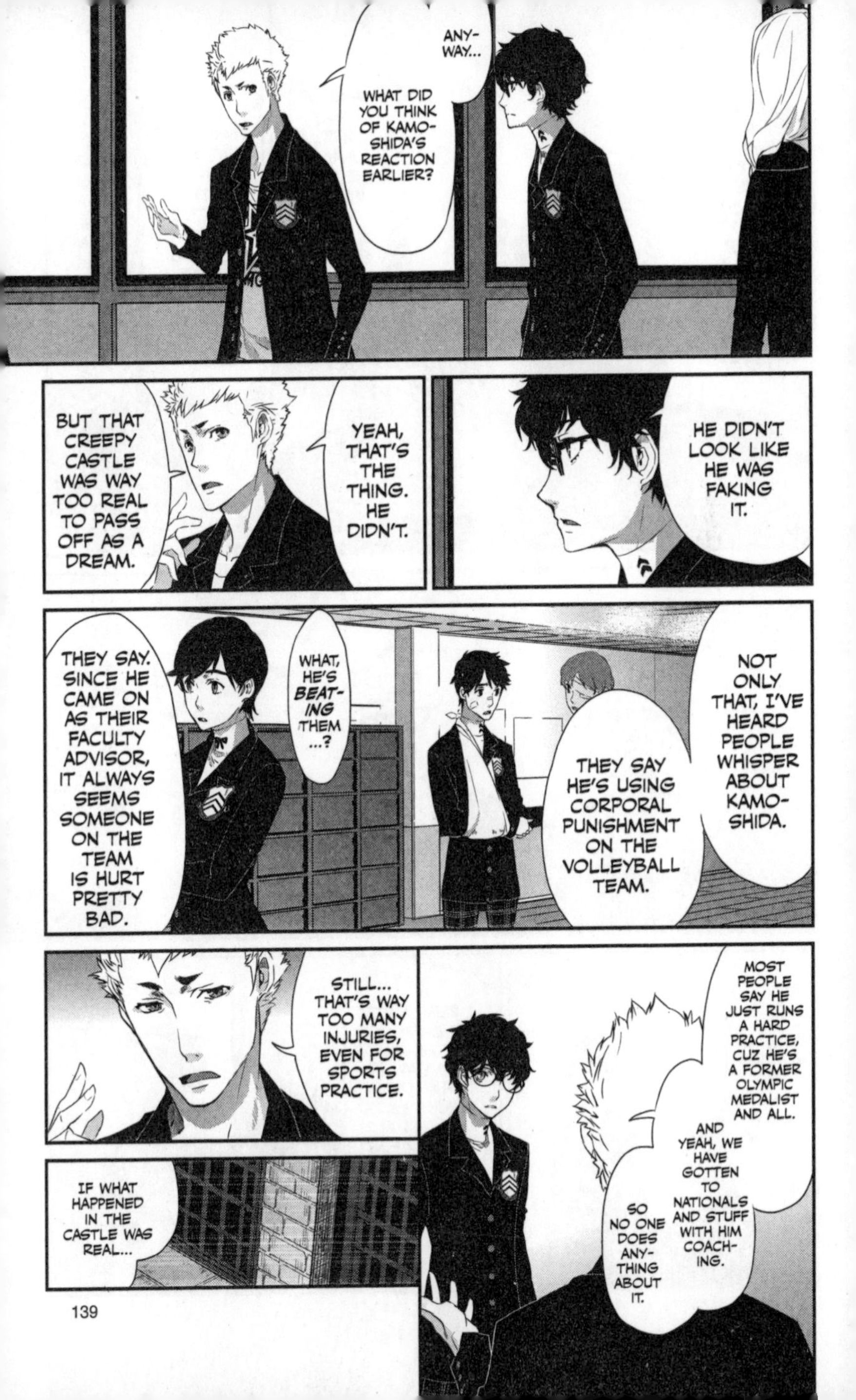
ANYWAY...
WHAT DID YOU THINK OF KAMOSHIDA'S REACTION EARLIER?
HE DIDN'T LOOK LIKE HE WAS FAKING IT.
YEAH, THAT'S THE THING. HE DIDN'T.
BUT THAT CREEPY CASTLE WAS WAY TOO REAL TO PASS OFF AS A DREAM.
NOT ONLY THAT, I'VE HEARD PEOPLE WHISPER ABOUT KAMOSHIDA.
THEY SAY HE'S USING CORPORAL PUNISHMENT ON THE VOLLEYBALL TEAM.
WHAT, HE'S *BEATING* THEM...?
THEY SAY. SINCE HE CAME ON AS THEIR FACULTY ADVISOR, IT ALWAYS SEEMS SOMEONE ON THE TEAM IS HURT PRETTY BAD.
MOST PEOPLE SAY HE JUST RUNS A HARD PRACTICE, CUZ HE'S A FORMER OLYMPIC MEDALIST AND ALL.
AND YEAH, WE HAVE GOTTEN TO NATIONALS AND STUFF WITH HIM COACHING.
SO NO ONE DOES ANYTHING ABOUT IT.
STILL... THAT'S WAY TOO MANY INJURIES, EVEN FOR SPORTS PRACTICE.
IF WHAT HAPPENED IN THE CASTLE WAS REAL...

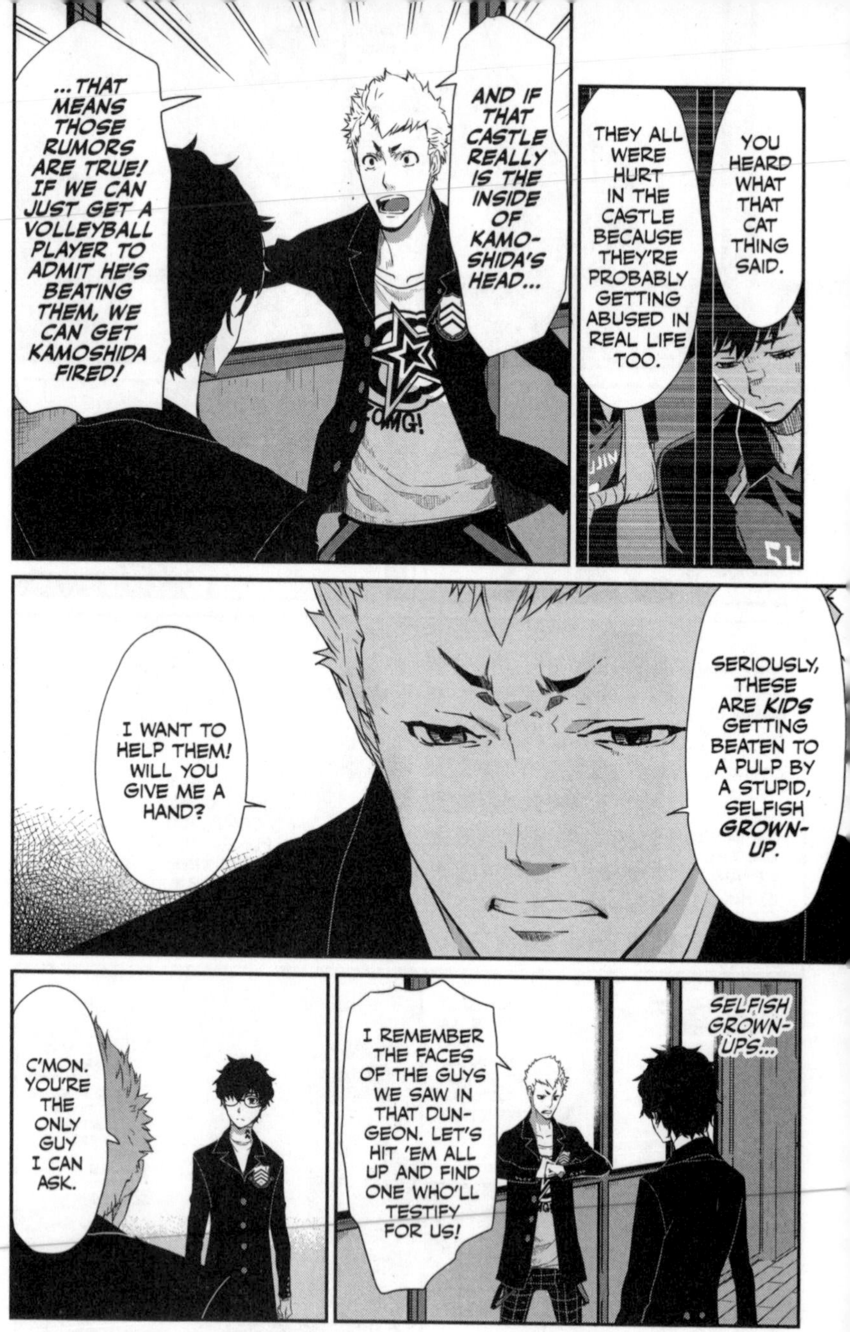
YOU HEARD WHAT THAT CAT THING SAID.
THEY ALL WERE HURT IN THE CASTLE BECAUSE THEY'RE PROBABLY GETTING ABUSED IN REAL LIFE TOO.
AND IF THAT CASTLE REALLY IS THE INSIDE OF KAMOSHIDA'S HEAD...
...THAT MEANS THOSE RUMORS ARE TRUE! IF WE CAN JUST GET A VOLLEYBALL PLAYER TO ADMIT HE'S BEATING THEM, WE CAN GET KAMOSHIDA FIRED!
SERIOUSLY, THESE ARE *KIDS* GETTING BEATEN TO A PULP BY A STUPID, SELFISH *GROWN-UP*.
I WANT TO HELP THEM! WILL YOU GIVE ME A HAND?
SELFISH GROWN-UPS...
I REMEMBER THE FACES OF THE GUYS WE SAW IN THAT DUNGEON. LET'S HIT 'EM ALL UP AND FIND ONE WHO'LL TESTIFY FOR US!
C'MON. YOU'RE THE ONLY GUY I CAN ASK.

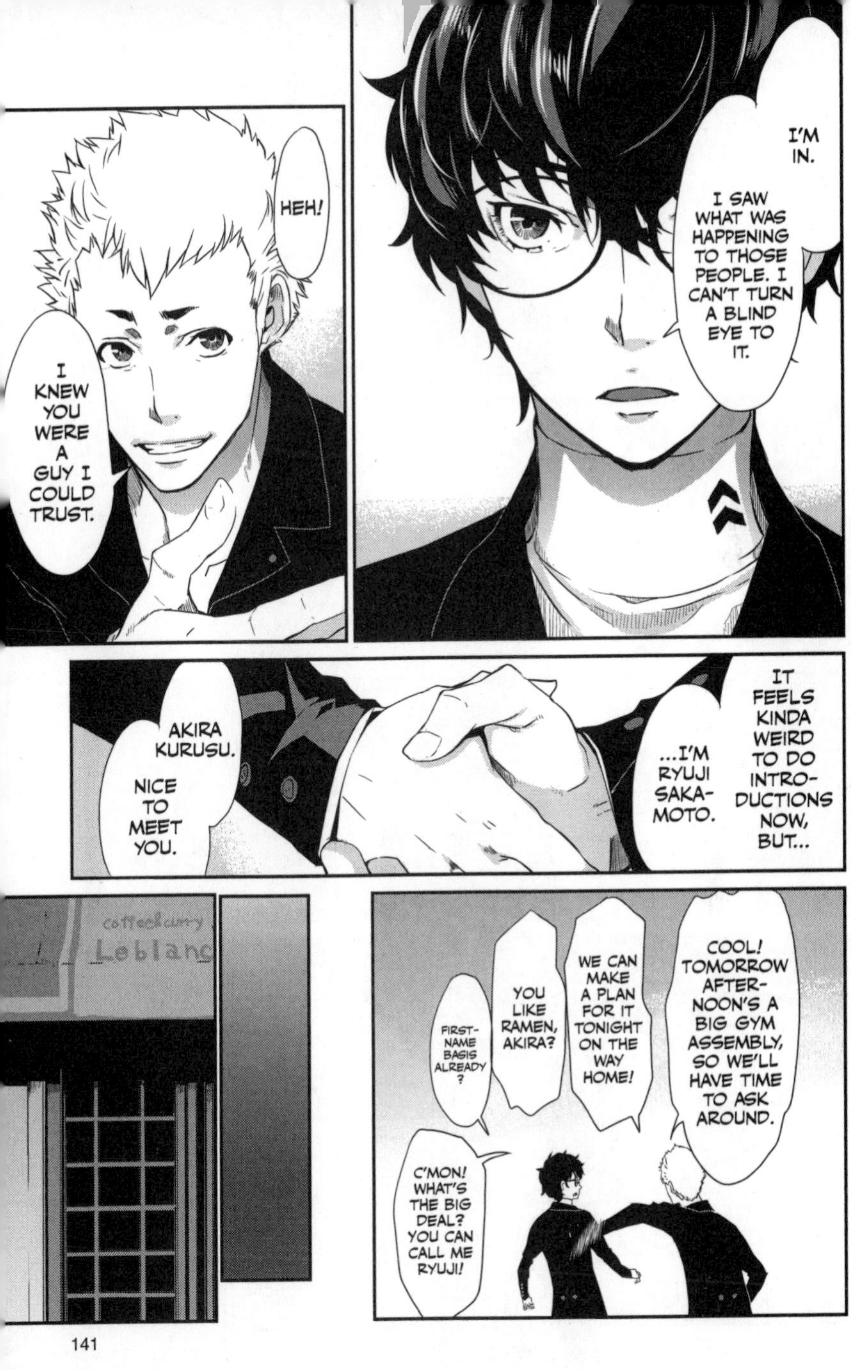
I'M IN.
I SAW WHAT WAS HAPPENING TO THOSE PEOPLE. I CAN'T TURN A BLIND EYE TO IT.
HEH!
I KNEW YOU WERE A GUY I COULD TRUST.
IT FEELS KINDA WEIRD TO DO INTRO-DUCTIONS NOW, BUT...
...I'M RYUJI SAKA-MOTO.
AKIRA KURUSU.
NICE TO MEET YOU.
COOL! TOMORROW AFTER-NOON'S A BIG GYM ASSEMBLY, SO WE'LL HAVE TIME TO ASK AROUND.
WE CAN MAKE A PLAN FOR IT TONIGHT ON THE WAY HOME!
YOU LIKE RAMEN, AKIRA?
FIRST-NAME BASIS ALREADY?
C'MON! WHAT'S THE BIG DEAL? YOU CAN CALL ME RYUJI!
coffee&curry
Leblanc

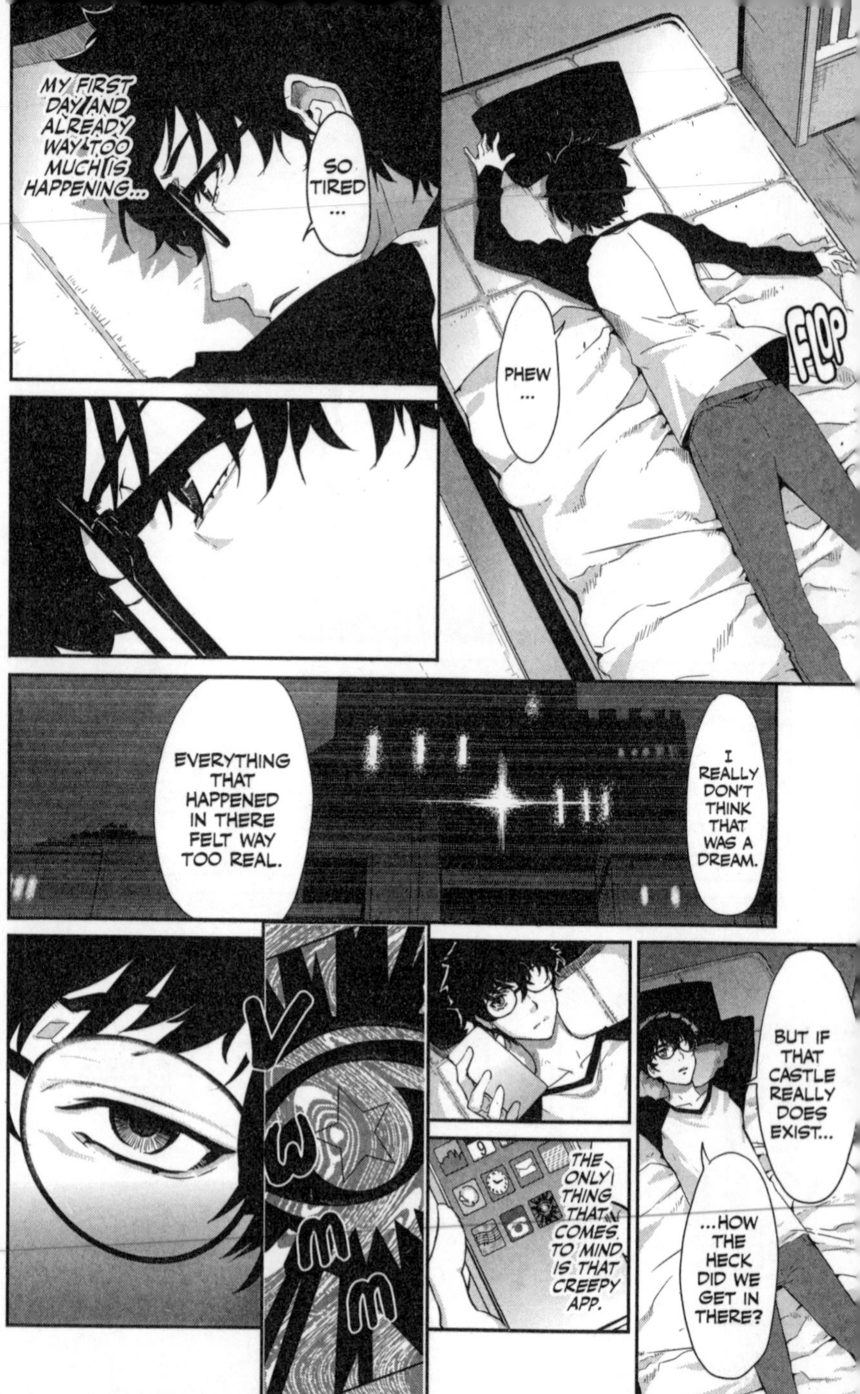
PHEW ...
FLOP
SO TIRED ...
MY FIRST DAY AND ALREADY WAY TOO MUCH IS HAPPENING...
I REALLY DON'T THINK THAT WAS A DREAM.
EVERYTHING THAT HAPPENED IN THERE FELT WAY TOO REAL.
BUT IF THAT CASTLE REALLY DOES EXIST...
...HOW THE HECK DID WE GET IN THERE?
THE ONLY THING THAT COMES TO MIND IS THAT CREEPY APP.

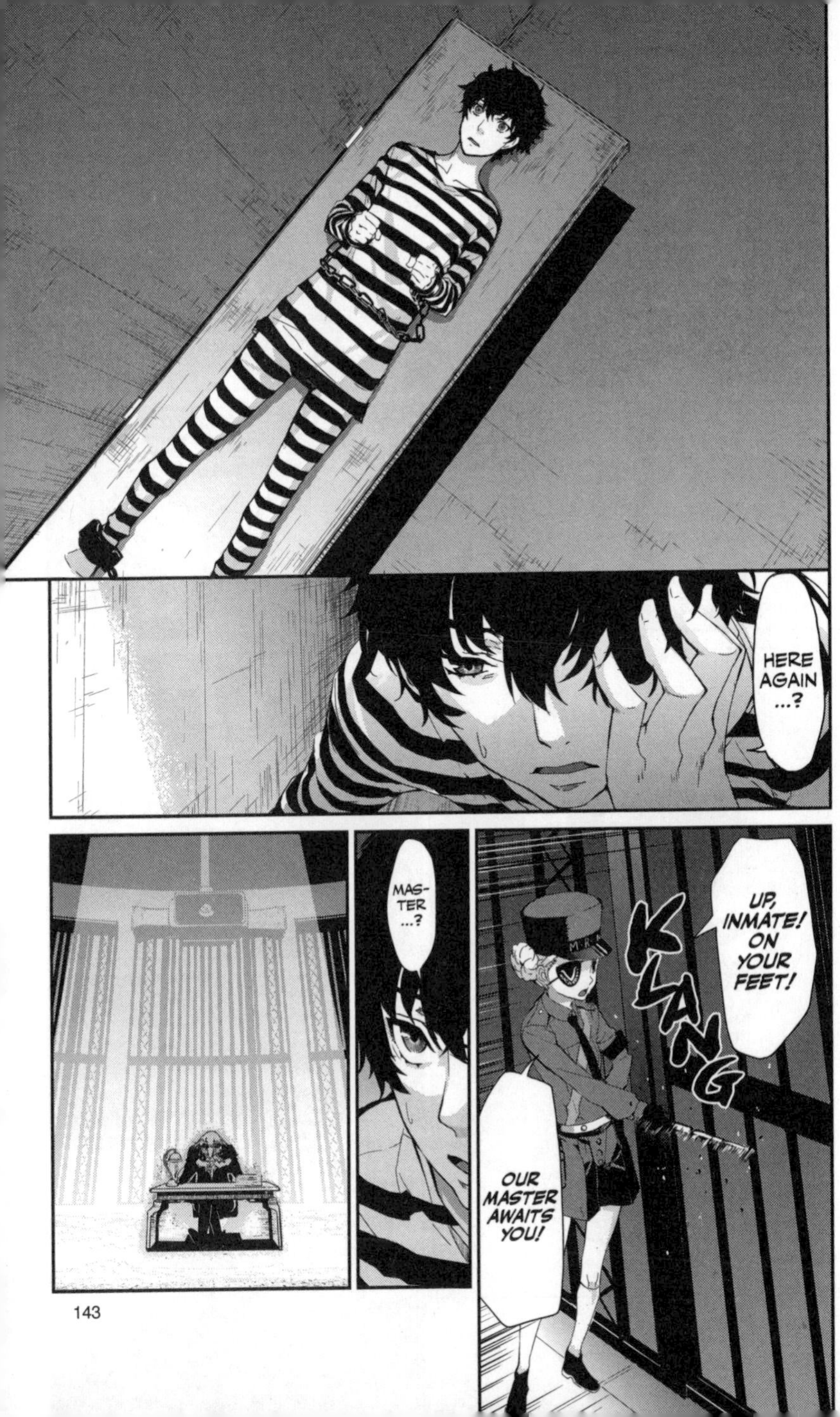
HERE AGAIN ...?
UP, INMATE! ON YOUR FEET!
KLANG
OUR MASTER AWAITS YOU!
MAS-TER ...?

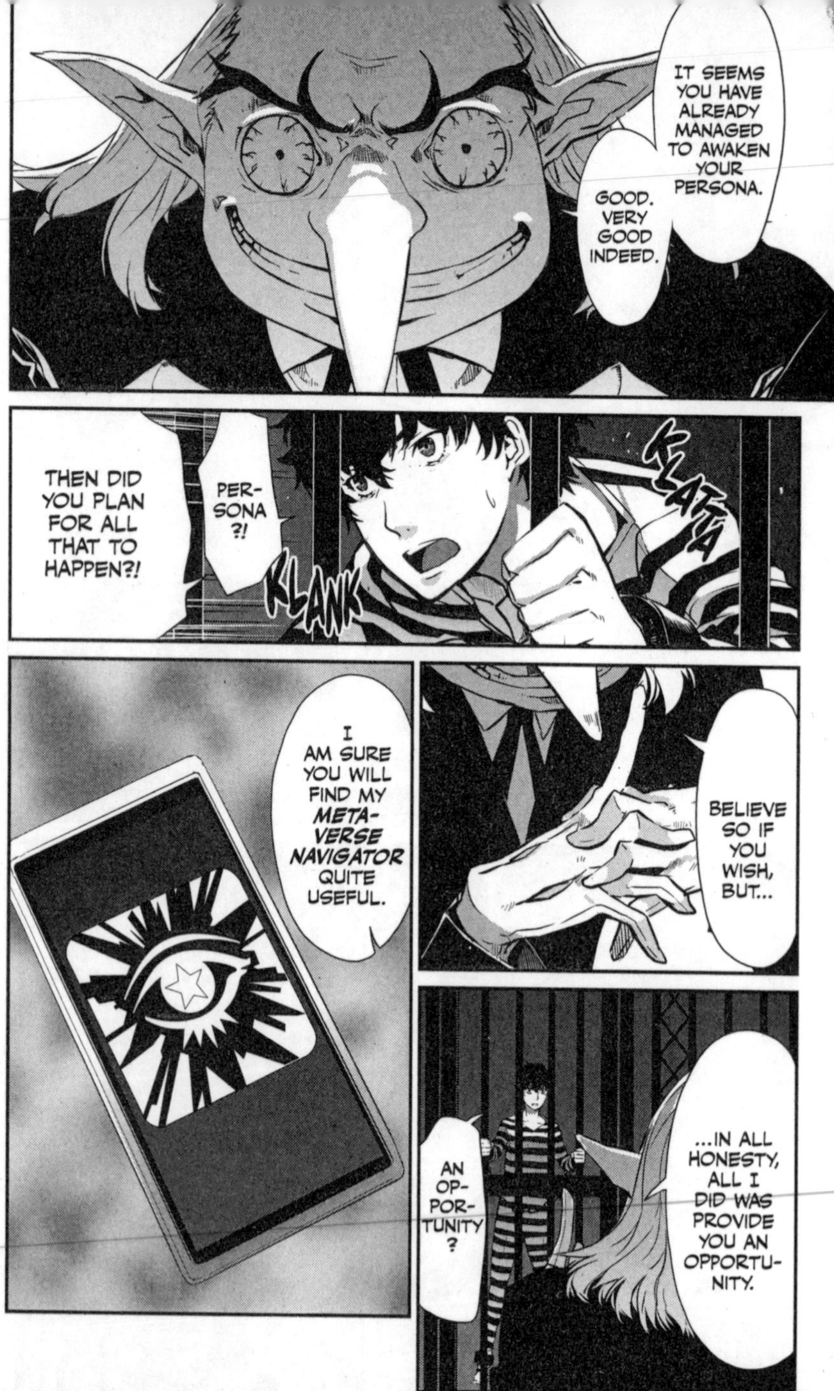
IT SEEMS YOU HAVE ALREADY MANAGED TO AWAKEN YOUR PERSONA.
GOOD. VERY GOOD INDEED.
KLATTA
PER-SONA?!
THEN DID YOU PLAN FOR ALL THAT TO HAPPEN?!
KLANK
BELIEVE SO IF YOU WISH, BUT...
...IN ALL HONESTY, ALL I DID WAS PROVIDE YOU AN OPPORTU-NITY.
AN OP-POR-TUNITY?
I AM SURE YOU WILL FIND MY *META-VERSE NAVIGATOR* QUITE USEFUL.

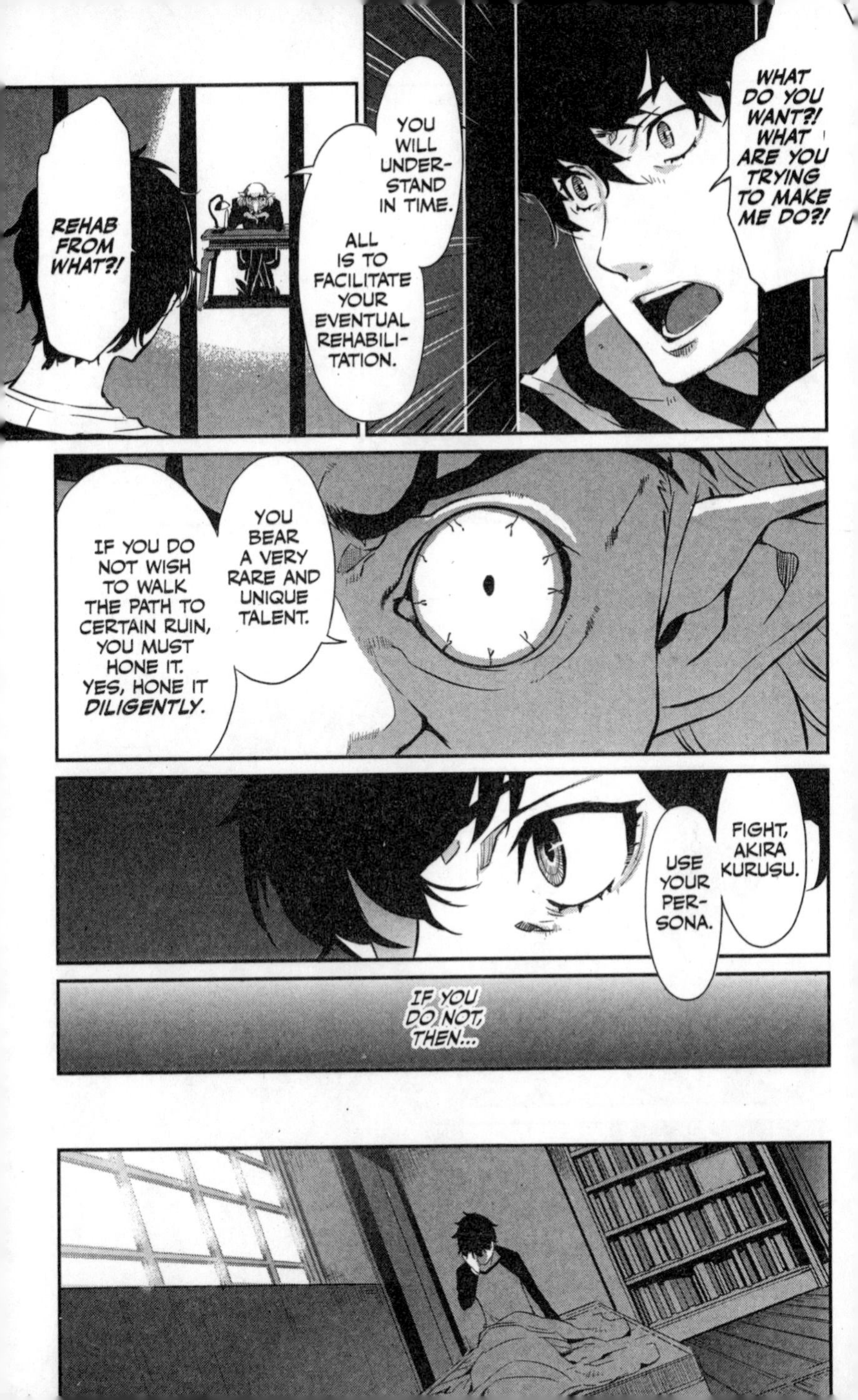
WHAT DO YOU WANT?! WHAT ARE YOU TRYING TO MAKE ME DO?!
YOU WILL UNDER-STAND IN TIME.
ALL IS TO FACILITATE YOUR EVENTUAL REHABILI-TATION.
REHAB FROM WHAT?!
YOU BEAR A VERY RARE AND UNIQUE TALENT.
IF YOU DO NOT WISH TO WALK THE PATH TO CERTAIN RUIN, YOU MUST HONE IT. YES, HONE IT *DILIGENTLY*.
FIGHT, AKIRA KURUSU.
USE YOUR PER-SONA.
IF YOU DO NOT, THEN...

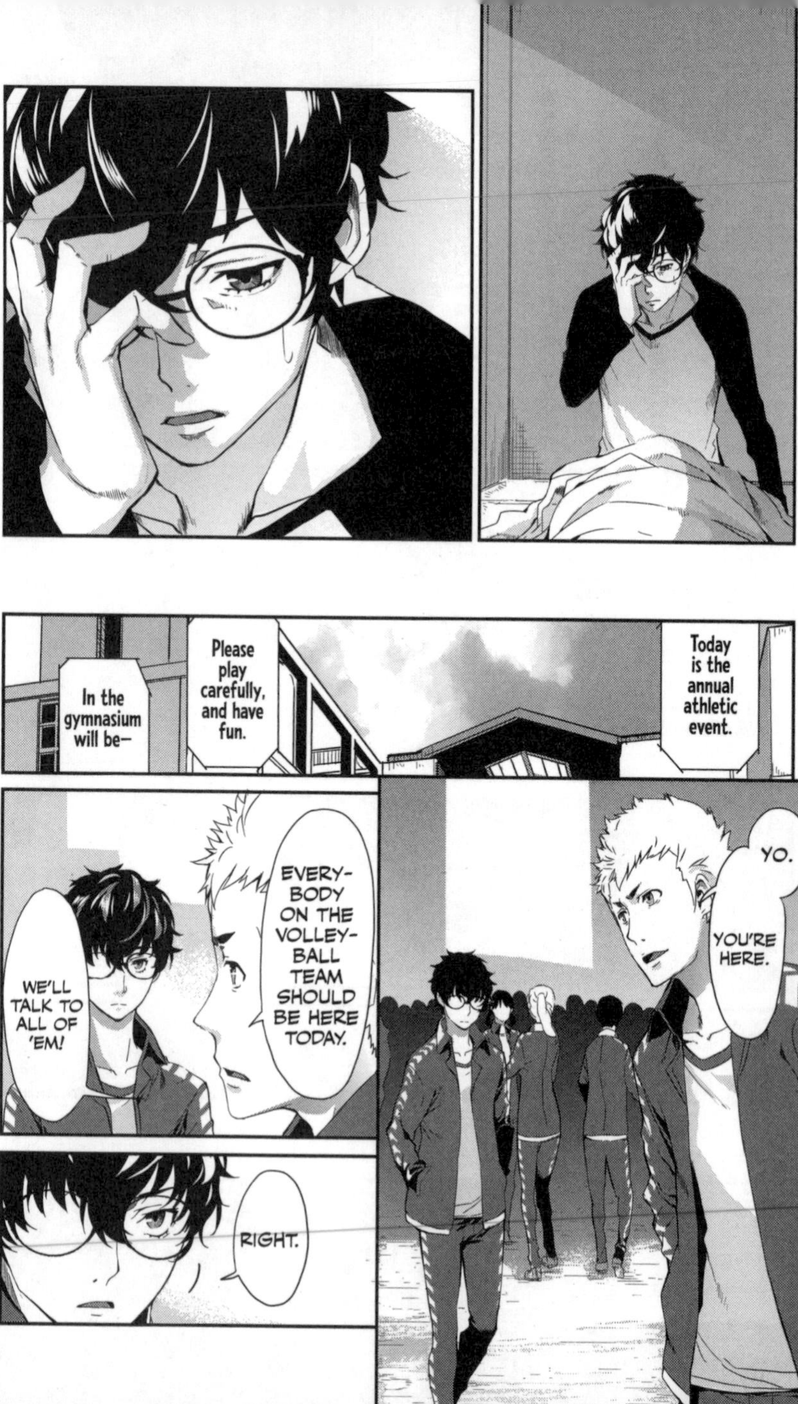

Today is the annual athletic event.
Please play carefully, and have fun.
In the gymnasium will be—
YO.
YOU'RE HERE.
EVERY-BODY ON THE VOLLEY-BALL TEAM SHOULD BE HERE TODAY.
WE'LL TALK TO ALL OF 'EM!
RIGHT.

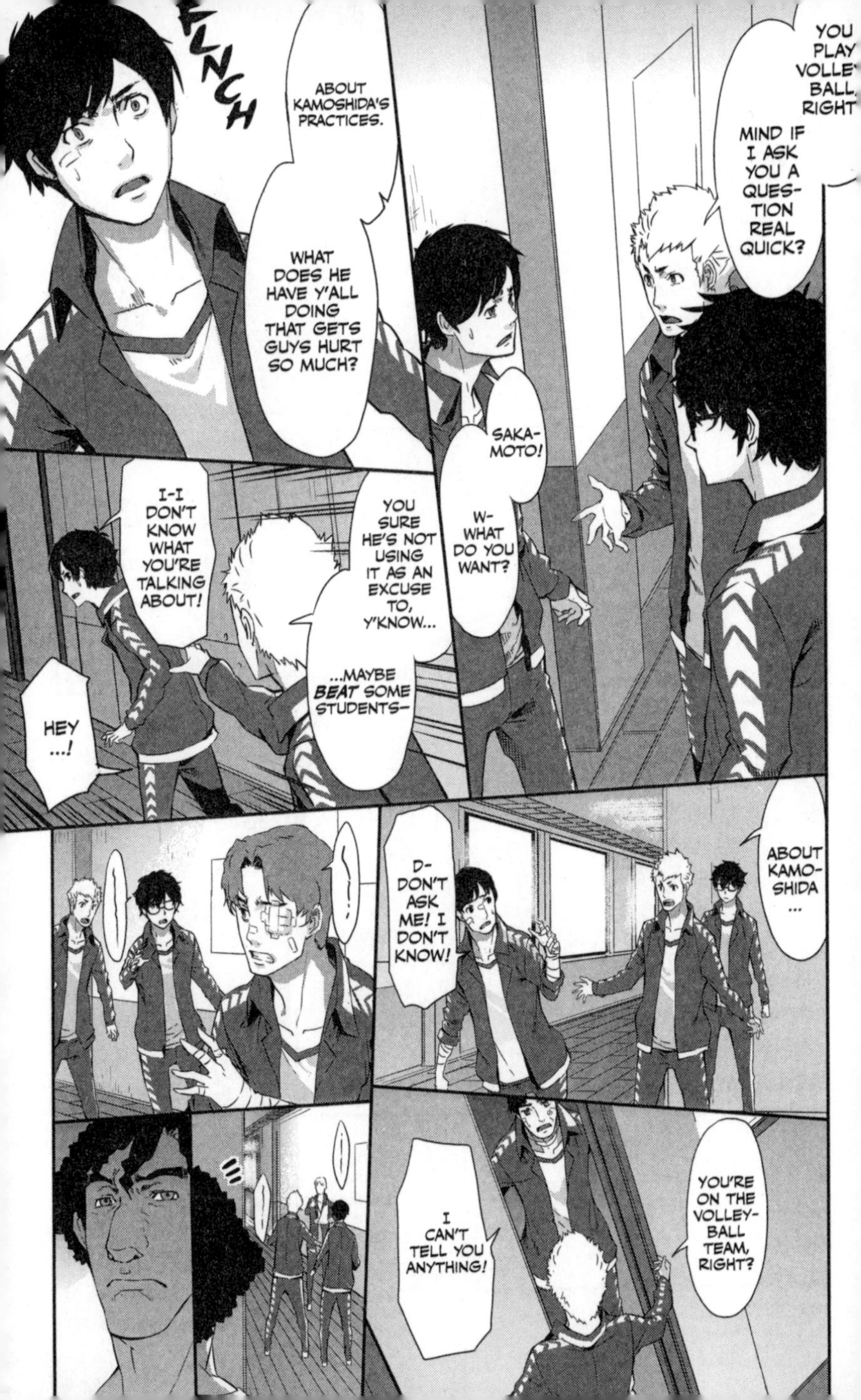
YOU PLAY VOLLEYBALL, RIGHT
MIND IF I ASK YOU A QUESTION REAL QUICK?
SAKA-MOTO!
W-WHAT DO YOU WANT?
ABOUT KAMOSHIDA'S PRACTICES.
WHAT DOES HE HAVE Y'ALL DOING THAT GETS GUYS HURT SO MUCH?
FLINCH
YOU SURE HE'S NOT USING IT AS AN EXCUSE TO, Y'KNOW...
...MAYBE *BEAT* SOME STUDENTS—
I-I DON'T KNOW WHAT YOU'RE TALKING ABOUT!
HEY ...!
ABOUT KAMO-SHIDA ...
D-DON'T ASK ME! I DON'T KNOW!
!
!
YOU'RE ON THE VOLLEY-BALL TEAM, RIGHT?
I CAN'T TELL YOU ANYTHING!
!
!

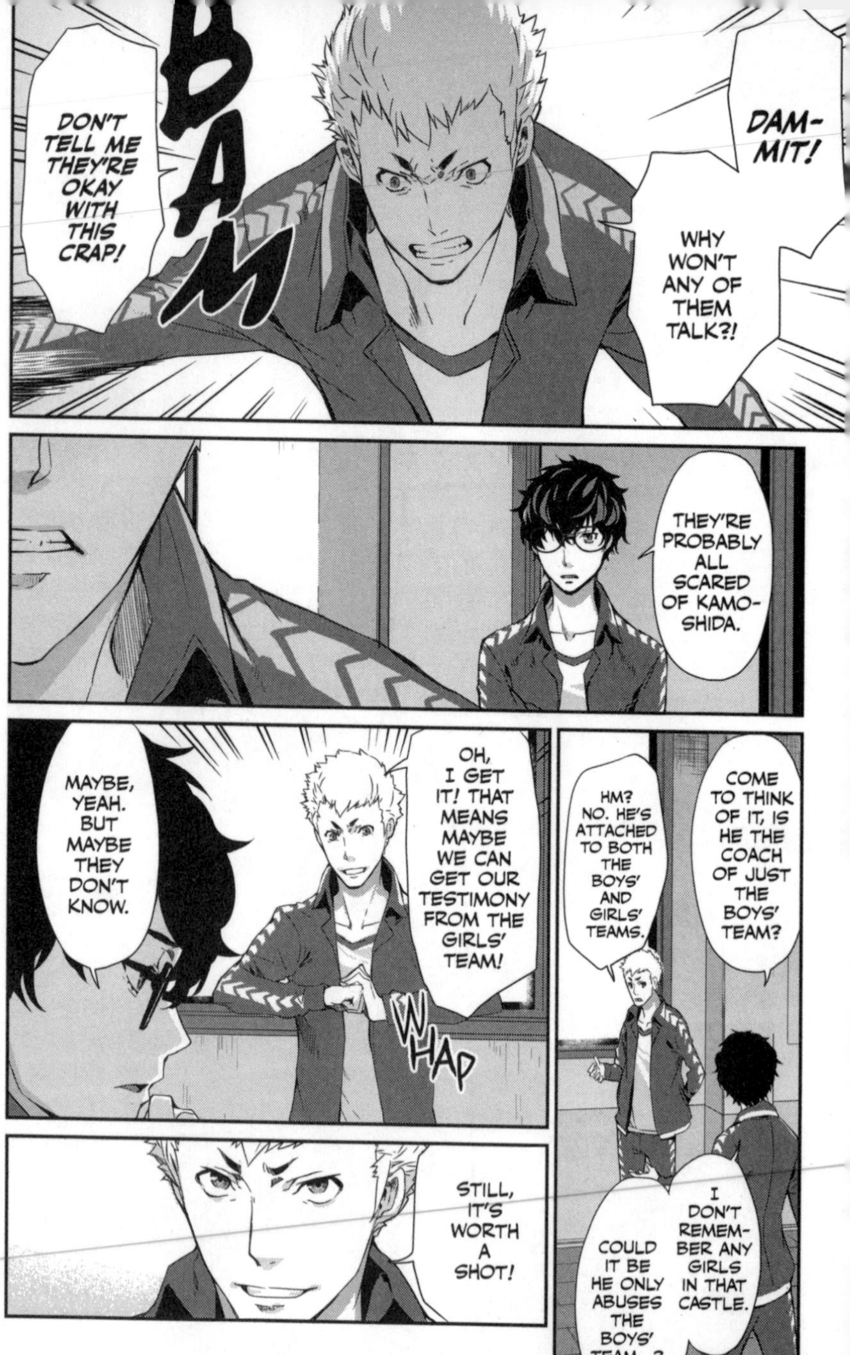
DAM-MIT!
WHY WON'T ANY OF THEM TALK?!
DON'T TELL ME THEY'RE OKAY WITH THIS CRAP!
BAM
THEY'RE PROBABLY ALL SCARED OF KAMO-SHIDA.
COME TO THINK OF IT, IS HE THE COACH OF JUST THE BOYS' TEAM?
HM? NO. HE'S ATTACHED TO BOTH THE BOYS' AND GIRLS' TEAMS.
I DON'T REMEM-BER ANY GIRLS IN THAT CASTLE.
COULD IT BE HE ONLY ABUSES THE BOYS' TEAM...?
OH, I GET IT! THAT MEANS MAYBE WE CAN GET OUR TESTIMONY FROM THE GIRLS' TEAM!
MAYBE, YEAH. BUT MAYBE THEY DON'T KNOW.
WHAP
STILL, IT'S WORTH A SHOT!

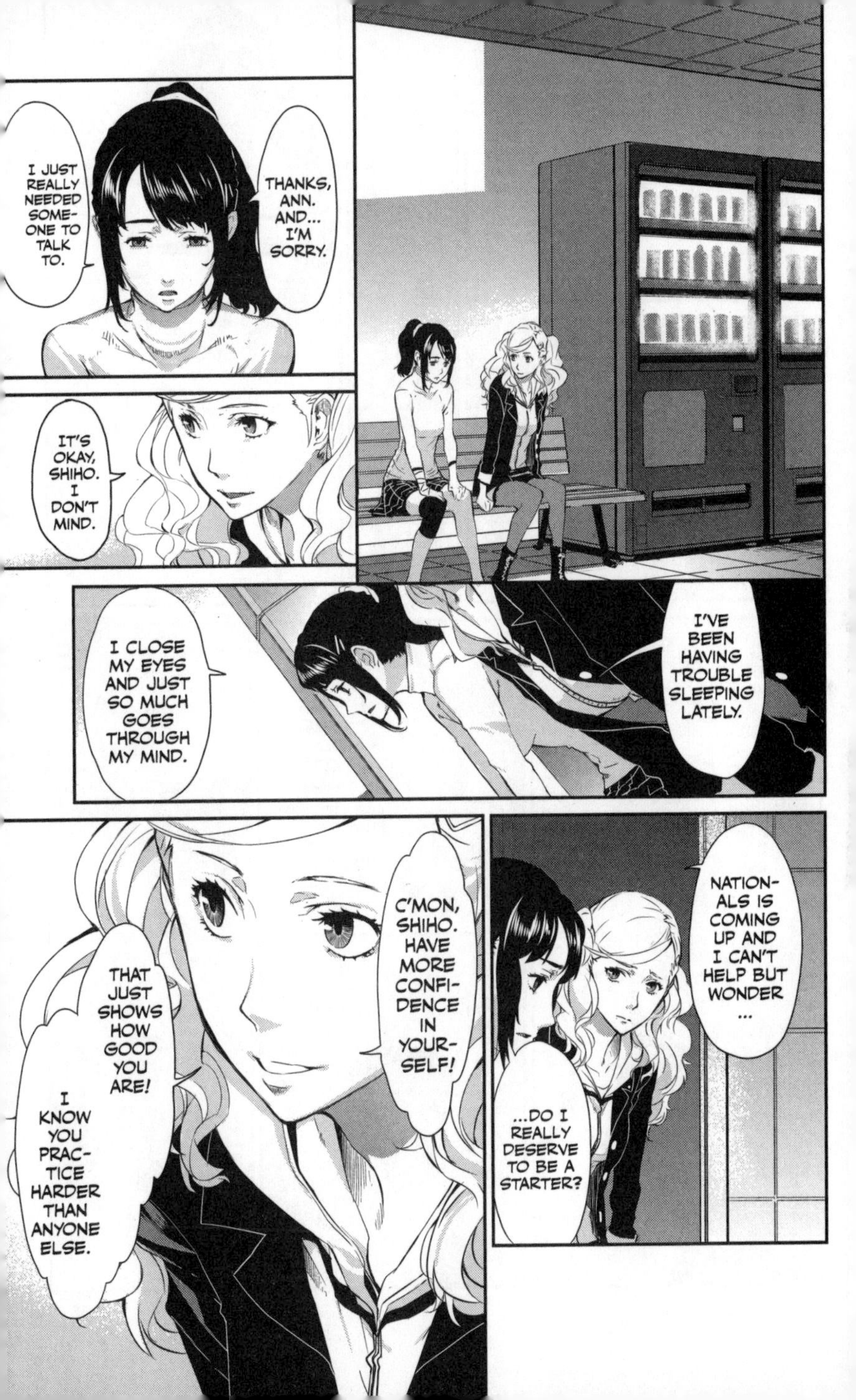
THANKS, ANN. AND... I'M SORRY.
I JUST REALLY NEEDED SOMEONE TO TALK TO.
IT'S OKAY, SHIHO. I DON'T MIND.
I'VE BEEN HAVING TROUBLE SLEEPING LATELY.
I CLOSE MY EYES AND JUST SO MUCH GOES THROUGH MY MIND.
NATIONALS IS COMING UP AND I CAN'T HELP BUT WONDER...
...DO I REALLY DESERVE TO BE A STARTER?
C'MON, SHIHO. HAVE MORE CONFIDENCE IN YOURSELF!
THAT JUST SHOWS HOW GOOD YOU ARE!
I KNOW YOU PRACTICE HARDER THAN ANYONE ELSE.

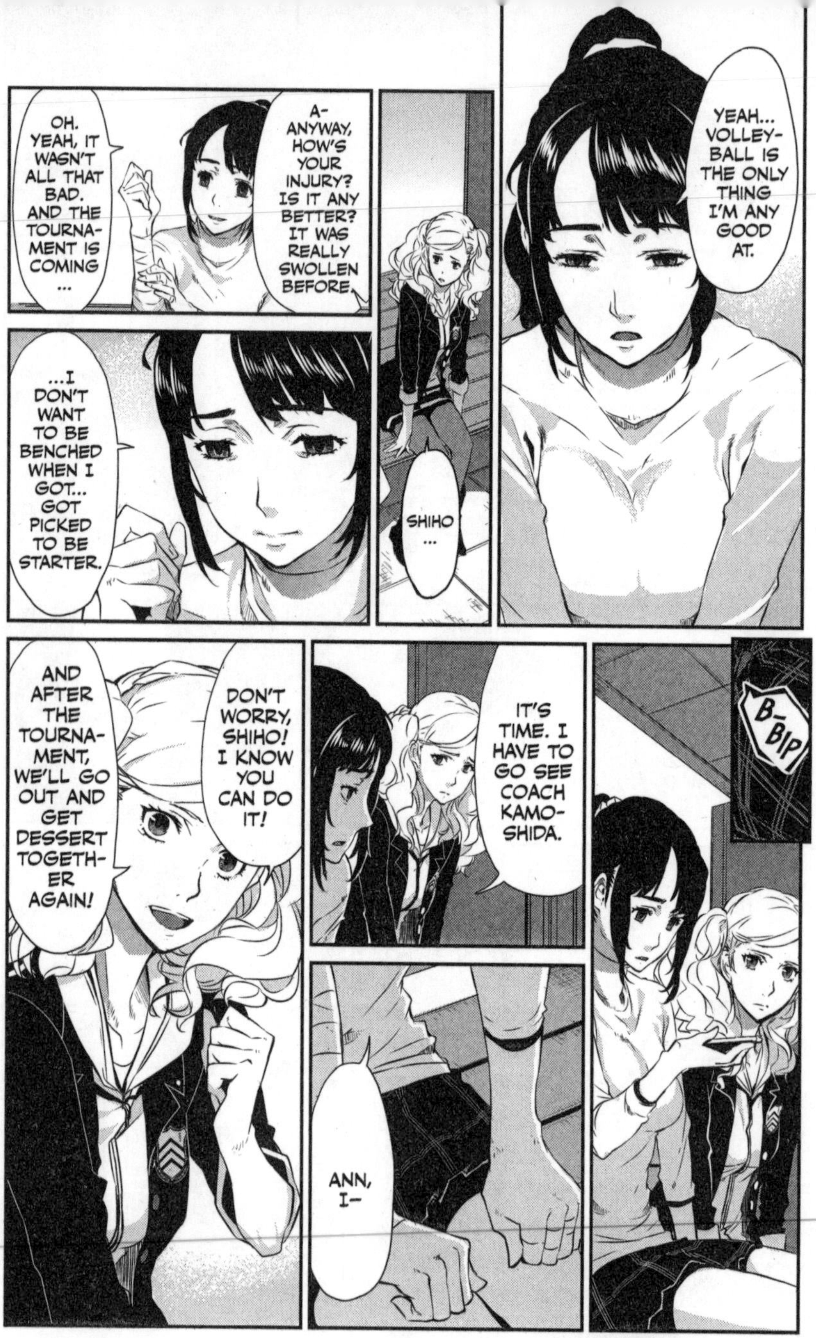
YEAH... VOLLEYBALL IS THE ONLY THING I'M ANY GOOD AT.
A- ANYWAY, HOW'S YOUR INJURY? IS IT ANY BETTER? IT WAS REALLY SWOLLEN BEFORE.
OH. YEAH, IT WASN'T ALL THAT BAD. AND THE TOURNAMENT IS COMING ...
...I DON'T WANT TO BE BENCHED WHEN I GOT... GOT PICKED TO BE STARTER.
SHIHO ...
B-BIP
IT'S TIME. I HAVE TO GO SEE COACH KAMOSHIDA.
ANN, I—
DON'T WORRY, SHIHO! I KNOW YOU CAN DO IT!
AND AFTER THE TOURNAMENT, WE'LL GO OUT AND GET DESSERT TOGETHER AGAIN!

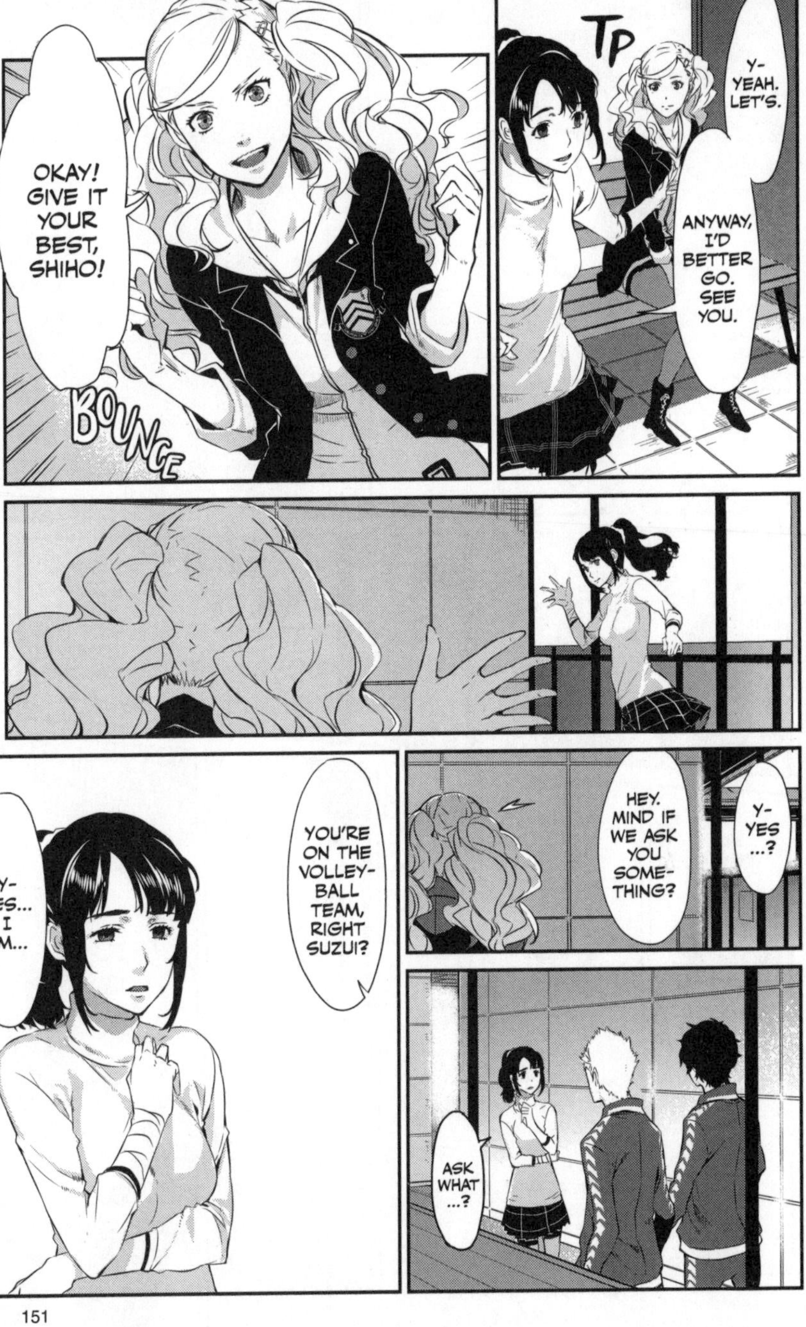
TP
Y-YEAH. LET'S.
ANYWAY, I'D BETTER GO. SEE YOU.
OKAY! GIVE IT YOUR BEST, SHIHO!
BOUNCE
HEY. MIND IF WE ASK YOU SOME-THING?
Y-YES ...?
ASK WHAT ...?
YOU'RE ON THE VOLLEY-BALL TEAM, RIGHT SUZUI?
Y-YES... I AM...

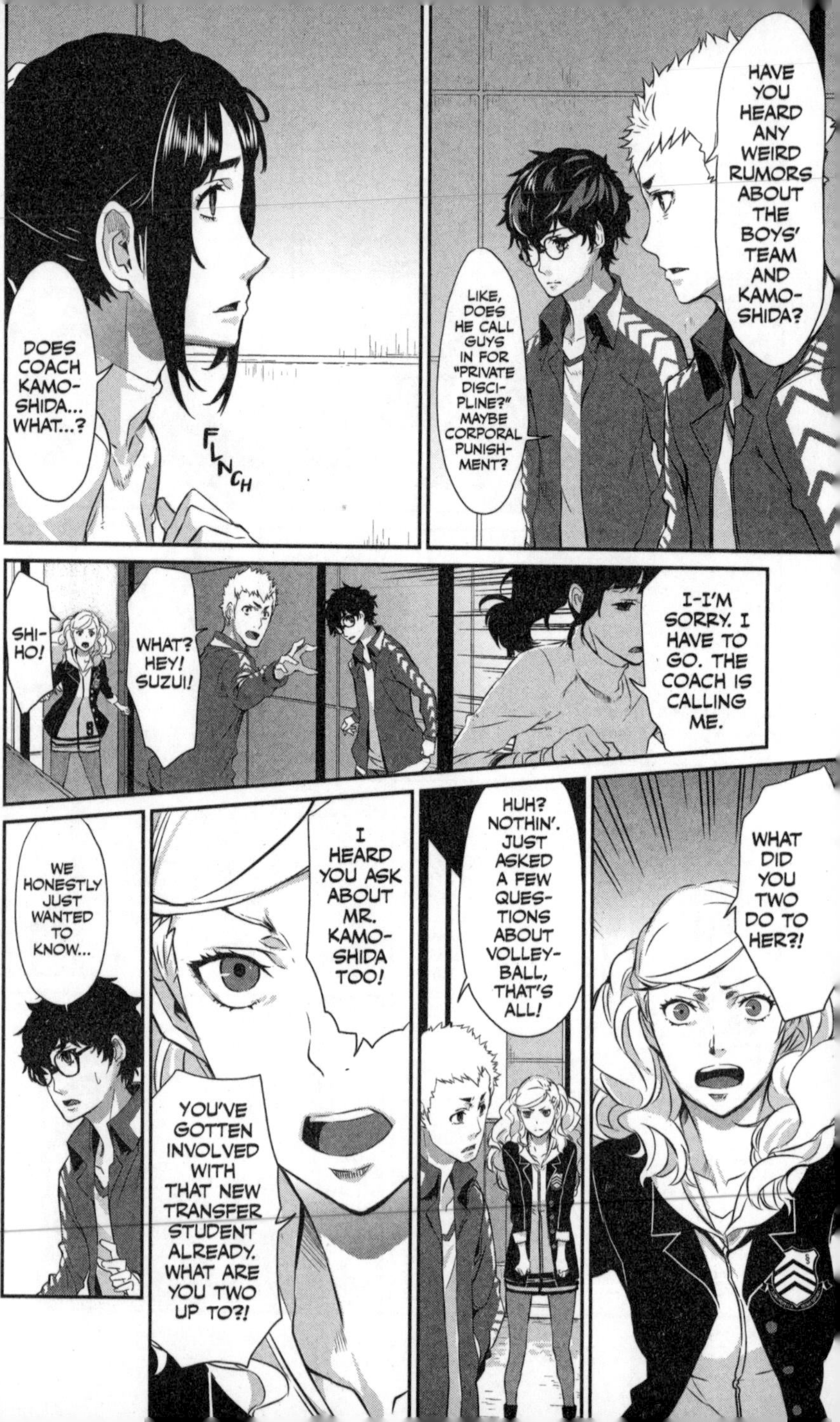
HAVE YOU HEARD ANY WEIRD RUMORS ABOUT THE BOYS' TEAM AND KAMO-SHIDA?
LIKE, DOES HE CALL GUYS IN FOR "PRIVATE DISCI-PLINE?" MAYBE CORPORAL PUNISH-MENT?
FLNCH
DOES COACH KAMO-SHIDA... WHAT...?
I-I'M SORRY. I HAVE TO GO. THE COACH IS CALLING ME.
WHAT? HEY! SUZUI!
SHI-HO!
WHAT DID YOU TWO DO TO HER?!
HUH? NOTHIN'. JUST ASKED A FEW QUES-TIONS ABOUT VOLLEY-BALL, THAT'S ALL!
I HEARD YOU ASK ABOUT MR. KAMO-SHIDA TOO!
YOU'VE GOTTEN INVOLVED WITH THAT NEW TRANSFER STUDENT ALREADY. WHAT ARE YOU TWO UP TO?!
WE HONESTLY JUST WANTED TO KNOW...

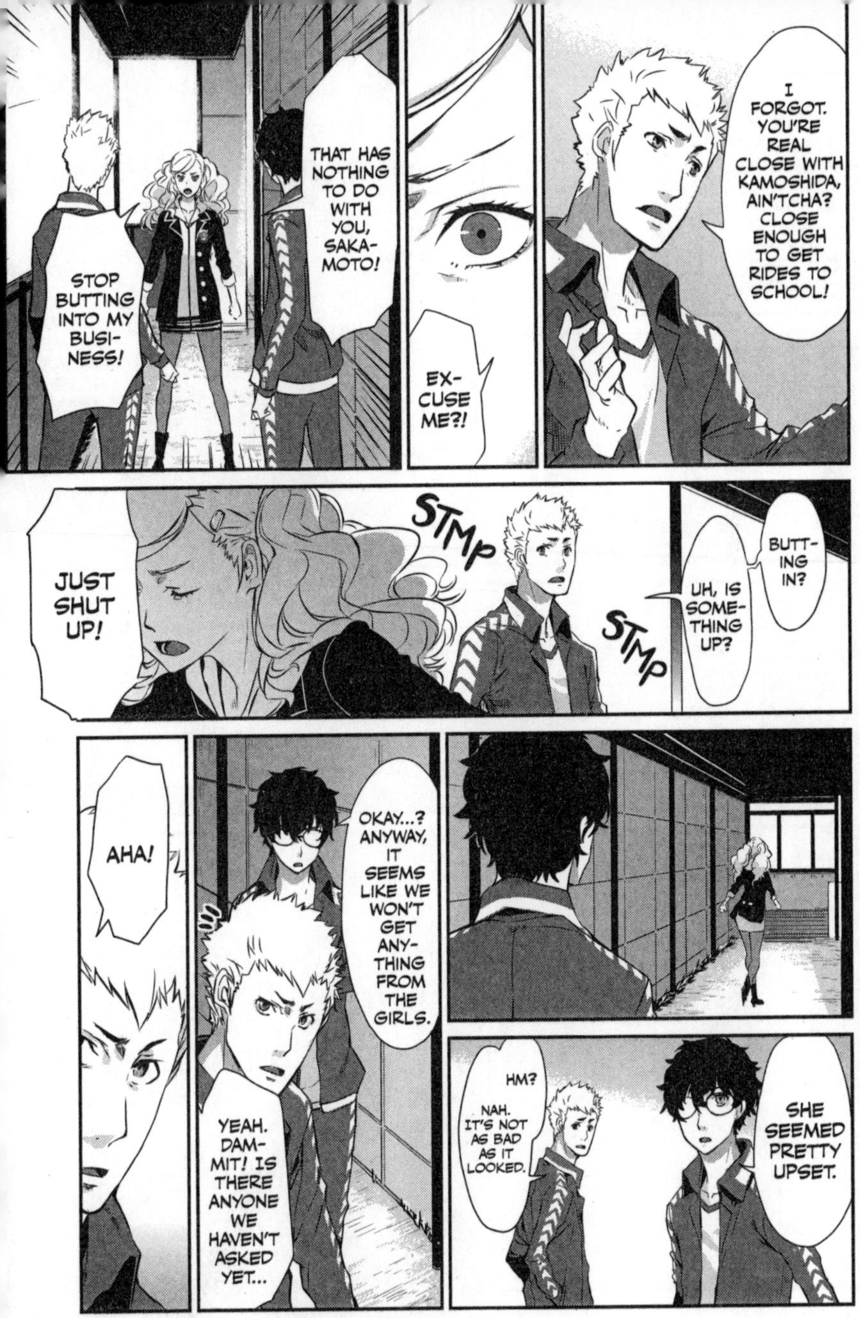
I FORGOT. YOU'RE REAL CLOSE WITH KAMOSHIDA, AIN'TCHA? CLOSE ENOUGH TO GET RIDES TO SCHOOL!
EXCUSE ME?!
THAT HAS NOTHING TO DO WITH YOU, SAKAMOTO!
STOP BUTTING INTO MY BUSINESS!
BUTTING IN?
UH, IS SOMETHING UP?
STMP
STMP
JUST SHUT UP!
SHE SEEMED PRETTY UPSET.
HM?
NAH. IT'S NOT AS BAD AS IT LOOKED.
OKAY...? ANYWAY, IT SEEMS LIKE WE WON'T GET ANYTHING FROM THE GIRLS.
YEAH. DAMMIT! IS THERE ANYONE WE HAVEN'T ASKED YET...
AHA!

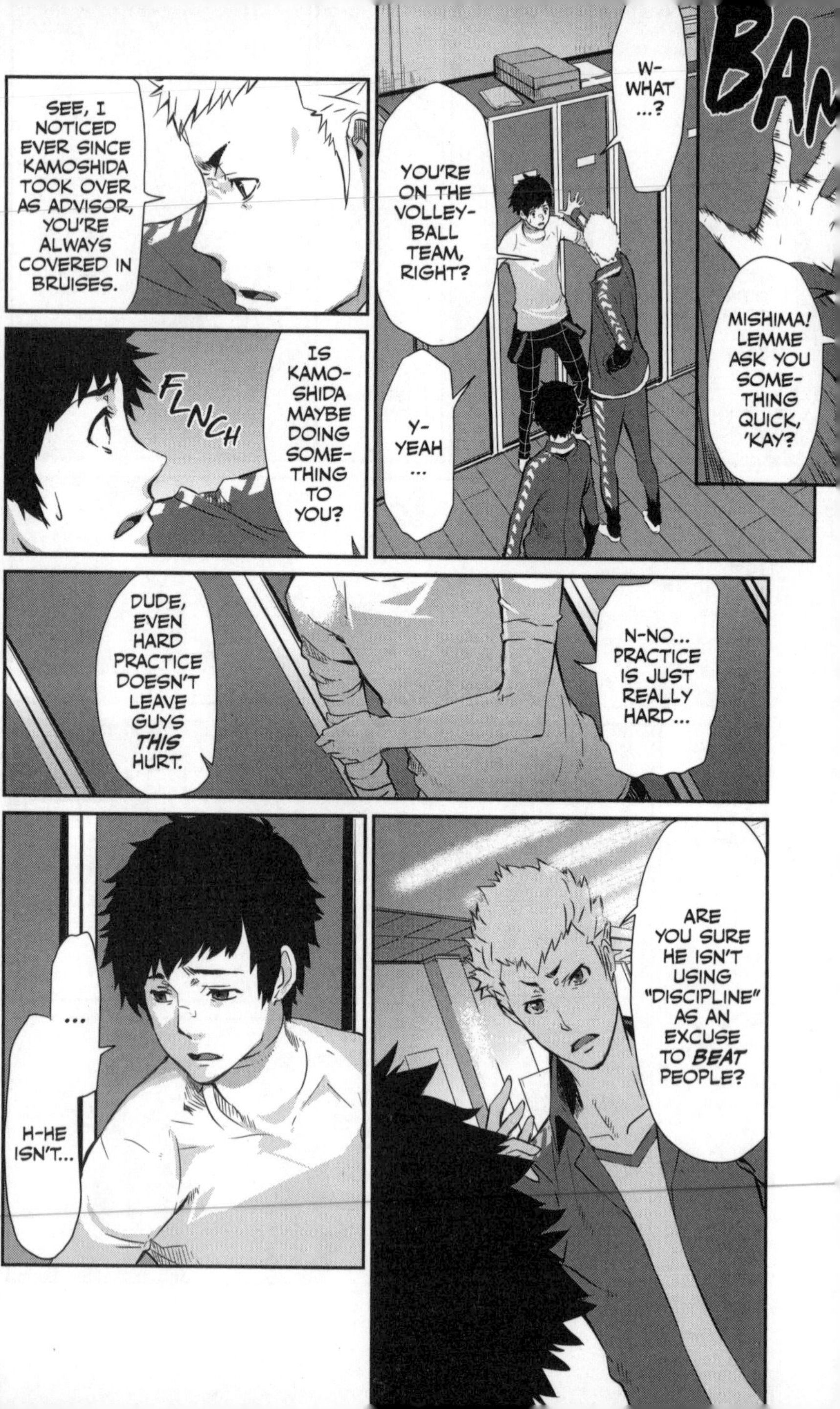
BAM
MISHIMA! LEMME ASK YOU SOMETHING QUICK, 'KAY?
W-WHAT ...?
YOU'RE ON THE VOLLEYBALL TEAM, RIGHT?
Y-YEAH ...
SEE, I NOTICED EVER SINCE KAMOSHIDA TOOK OVER AS ADVISOR, YOU'RE ALWAYS COVERED IN BRUISES.
FLNCH
IS KAMOSHIDA MAYBE DOING SOMETHING TO YOU?
N-NO... PRACTICE IS JUST REALLY HARD...
DUDE, EVEN HARD PRACTICE DOESN'T LEAVE GUYS THIS HURT.
ARE YOU SURE HE ISN'T USING "DISCIPLINE" AS AN EXCUSE TO BEAT PEOPLE?
...
H-HE ISN'T...

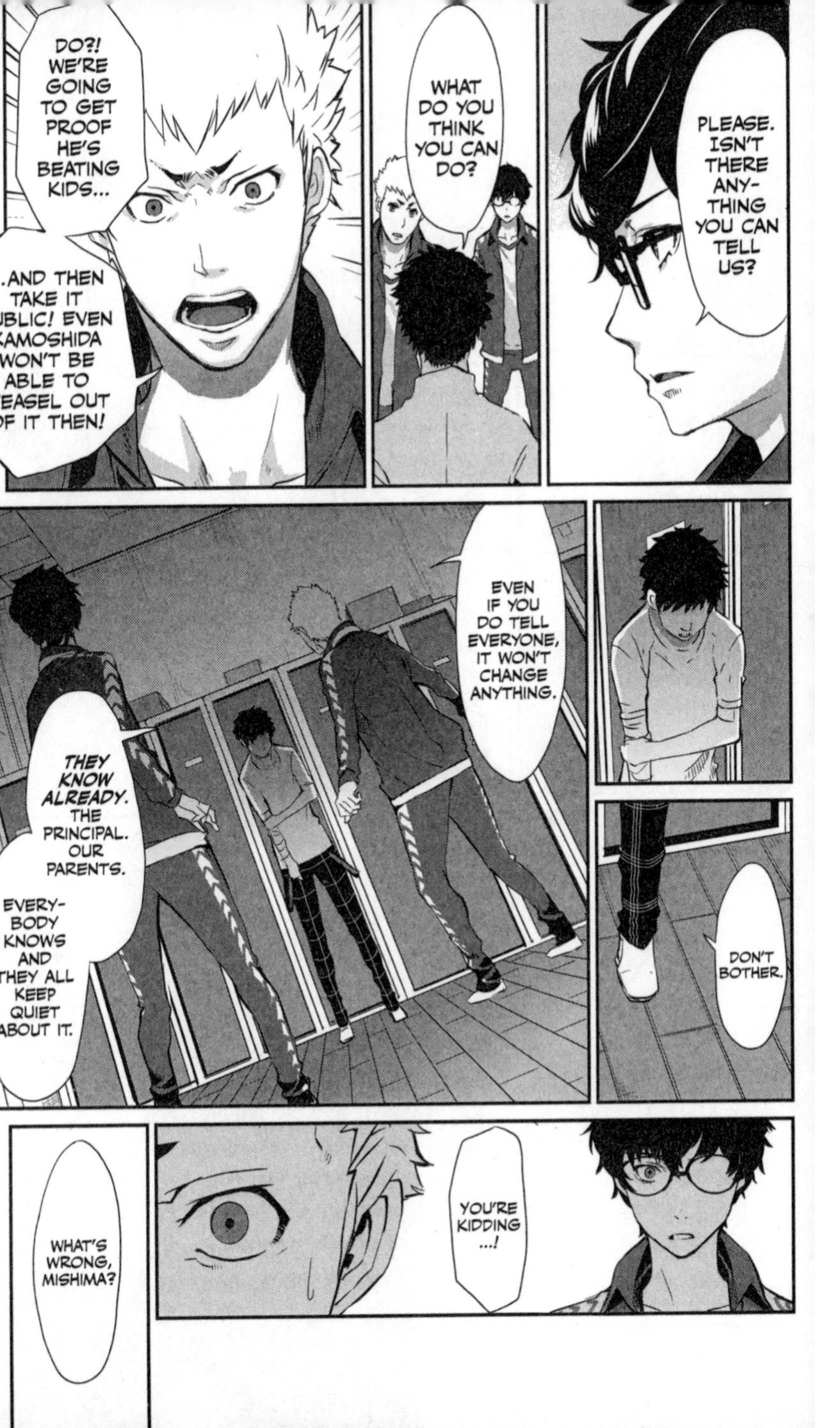
PLEASE. ISN'T THERE ANYTHING YOU CAN TELL US?
WHAT DO YOU THINK YOU CAN DO?
DO?! WE'RE GOING TO GET PROOF HE'S BEATING KIDS...
...AND THEN TAKE IT PUBLIC! EVEN KAMOSHIDA WON'T BE ABLE TO WEASEL OUT OF IT THEN!
DON'T BOTHER.
EVEN IF YOU DO TELL EVERYONE, IT WON'T CHANGE ANYTHING.
THEY KNOW ALREADY. THE PRINCIPAL. OUR PARENTS.
EVERYBODY KNOWS AND THEY ALL KEEP QUIET ABOUT IT.
YOU'RE KIDDING ...!
WHAT'S WRONG, MISHIMA?

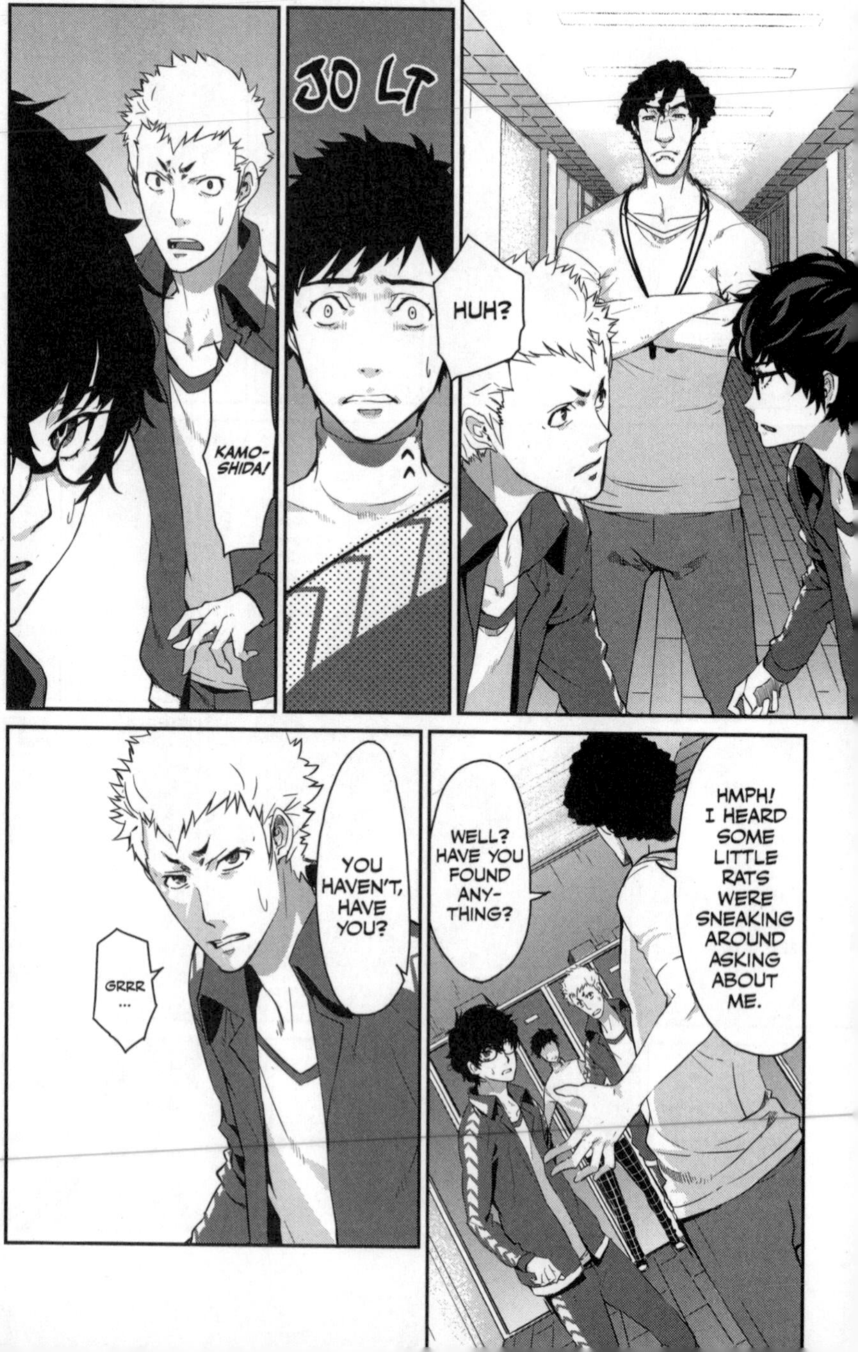
HUH?
JOLT
KAMO-SHIDA!
HMPH! I HEARD SOME LITTLE RATS WERE SNEAKING AROUND ASKING ABOUT ME.
WELL? HAVE YOU FOUND ANY-THING?
YOU HAVEN'T, HAVE YOU?
GRRR ...

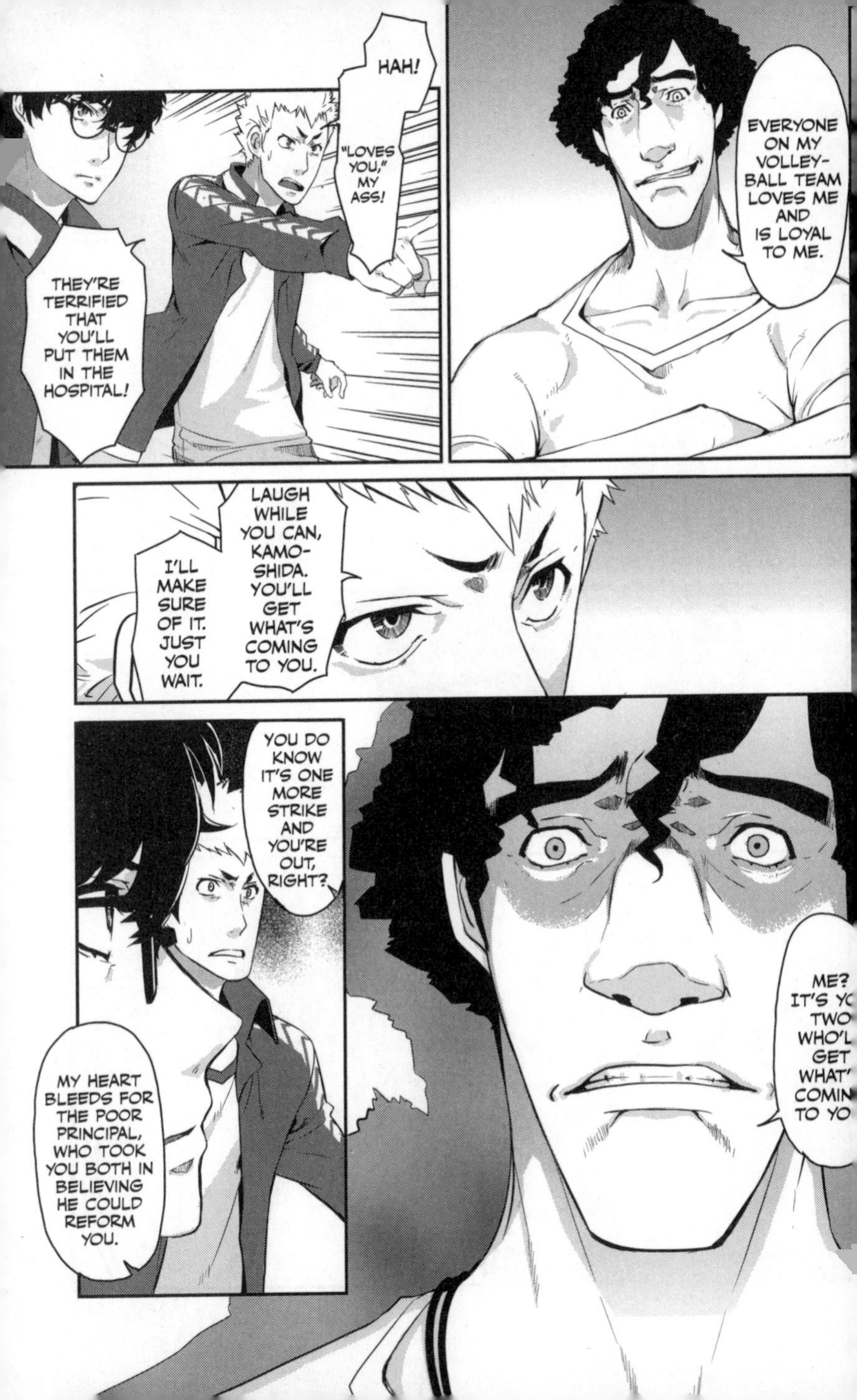

EVERYONE ON MY VOLLEY-BALL TEAM LOVES ME AND IS LOYAL TO ME.
HAH!
"LOVES YOU," MY ASS!
THEY'RE TERRIFIED THAT YOU'LL PUT THEM IN THE HOSPITAL!
LAUGH WHILE YOU CAN, KAMO-SHIDA. YOU'LL GET WHAT'S COMING TO YOU.
I'LL MAKE SURE OF IT. JUST YOU WAIT.
YOU DO KNOW IT'S ONE MORE STRIKE AND YOU'RE OUT, RIGHT?
ME? IT'S YO TWO WHO'L GET WHAT' COMIN TO YO
MY HEART BLEEDS FOR THE POOR PRINCIPAL, WHO TOOK YOU BOTH IN BELIEVING HE COULD REFORM YOU.

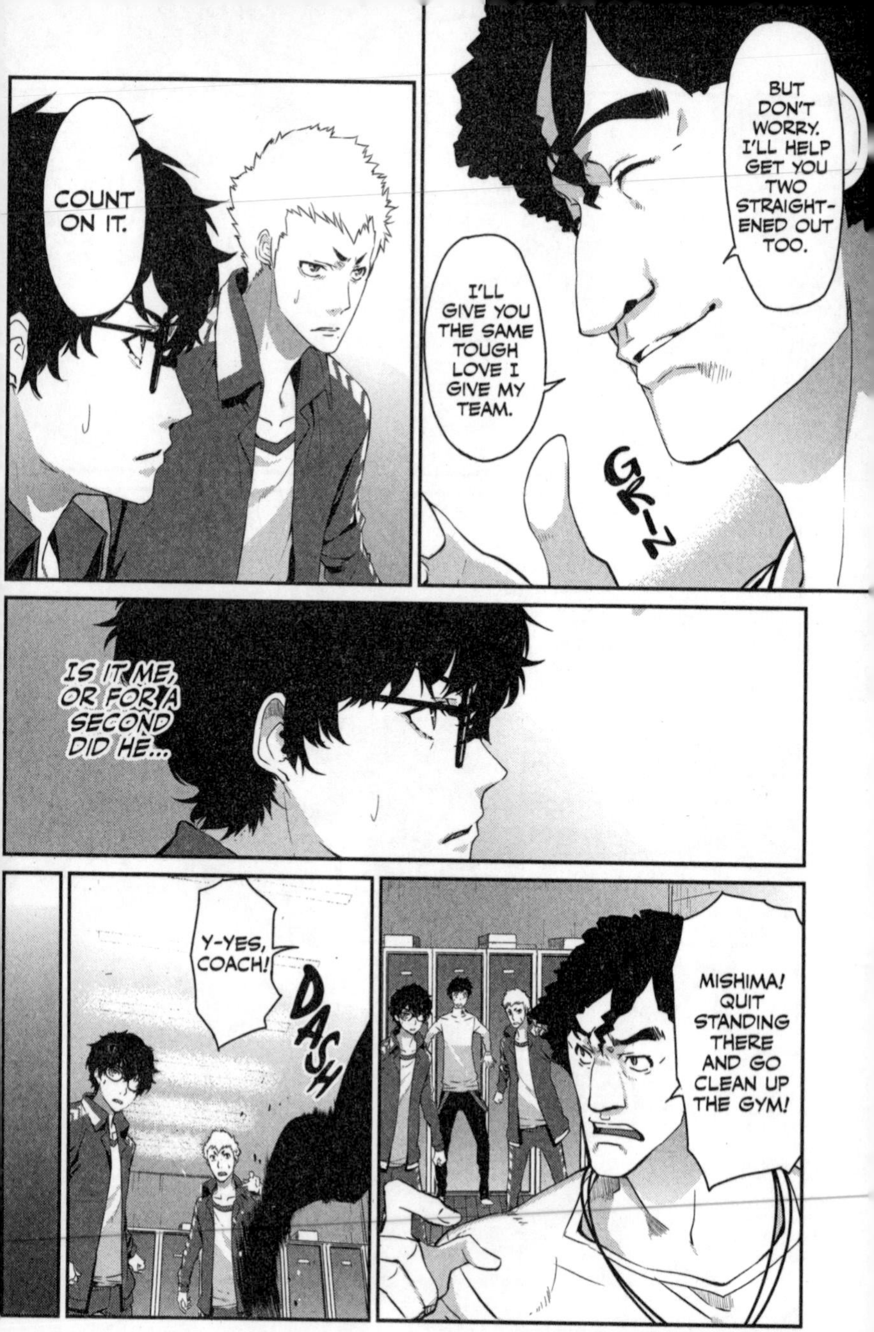
BUT DON'T WORRY. I'LL HELP GET YOU TWO STRAIGHT-ENED OUT TOO.
I'LL GIVE YOU THE SAME TOUGH LOVE I GIVE MY TEAM.
GRIN
COUNT ON IT.
IS IT ME, OR FOR A SECOND DID HE...
MISHIMA! QUIT STANDING THERE AND GO CLEAN UP THE GYM!
Y-YES, COACH!
DASH

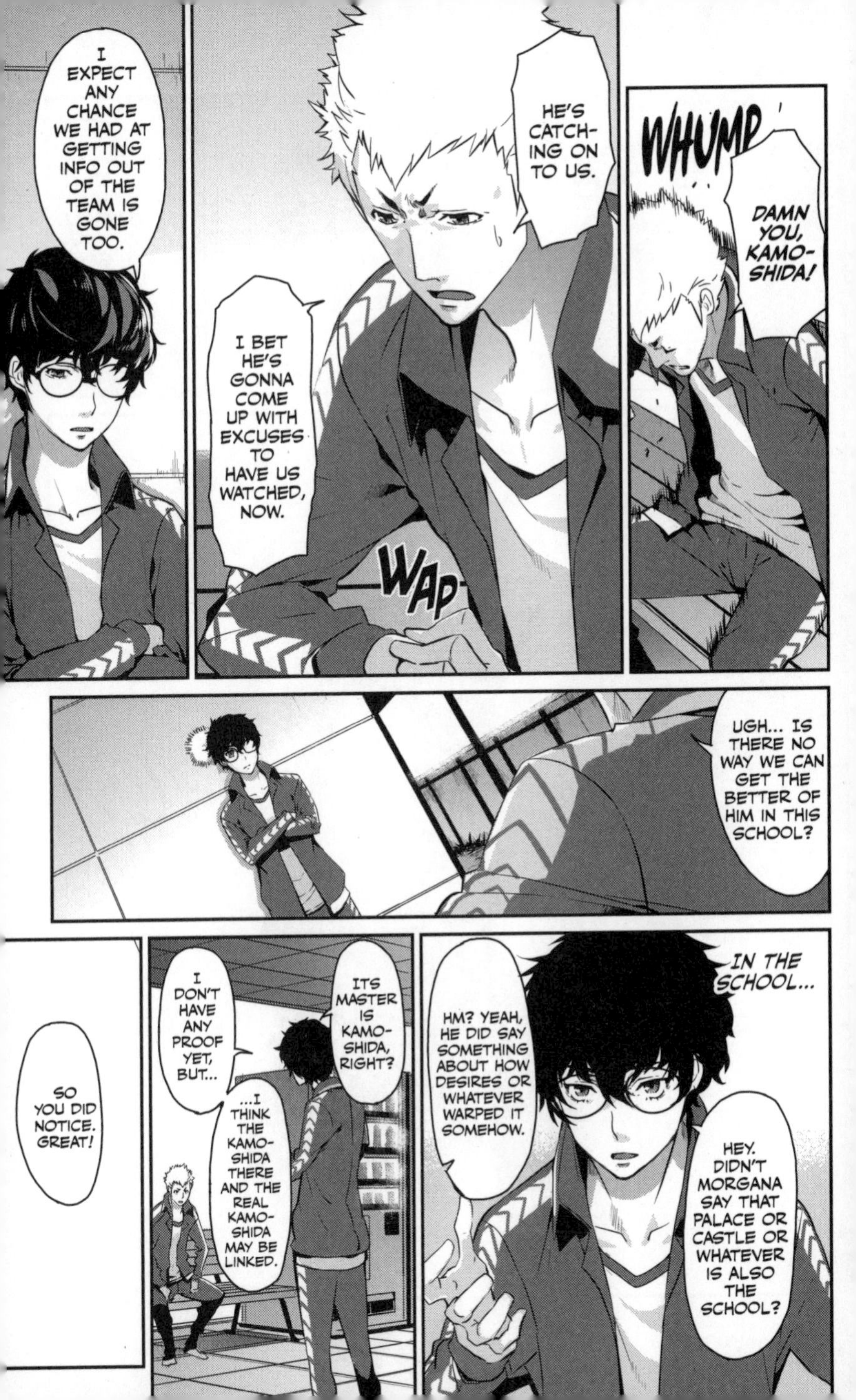
WHUMP
DAMN YOU, KAMOSHIDA!
HE'S CATCHING ON TO US.
I BET HE'S GONNA COME UP WITH EXCUSES TO HAVE US WATCHED, NOW.
WAP
I EXPECT ANY CHANCE WE HAD AT GETTING INFO OUT OF THE TEAM IS GONE TOO.
UGH... IS THERE NO WAY WE CAN GET THE BETTER OF HIM IN THIS SCHOOL?
IN THE SCHOOL...
HEY. DIDN'T MORGANA SAY THAT PALACE OR CASTLE OR WHATEVER IS ALSO THE SCHOOL?
HM? YEAH, HE DID SAY SOMETHING ABOUT HOW DESIRES OR WHATEVER WARPED IT SOMEHOW.
ITS MASTER IS KAMOSHIDA, RIGHT?
I DON'T HAVE ANY PROOF YET, BUT...
...I THINK THE KAMOSHIDA THERE AND THE REAL KAMOSHIDA MAY BE LINKED.
SO YOU DID NOTICE. GREAT!

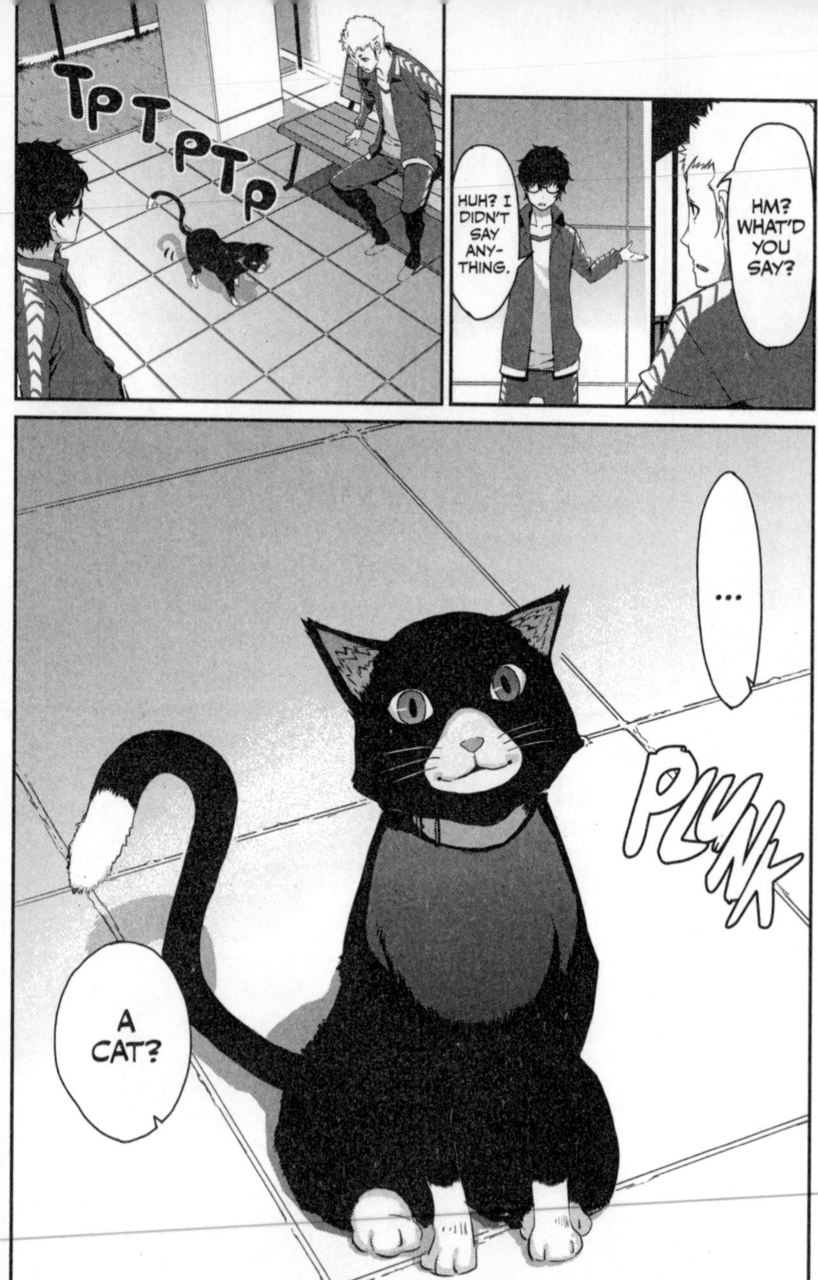
HM? WHAT'D YOU SAY?
HUH? I DIDN'T SAY ANY-THING.
TPTPTP
...
PLUNK
A CAT?

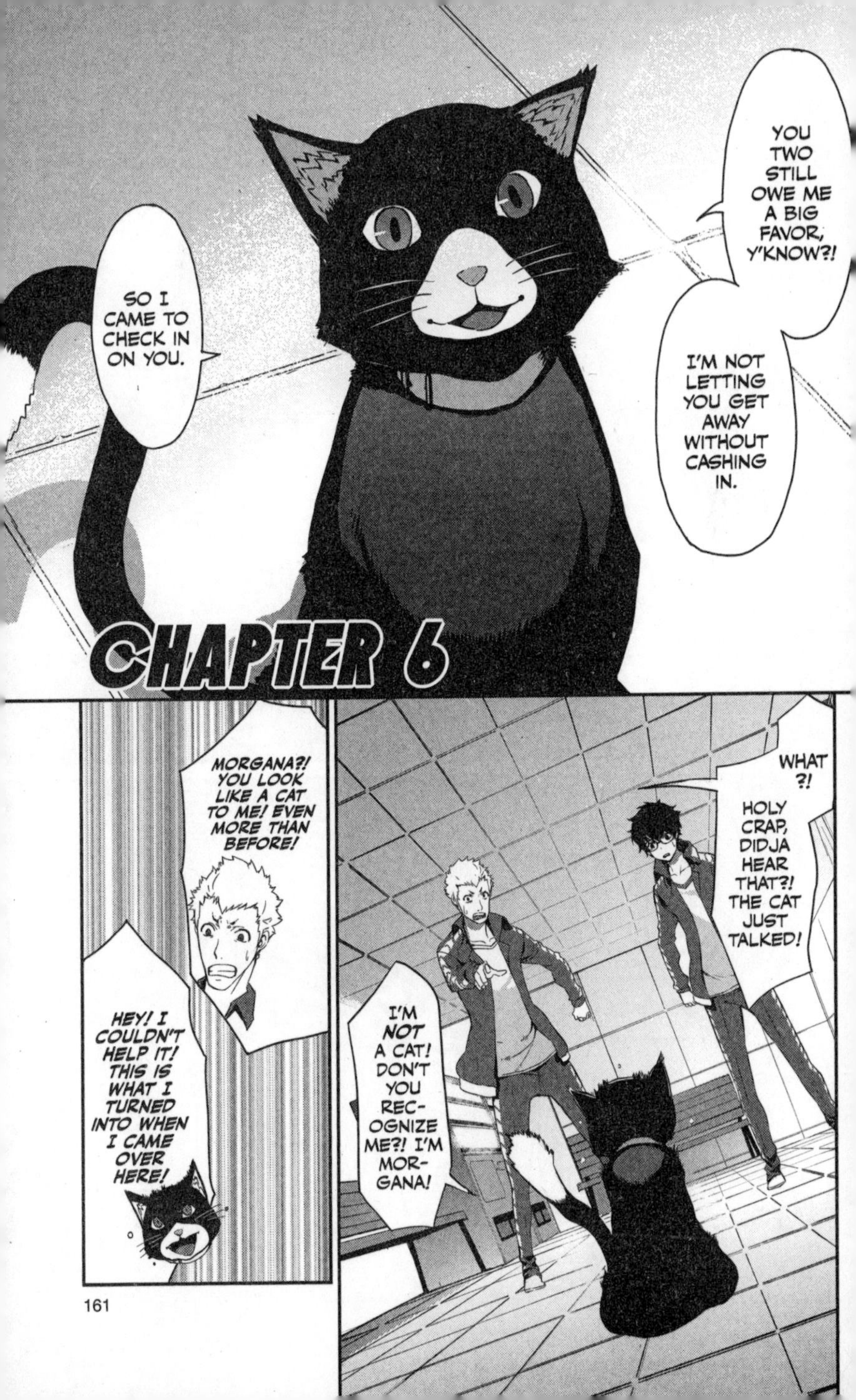
YOU TWO STILL OWE ME A BIG FAVOR, Y'KNOW?!
I'M NOT LETTING YOU GET AWAY WITHOUT CASHING IN.
SO I CAME TO CHECK IN ON YOU.
CHAPTER 6
WHAT?!
HOLY CRAP, DIDJA HEAR THAT?! THE CAT JUST TALKED!
I'M NOT A CAT! DON'T YOU REC-OGNIZE ME?! I'M MOR-GANA!
MORGANA?! YOU LOOK LIKE A CAT TO ME! EVEN MORE THAN BEFORE!
HEY! I COULDN'T HELP IT! THIS IS WHAT I TURNED INTO WHEN I CAME OVER HERE!

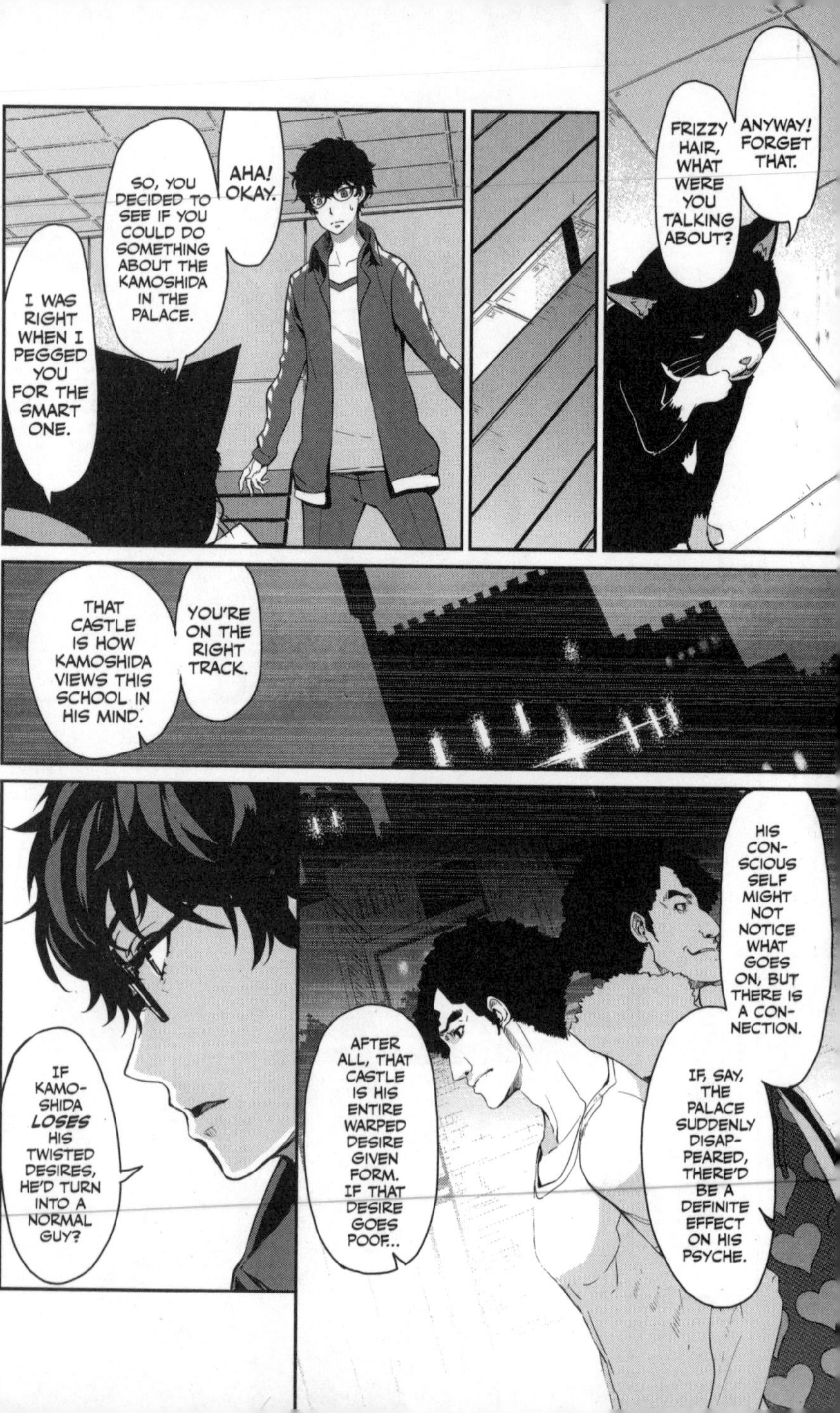
ANYWAY! FORGET THAT.
FRIZZY HAIR, WHAT WERE YOU TALKING ABOUT?
AHA! OKAY.
SO, YOU DECIDED TO SEE IF YOU COULD DO SOMETHING ABOUT THE KAMOSHIDA IN THE PALACE.
I WAS RIGHT WHEN I PEGGED YOU FOR THE SMART ONE.
YOU'RE ON THE RIGHT TRACK.
THAT CASTLE IS HOW KAMOSHIDA VIEWS THIS SCHOOL IN HIS MIND.
HIS CONSCIOUS SELF MIGHT NOT NOTICE WHAT GOES ON, BUT THERE IS A CONNECTION.
IF, SAY, THE PALACE SUDDENLY DISAPPEARED, THERE'D BE A DEFINITE EFFECT ON HIS PSYCHE.
AFTER ALL, THAT CASTLE IS HIS ENTIRE WARPED DESIRE GIVEN FORM. IF THAT DESIRE GOES POOF...
IF KAMOSHIDA *LOSES* HIS TWISTED DESIRES, HE'D TURN INTO A NORMAL GUY?

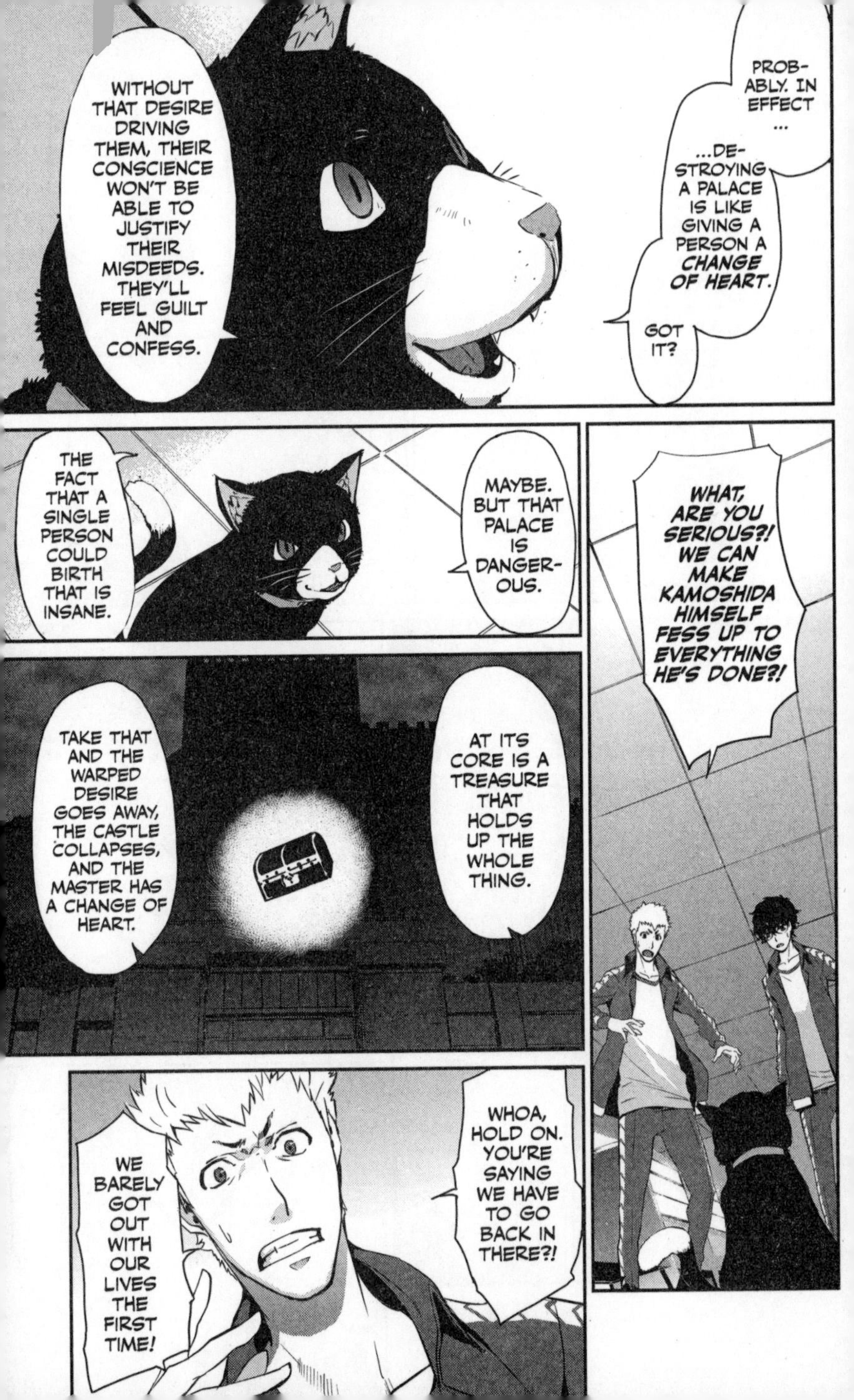
PROB-ABLY. IN EFFECT ...
...DE-STROYING A PALACE IS LIKE GIVING A PERSON A *CHANGE OF HEART*.
GOT IT?
WITHOUT THAT DESIRE DRIVING THEM, THEIR CONSCIENCE WON'T BE ABLE TO JUSTIFY THEIR MISDEEDS. THEY'LL FEEL GUILT AND CONFESS.
WHAT, ARE YOU SERIOUS?! WE CAN MAKE KAMOSHIDA HIMSELF FESS UP TO EVERYTHING HE'S DONE?!
MAYBE. BUT THAT PALACE IS DANGER-OUS.
THE FACT THAT A SINGLE PERSON COULD BIRTH THAT IS INSANE.
AT ITS CORE IS A TREASURE THAT HOLDS UP THE WHOLE THING.
TAKE THAT AND THE WARPED DESIRE GOES AWAY, THE CASTLE COLLAPSES, AND THE MASTER HAS A CHANGE OF HEART.
WHOA, HOLD ON. YOU'RE SAYING WE HAVE TO GO BACK IN THERE?!
WE BARELY GOT OUT WITH OUR LIVES THE FIRST TIME!

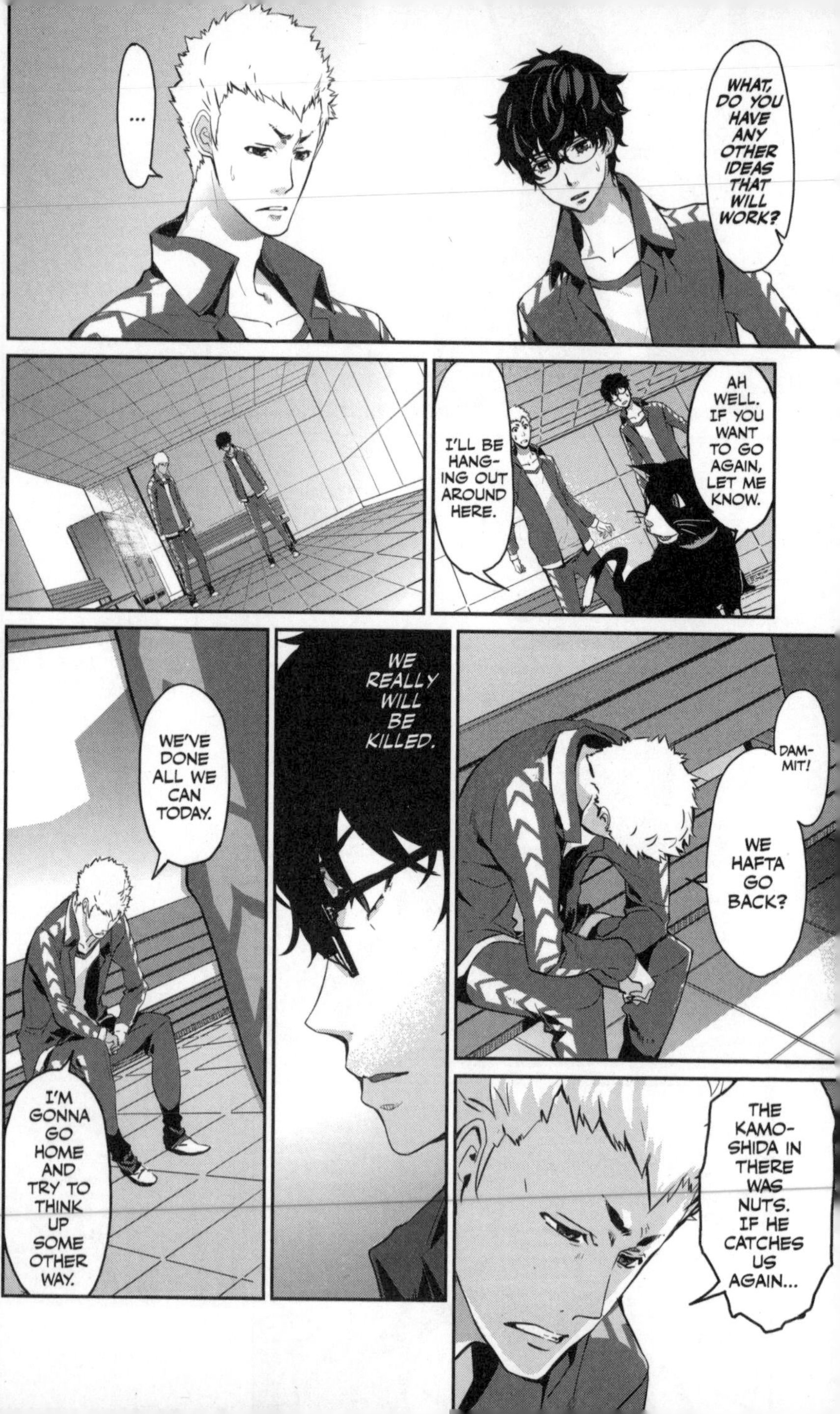
WHAT, DO YOU HAVE ANY OTHER IDEAS THAT WILL WORK?
...
AH WELL. IF YOU WANT TO GO AGAIN, LET ME KNOW.
I'LL BE HANGING OUT AROUND HERE.
DAMMIT!
WE HAFTA GO BACK?
THE KAMOSHIDA IN THERE WAS NUTS. IF HE CATCHES US AGAIN...
WE REALLY WILL BE KILLED.
WE'VE DONE ALL WE CAN TODAY.
I'M GONNA GO HOME AND TRY TO THINK UP SOME OTHER WAY.

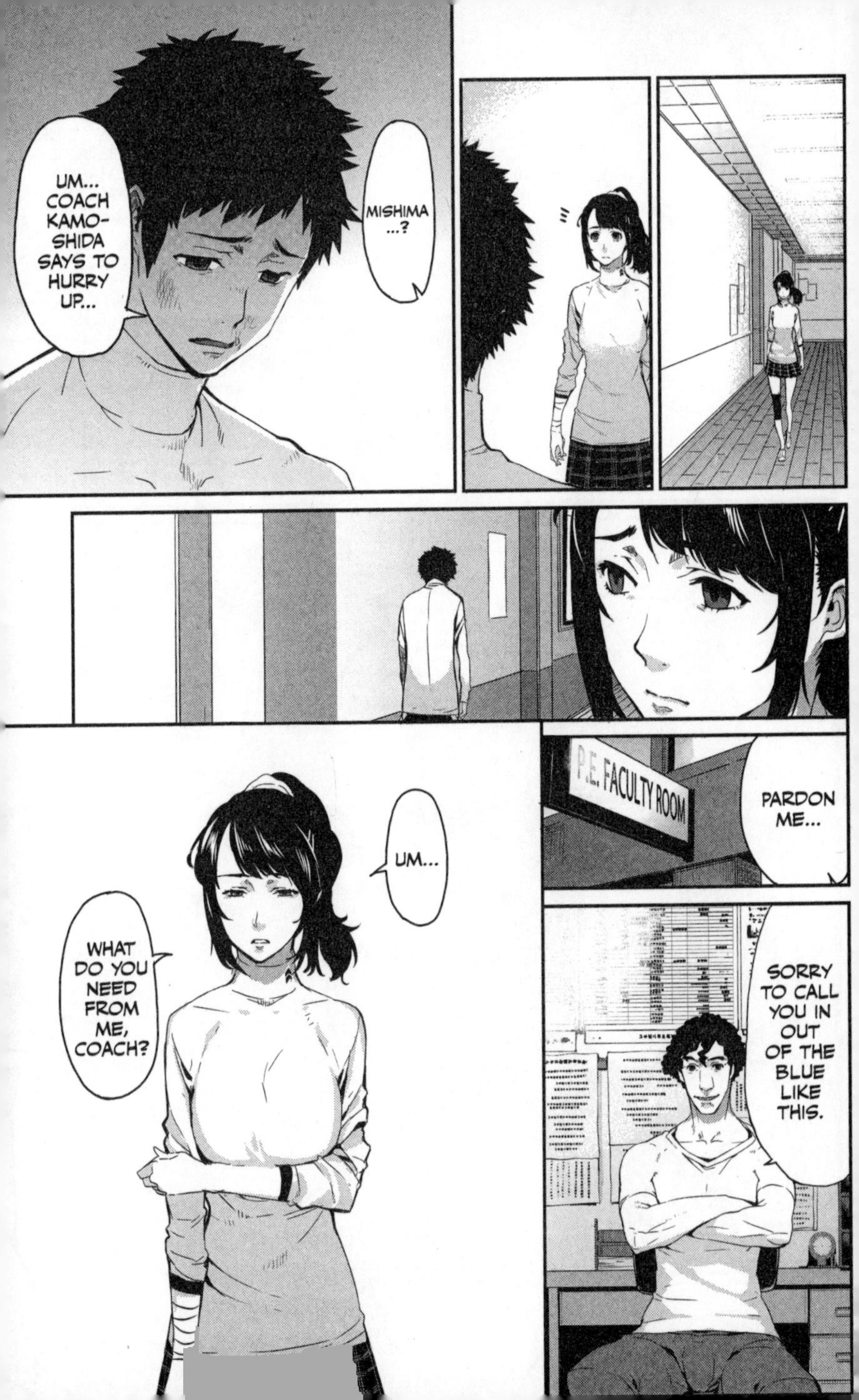
MISHIMA ...?
UM... COACH KAMO-SHIDA SAYS TO HURRY UP...
P.E. FACULTY ROOM
PARDON ME...
SORRY TO CALL YOU IN OUT OF THE BLUE LIKE THIS.
UM...
WHAT DO YOU NEED FROM ME, COACH?

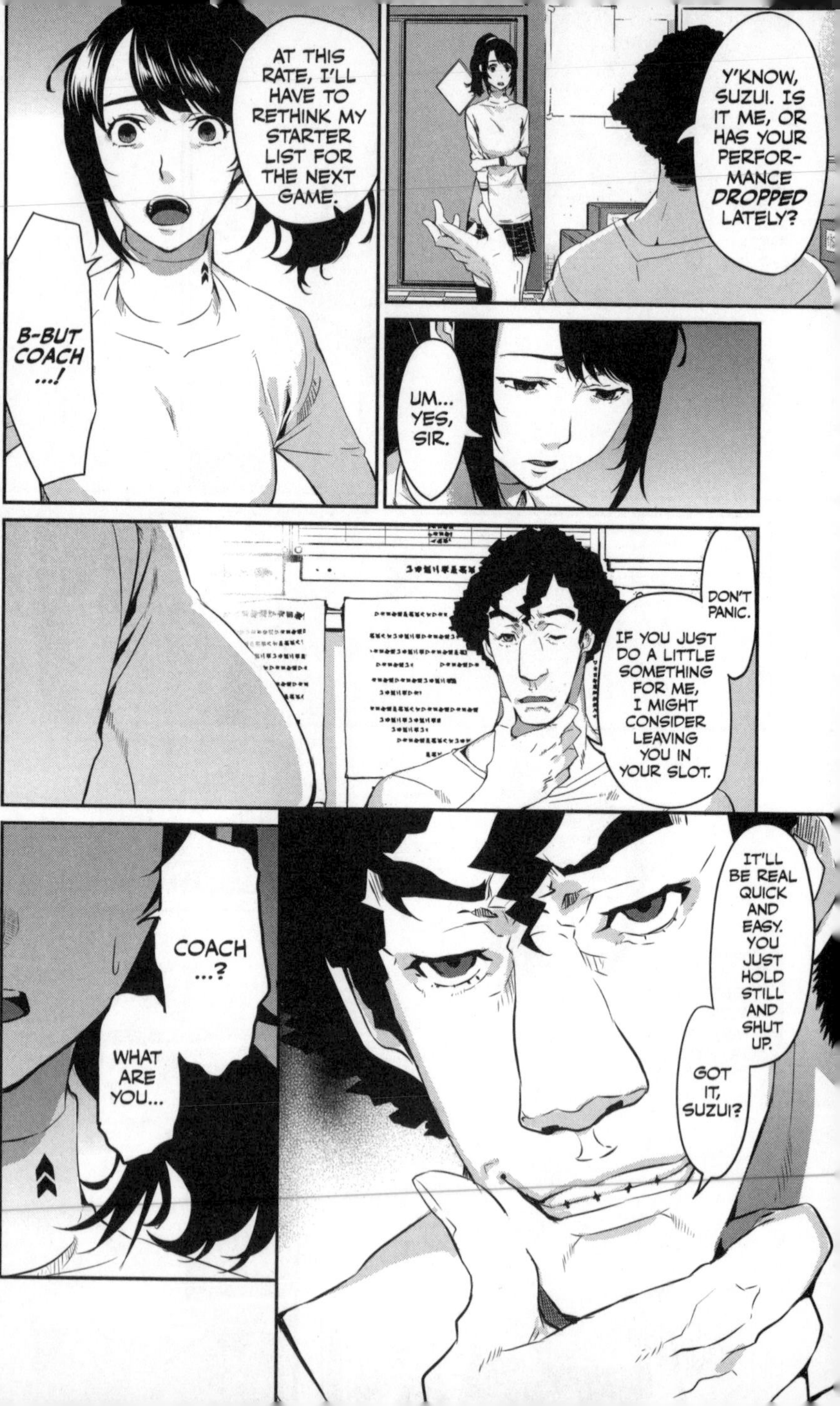
Y'KNOW, SUZUI. IS IT ME, OR HAS YOUR PERFORMANCE **DROPPED** LATELY?
UM... YES, SIR.
AT THIS RATE, I'LL HAVE TO RETHINK MY STARTER LIST FOR THE NEXT GAME.
B-BUT COACH ...!
DON'T PANIC.
IF YOU JUST DO A LITTLE SOMETHING FOR ME, I MIGHT CONSIDER LEAVING YOU IN YOUR SLOT.
IT'LL BE REAL QUICK AND EASY. YOU JUST HOLD STILL AND SHUT UP.
GOT IT, SUZUI?
COACH ...?
WHAT ARE YOU...

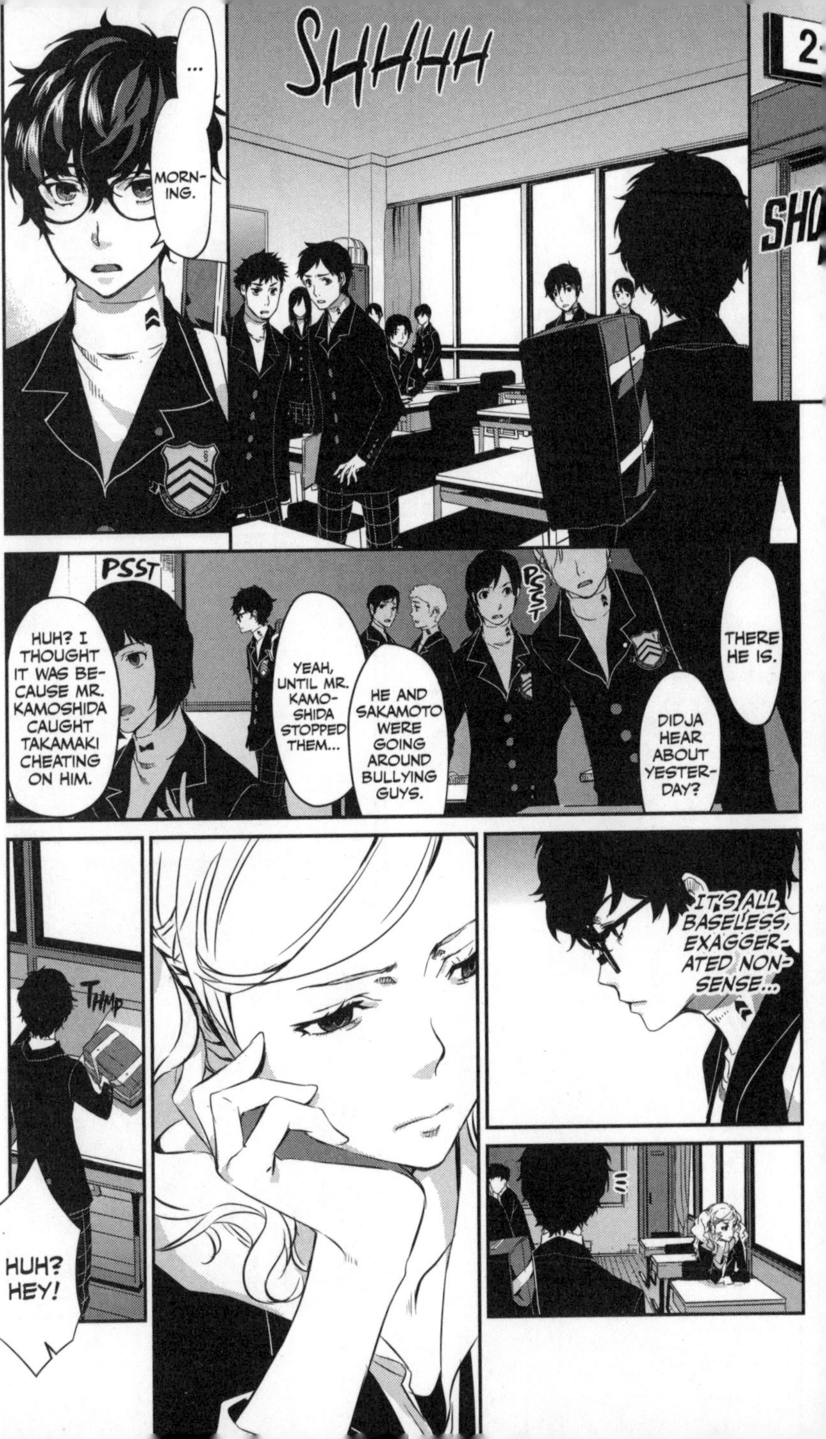
2-
SHO
SHHHH
...
MORNING.
THERE HE IS.
DIDJA HEAR ABOUT YESTERDAY?
PSST
HE AND SAKAMOTO WERE GOING AROUND BULLYING GUYS.
YEAH, UNTIL MR. KAMOSHIDA STOPPED THEM...
PSST
HUH? I THOUGHT IT WAS BECAUSE MR. KAMOSHIDA CAUGHT TAKAMAKI CHEATING ON HIM.
IT'S ALL BASELESS, EXAGGERATED NONSENSE...
THMP
HUH? HEY!

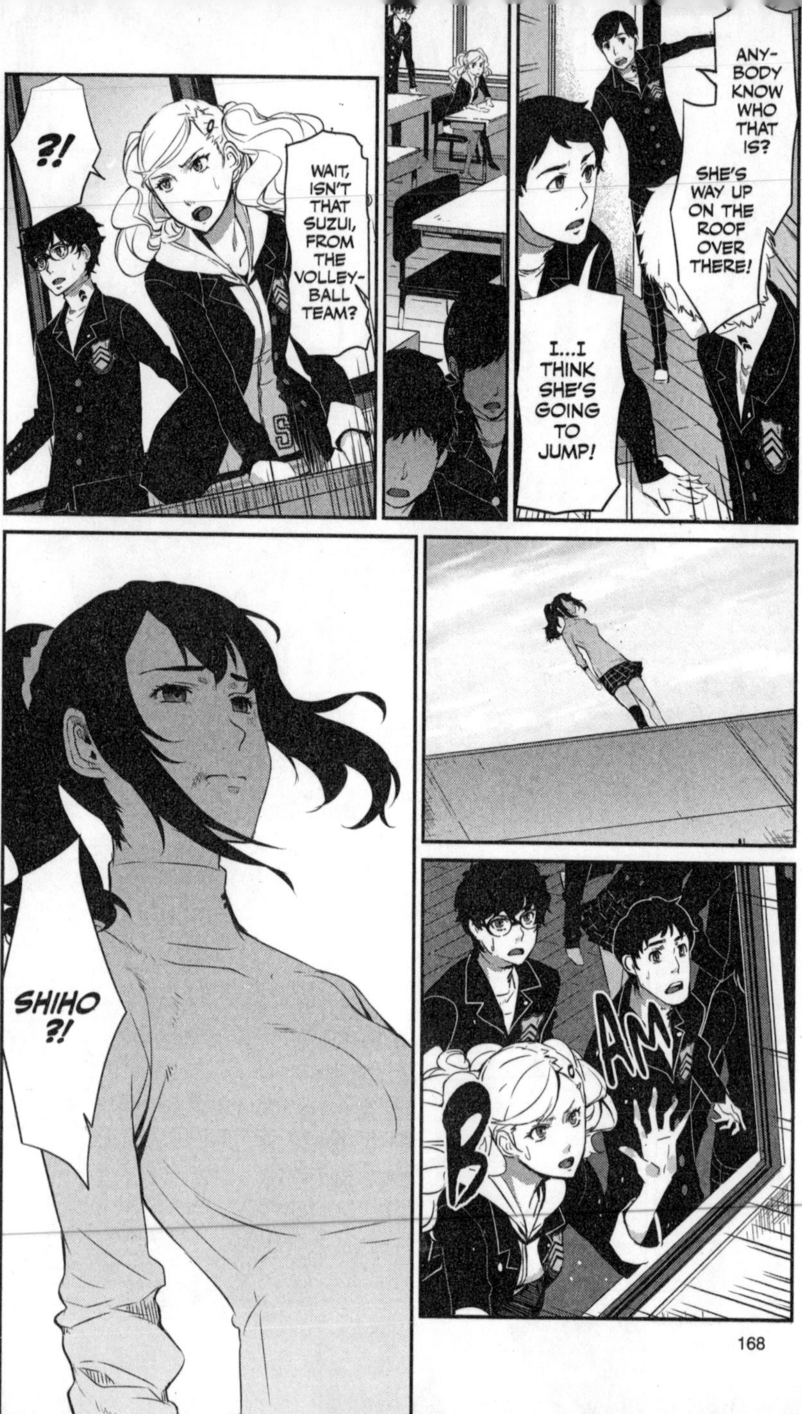
ANY-BODY KNOW WHO THAT IS?
SHE'S WAY UP ON THE ROOF OVER THERE!
I...I THINK SHE'S GOING TO JUMP!
WAIT, ISN'T THAT SUZUI, FROM THE VOLLEY-BALL TEAM?
?!
BAM
SHIHO ?!

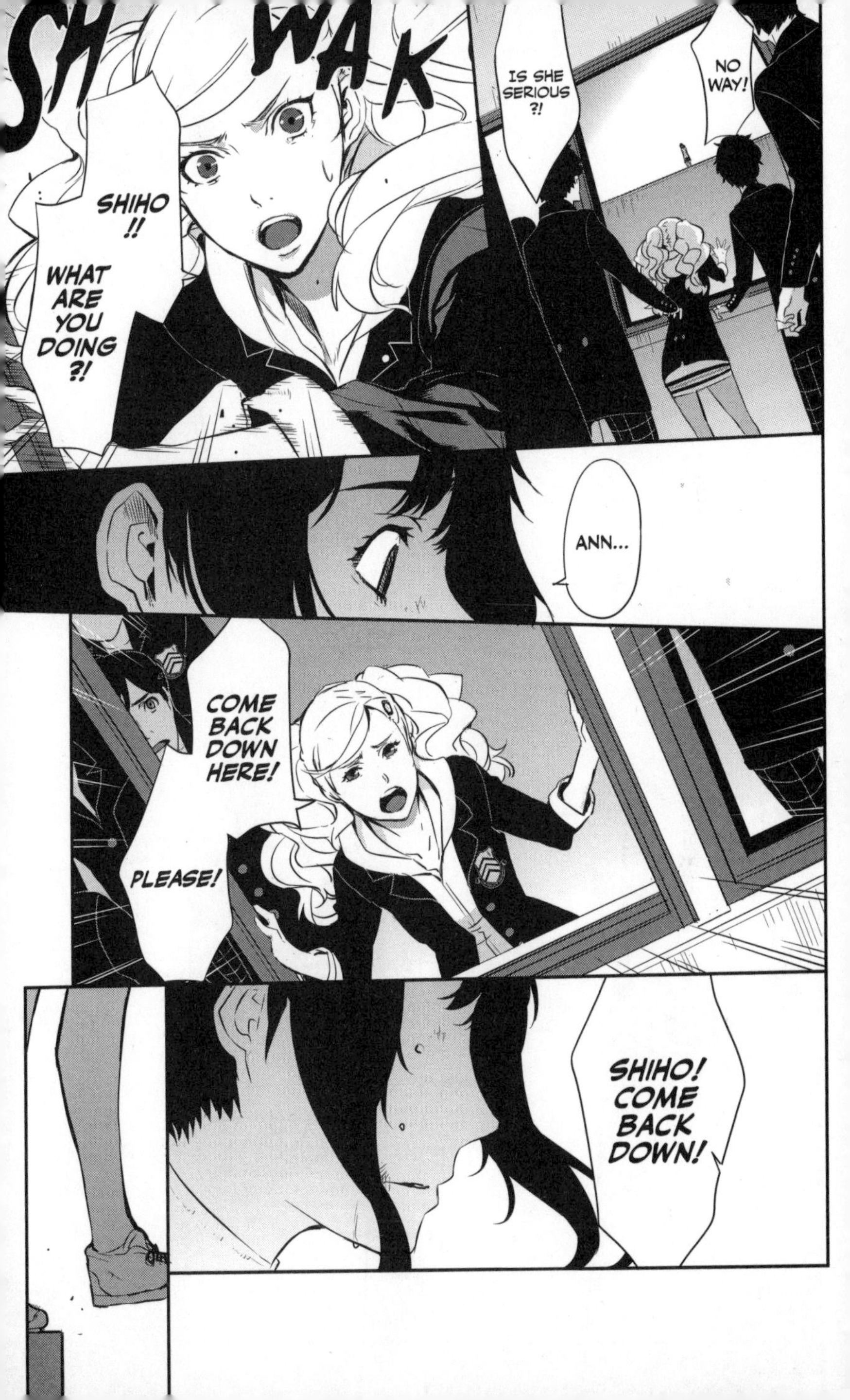
NO WAY!
IS SHE SERIOUS?!
SHWAK
SHIHO!!
WHAT ARE YOU DOING?!
ANN...
COME BACK DOWN HERE!
PLEASE!
SHIHO! COME BACK DOWN!

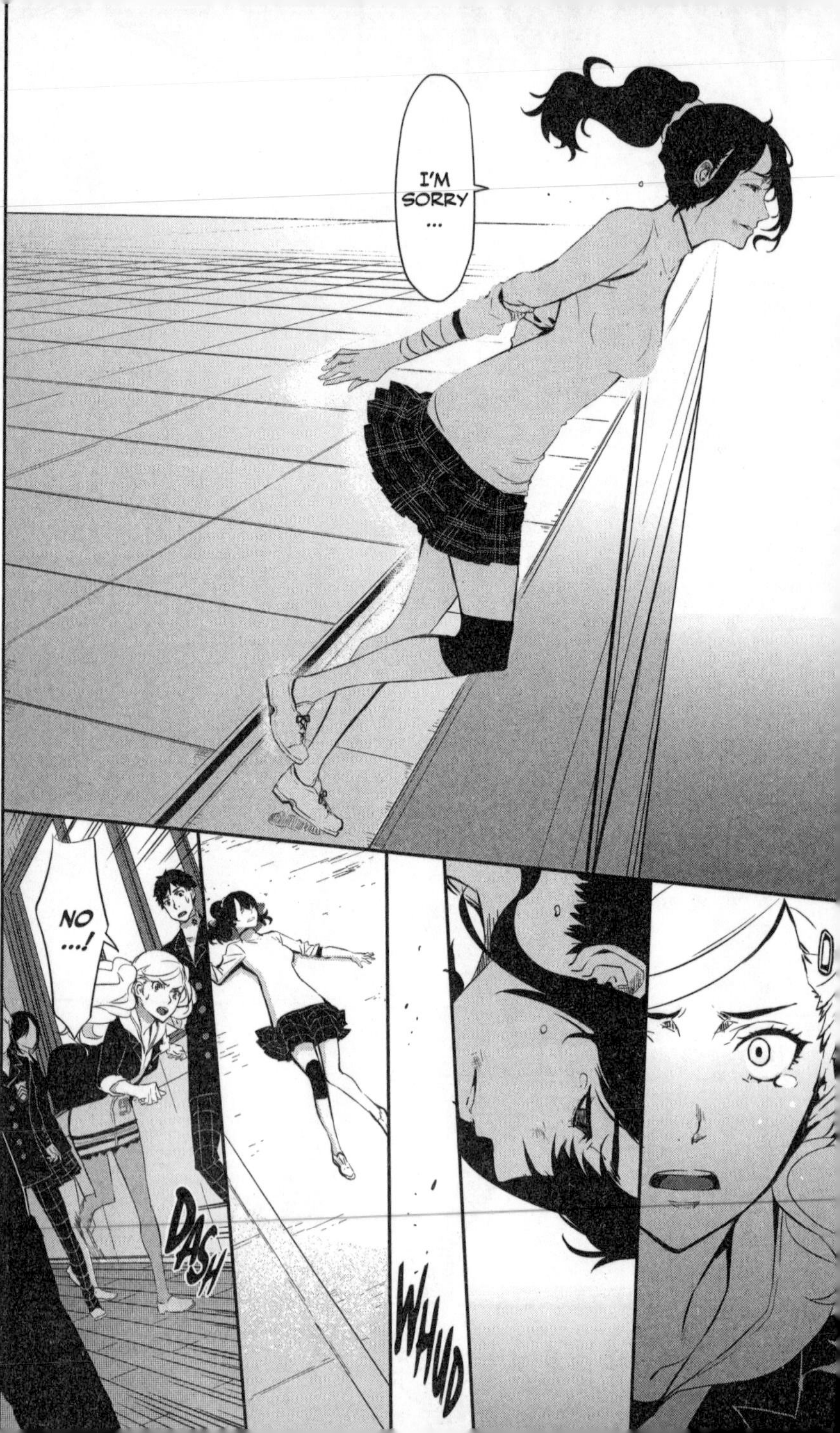
I'M SORRY ...
NO ...!
DASH
WHUD

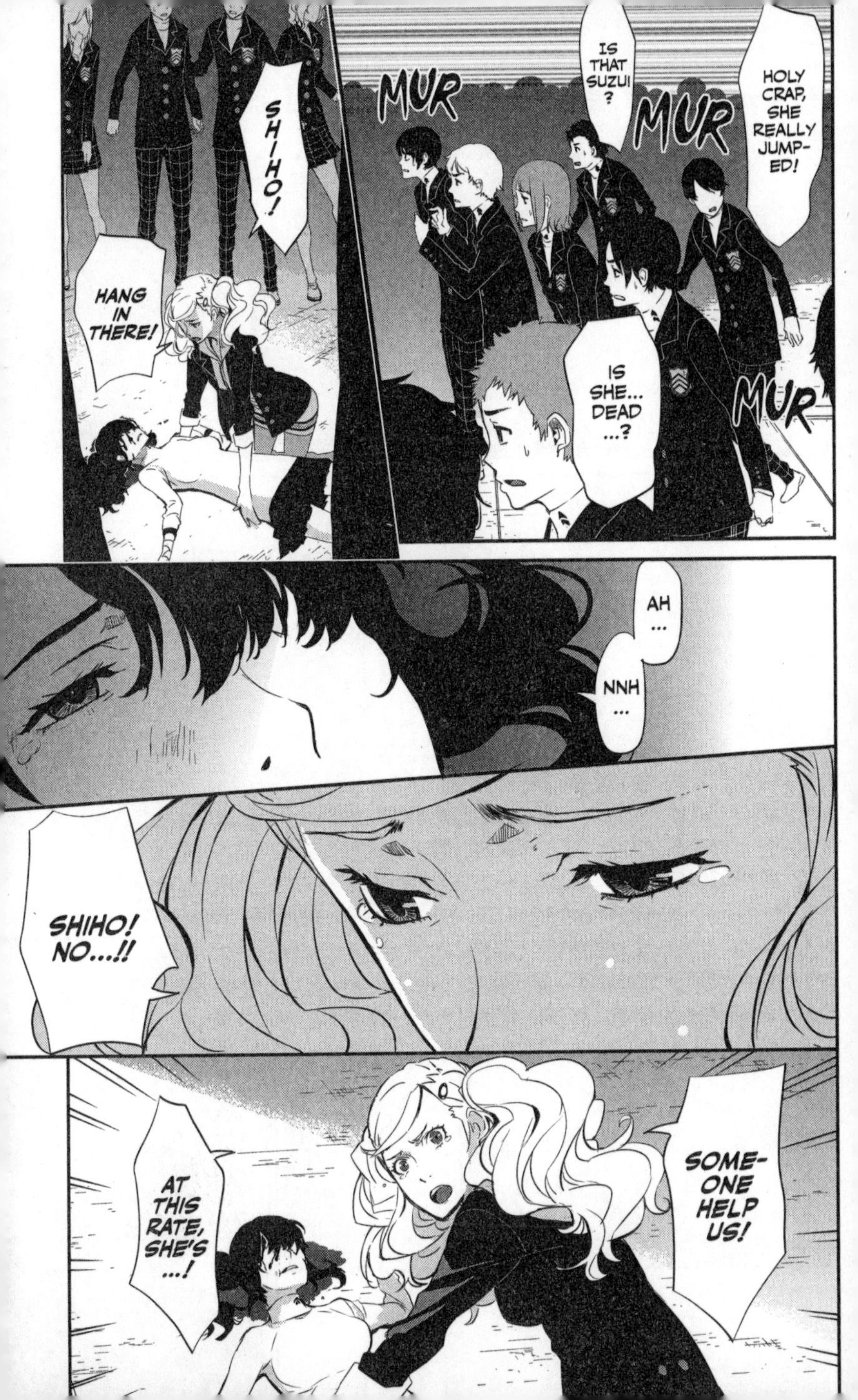
HOLY CRAP, SHE REALLY JUMPED!
IS THAT SUZUI?
MUR
MUR
MUR
IS SHE... DEAD...?
SHIHO!
HANG IN THERE!
AH...
NNH...
SHIHO! NO...!!
SOMEONE HELP US!
AT THIS RATE, SHE'S...!

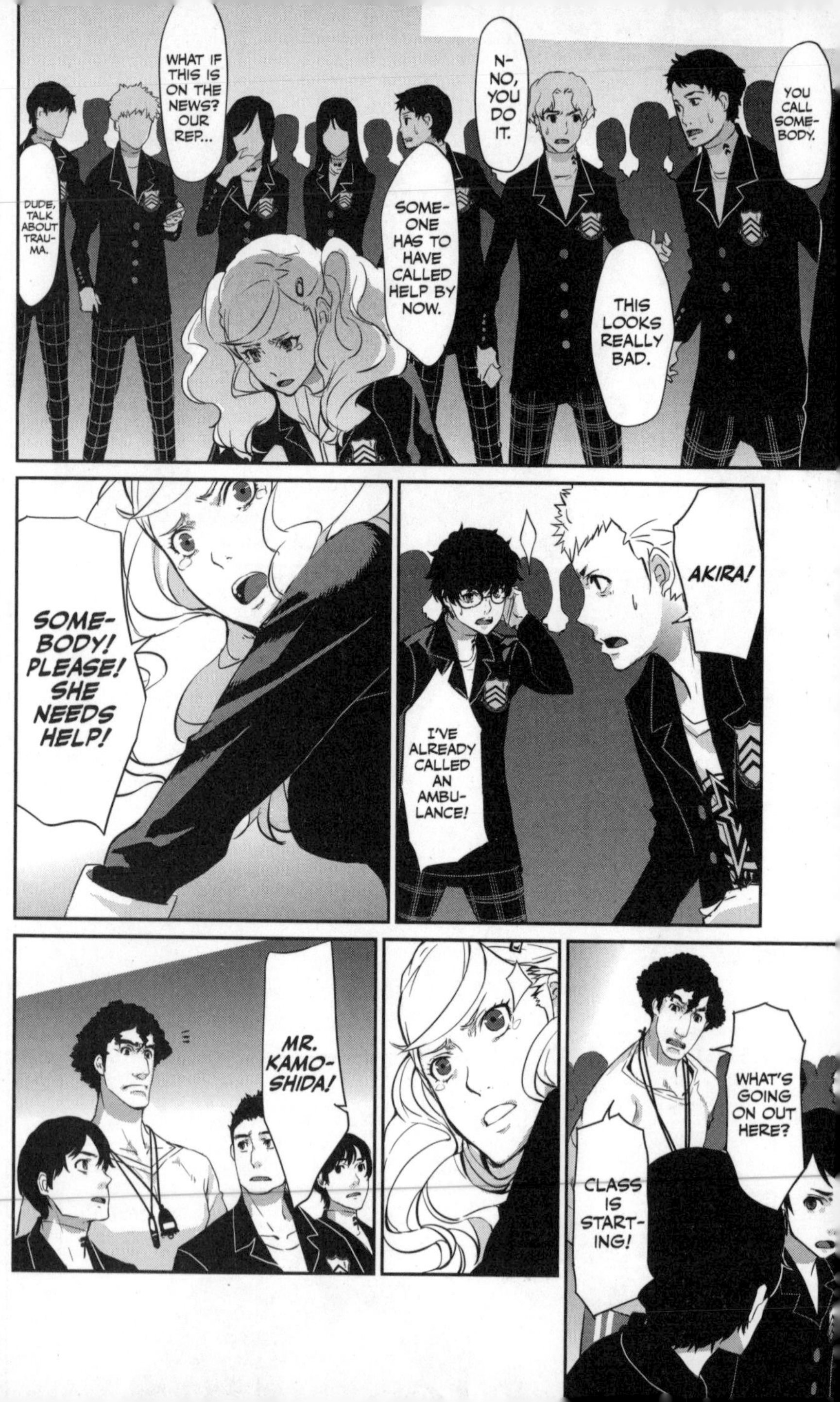
YOU CALL SOMEBODY.
N-NO, YOU DO IT.
THIS LOOKS REALLY BAD.
SOMEONE HAS TO HAVE CALLED HELP BY NOW.
WHAT IF THIS IS ON THE NEWS? OUR REP...
DUDE, TALK ABOUT TRAUMA.
AKIRA!
I'VE ALREADY CALLED AN AMBULANCE!
SOMEBODY! PLEASE! SHE NEEDS HELP!
WHAT'S GOING ON OUT HERE?
CLASS IS STARTING!
MR. KAMOSHIDA!

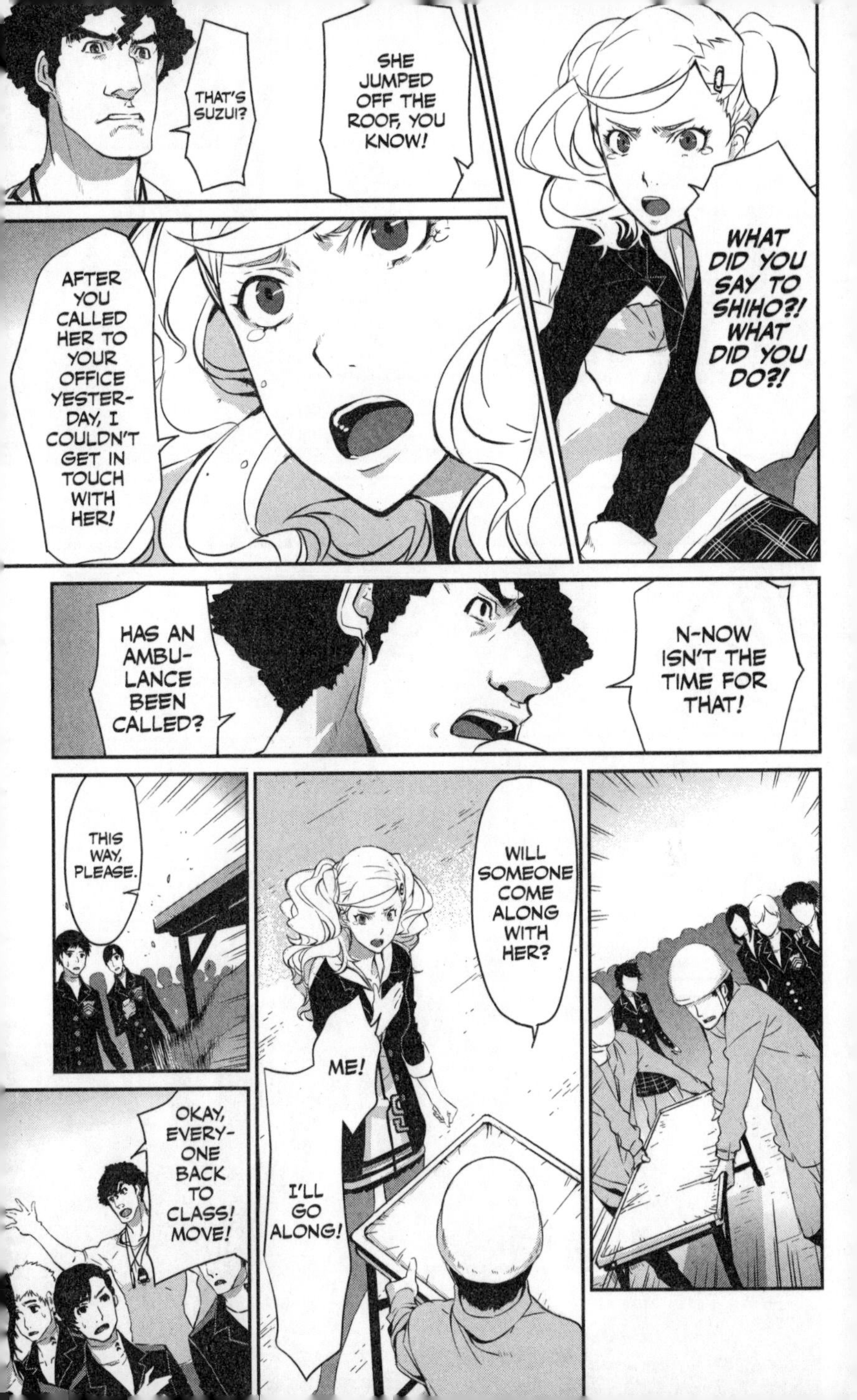
THAT'S SUZUI?
SHE JUMPED OFF THE ROOF, YOU KNOW!
AFTER YOU CALLED HER TO YOUR OFFICE YESTER-DAY, I COULDN'T GET IN TOUCH WITH HER!
WHAT DID YOU SAY TO SHIHO?! WHAT DID YOU DO?!
N-NOW ISN'T THE TIME FOR THAT!
HAS AN AMBU-LANCE BEEN CALLED?
WILL SOMEONE COME ALONG WITH HER?
ME!
I'LL GO ALONG!
THIS WAY, PLEASE.
OKAY, EVERY-ONE BACK TO CLASS! MOVE!

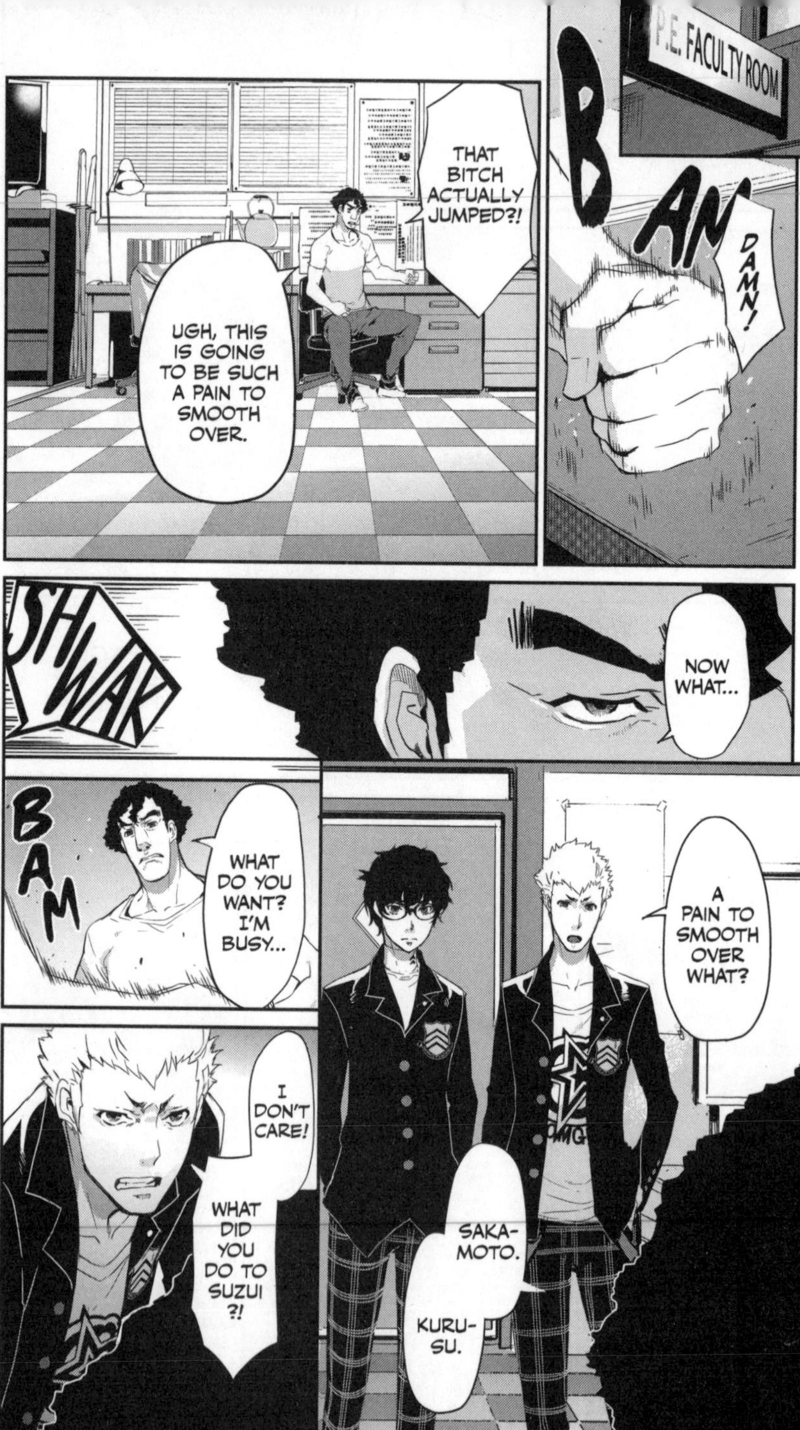
P.E. FACULTY ROOM
BAM
DAMN!
THAT BITCH ACTUALLY JUMPED?!
UGH, THIS IS GOING TO BE SUCH A PAIN TO SMOOTH OVER.
NOW WHAT...
SHWAK
A PAIN TO SMOOTH OVER WHAT?
SAKA-MOTO.
KURU-SU.
BAM
WHAT DO YOU WANT? I'M BUSY...
I DON'T CARE!
WHAT DID YOU DO TO SUZUI?!

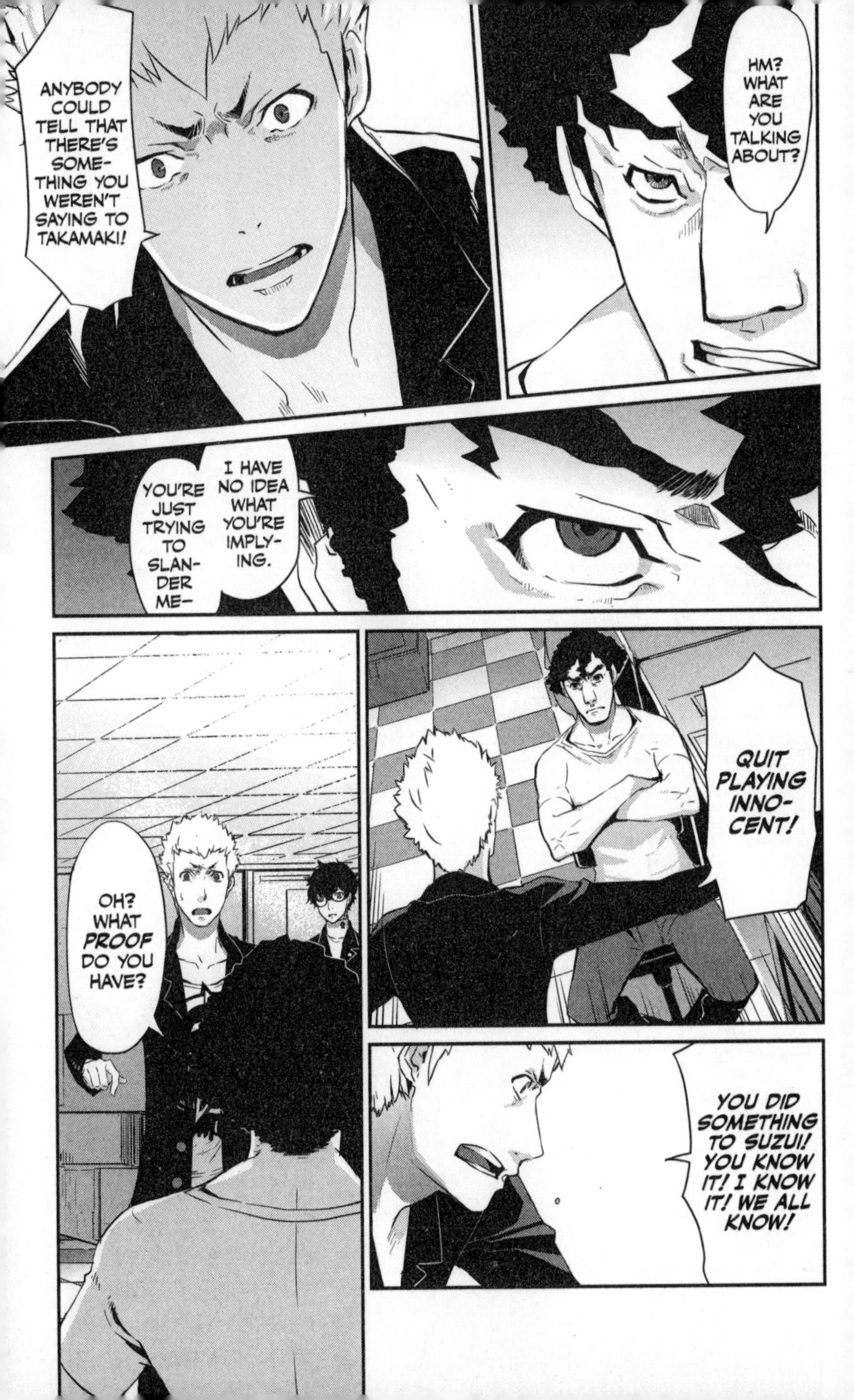
HM? WHAT ARE YOU TALKING ABOUT?
ANYBODY COULD TELL THAT THERE'S SOME-THING YOU WEREN'T SAYING TO TAKAMAKI!
I HAVE NO IDEA WHAT YOU'RE IMPLY-ING.
YOU'RE JUST TRYING TO SLAN-DER ME—
QUIT PLAYING INNO-CENT!
YOU DID SOMETHING TO SUZUI! YOU KNOW IT! I KNOW IT! WE ALL KNOW!
OH? WHAT *PROOF* DO YOU HAVE?

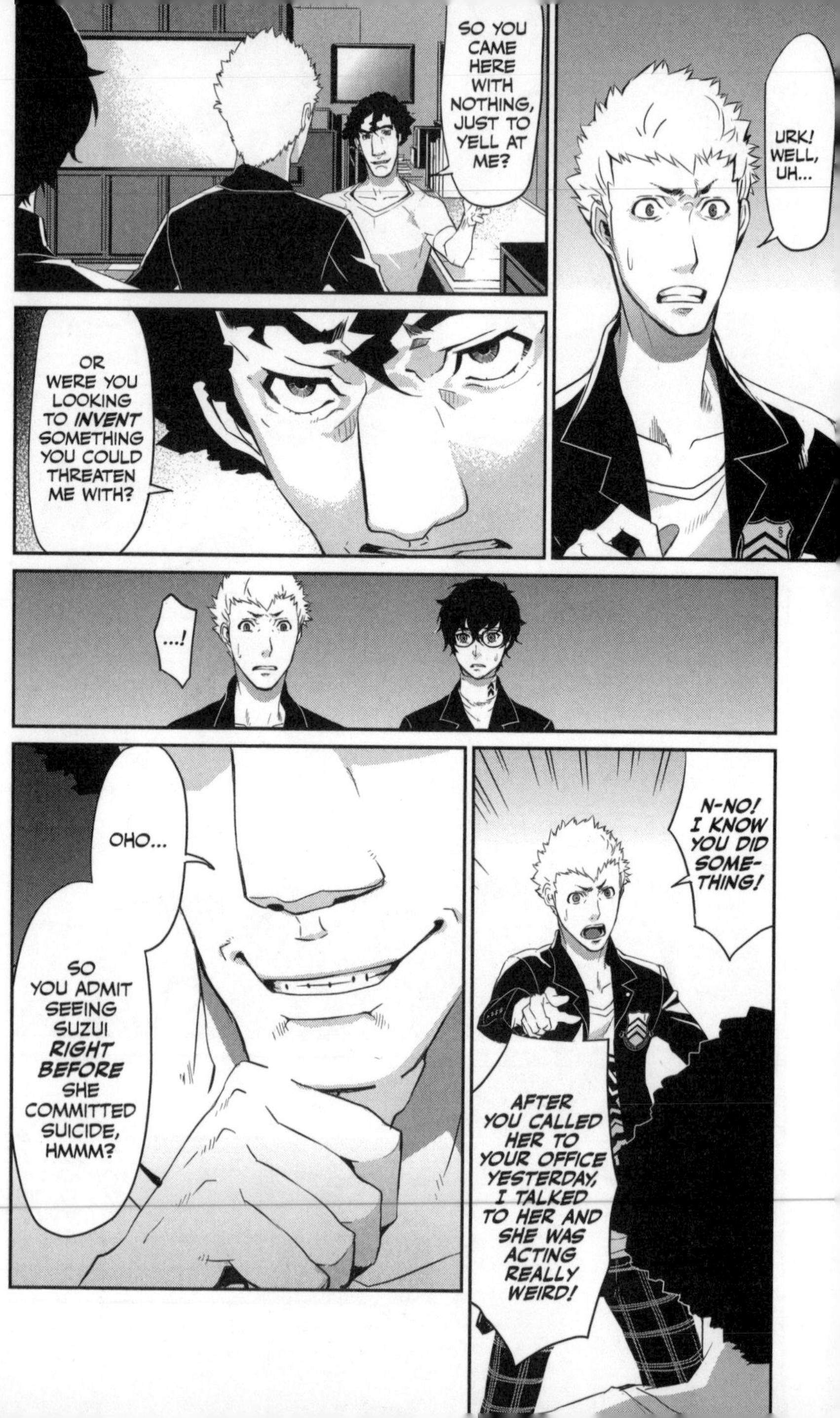
URK! WELL, UH...
SO YOU CAME HERE WITH NOTHING, JUST TO YELL AT ME?
OR WERE YOU LOOKING TO *INVENT* SOMETHING YOU COULD THREATEN ME WITH?
...!
N-NO! I KNOW YOU DID SOME-THING!
AFTER YOU CALLED HER TO YOUR OFFICE YESTERDAY, I TALKED TO HER AND SHE WAS ACTING REALLY WEIRD!
OHO...
SO YOU ADMIT SEEING SUZUI *RIGHT BEFORE* SHE COMMITTED SUICIDE, HMMM?

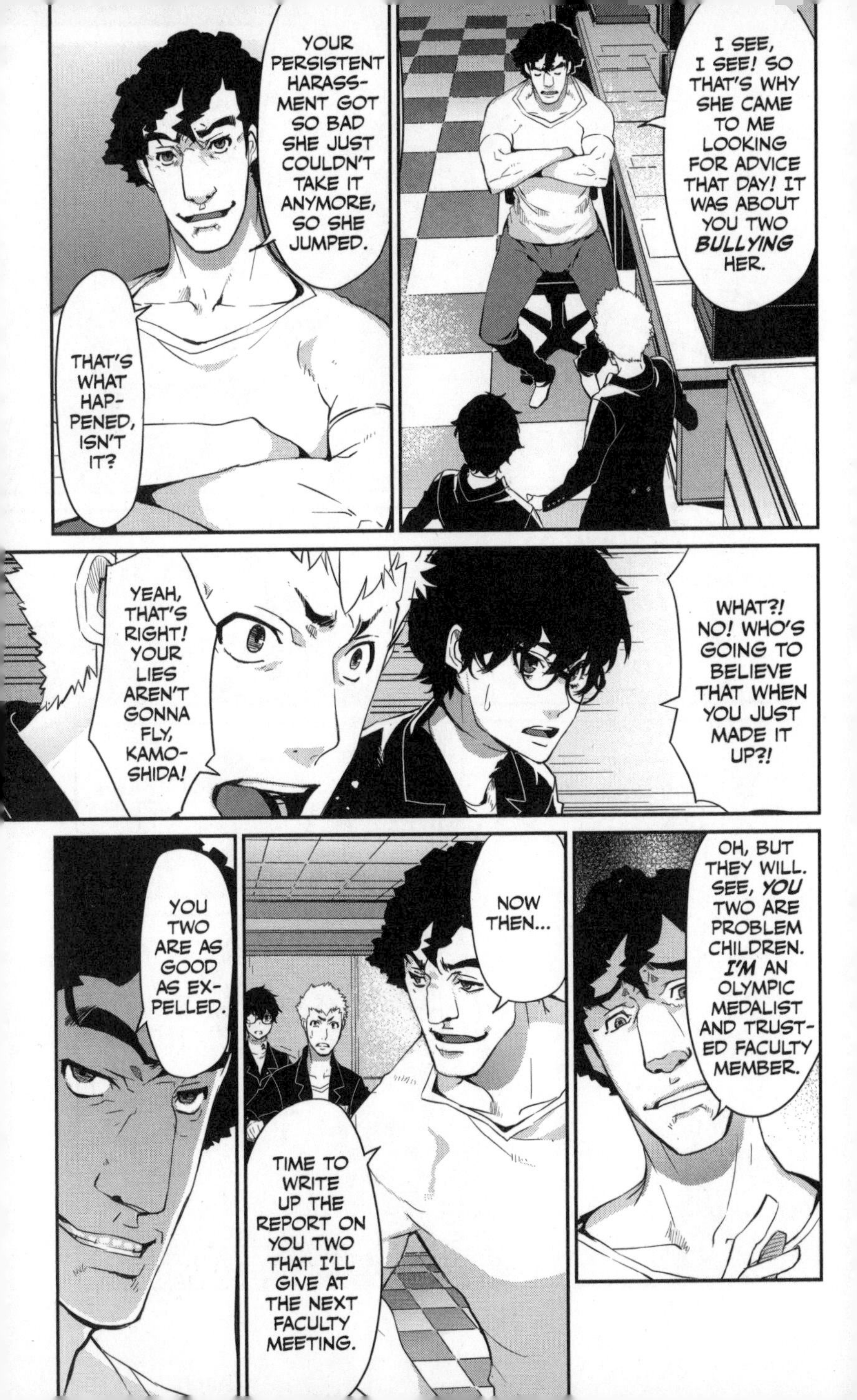
I SEE, I SEE! SO THAT'S WHY SHE CAME TO ME LOOKING FOR ADVICE THAT DAY! IT WAS ABOUT YOU TWO BULLYING HER.
YOUR PERSISTENT HARASSMENT GOT SO BAD SHE JUST COULDN'T TAKE IT ANYMORE, SO SHE JUMPED.
THAT'S WHAT HAPPENED, ISN'T IT?
WHAT?! NO! WHO'S GOING TO BELIEVE THAT WHEN YOU JUST MADE IT UP?!
YEAH, THAT'S RIGHT! YOUR LIES AREN'T GONNA FLY, KAMOSHIDA!
OH, BUT THEY WILL. SEE, YOU TWO ARE PROBLEM CHILDREN. I'M AN OLYMPIC MEDALIST AND TRUSTED FACULTY MEMBER.
NOW THEN...
TIME TO WRITE UP THE REPORT ON YOU TWO THAT I'LL GIVE AT THE NEXT FACULTY MEETING.
YOU TWO ARE AS GOOD AS EXPELLED.

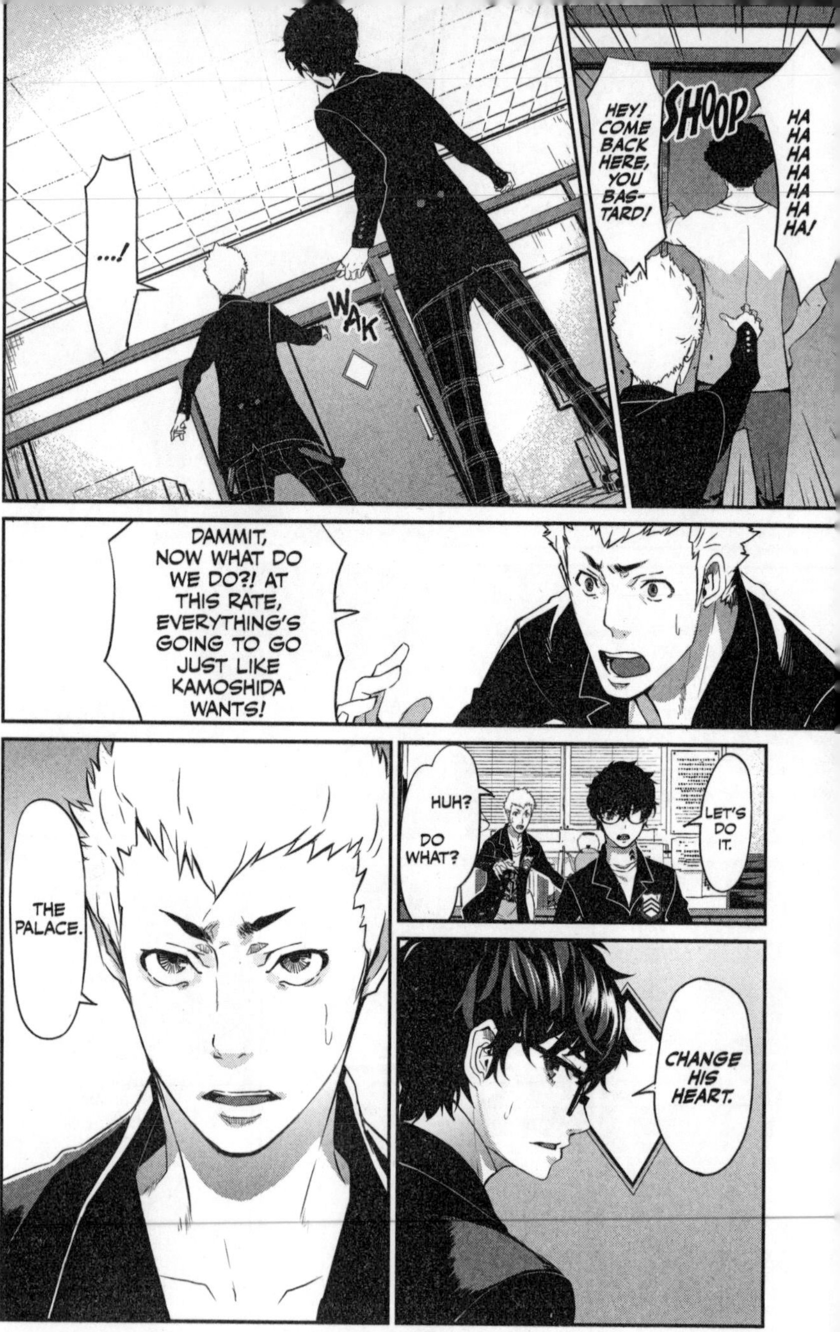
HA HA HA HA HA HA HA HA!
SHOOP
HEY! COME BACK HERE, YOU BAS-TARD!
...!
WAK
DAMMIT, NOW WHAT DO WE DO?! AT THIS RATE, EVERYTHING'S GOING TO GO JUST LIKE KAMOSHIDA WANTS!
LET'S DO IT.
HUH?
DO WHAT?
CHANGE HIS HEART.
THE PALACE.

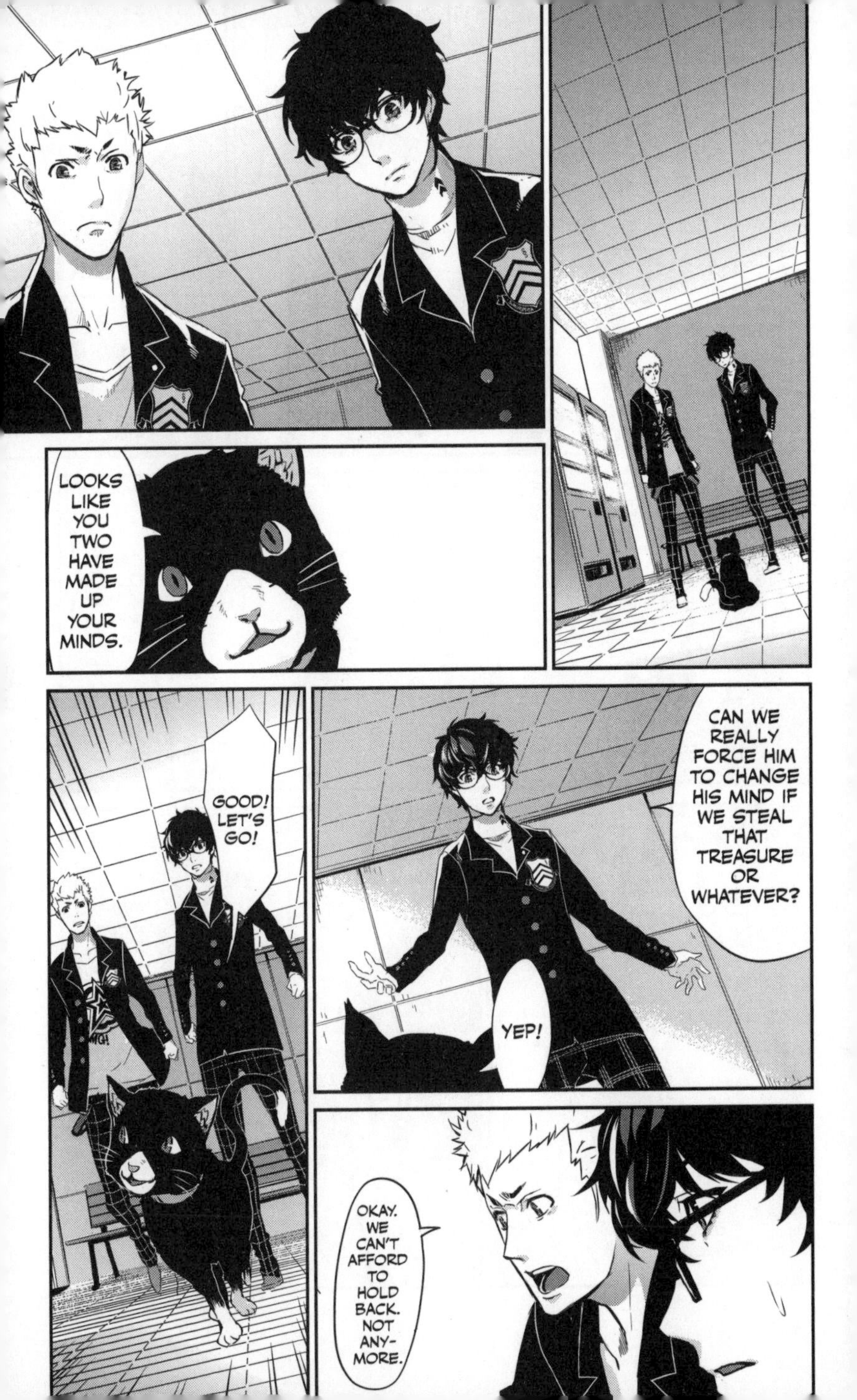
LOOKS LIKE YOU TWO HAVE MADE UP YOUR MINDS.
CAN WE REALLY FORCE HIM TO CHANGE HIS MIND IF WE STEAL THAT TREASURE OR WHATEVER?
YEP!
OKAY. WE CAN'T AFFORD TO HOLD BACK. NOT ANY-MORE.
GOOD! LET'S GO!

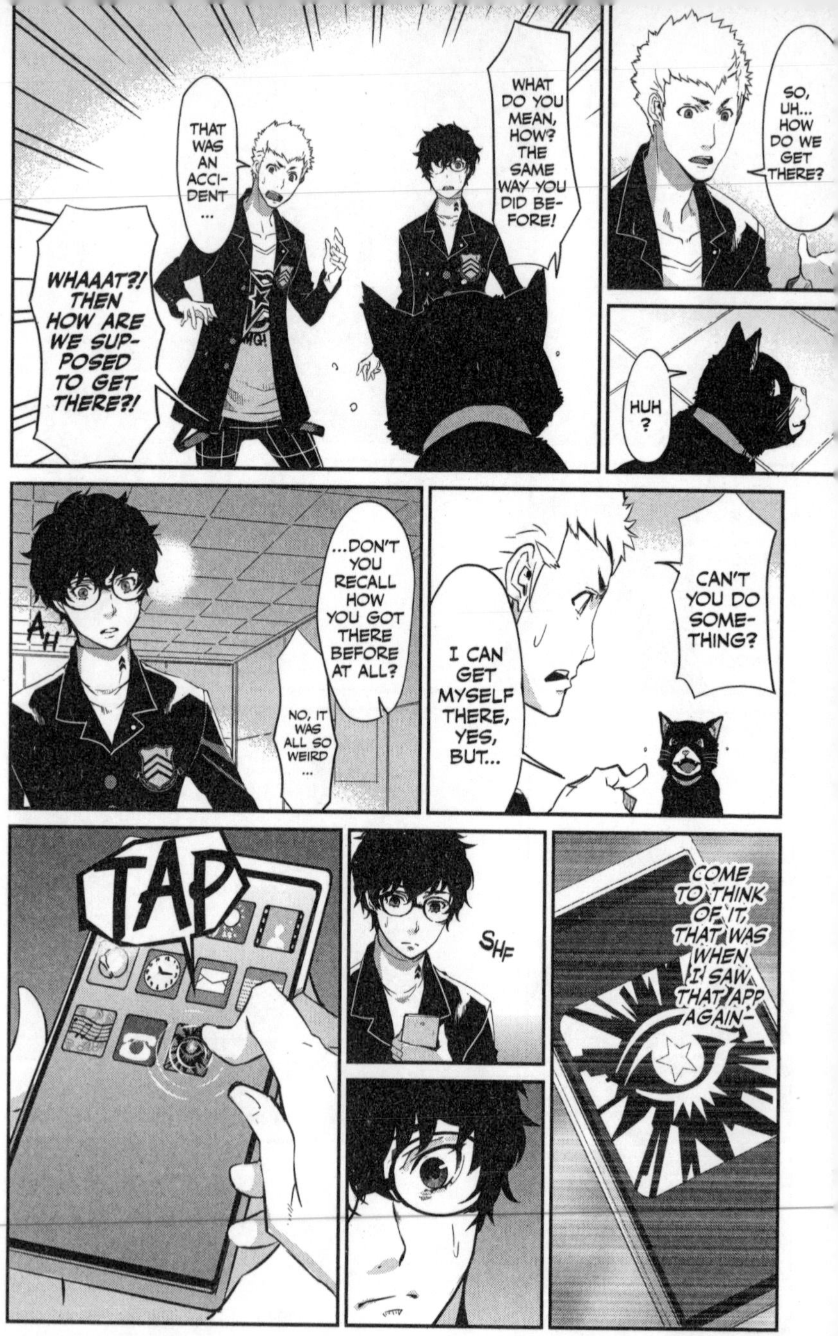
SO, UH... HOW DO WE GET THERE?
HUH?
WHAT DO YOU MEAN, HOW? THE SAME WAY YOU DID BEFORE!
THAT WAS AN ACCIDENT...
WHAAAT?! THEN HOW ARE WE SUPPOSED TO GET THERE?!
CAN'T YOU DO SOMETHING?
I CAN GET MYSELF THERE, YES, BUT...
...DON'T YOU RECALL HOW YOU GOT THERE BEFORE AT ALL?
NO, IT WAS ALL SO WEIRD...
AH
COME TO THINK OF IT, THAT WAS WHEN I SAW THAT APP AGAIN–
SHF
TAP

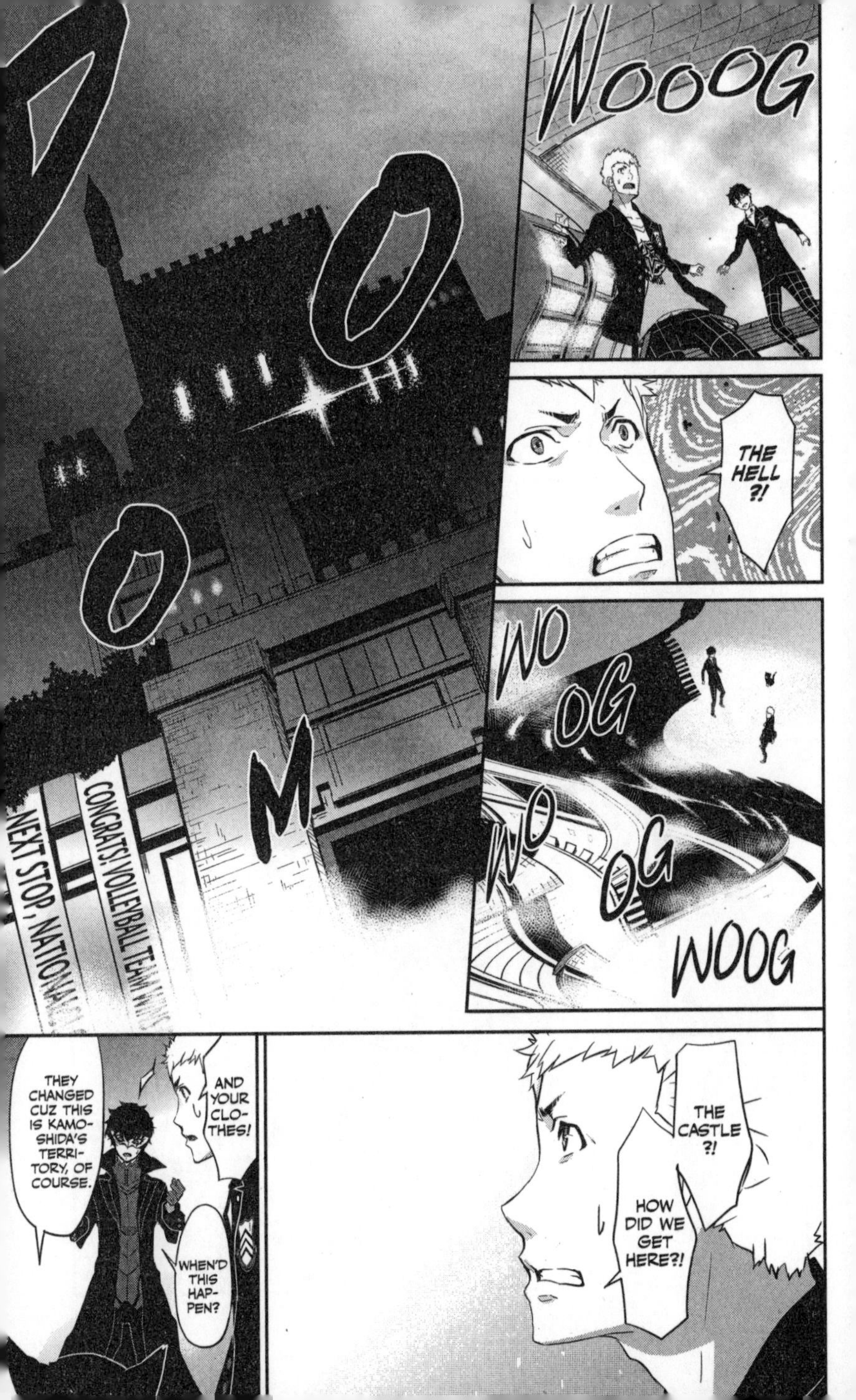
WOOOG
THE HELL?!
WOO
OG
WOO
OG
WOOG
DOOOM
CONGRATS! VOLLEYBALL TEAM
NEXT STOP,
THE CASTLE?!
HOW DID WE GET HERE?!
AND YOUR CLOTHES!
WHEN'D THIS HAPPEN?
THEY CHANGED CUZ THIS IS KAMOSHIDA'S TERRITORY, OF COURSE.

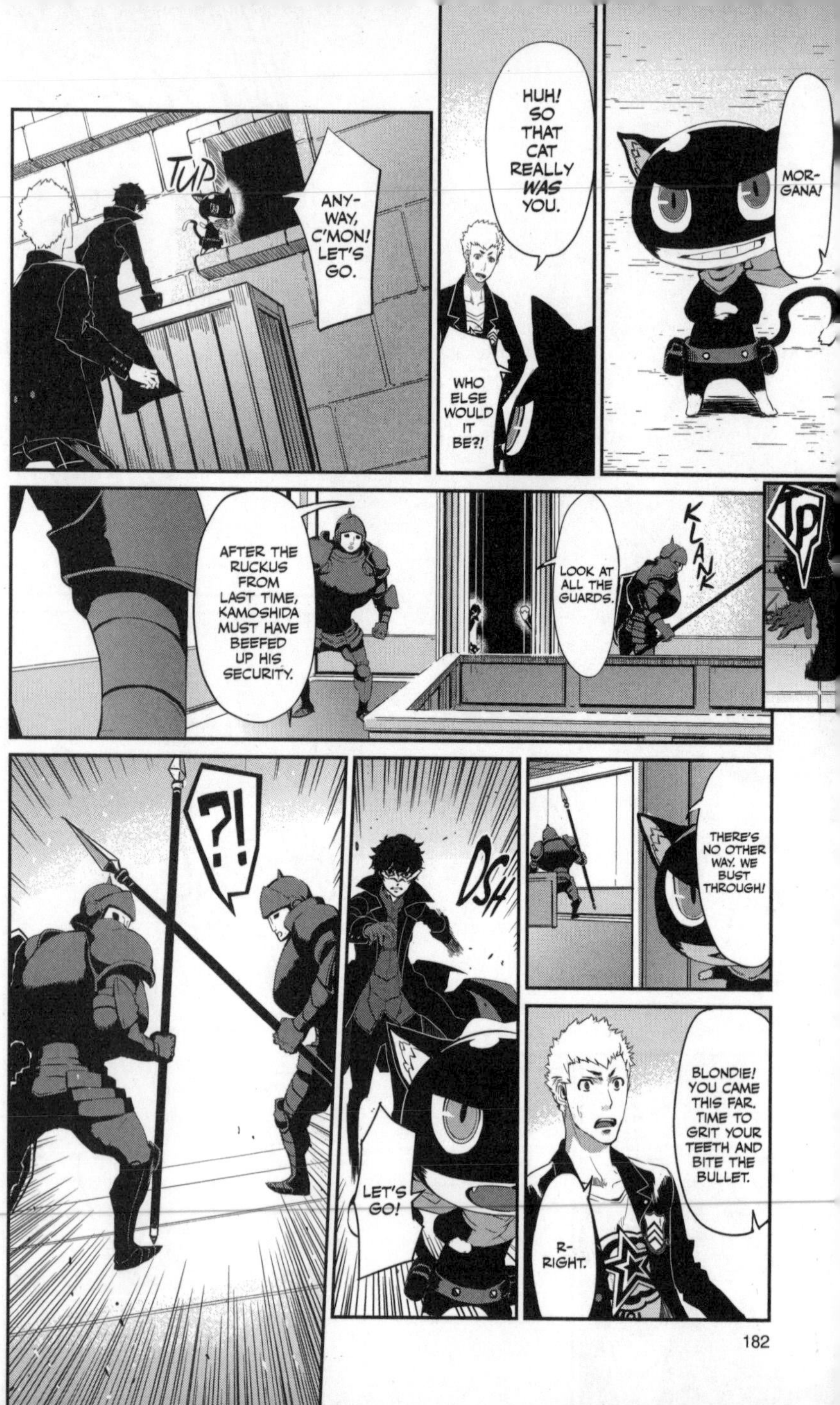
MOR-GANA!
HUH! SO THAT CAT REALLY WAS YOU.
WHO ELSE WOULD IT BE?!
TUP
ANY-WAY, C'MON! LET'S GO.
TP
KLANK
LOOK AT ALL THE GUARDS.
AFTER THE RUCKUS FROM LAST TIME, KAMOSHIDA MUST HAVE BEEFED UP HIS SECURITY.
THERE'S NO OTHER WAY. WE BUST THROUGH!
BLONDIE! YOU CAME THIS FAR. TIME TO GRIT YOUR TEETH AND BITE THE BULLET.
R-RIGHT.
DSH
LET'S GO!
?!

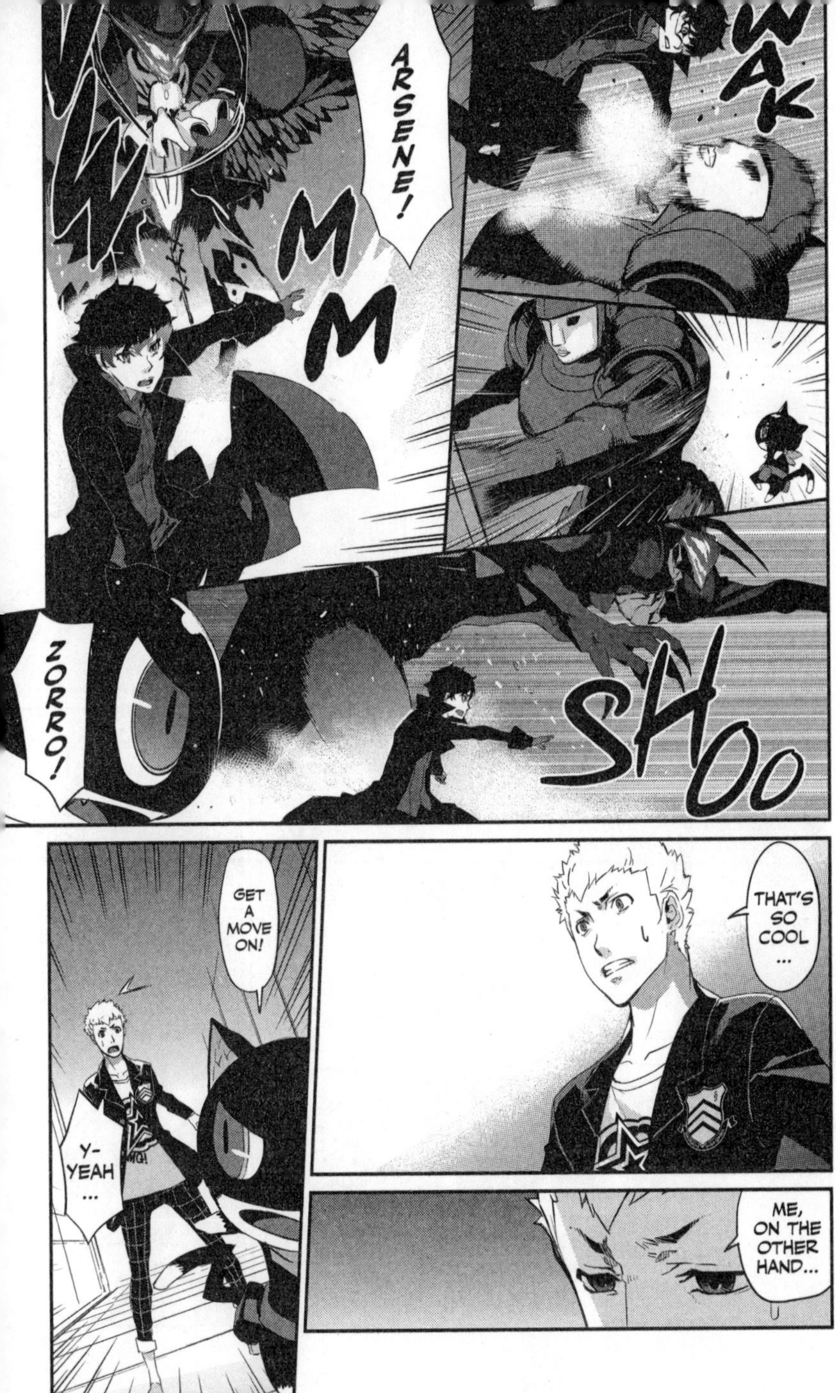
WAK
ARSENE!
WMMM
ZORRO!
SHOO
THAT'S SO COOL ...
ME, ON THE OTHER HAND...
GET A MOVE ON!
Y-YEAH ...

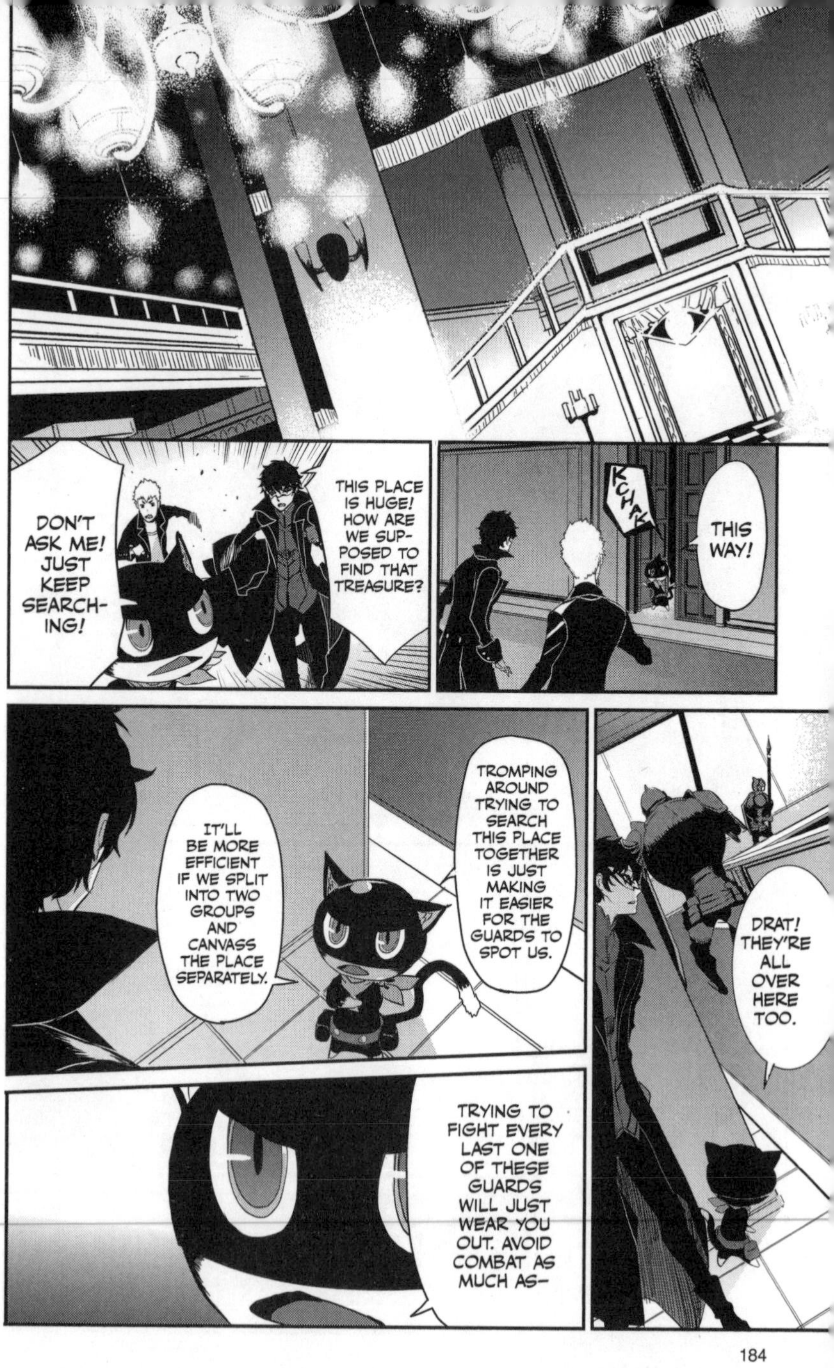
KCHAK
THIS WAY!
THIS PLACE IS HUGE! HOW ARE WE SUP-POSED TO FIND THAT TREASURE?
DON'T ASK ME! JUST KEEP SEARCH-ING!
DRAT! THEY'RE ALL OVER HERE TOO.
TROMPING AROUND TRYING TO SEARCH THIS PLACE TOGETHER IS JUST MAKING IT EASIER FOR THE GUARDS TO SPOT US.
IT'LL BE MORE EFFICIENT IF WE SPLIT INTO TWO GROUPS AND CANVASS THE PLACE SEPARATELY.
TRYING TO FIGHT EVERY LAST ONE OF THESE GUARDS WILL JUST WEAR YOU OUT. AVOID COMBAT AS MUCH AS–

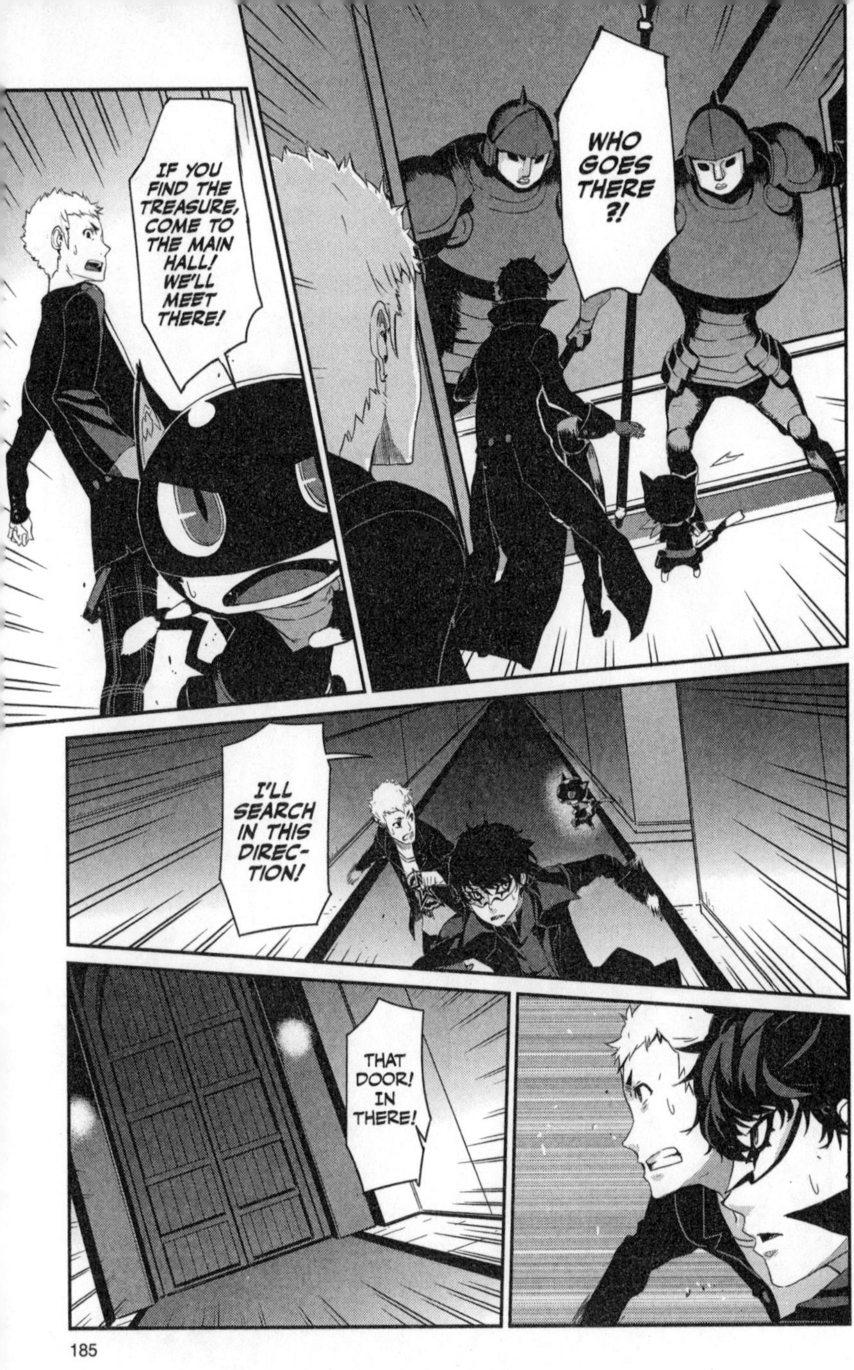
WHO GOES THERE ?!
IF YOU FIND THE TREASURE, COME TO THE MAIN HALL! WE'LL MEET THERE!
I'LL SEARCH IN THIS DIREC- TION!
THAT DOOR! IN THERE!

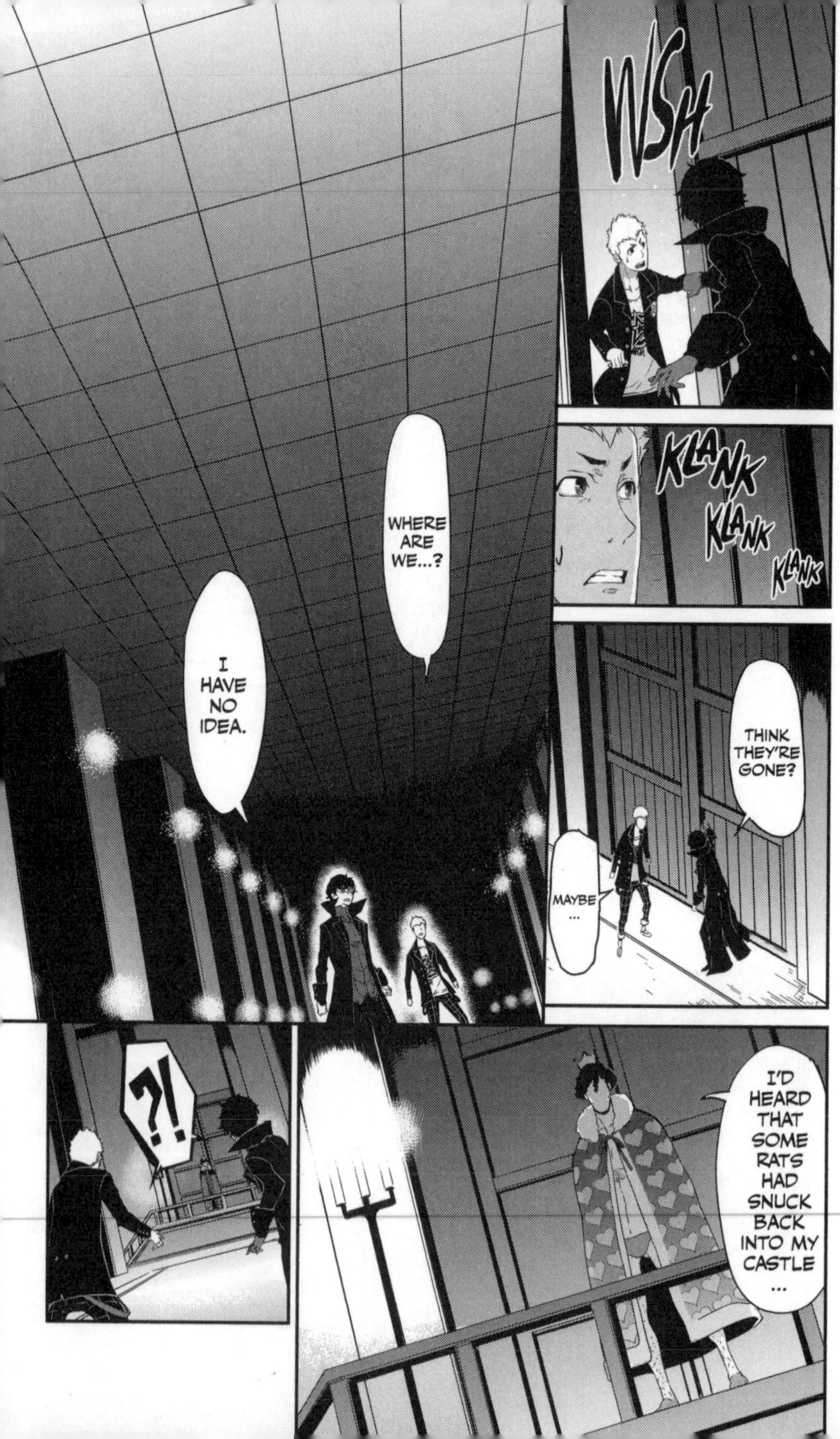
WSH
KLANK KLANK KLANK
THINK THEY'RE GONE?
MAYBE...
WHERE ARE WE...?
I HAVE NO IDEA.
I'D HEARD THAT SOME RATS HAD SNUCK BACK INTO MY CASTLE...
?!

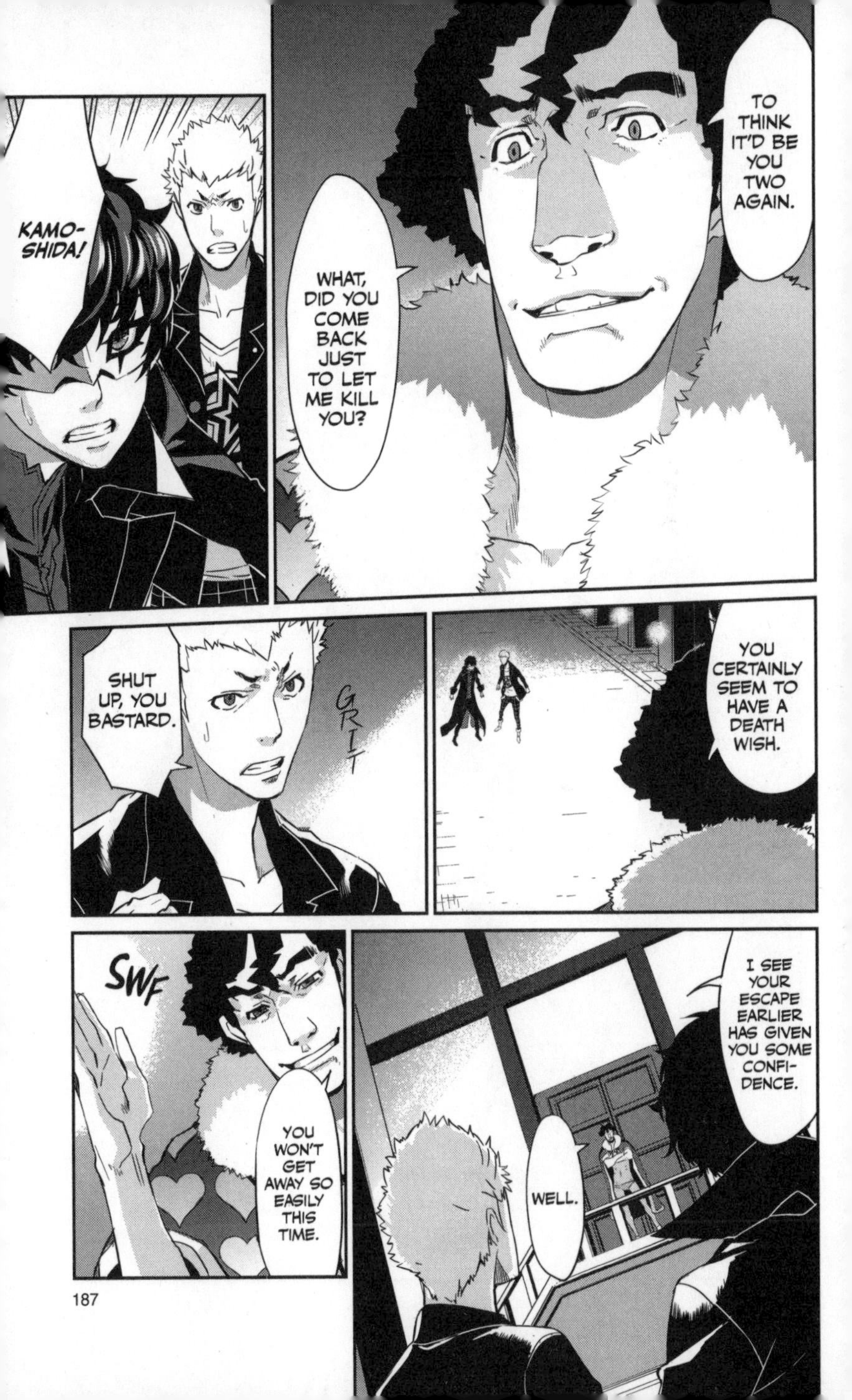
TO THINK IT'D BE YOU TWO AGAIN.
WHAT, DID YOU COME BACK JUST TO LET ME KILL YOU?
KAMO-SHIDA!
YOU CERTAINLY SEEM TO HAVE A DEATH WISH.
GRIT
SHUT UP, YOU BASTARD.
I SEE YOUR ESCAPE EARLIER HAS GIVEN YOU SOME CONFI-DENCE.
WELL.
SWF
YOU WON'T GET AWAY SO EASILY THIS TIME.

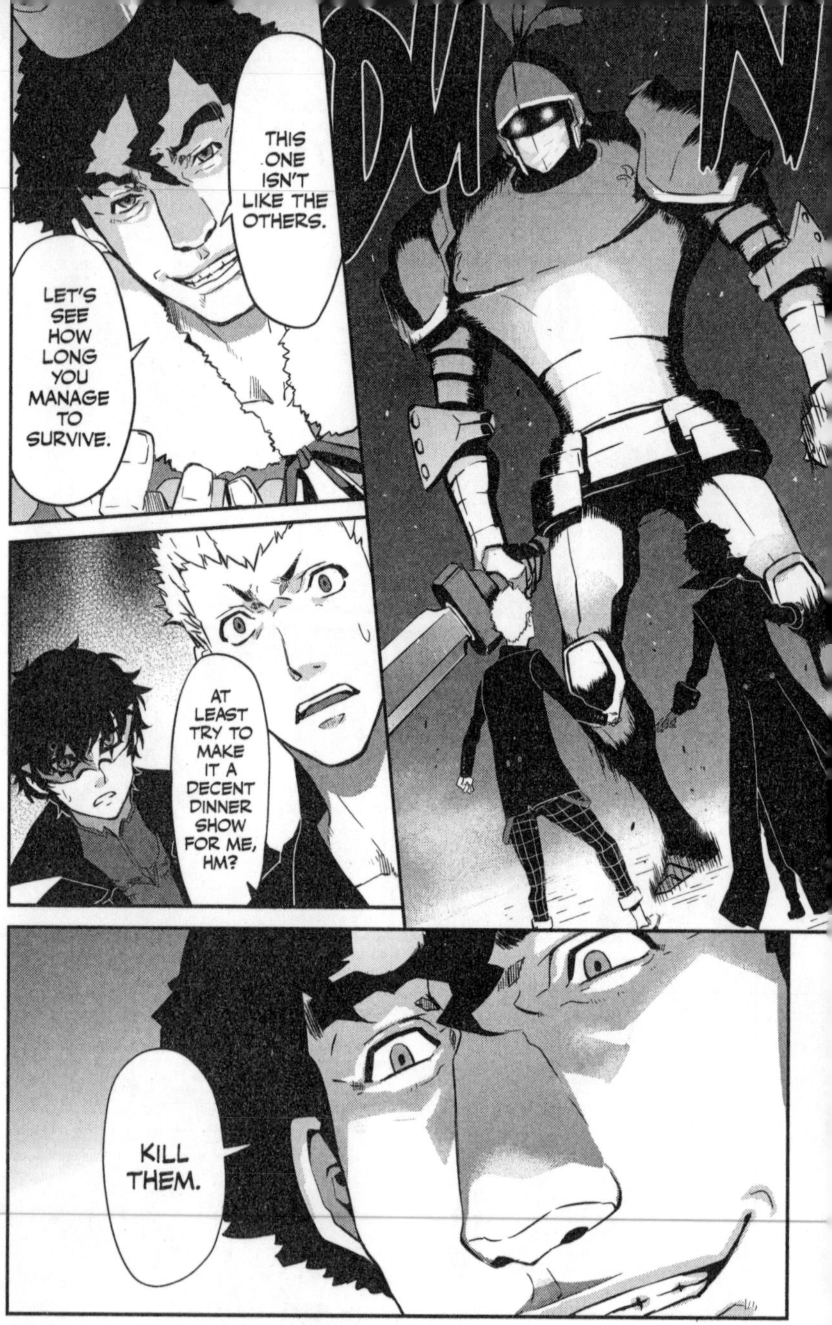
THIS ONE ISN'T LIKE THE OTHERS.
LET'S SEE HOW LONG YOU MANAGE TO SURVIVE.
AT LEAST TRY TO MAKE IT A DECENT DINNER SHOW FOR ME, HM?
KILL THEM.

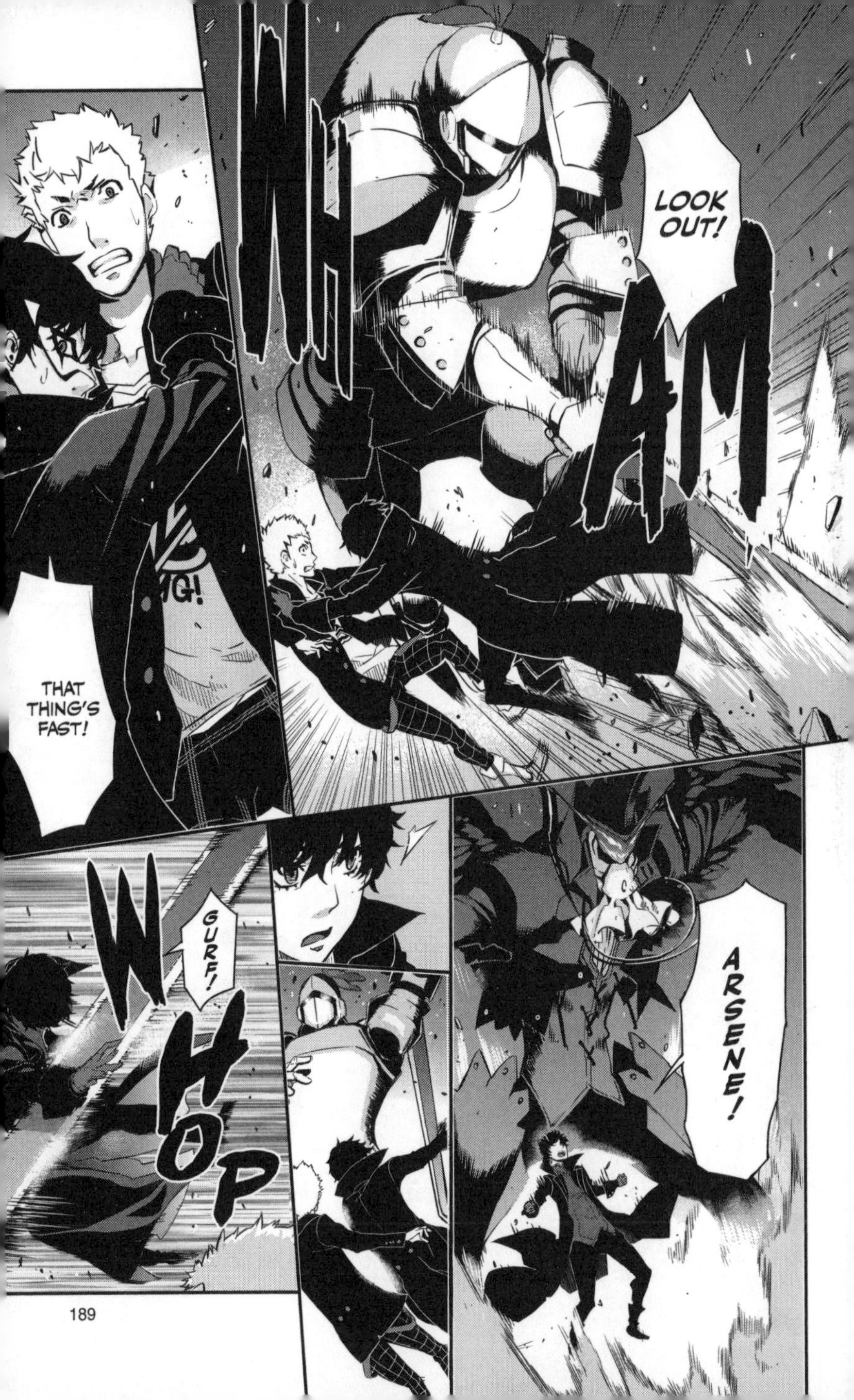
LOOK OUT!
WHAM
NG!
THAT THING'S FAST!
ARSENE!
GURF!
WHOP

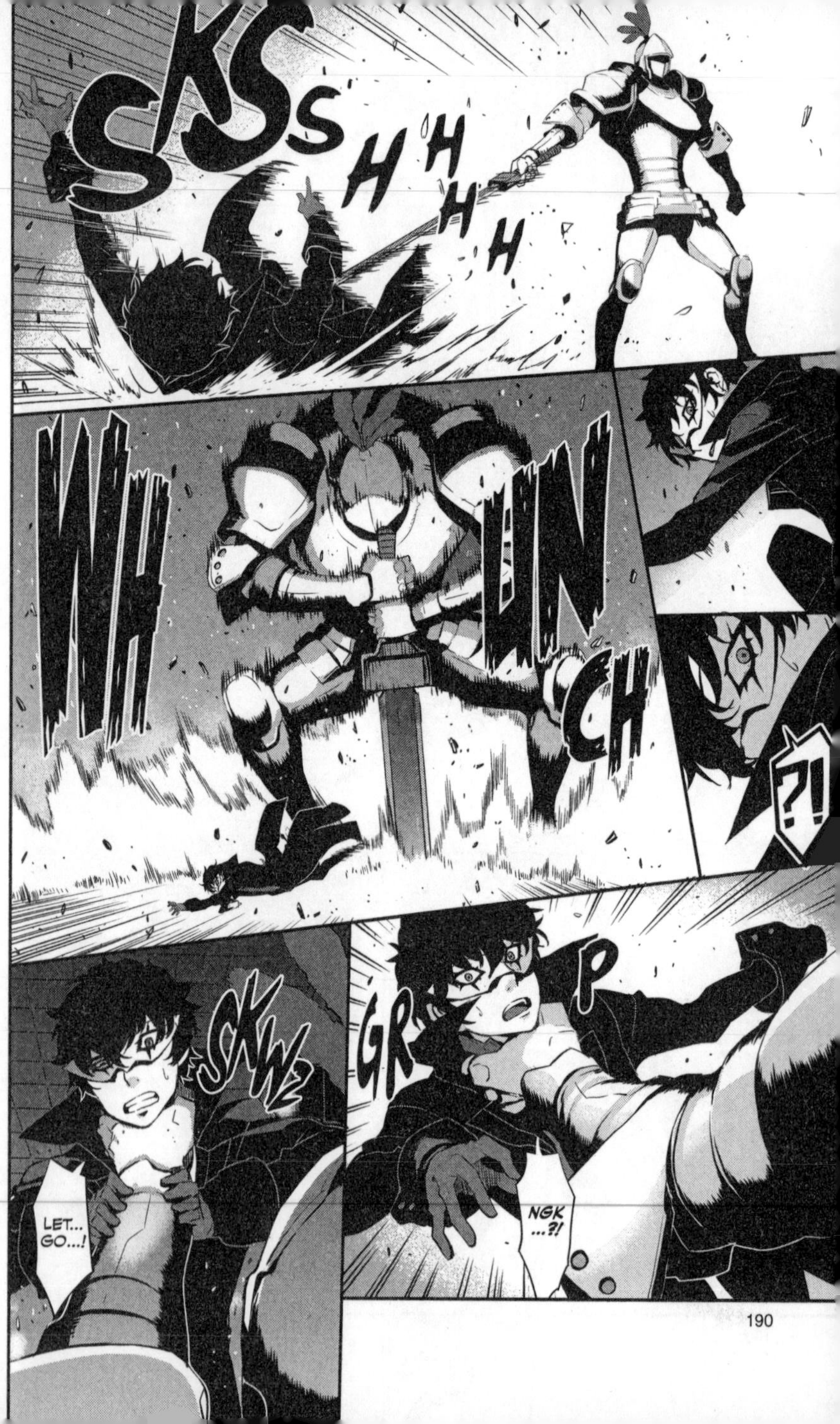

SKSSHHHH
?!
WHUNCH
GRP
NGK ...?!
SKW
LET... GO...!

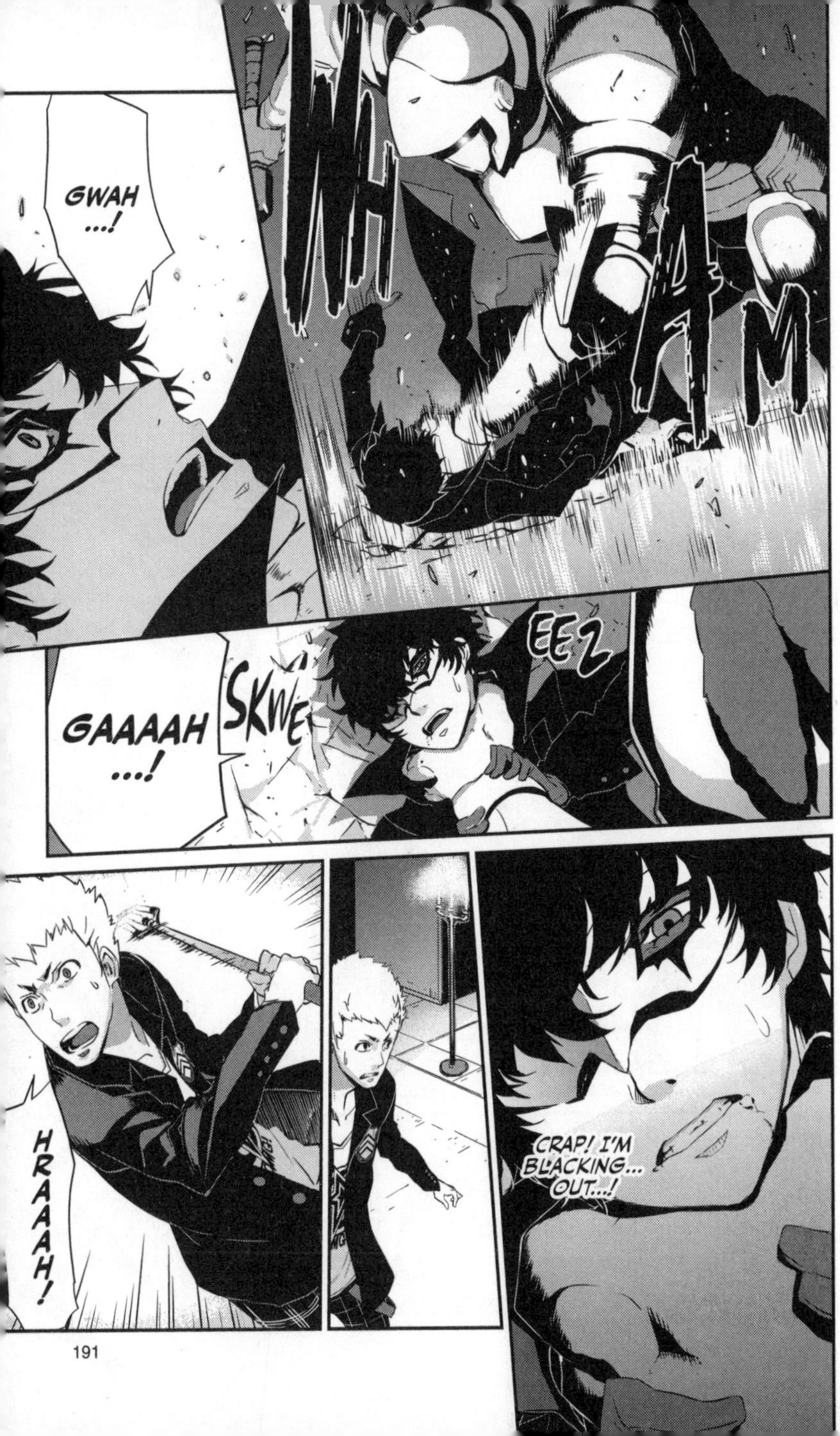
WHAM
GWAH ...!
SKWEEZ
GAAAAH ...!
CRAP! I'M BLACKING... OUT...!
HRAAAAH!

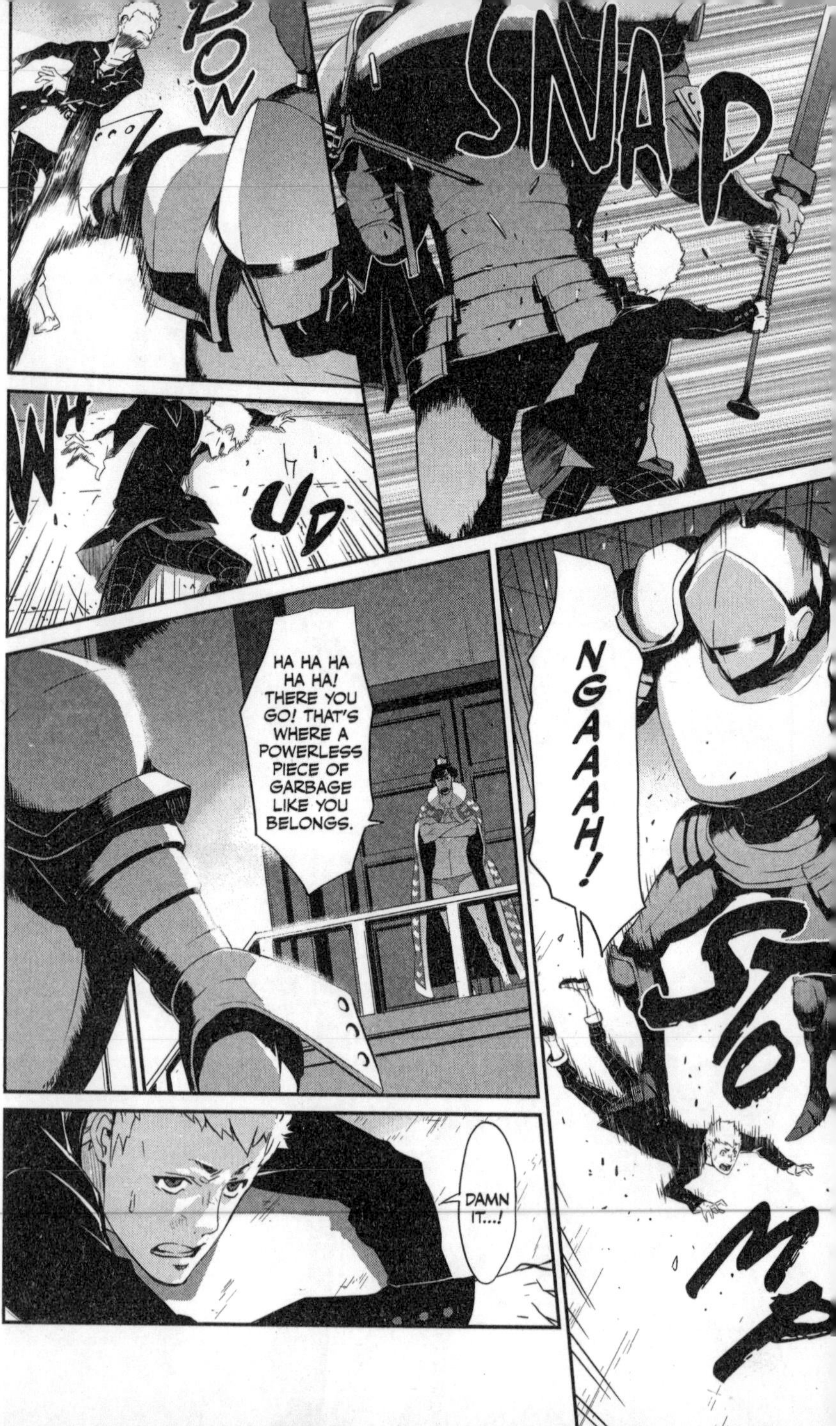
SNAP
POW
WHUD
NGAAAH!
STOMP
HA HA HA HA HA! THERE YOU GO! THAT'S WHERE A POWERLESS PIECE OF GARBAGE LIKE YOU BELONGS.
DAMN IT...!

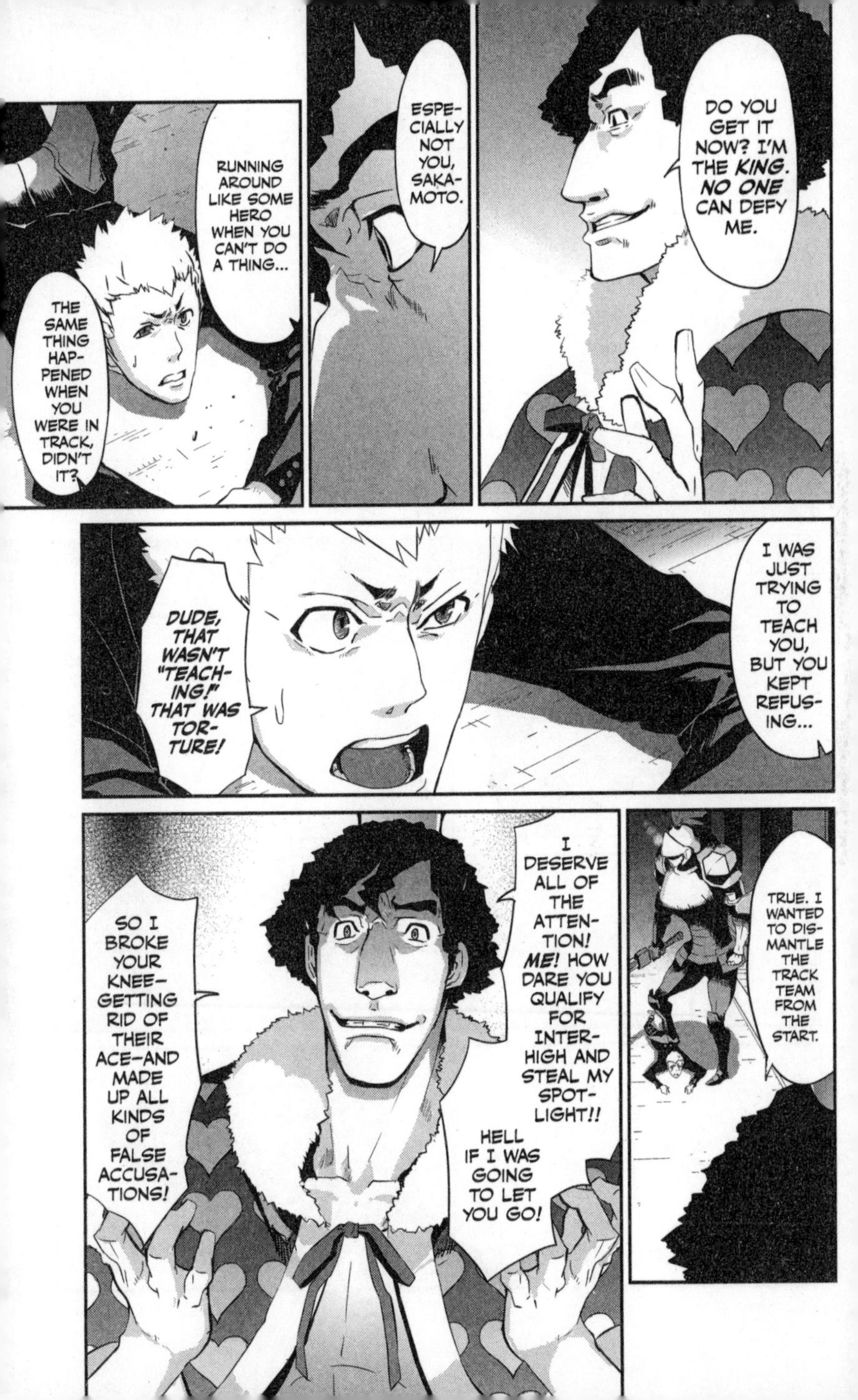
DO YOU GET IT NOW? I'M THE *KING*. *NO ONE* CAN DEFY ME.
ESPECIALLY NOT YOU, SAKAMOTO.
RUNNING AROUND LIKE SOME HERO WHEN YOU CAN'T DO A THING...
THE SAME THING HAPPENED WHEN YOU WERE IN TRACK, DIDN'T IT?
I WAS JUST TRYING TO TEACH YOU, BUT YOU KEPT REFUSING...
DUDE, THAT WASN'T "TEACHING!" THAT WAS TORTURE!
TRUE. I WANTED TO DISMANTLE THE TRACK TEAM FROM THE START.
I DESERVE ALL OF THE ATTENTION! *ME!* HOW DARE YOU QUALIFY FOR INTER-HIGH AND STEAL MY SPOTLIGHT!!
HELL IF I WAS GOING TO LET YOU GO!
SO I BROKE YOUR KNEE—GETTING RID OF THEIR ACE—AND MADE UP ALL KINDS OF FALSE ACCUSATIONS!

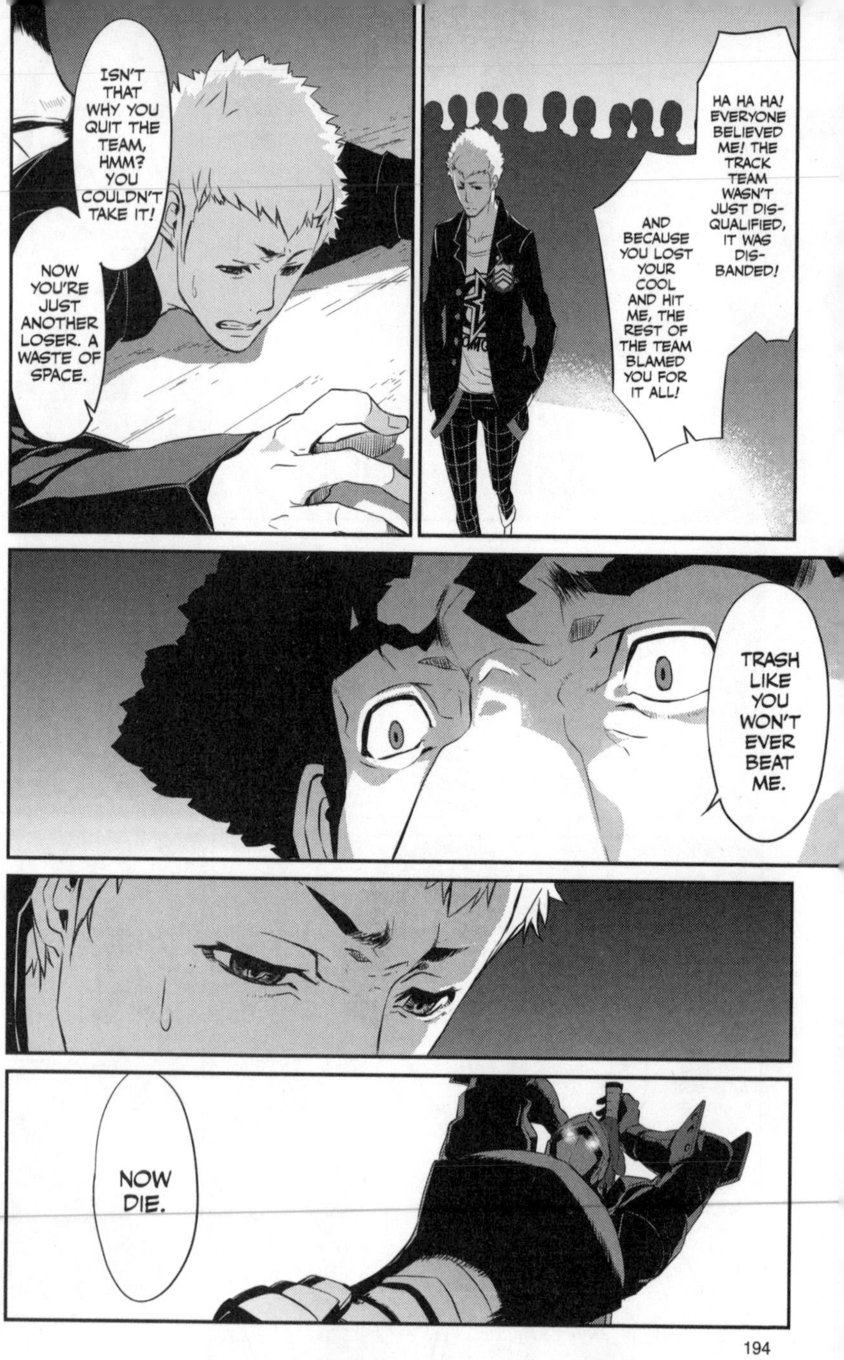
HA HA HA! EVERYONE BELIEVED ME! THE TRACK TEAM WASN'T JUST DIS-QUALIFIED, IT WAS DIS-BANDED!
AND BECAUSE YOU LOST YOUR COOL AND HIT ME, THE REST OF THE TEAM BLAMED YOU FOR IT ALL!
ISN'T THAT WHY YOU QUIT THE TEAM, HMM? YOU COULDN'T TAKE IT!
NOW YOU'RE JUST ANOTHER LOSER. A WASTE OF SPACE.
TRASH LIKE YOU WON'T EVER BEAT ME.
NOW DIE.

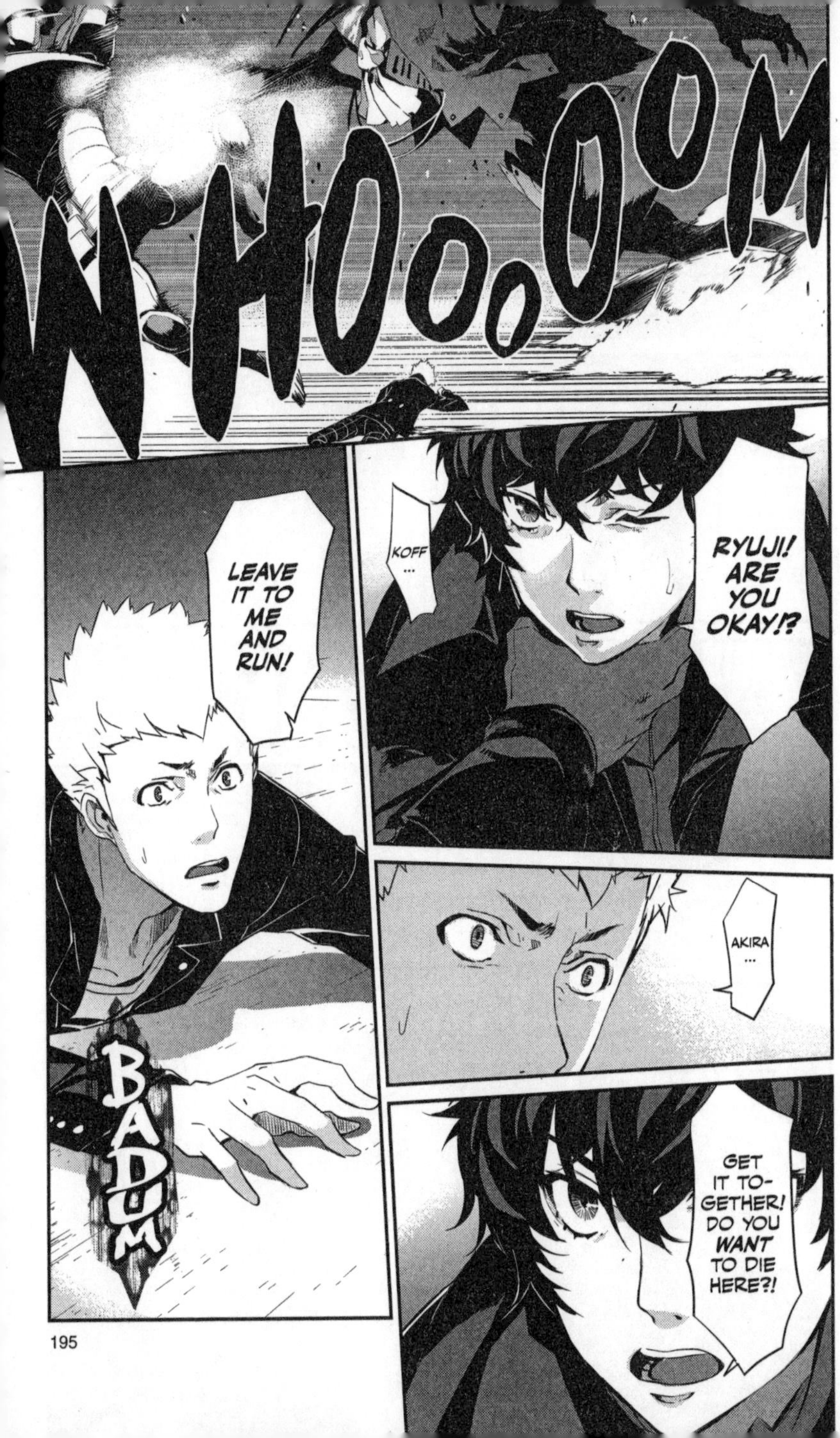
WHOOOOOM
RYUJI! ARE YOU OKAY!?
KOFF...
AKIRA...
GET IT TO-GETHER! DO YOU WANT TO DIE HERE?!
LEAVE IT TO ME AND RUN!
BADUM

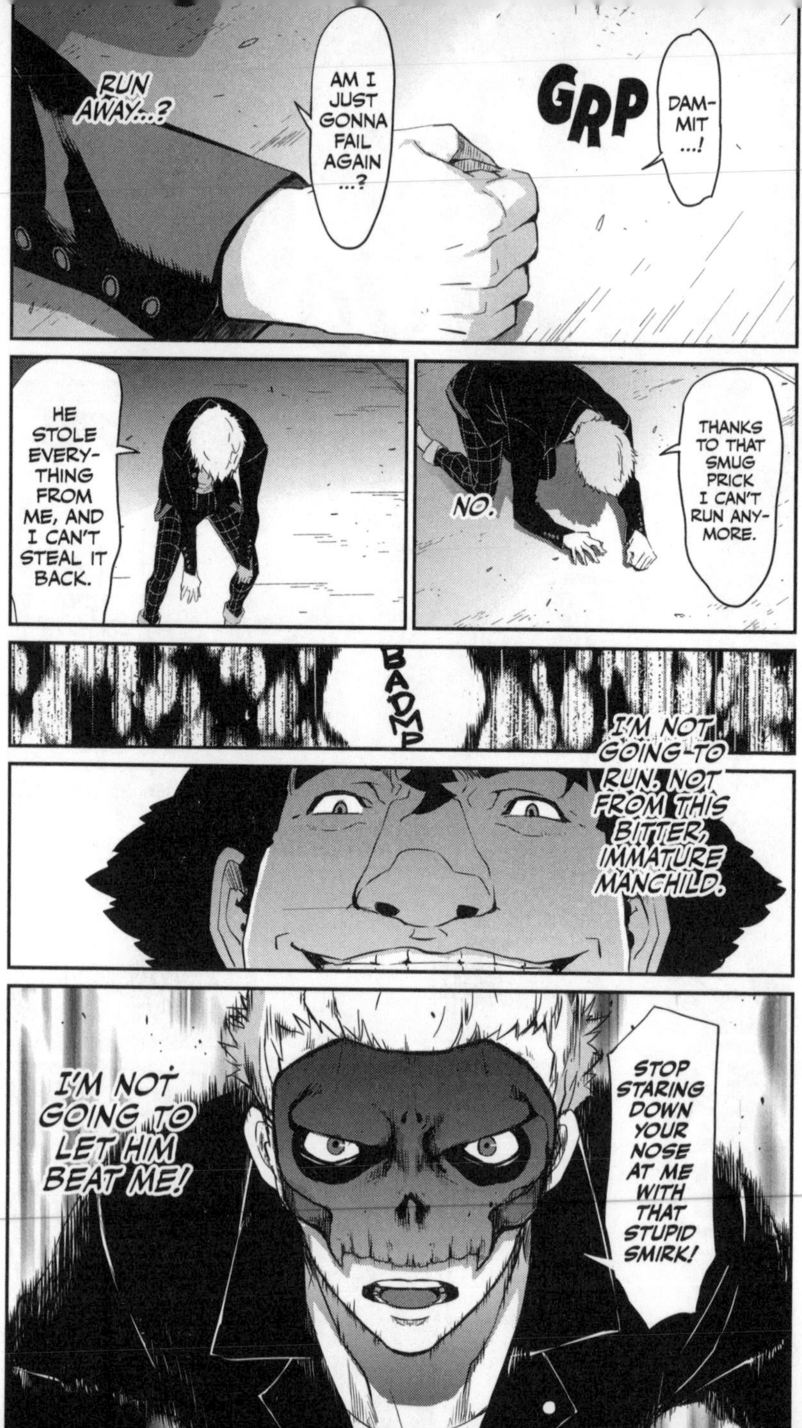
DAM-MIT ...!
GRP
AM I JUST GONNA FAIL AGAIN ...?
RUN AWAY...?
THANKS TO THAT SMUG PRICK I CAN'T RUN ANY-MORE.
NO.
HE STOLE EVERY-THING FROM ME, AND I CAN'T STEAL IT BACK.
BADMP
I'M NOT GOING TO RUN. NOT FROM THIS BITTER, IMMATURE MANCHILD.
STOP STARING DOWN YOUR NOSE AT ME WITH THAT STUPID SMIRK!
I'M NOT GOING TO LET HIM BEAT ME!

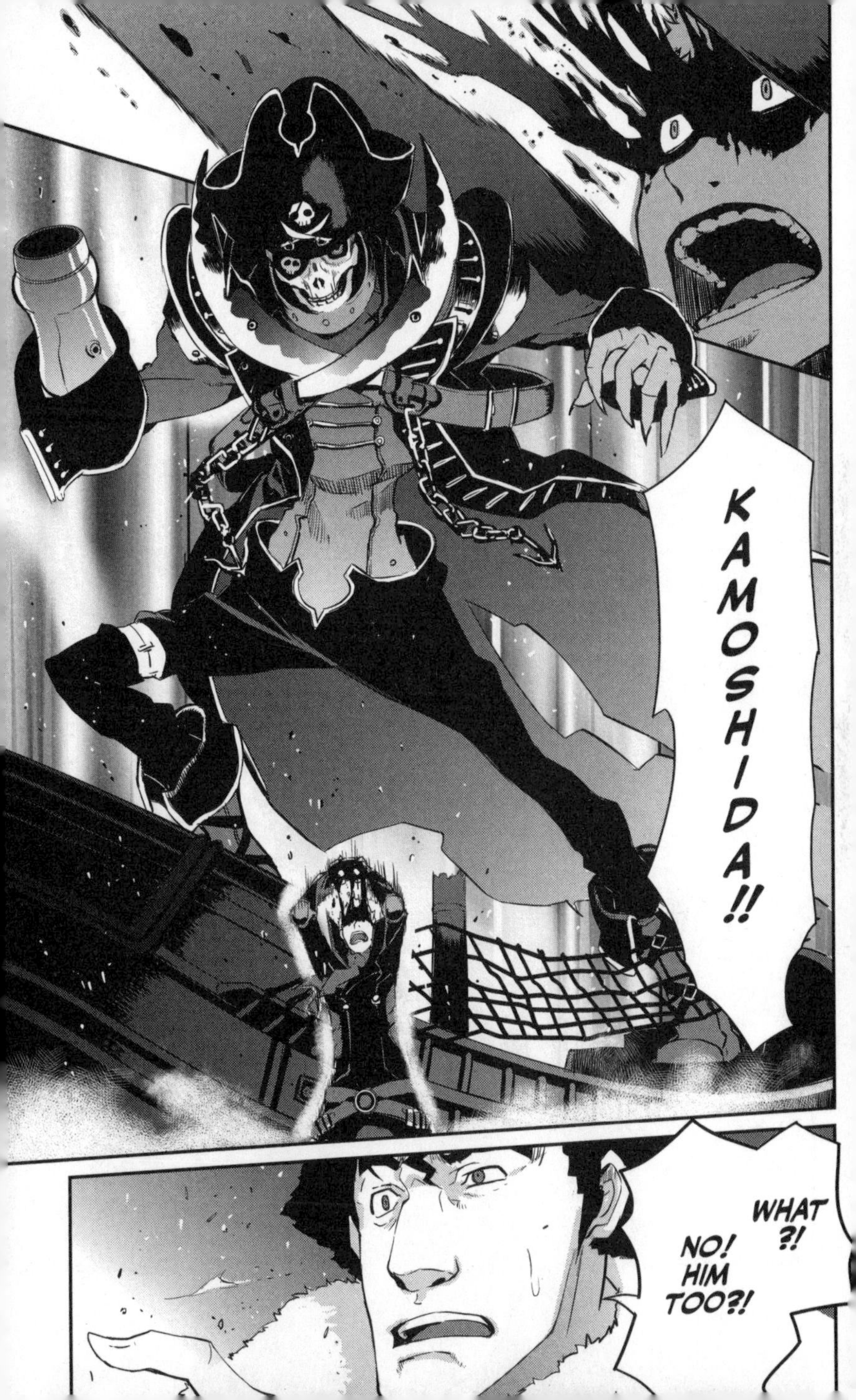
KAMOSHIDA!!
WHAT?!
NO! HIM TOO?!

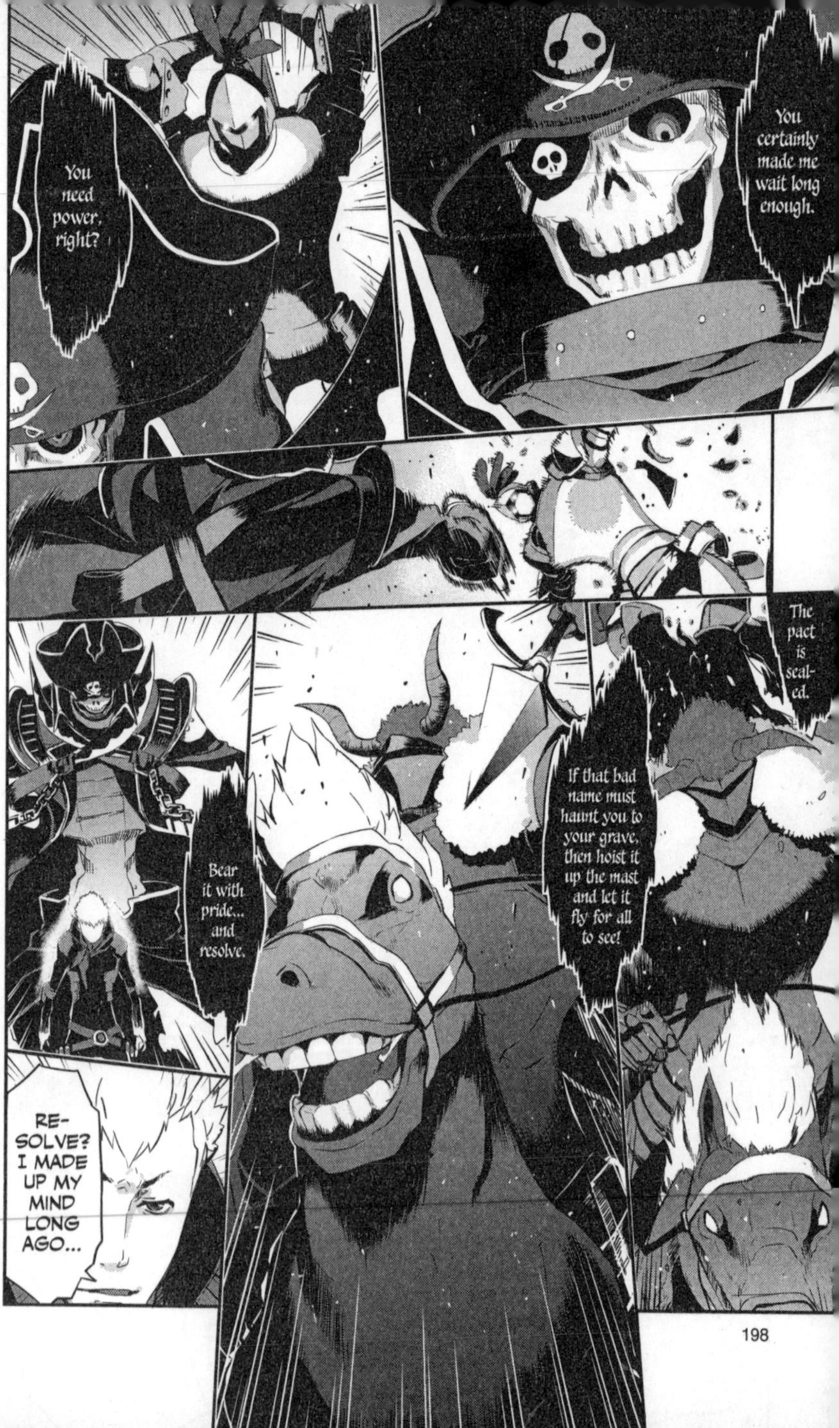

You certainly made me wait long enough.
You need power, right?
The pact is seal-ed.
If that bad name must haunt you to your grave, then hoist it up the mast and let it fly for all to see!
Bear it with pride... and resolve.
RE-SOLVE? I MADE UP MY MIND LONG AGO...

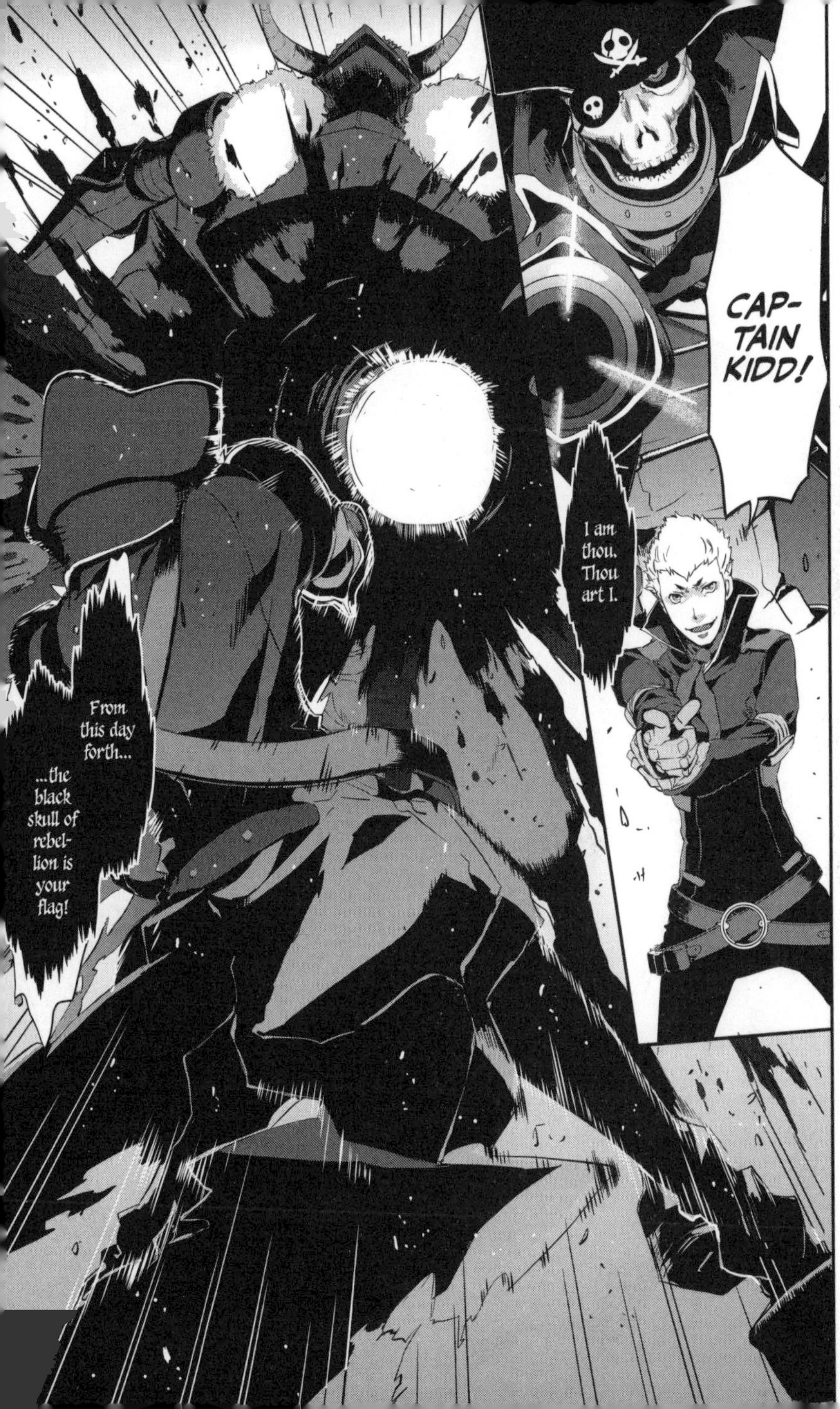
CAP-TAIN KIDD!
I am thou. Thou art I.
From this day forth...
...the black skull of rebellion is your flag!

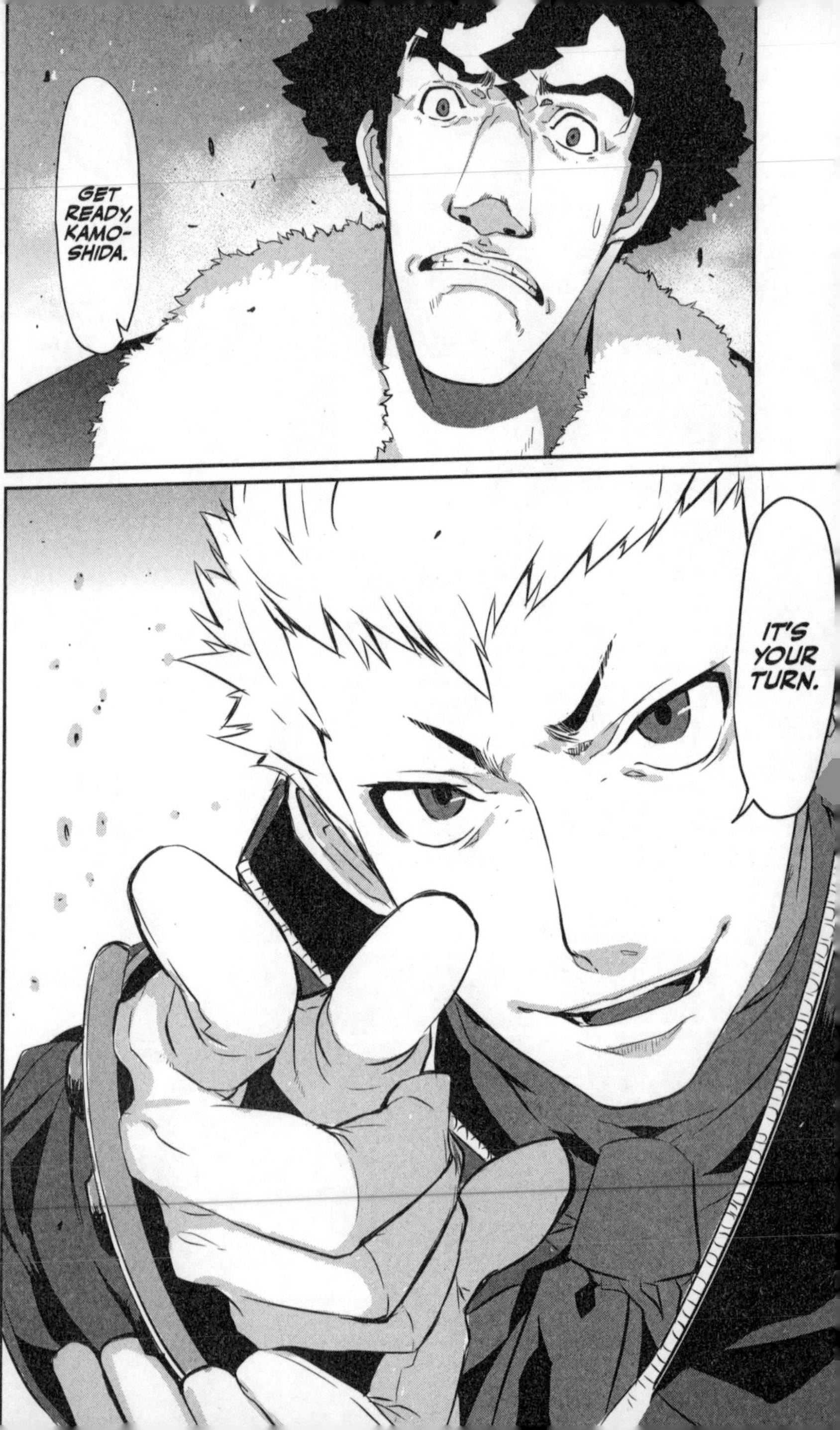
GET READY, KAMO-SHIDA.
IT'S YOUR TURN.

SUSHI TEN
風信寿合

Conveyor Belt
Sushi TEN
回転寿司天

SORRY TO CALL ON YOU WITH NO ADVANCE WARNING.

NO, NO. I'M ONLY TOO HAPPY TO OBLIGE. ESPECIALLY IF IT'S YOUR TREAT, MISS SAE.

AH WELL. I'LL CUT TO THE CHASE. I'D LIKE TO ASK A FAVOR OF YOU.

UH-HUH. OF COURSE YOU DID.

TINK

WHAT ABOUT SCHOOL? SHOULDN'T YOU HAVE BEEN IN CLASS?

WE HAD THE DAY OFF TODAY.

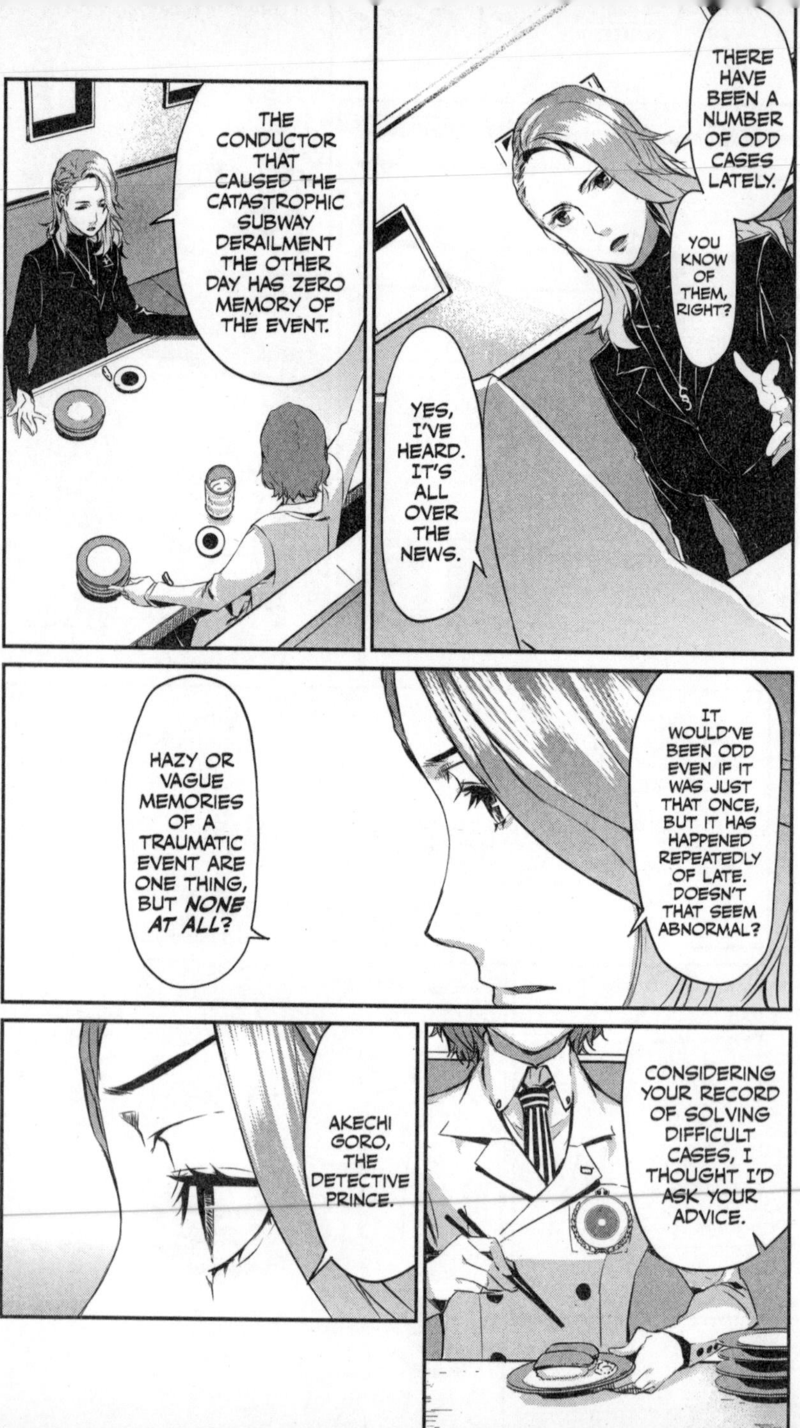
THERE HAVE BEEN A NUMBER OF ODD CASES LATELY.
YOU KNOW OF THEM, RIGHT?
YES, I'VE HEARD. IT'S ALL OVER THE NEWS.
THE CONDUCTOR THAT CAUSED THE CATASTROPHIC SUBWAY DERAILMENT THE OTHER DAY HAS ZERO MEMORY OF THE EVENT.
IT WOULD'VE BEEN ODD EVEN IF IT WAS JUST THAT ONCE, BUT IT HAS HAPPENED REPEATEDLY OF LATE. DOESN'T THAT SEEM ABNORMAL?
HAZY OR VAGUE MEMORIES OF A TRAUMATIC EVENT ARE ONE THING, BUT *NONE AT ALL*?
CONSIDERING YOUR RECORD OF SOLVING DIFFICULT CASES, I THOUGHT I'D ASK YOUR ADVICE.
AKECHI GORO, THE DETECTIVE PRINCE.

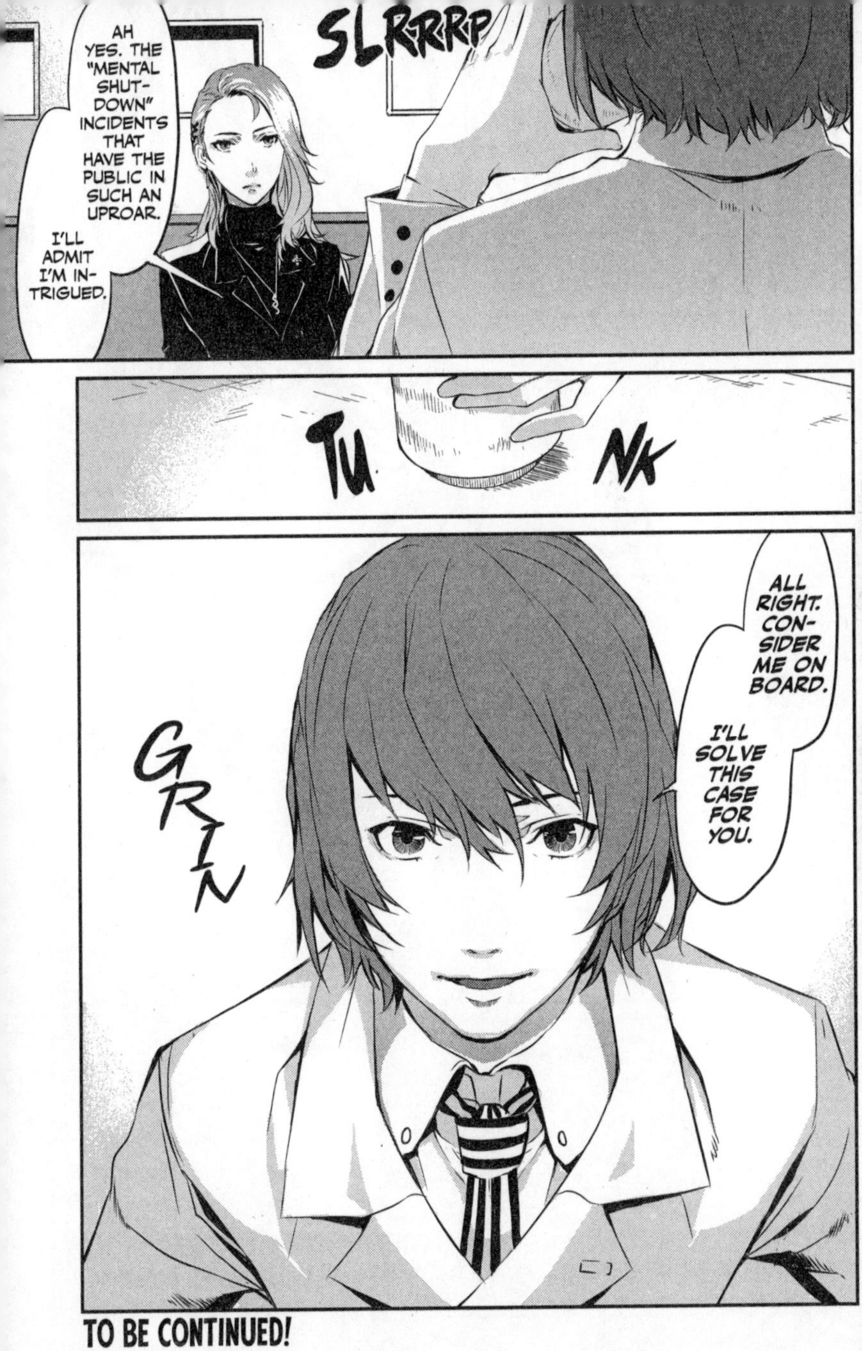
SLRRRP
AH YES. THE "MENTAL SHUT-DOWN" INCIDENTS THAT HAVE THE PUBLIC IN SUCH AN UPROAR.
I'LL ADMIT I'M IN-TRIGUED.
TU NK
ALL RIGHT. CON-SIDER ME ON BOARD.
I'LL SOLVE THIS CASE FOR YOU.
GRIN

TO BE CONTINUED!

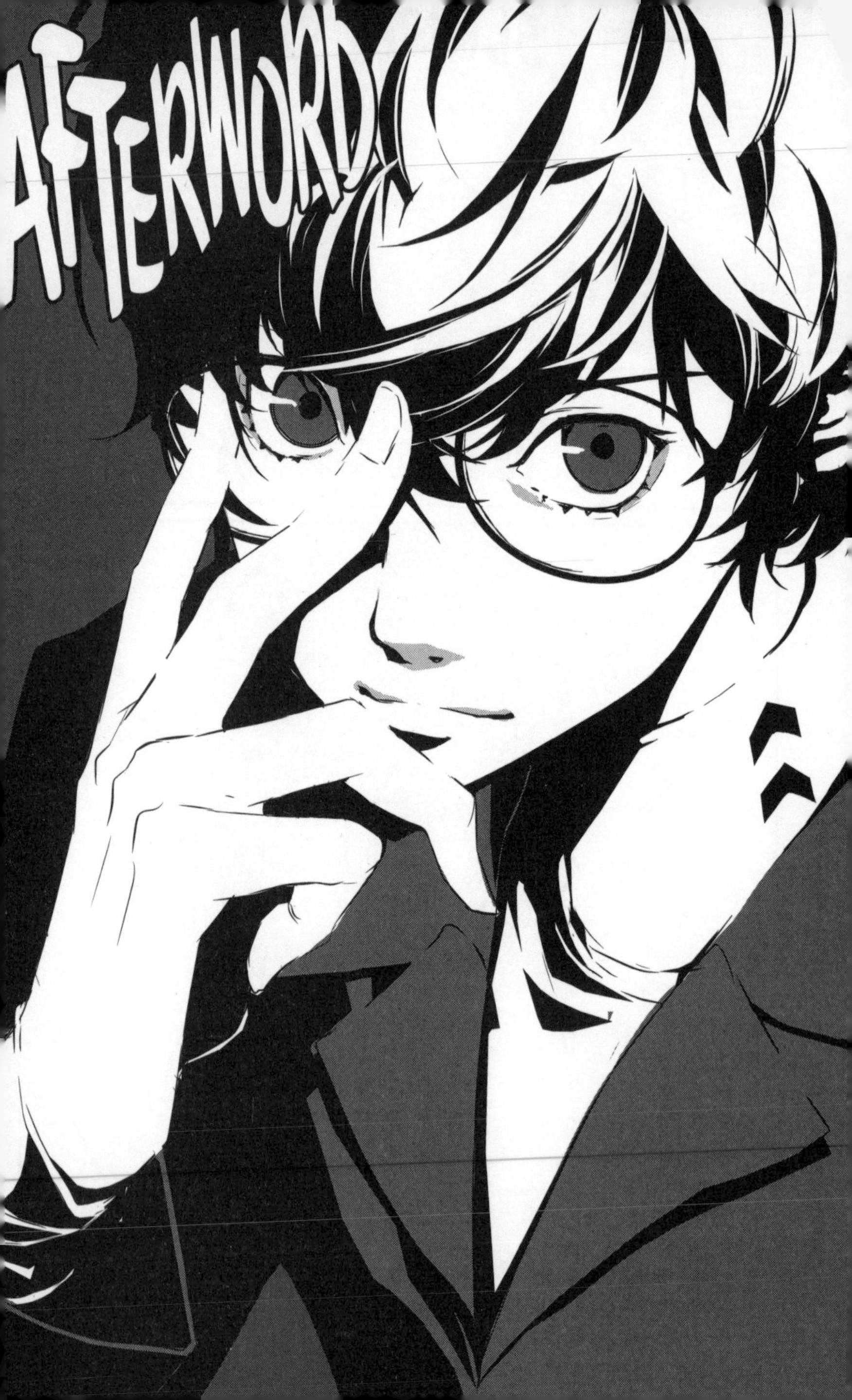
AFTERWORD

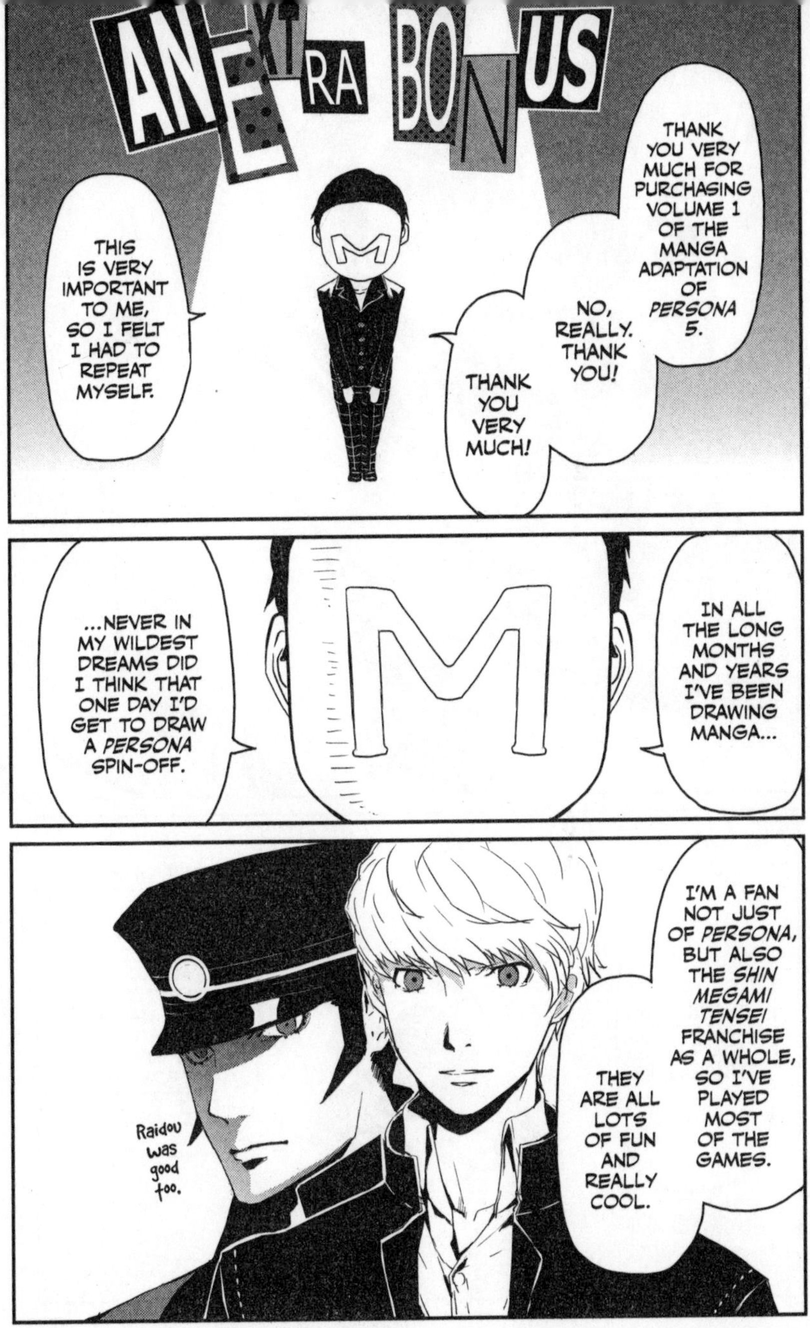
AN EXTRA BONUS
THANK YOU VERY MUCH FOR PURCHASING VOLUME 1 OF THE MANGA ADAPTATION OF *PERSONA* 5.
NO, REALLY. THANK YOU!
THANK YOU VERY MUCH!
THIS IS VERY IMPORTANT TO ME, SO I FELT I HAD TO REPEAT MYSELF.
IN ALL THE LONG MONTHS AND YEARS I'VE BEEN DRAWING MANGA...
...NEVER IN MY WILDEST DREAMS DID I THINK THAT ONE DAY I'D GET TO DRAW A *PERSONA* SPIN-OFF.
I'M A FAN NOT JUST OF *PERSONA*, BUT ALSO THE *SHIN MEGAMI TENSEI* FRANCHISE AS A WHOLE, SO I'VE PLAYED MOST OF THE GAMES.
THEY ARE ALL LOTS OF FUN AND REALLY COOL.
Raidou was good too.

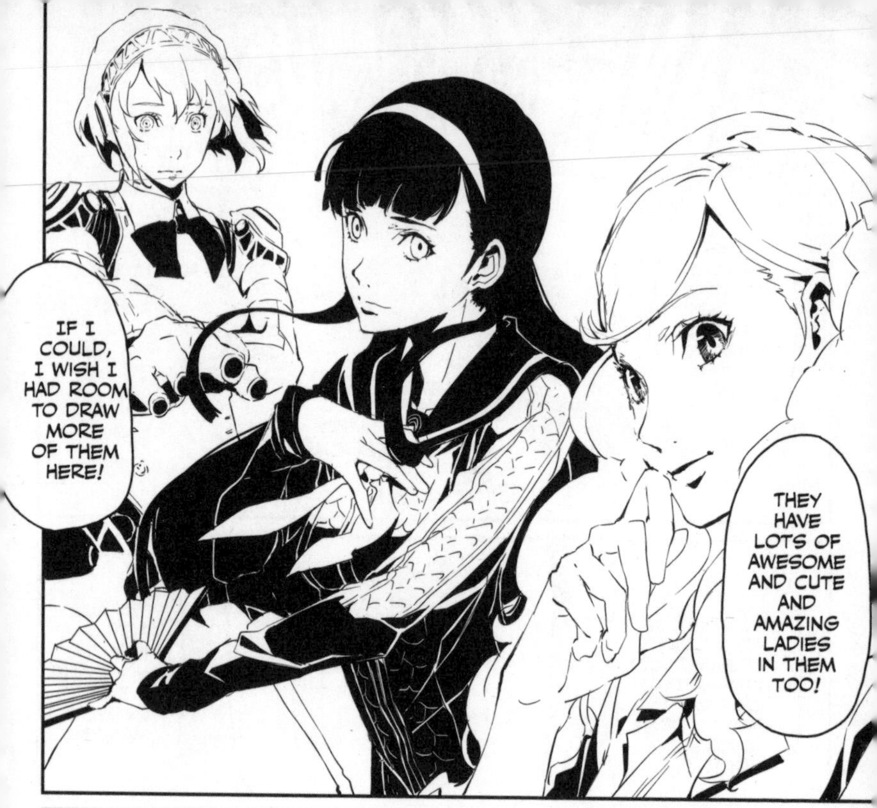
THEY HAVE LOTS OF AWESOME AND CUTE AND AMAZING LADIES IN THEM TOO!
IF I COULD, I WISH I HAD ROOM TO DRAW MORE OF THEM HERE!

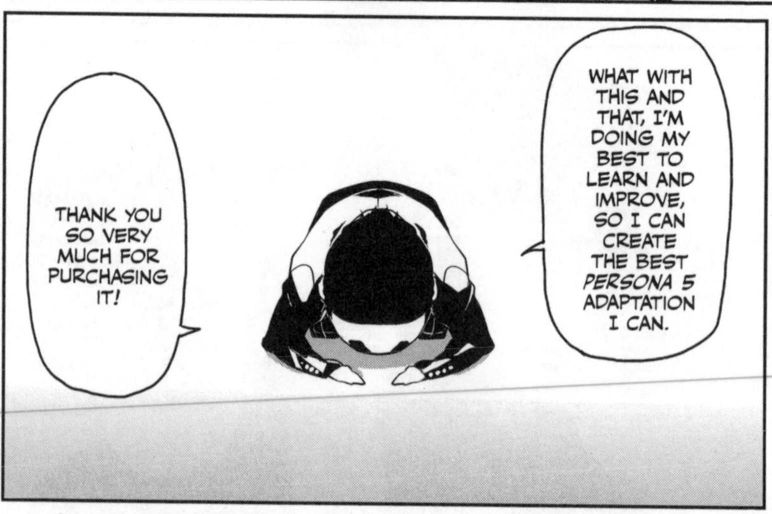
WHAT WITH THIS AND THAT, I'M DOING MY BEST TO LEARN AND IMPROVE, SO I CAN CREATE THE BEST *PERSONA 5* ADAPTATION I CAN.
THANK YOU SO VERY MUCH FOR PURCHASING IT!

Staff

Chie Soraku

Satoshi Yagotoki

Aya Shimeji

Nemu Kurusu

Ikuko Deluxe

tetra

And...
Atlus, and everyone else who has
assisted with the adaptation of
Persona 5.

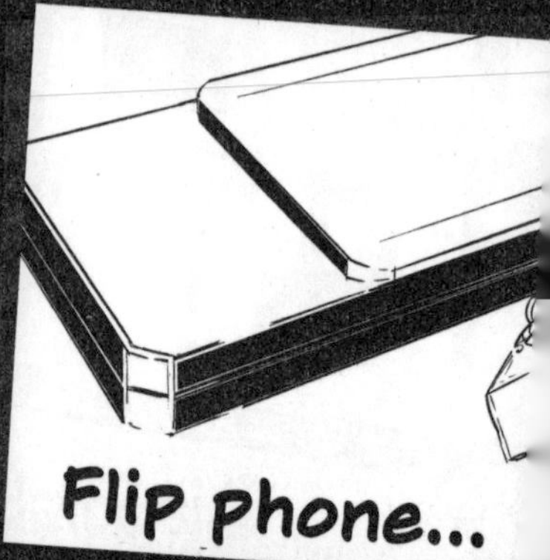
Flip phone...

Hisato MuRAs

Hello! I'm Hisato Murasaki, and it's my honor t
you the manga adaptation of *Persona 5*! Volun
together and ready to go on sale. It took a lot
error, but I somehow managed to reach a whc
worth of content. I'm sure there are many spc
use more work, but I hope you will still enjoy
to seeing you again!

Hisato Murasaki is a manga artist and illus
He has created illustrations for a number o
series, including *Hyakume no Kishi* (*Knight*
Case-Book of ENA, the *D-Crackers* series
D's Report. He also wrote the manga, *Boku*
Uchuujin (*The Alien Around Me*). He startec
in 2016.

PERSONA5 5 1

BY **HISATO MURASAKI**
ORIGINAL CONCEPT BY **ATLUS**

Translation/Adrienne Beck
Touch-Up Art & Lettering/Annaliese Christman
Design/Kam Li
Editor/Marlene First
Approval Cooperation/Shinji Yamamoto (ATLUS),
Miki Iwata (ATLUS)

PERSONA 5 Vol. 1
by Hisato MURASAKI
Original Concept by ATLUS
© ATLUS © SEGA All rights reserved.
© 2017 Hisato MURASAKI
All rights reserved.
Original Japanese edition published by SHOGAKUKAN.
English translation rights in the United States of America, Canada, the United
Kingdom, Ireland, Australia and New Zealand arranged with SHOGAKUKAN.

Original cover design: Kenro YOKOYAMA (Beeworks)

Printed in Italy
Published by VIZ Media, LLC
P.O. Box 77010
San Francisco, CA 94107

10 9 8 7 6 5 4
First printing, January 2020
Fourth printing, June 2021

VIZ MEDIA
viz.com

PARENTAL ADVISORY
PERSONA 5 is rated T+ for Older Teen and
is recommended for ages 16 and up for
fantasy violence and sexual themes.

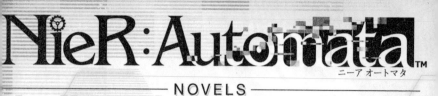

NieR:Automata™

ニーア オートマタ

NOVELS

Written by Jun Eishima and Yoko Taro

Original Story by Yoko Taro

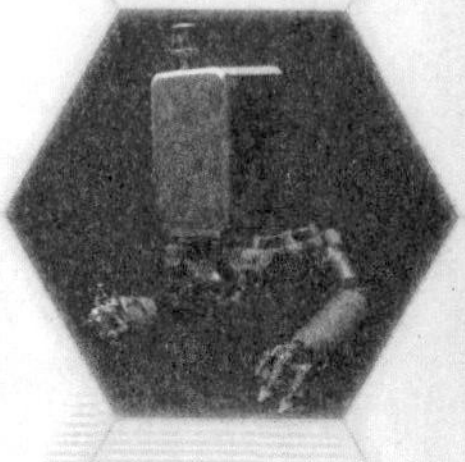

EXPERIENCE THE WORLD AND CHARACTERS OF THE HIT VIDEO GAME FRANCHISE!

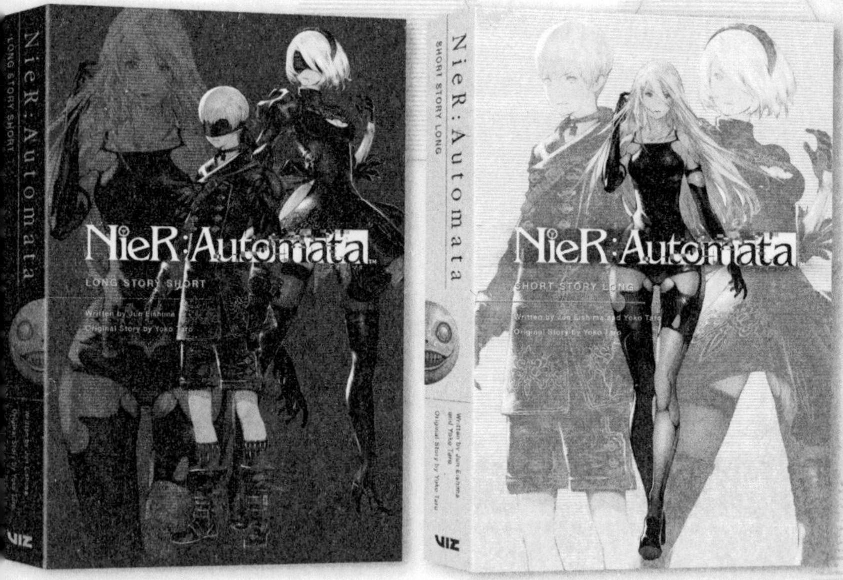
NieR:Automata
LONG STORY SHORT
VIZ
NieR:Automata
SHORT STORY LONG
VIZ

When alien forces invade with an army of Machines, the remnants of humanity must depend on Androids of their own design—the placid 2B and the excitable 9S—to survive.

VIZ

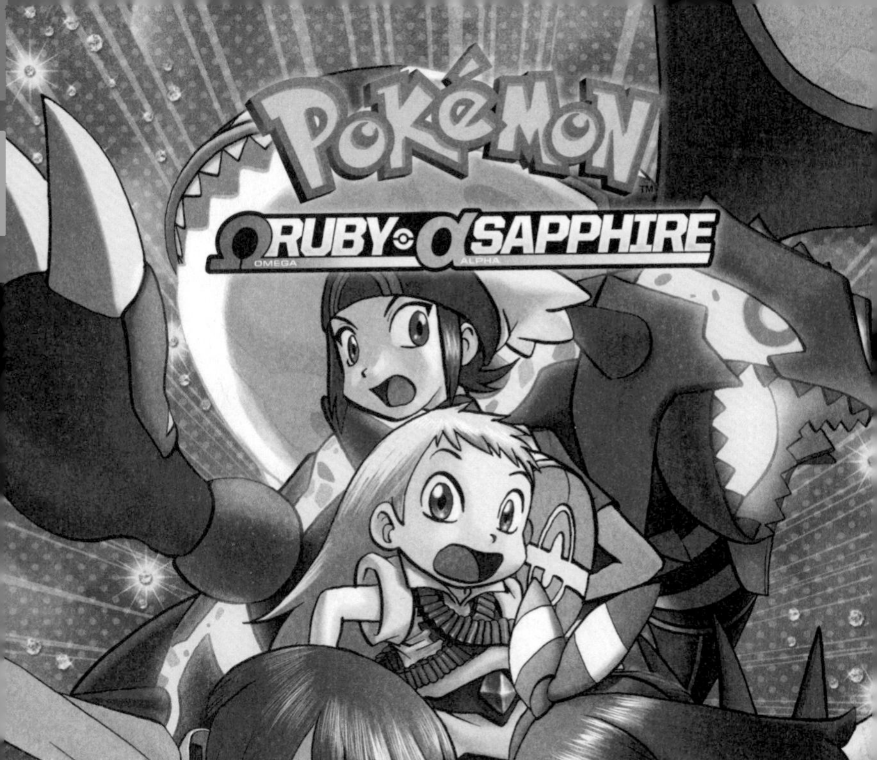
POKÉMON™
ΩRUBY OMEGA · αSAPPHIRE ALPHA
STORY BY
HIDENORI KUSAKA
ART BY
SATOSHI YAMAMOTO

Awesome adventures inspired by the best-selling Pokémon Omega Ruby and Pokémon Alpha Sapphire video games that pick up where the *Pokémon Adventures Ruby & Sapphire* saga left off!

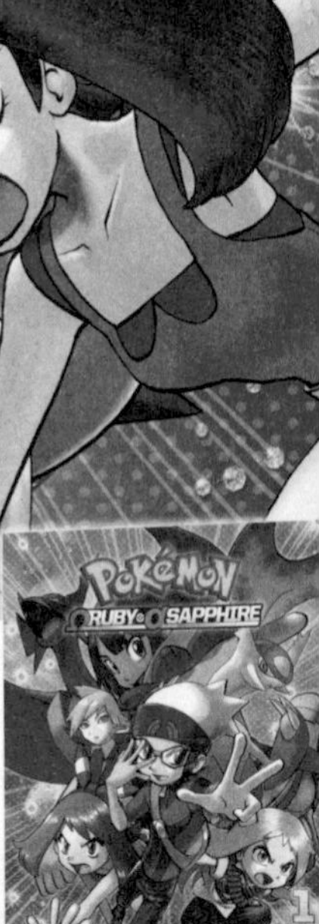
POKÉMON
ΩRUBY·αSAPPHIRE
1

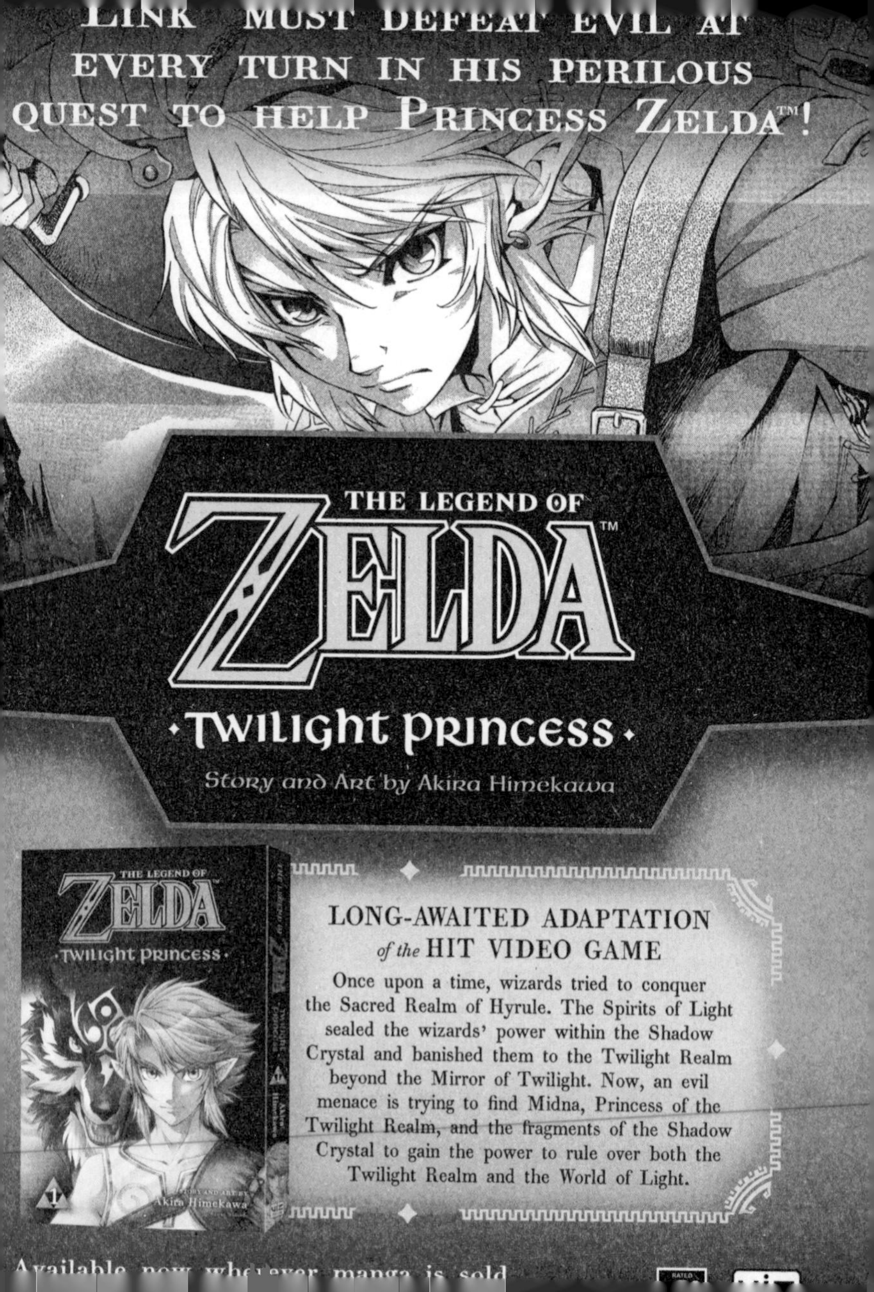
LINK MUST DEFEAT EVIL AT EVERY TURN IN HIS PERILOUS QUEST TO HELP PRINCESS ZELDA™!
THE LEGEND OF ZELDA™
·TWILIGHT PRINCESS·
Story and Art by Akira Himekawa
LONG-AWAITED ADAPTATION of the HIT VIDEO GAME
Once upon a time, wizards tried to conquer the Sacred Realm of Hyrule. The Spirits of Light sealed the wizards' power within the Shadow Crystal and banished them to the Twilight Realm beyond the Mirror of Twilight. Now, an evil menace is trying to find Midna, Princess of the Twilight Realm, and the fragments of the Shadow Crystal to gain the power to rule over both the Twilight Realm and the World of Light.
Available now wherever manga is sold.

THE LEGEND OF ZELDA

LEGENDARY EDITION

STORY AND ART BY

AKIRA HIMEKAWA

The Legendary Editions of *The Legend of Zelda*™ contain
two volumes of the beloved manga series, presented in a
deluxe format featuring new covers and color art pieces.

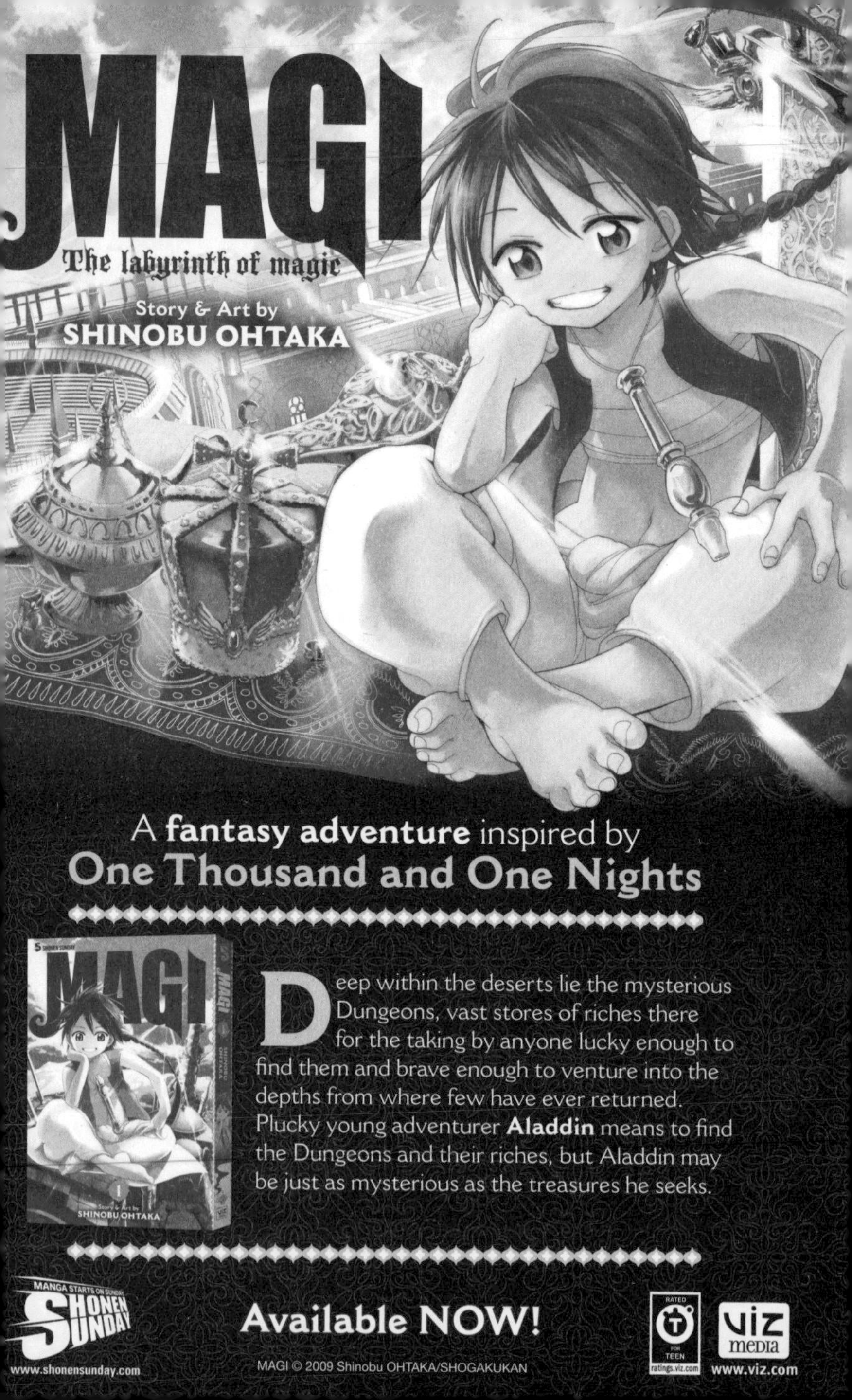
MAGI
The labyrinth of magic
Story & Art by
SHINOBU OHTAKA
A fantasy adventure inspired by
One Thousand and One Nights
MAGI
Story & Art by
SHINOBU OHTAKA
Deep within the deserts lie the mysterious Dungeons, vast stores of riches there for the taking by anyone lucky enough to find them and brave enough to venture into the depths from where few have ever returned. Plucky young adventurer Aladdin means to find the Dungeons and their riches, but Aladdin may be just as mysterious as the treasures he seeks.
MANGA STARTS ON SUNDAY
SHONEN SUNDAY
www.shonensunday.com
Available NOW!
MAGI © 2009 Shinobu OHTAKA/SHOGAKUKAN
RATED
T
FOR
TEEN
ratings.viz.com
viz media
www.viz.com

K
idnapped by the Demon King and imprisoned in his castle, Princess Syalis is...bored.

SLEEPY PRINCESS IN THE DEMON CASTLE

Story & Art by

KAGIJI KUMANOMATA

C
aptured princess Syalis decides to while away her hours in the Demon Castle by sleeping, but getting a good night's rest turns out to be a lot of work! She begins by fashioning a DIY pillow out of the fur of her Teddy Demon guards and an "air mattress" from the magical Shield of the Wind. Things go from bad to worse—for her captors—when some of Princess Syalis's schemes end in her untimely—if temporary—demise and she chooses the Forbidden Grimoire for her bedtime reading...

This is the LAST PAGE!

You're Reading the WRONG WAY!

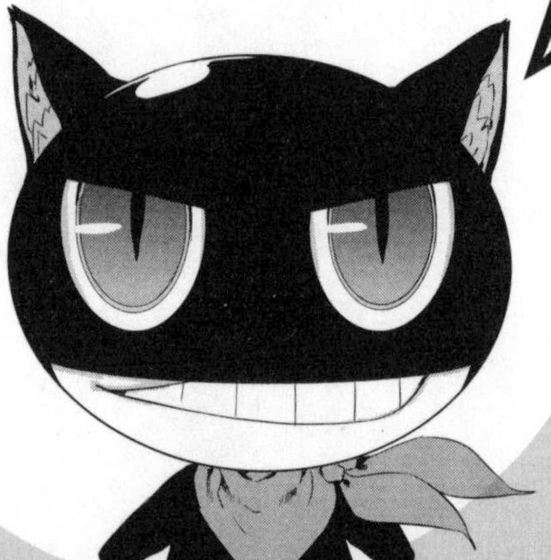

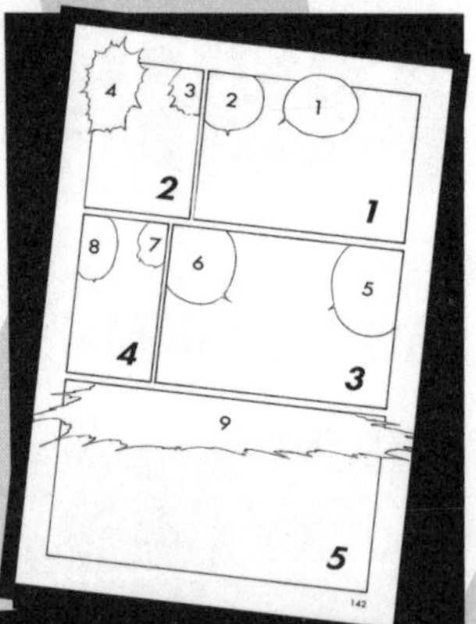
1
2
3
4
1
2
5
6
7
8
3
4
9
5
142

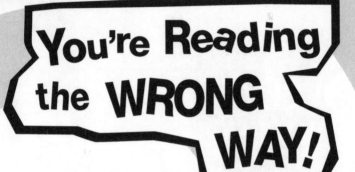

PERSONA 5 reads from right to left, starting in the upper-right corner. Japanese is read from right to left, meaning that action, sound effects, and word-balloon order are completely reversed from English order.